ORTHODOXY, ROMAN CATHOLICISM
AND ANGLICANISM

ORTHODOXY
ROMAN CATHOLICISM
AND ANGLICANISM

By

METHODIOS FOUYAS,
Ph.D.(Man.), Hon. D.D.(Edin.)

Greek Orthodox Archbishop of Aksum

LONDON
OXFORD UNIVERSITY PRESS
NEW YORK   TORONTO

1972

Oxford University Press, Ely House, London W.1

GLASGOW NEW YORK TORONTO MELBOURNE WELLINGTON
CAPE TOWN IBADAN NAIROBI DAR ES SALAAM LUSAKA ADDIS ABABA
DELHI BOMBAY CALCUTTA MADRAS KARACHI LAHORE DACCA
KUALA LUMPUR SINGAPORE HONG KONG TOKYO

ISBN 0 19 213947 9

© Oxford University Press, 1972

Printed in Northern Ireland at
The Universities Press, Belfast

TO
HIS BEATITUDE
NICHOLAOS VI
POPE AND PATRIARCH
OF ALEXANDRIA AND ALL AFRICA

In affectionate acknowledgement
of our long spiritual friendship

FOREWORD

This book is written from an unusual angle. It is not limited to a study of doctrine alone, nor is it simply a history of the three Churches. It gives a historical account of the Churches which emphasizes the reasons for their separation and the common elements which keep them doctrinally together. This is in my opinion the ecumenical way of learning. We must not look in isolation at what our fellow Christians say for themselves or what we say for ourselves. We must put these together and attempt to understand one another, so that we can see the Christian tradition as a whole.

As these three Churches have now entered into fuller relations with each other, this comparative study of their doctrine and their attitudes towards one another may be of some value.

The book is divided into three main parts. The first part discusses the origin of the divisions within the one Church, the reasons for them, and the developments of these divisions; together with an account of some attempts at reconciliation. The second part is a comparative analysis of Christian doctrine as held in the three Churches. The third and last part is entitled 'Towards Unity', and tries to give a comprehensive survey of the present situation in the relations between the three Churches. It is in this part that I contribute my own comments on the prospects for unity.

I am afraid that I am perhaps out of fashion in that I am not always as kind as I would have liked to be towards the Roman Church. This is not because I dislike that Church, but because I wish to portray the true facts which so many contemporary ecumenists play down or ignore. There are many points concerning the relations of the three Churches which are not stressed by contemporary authors. We live in a time of apparent Christian charity which, I think, could destroy the vitality of the Christian Churches. I know that this is a paradox, but I am sure that all too often we are satisfied with a charitable ambiguity at the expense of truth.

I feel sometimes that I am amongst the few non-Anglicans who have attempted to know and appreciate the true greatness of

Anglicanism which, with its typically English liberalism and comprehensiveness, was perhaps born out of due time. Ordinary people are unable to distinguish between traditions and beliefs, or between institutions and principles. For these reasons the Anglican Church's reputation has often suffered in both East and West.

I have tried to be as impartial as I can towards the Orthodox Church. The unfortunate circumstances which have beset Orthodoxy during the last five hundred years have made very little impression on most non-Orthodox who have written about it. I am glad however that the West is now becoming more aware of what happened during this period.

Since this book was begun a series of historic meetings between heads and representatives of Churches has been taking place. Some account of them is included in Chapter VIII. But a very long time will elapse before there will be any alteration in the present form of the three Churches, Anglican, Orthodox and Roman Catholic, since none of them is yet prepared to make any changes in its doctrine and tradition.

I am grateful to two advisers who read the manuscript after it was accepted for publication, the Rev. Colin Davey and the late Rev. Canon John Findlow, whose suggestions I have generally been glad to accept.

I would like to make mention of the late Rev. Dr. Arnold Ehrhardt. Dr. Ehrhardt was a great scholar and a great man. He suffered during Hitler's regime in Germany and finally found shelter in England, and a spiritual home in the Church of England. He and Professor Gordon Rupp inspired me greatly during my stay in Manchester.

Addis Ababa   M.F.
August 1971

CONTENTS

PART THREE

ABBREVIATIONS USED IN FOOTNOTES

C.   *Concilium. An International Review of Theology.* Formerly published by Burns and Oates, London; now Antony Clark Books, Wheathampstead.

C.E.   *The Christian East. A Quarterly Review devoted to the Study of the Eastern Churches.* Published by the Anglican and Eastern Churches Association, London.

D.E.W. *Dialogue East and West.* The Faith Press, London, 1963.

Eccl.   *Ecclesia. Official Bulletin of the Church of Greece.*

E.C.Q.   *Eastern Churches Quarterly.* Ed. by Dom Bede Winslow of St. Augustine Abbey, Ramsgate.

E.E.   *Ecumenical Experiences.* Ed. by Luis V. Romeu. Burns and Oates, London, 1965.

E.R.   *Ecumenical Review.* The World Council of Churches, Geneva.

H.E.M. *A History of the Ecumenical Movement,* 1517–1948. Ed. by Ruth Rouse and Stephen Charles Neill. S.P.C.K., London, 1954.

O.I.C.   *One in Christ. A Catholic Ecumenical Review.* London.

P.A.   *Problems of Authority.* Ed. by John M. Todd, London, 1962.

P.G.   Migne, *Patrologia Graeca.*

P.L.   Migne, *Patrologia Latina.*

R.E.C.   *Rediscovering Eastern Christendom. Essays in Memory of Dom Winslow.* Ed. by E. L. B. Fry and A. H. Armstrong, London, 1963.

S.   *Sobornost. The Journal of the Fellowship of St. Alban and St. Sergius.* London.

S.C.U.   *Steps to Christian Unity.* Ed. by John O'Brien. Collins, London, 1965.

TH.   *Theologia. Official Quarterly Review of the Holy Synod of the Church of Greece.*

For other works referred to, see the Bibliography, pages 260–72.

INTRODUCTION

The Second Vatican Council and the Pan-Orthodox Conferences held on the Island of Rhodes, at Belgrade, and at Chambésy have considerably furthered the dialogue between the Orthodox, Roman, and Anglican Churches.

In past centuries it was almost impossible for any of the three Churches to know what the others really stood for. Prejudice, geography and politics made communication between them almost impossible—for polemics and controversy are not true communication. Today, however, frequent contacts, friendship between Christians, and study of each other's religious life stimulates a desire for *rapprochement* without the fear of being forced to accept the other's religious ideology. Indeed these frequent contacts have in many cases mitigated the extremism which so often separates one Church from the other. Emigration has led to contacts between clergy and people, and many conferences, pilgrimages, etc., have been organized. It is interesting that Church leaders show a great desire for Christian dialogue, although they may not share the same doctrinal approach to co-operation or Christian unity. Even though they differ doctrinally, psychologically, racially and educationally, they seem to want to know what the situation is in the rest of the Christian world.

For many centuries the Orthodox Church was virtually unknown to the majority of Western Europeans. What they knew about Orthodoxy was obtained from books, mainly written by diplomats, chaplains, or travellers, who had an inadequate knowledge of the Orthodox Church. I feel great shame when I read, for example, the book written by Dr. Adrian Fortescue on the Orthodox Church, because apart from his violation of the facts, he presents the Greek Church as a very primitive one. Most of the earlier scholars who dealt with the Orthodox Church expressed the opinion that there was nothing to be learned from the Orthodox, or that this Church needed to be reformed. Opinions like these predominate in Europe and are very difficult to change. Möhler, for instance, wrote that 'the Eastern Church appears

to be a static Tradition'.[1] A contemporary Roman Catholic[2] makes
an attempt to mitigate Möhler's impression saying that 'if Möhler had
not died so young, he would undoubtedly have taken account of the
genuine interest that Eastern Theology always presents. His concern
about a patristic theology brought him very close to the Orthodox
turn of mind. Actually, there could be no better way of approaching
Orthodoxy than by starting out with Möhler's theology.' Although
it is true that Möhler's theology is very close to the Orthodox, he had
nothing good to say about the Orthodox Church itself. 'The fact is
that there is no interest nowadays in turning towards the Eastern
Church and its tributaries for, although the old feud between these
communities and the Catholic and Protestant Churches still exists, it
does not have any really vital influence at present.'[3]

   After Möhler, the great German theologian Adolf Harnack (1851–
1930) in his *History of Dogma* (Vol. iv), shared these opinions. Harnack
was born in the Baltic Province of Estonia, which was under Russian
domination; and, being influenced by the German Turcophilia of his
time, he had a very distorted opinion of the Orthodox Church. He
was also influenced by the general Russophobia of his age and by
liberal Protestant theology, which denied precisely all those elements
which form the foundation of Orthodox life, especially the mystical
pragmatism of Orthodox worship. So great was the distortion of the
facts about the Orthodox Church made by Harnack that the German
writer G. Wunderle says that 'it is seldom that the Eastern Church
was condemned by a Christian Professor of Theology so violently
and without understanding as Harnack did in his unhappy declarations'.[4] W. A. Visser 't Hooft likewise deplores that Harnack, 'such a
great and broadminded thinker . . . has sometimes made extremely
unfair statements about Orthodoxy'.[5] From Harnack onwards it was
held that the Orthodox Church had nothing in common with the
Early Church except the name, that it was in fact a petrified form of
ancient syncretism.[6] On the other hand there are scholars who,

---

   [1] W. Niesel, *Reformed Symbolics* (London, 1962), pp. 23, 32, 198.

   [2] G. H. Tavard, *Two Centuries of Ecumenism* (Burns & Oates), pp. 77–78.

   [3] Möhler's *Symbolik*, transl. into English by J. B. Roberston (New York,
1906), p. 3; elsewhere I use the London edition (1843).

   [4] *Ueber die Religiöse Bedeutung der Ostkirchlichen Studien* (1939), p. 12.

   [5] *Anglo-Catholicism and Orthodoxy* (London, 1933), p. 93.

   [6] Like Harnack, K. Lubeck writes that 'the Eastern Church was torpid, ignorant
and at a generally low level'. *Die Christlichen Kirchen des Orient* (1911), quoted
in F. Heiler, *Urkirche und Ostkirche* (1937), pp. 555 ff.

although they have good will towards Orthodoxy, nevertheless present things incorrectly from an historical point of view.[7] Others, fewer in number, have tried to work for a proper *rapprochement*, like F. de Baader (1765–1841),[8] who attempted to overcome the misunderstanding and prejudice against the Orthodox Church prevailing in Germany.[9] And Pope Pius XI in his Encyclical *Ecclesiam Dei* (1923) saw that 'Latins must acquire a better and deeper knowledge of Eastern matters and usages. An exact knowledge of things will lead to a true appreciation of persons and at the same time a sincere good will towards them.' On another occasion when he asked the Cardinals to work for unity with the East he used words which show that knowledge of one another will lead to common understanding. 'It is evident' he said, 'that we must, on the one hand, abandon the false idea that has become common in the course of centuries regarding Orthodox institutions and doctrines. On the other hand, we must give ourselves up to a profound study that will show up the agreement between their Fathers and the Latin Fathers, resulting in one and the same faith.'[10]

In the West there has been a continuous reformation, whereas in the East the Orthodox have not changed but have simply interpreted and expounded the dogmas which were formulated by the ancient and undivided Church. On this matter a distinguished German Professor in the University of Heidelberg has written: 'Reluctance to formulate dogmas is not, in itself, any more a weakness than a steady sanguine advance towards new and ever more intricate dogmas is necessarily a sign of spiritual and theological strength. It could very well be just the opposite for, as the history of dogma in the Roman Church shows, dogmas which are continually increasing in intricacy and detail prove in time to be so cumbersome that theological thinking becomes increasingly hampered in its movement and loses its broad catholicity.[11]

---

[7] cf. Konrad Algermissen, *Konfessionskunde* (5th ed. 1910), p. 349, who says that the present Orthodox Church is not the same as the Byzantine Church because, he says, this was united with Rome!

[8] cf. *Der Morgenländische Katholizismus in seinem wesentlichen als in seinem äusserlichen Verhältnisse dargestellt*, Stuttgart, 1841. This book seems to be the most significant writing of nineteenth century from an ecumenical point of view.

[9] In our time this task has been undertaken especially by Ernst Benz, Professor at the University of Marburg, in many works.

[10] G. H. Tavard, *Two Centuries of Ecumenism*, p. 120.

[11] Edm. Schlink, 'Changes in Protestant thinking about the Eastern Church', *E.R.* x (1958), p. 395.

On the Orthodox side there has been a reluctance to study the life and faith of the Roman Church because the latter constantly tried to convert the Orthodox peoples of the East to Catholicism and to subordinate the Orthodox Church to the Roman Pontiff.[12] Over the centuries many Orthodox studied in Roman Catholic schools, both in Rome and elsewhere. Some simply wanted to learn how to resist Romanism, in order to pass on this knowledge to their fellow-Orthodox. Others, alas, submitted to Rome and became the embittered enemies of Orthodoxy.[13]

Today we witness a new trend in the relations between Orthodox and Roman Catholics.[14] Yet although their attitudes are changing, the gap is still wide, and ignorance great. As Fr. Congar writes 'There are very valuable books on the level of information and documentation, and often in sheer erudition; but if we want to understand the Orthodox, we must go beyond them'.[15] Certainly the Second Vatican Council not only permits but advises Roman Catholics to make approaches to the Orthodox. Yet in order to understand the present situation, we must also refer to many earlier events in the history of the Church.

The relations between Orthodox and Anglicans have always been marked by a spirit of sincerity and cordiality. But, because of the political situation in the East, no personal contacts were made until the

[12] For the methods used for the successful conversion of the Orthodox see the recent book: *Christian Unity, A Catholic View*, ed. by John C. Heenan, and the article by Maurice Bévenot, entitled 'Communicatio in Sacris', pp. 114–39. For the purpose of converting the Orthodox Church, the Roman Church has founded: *Congregatio de rebus Graecorum* (by Pope Gregory XIII), *Congregatio de Propaganda Fide pro negotiis ritus orientalis* (by Pope Pius IX), *Congregatio pro Ecclesia Orientalis* (by Pope Benedict XX). The foundation of *Congregatio de Propaganda Fide*, by Pope Gregory XV, in the year 1622, calls for special mention because its mission was to extend the Christian faith in the Orthodox East, which he regarded as *Ecclesia in partibus infidelium* (Church in Non-Christian Regions). The Popes and the Jesuits did not hesitate to include the 'Schismatic' Greeks amongst those who ought to be converted.

[13] For that purpose in the year 1577 the Romans founded the Roman College of St. Athanasius, especially for Greek students. This kind of education Fr. Florovsky calls the root of 'pseudomorphosis' and considers it very dangerous as it leads to a kind of schism in the soul. *H.E.M.*, p. 183.

[14] Dom BedeWinslow, of St. Augustine's Abbey, Ramsgate, tried to establish a friendly dialogue with Roman, Orthodox and Anglicans. For many years his *Eastern Churches Quarterly* spread a sympathetic understanding of Orthodox Churches and theology.

[15] Y. Congar, 'My first step in Ecumenism', *E.E.*, p. 28.

early seventeenth century. Some of the Reformers borrowed material from the Orthodox Church, and their appeal to 'sound learning' included a study of the Fathers; but their sources were the liturgical and other books and documents that were available in England. However, the opening of English trade in the Middle East, and the establishment of an Embassy in Constantinople, made possible considerable contacts over the years between Anglicans and Orthodox both in the East and in England. Diplomats, clergy, scholars and travellers came to know the Orthodox at first hand. Orthodox bishops and clergy visited or studied in England. Anglican Archbishops and Bishops corresponded with Orthodox Patriarchs and Church leaders. Yet the majority of Anglicans and Orthodox have usually remained ignorant of each other's churches, for, as Fr. Florovsky wrote, 'the average Churchman, in all denominations, is still hardly aware of ecumenical problems and ecumenical progress'.[16] Furthermore, many Anglican theologians have had an extremely limited view of Orthodoxy, while most Orthodox have failed to understand the mentality of Anglicanism, with its dislike of dogmatism and legalism, and have been unaware of the Caroline divines and their Catholic, but non-Roman, conception of the Church. Nevertheless much progress has been made; but much remains still to be done.

Anglican–Roman relations have of course been the subject of an immense literature, ever since the Reformation. There were, first, the writings of the Reformation period in the sixteenth century, with its political factors and the complications of Henry VIII's divorce, Mary Tudor's marriage to Philip of Spain; the accession of Elizabeth I and the Pope's excommunication and 'deposition' of her, with the Spanish Armada, the Recusants, the Jesuit missionary priests, whose activity was regarded as treasonable, and so on. There was then a period in the seventeenth century when political considerations were not so pressing and matters of doctrine and church order could be debated, as between Archbishop Laud and Fisher the Jesuit. With James II and the Jacobite movement in favour of the exiled Stuarts, political tension returned, although this did not prevent a man as distinguished as William Wake (Archbishop of Canterbury 1716–37) from making serious contacts, which we should now call 'ecumenical', with French Roman Catholics in the hope of a 'Gallican-Anglican' *rapprochement*. Then in the Napoleonic period the French Revolution and the sufferings of the Catholic *emigré* priests and faithful laity, many of whom found refuge in England,

[16] George Florovsky, 'The Ecumenical Dialogue', *E.E.* p. 45.

led to increased friendliness. This was succeeded by the Tractarian Movement and the mid-nineteenth-century renaissance of Roman Catholicism in England, coupled with the rise of Ultramontanism, the first Vatican Council (1870), the dogma of Papal Infallibility, the condemnation of Anglican Orders (1896), and the suppression of Roman Catholic Modernism by the Bull *Lamentabili* (1907), and connected events. All this made the Roman Church appear to Anglicans in the guise of an implacable adversary: welcoming, or even 'seducing', converts from Anglicanism who followed Newman into the Roman fold; teaching aggressively that only the Papal Communion was the true Catholic Church, and that Anglican sacraments (even, it seems, baptism) were therefore invalid and Anglicans 'outside the church' and little better than non-Christians; obscurantist in biblical criticism, maintaining views of inspiration and the Old Testament which were critically indefensible; superstitious in popular piety, with regard to such matters as the Holy House of Loreto, and the appearances of the Virgin Mary at Lourdes and at Fatima; and over-dogmatic in its Mariology by the definitions of the Immaculate Conception and the Bodily Assumption as *de fide*. All this meant that, until very recent years, literature on Anglican–Roman relations was predominantly *controversial*. Typical of it were such works as that by Archbishop Salmon (Protestant Archbishop of Dublin) on *Infallibility*; on the other side were many substantial Roman works and hundreds of popular writings, from the urbane books of cultivated priests like Mgr. Ronald Knox to the pamphlets of the Catholic Truth Society, which were matched on the other side by the extreme low-church productions of the Protestant Truth Society directed by Mr. Kensit— the arch-protestant Anglican lay polemicist. Only with the work of men like Fr. Yves Congar and Dom Gregory Dix did a better age dawn, and they were lone pioneers until John XXIII and the Second Vatican Council changed the atmosphere completely.

Dealing with three Christian Churches which claim to be Catholic[17] does not mean that I belittle the importance of the Protestant Churches. On the contrary, as an Orthodox I believe that they are of great importance and they deserve all our love and veneration. Already we see the beginning of the dialogue between Orthodox and Methodists in the Lectures of the Rev. Dr. Marcus Ward[18] and Professor E. Gordon

---

[17] W. A. Visser 't Hooft, *Anglo-Catholicism and Orthodoxy*, p. 111, says that Anglicanism, Orthodoxy and Old Catholicism represent together the Catholic family outside the Roman Communion.

[18] *D.E.W.* p. 41–44.

Rupp.[19] The first says 'I suppose there is no greater gap in the whole of Christendom than between the Methodist Tradition and the Orthodox, and I am to speak not so much of what I and those like me can learn, but what as a matter of fact, I, a Methodist, have learned from Orthodoxy.'[20] Professor Rupp, more close to the Orthodox Tradition and an authority on the Reformation, says 'the resemblances between Methodism and Rome are occidental, and the resemblances to Orthodoxy are accidental.'[21] He emphasizes the fact that John Wesley 'has to be seen within the Augustinian tradition, and in many ways his temper of mind and outlook was like that of the Cappadocian Fathers. He has the same concern for the life of the soul, for inward religion, the practical philanthropy and care for the poor which mark St. Basil. His forthright moralism and his ethical Puritanism I suppose, of all Fathers, is most like St. Chrysostom, that other John.'[22] Speaking on Calvinism and Orthodoxy, Professor Rupp says: 'There are deep resemblances on some points between Calvinism and Orthodoxy in Calvin's very rich doctrine on the Holy Spirit'. Finally on the Lutheran tradition, Professor Rupp points out that 'there are very profound resemblances between Lutheran theology and that of Orthodoxy.'[23] This is the reason why I believe that the presence of the Orthodox Church in Ecumenical discussions provides an indispensable link between the various Christian traditions. As Professor Rupp suggests: 'I believe that there are some grounds for supposing that the united Anglican and Methodist Church in England would form a new kind of Church which in some ways would be much more like Orthodoxy than it is like the Church of England as it is today, or the Church of Rome as it is today.'[24]

[19] *We Belong to One Another*. Methodist, Anglican and Orthodox Essays. Ed. by A. M. Allchin (Epworth Press, London, 1965), pp. 13–47.

[20] *D.E.W.* p. 41.

[21] *We Belong to One Another*, p. 15.

[22] ibid. pp. 18–19.

[23] ibid. p. 21.

[24] ibid. p. 22; cf. also Gordon Rupp, *Methodists, Anglicans and Orthodoxy*. S. Series 4: No. 10 (Winter-Spring 1964), p. 566.

PART ONE

Chapter I

THE ONE UNDIVIDED CHRISTIAN CHURCH

1. *Unity in Faith throughout Schisms and Divisions*

There have always been schisms and divisions among Christians: St. Paul's First Epistle to the Corinthians is in part a plea for unity in a divided community. Clement of Rome wrote in A.D. 97 to the Church of Corinth attacking rebellion and division. Ignatius of Antioch in his letters recommended to the representatives of the Churches of Ephesus, Magnesia and Tralles that they should be at peace with one another and obey their leaders. Polycarp of Smyrna wrote on the same lines to the Philippians. Irenaeus attacked the Gnostics, who were at first a great obstacle to the unity of the Church, though later, because much of their theological system was alien to Christian teaching, the Church parted company with them completely. Opposed to Gnosticism, and of course opposed to the Church, was another heretical and schismatic movement, that of Montanism. We can also see various schisms in the early Church of Rome. There was that between the followers of the anti-pope Hippolytus and those of Pope Callistus (A.D. c.217–c.223); and simultaneously another division occurred there between the followers of Novatian and Cornelius. Yet another schism appeared in Carthage under Felicissimus, which lasted for some time. At the beginning of the fourth century other schisms occurred, those of Melitius in Alexandria (A.D. 306) and of the Donatists in Carthage (A.D. 311). There were, then, in these early centuries, different parties and theological tendencies in the Church, but its unity was nevertheless maintained. For example, the great theologians Diodore of Tarsus, Theodore of Mopsuestia, and Theodoret of Cyrus lived in communion with the Catholic and Orthodox Church, although they were in conflict with Cyril of Alexandria, Rabbula of Edessa, and Proclus of Constantinople, over the question of the two natures of Christ.

The first schism between East and West occurred in the time of Bishop Victor of Rome (189–198) over the question of the date of Easter; and, as a result, the Churches of Asia Minor[1] were separated from the West until the first Ecumenical Council. The second schism between the two parts of Christendom appeared when the Westerners at the Council of Sardica (A.D. c.343) and the Easterners in Philippopolis excommunicated each other. There were schisms between Rome and Constantinople during the second and fourth Ecumenical Councils, when the Roman Primacy was threatened by the elevation of the See of Constantinople to equality with the See of Rome. Another schism occurred between these two Churches when St. John Chrysostom was condemned, and it lasted from A.D. 404 to 438. During the fifth century a new schism appeared between Rome and Constantinople, over the decree called the *Henoticon*, from 484 to 518 or 519. There was another rift in the year 649 when the Council at the Lateran condemned the Patriarchs of Constantinople, Sergius and Pyrrhus. Then in 692 the Council 'in Trullo', the *Quinisextum*, decided to recognize eighty-five Canons as Apostolic, whereas Rome recognized only fifty. This Council (Can. 36) also renewed the 28th Canon of the fourth Ecumenical Council, which granted to the See of Constantinople equal primacy of honour with Rome, and condemned the compulsory celibacy of the clergy and other customs of the Roman Church. Pope Sergius rejected the decisions of the Council 'in Trullo'. However, despite these controversies, and apart from the short-lived Photian schism of 867–870, the fundamental unity of the Church was maintained, until the schism of 1054.

2. The Differences between East and West

(i) Theological differences

Eastern Theology has as its basis the three Persons of the Holy Trinity, whose unity it then proceeds to explain. In the East Athanasius and Basil had to oppose the heresy which denied the divinity of Christ and held that the Son was a kind of demi-god and the Holy Spirit an offshoot from him, making both inferior to the Father. The Eastern Church had to insist that the Holy Spirit is absolutely equal with the Son and absolutely equal to the Father, and that there is no difference in the one-ness of the Divine Being; but that each person, Father, Son and Holy Ghost, is different in relation to the others.

---

[1] Eusebius, *Hist. Eccl.* v, 23–4.

On the other hand, Western Theology has as its basis the unity of God and proceeds from this to understand the three Persons in the Holy Trinity. It had to deal with Adoptionism, which said that Christ was the adopted son of God, no different in essence from all Christians who are adopted sons of God by grace. The Western Church replied that the Son is absolutely equal to the Father and he gives us the Holy Spirit as does the Father, and in order to protect the absolute equality of the Son and the Father they said that the Holy Spirit proceeds from the Son just as from the Father. It is from this point that Western theology has derived the phrase which describes the Holy Spirit as proceeding from the Father 'and from the Son' (*Filioque*). St. Augustine had realized that there was a difference between the Eastern and Western conceptions of the Holy Trinity.[1] Likewise St. Anselm says that the Latins talk of one substance and three persons, and the Greeks of one person and three substances.[2] Apart from these differences, there were many others. 'The school of Alexandria in the third century was producing a type of theology very different in tone from that of the Africans; and the difference of tone showed itself in opinions surprisingly different—for instance, about the destiny of the lost, or the meaning of the Body of Christ in the eucharist. Later, Alexandria and Antioch and Africa and Rome nourished very distinctive types of doctrine among theologians who were pillars of orthodoxy; and differences of opinion are sometimes marked.'[3] We must also observe that Jerome and Augustine not only tolerated such differences but demanded a like toleration from others—*Salvo jure communionis diversa sentire;* and Cyprian also had insisted on mutual respect between rival traditions.[4] These differences were not irreconcilable as long as the atmosphere remained favourable.[5]

(ii) *Ecclesiastical differences*

As in theology, so in administration, the Romans looked for unity and consequently the Popes claimed jurisdiction over the whole Church. This led almost inevitably to the separation between East and West. Here we come to the heart of the controversy between the two

[1] *De Trinitate*, vii, 4 (*P.L.* xlii, cols. 939–42).

[2] *De Fide Trinitatis* (*P.L.* clviii), col. 1144, cf. col. 284.

[3] C. Gore, *The Holy Spirit and the Church*, pp. 175–6. See especially Gore's *Roman Catholic Claims*, pp. 134 ff, where he treats this matter at greater length.

[4] Aug. *de Bapt.* ii, 3–6; Jerome, *Adv. Lucif.* 25; Cyprian: *De Cath. Eccl. Unit.* 5 and *Ep.* 68.4.

[5] Maurice Villain, *Unity. A History and some Reflections*. Transl. by J. R. Foster (Harvill Press, London, 1963), p. 153.

halves of Christendom. For their differing ecclesiologies sprang from their different views of the Holy Trinity. The Western side had a monarchical conception of the Church; the Eastern side had an oligarchical conception of it as a body of Bishops succeeding the Apostles. 'The two formulas', writes Maurice Villain (a Roman Catholic), 'were not necessarily irreconcilable. The Bishop of Rome was the first of the Patriarchs and received special honour, while Constantinople claimed its rightful autonomy. But it should be noted that the East had never been aware of any primacy of divine right granted to Peter by Christ; it was simply thought that Peter's successors drew their privilege from the privileged position of Rome (such was the view of Basil, John Chrysostom and John Damascene). The development of the Roman doctrine on this very important point took place outside the East.'[6] We should note, however, that a contrary view of the differences between Greeks and Latins over the Trinity is held by theologians like Fr. Bernard Leeming, for instance, who will not accept wide generalizations about them, and thinks that these differences have been exaggerated.[7] Cardinal Giacomo Lercaro, on the other hand, in an article on the Decree *De Ecumenismo* and the dialogue with non-Catholic [sic] Eastern Churches agrees that Eastern Orthodox ecclesiology reflects their conception of the Trinity. As a communion of sister-churches they consider the Trinity first as the Divine Persons and then proceed to affirm their one nature. In contrast, he continues, the West, following Tertullian and Augustine, begins with the divine Monarchy and then proceeds to affirm that this is a unity of three persons.[8]

(iii) *Political differences*

In addition to theological and ecclesiastical factors there were also important political influences at work in the separation of East and West. For instance, in the eighth century, Leo III (reigned A.D. 717–40) withdrew the provinces of Southern Italy and East Illyricum from the jurisdiction of the Pope and allocated them to the Patriarch of Constantinople. These two provinces were the bridges between East and West, because there Easterners and Westerners lived side by side. By this action Leo identified the ecclesiastical frontiers with the political frontiers.[9] He excluded from the Byzantine Empire all the

[6] Villain, op. cit., p. 154.   [7] 'Orthodox-Catholic Relations', *R.E.C.* p. 29.
[8] *C. v* (1965), p. 88.
[9] Runciman, *The Eastern Schism* (Oxford, Clarendon Press, 1956), p. 20.

non-Byzantine political and ecclesiastical leaders. And when the Popes founded the Papal State (754–6) they established their independence from the Byzantine Empire, and at the same time became political leaders in their own right, which Eastern Patriarchs had never been. Gradually we can see the separation of the Christian Church into two distinct blocs. The coronation of Charlemagne in 800, and the establishment of what was called the Holy Roman Empire, added yet another element to the political differences between East and West.

Patriarch Photius and Pope Nicolas I, who were responsible for the ninth-century schism, were at the same time typical products of the two worlds. Photius represented the Greeks, who excelled in speculative thought, in theology, and in art. Nicolas represented the Romans, who were good administrators, interested more in the practical running of the Church than 'in the subtleties of doctrinal definitions. The Greeks had a special love for the beauty of worship; the Romans valued discipline and order.'[10] A controversy over both jurisdiction and theology led to a split in relations between the two Churches. But, in spite of this division, the unity of faith was maintained and the breach between Photius and Nicolas was eventually healed.[11] By 1054, when a new division occurred, the significance of schism was forgotten, and at the time the new schism was considered a temporary affair of minor importance.

There were other reasons which at different times influenced the thought of the Eastern Church on the question of the unity of Christendom. Amongst these was the barbarous behaviour of the Crusaders, who tried to convert the Greeks to Latinism, treating them as infidels, confiscating their churches, and imprisoning their clergy. In the year 1185 the knights conquered Salonica and acted with great brutality, destroying every sacred and holy place of the Orthodox Church. The sack of Constantinople in the Fourth Crusade of 1204 dealt the final blow to brotherly relations between these two parts of the Christian Communion.

We have now come to understand that another major factor in the division of Christendom was nationalism. We can see its first appearance in North Africa in the so-called Donatist schism. The

---

[10] N. Zernov, *The Christian East* (London, S.P.C.K., 1956), p. 10 ff.

[11] For a new appreciation of Photius' policy in the schism between East and West during the 9th century, see: F. Dvornik, *The Photian Schism, History and Legend* (Cambridge, 1948).

Christians there belonged to two national groups, one formed by the natives of Africa, the other by the descendants of Latin colonists from Italy. These two elements in the Christian Church in North Africa were sharply opposed to each other. The conflict was so bitter that the schism was maintained until the seventh century, when both Churches disappeared, worn out by fratricidal struggles and finally overwhelmed by the Muslim invasions.

In the same way the conflicts in the fifth century between the Greeks and the Copts in Egypt acquired a national basis. The theological debate about the two *physeis* (natures) of Christ became virtually open warfare as a result of the national rivalry between the two parties. The rebellion of the Copts was supported by the Nestorians and the Armenians, who for political reasons broke off relations with the Byzantine Church and became independent national Churches.

Monophysitism became even more intolerant than Nestorianism towards anything Greek. The conflict over the two natures of Christ was interpreted as a war against Satan, who was identified with everything in society reflecting the influence of the wealthy Greco–Roman 'exploiters'. The nationalism and isolation of the different Eastern Churches was increased by Muslim domination. The Churches became self-contained, self-satisfied, and introspective. Slowly over the centuries they acquired the characteristics of national groups, and this led eventually to the complete identification of Church and Nation. The result has been the Eastern Christian concept of a single religious and national community.[12]

3. *Independence and Disunity*

Even today Roman Catholic writers insist that the independence (autonomy) of the Eastern Patriarchs was not a complete one because this 'would be contrary to the dogma of the Pope's primacy of jurisdiction.'[1] To support their view these Roman Catholic authors speak of appeals made by Easterners to the Popes. 'We can cite about fifteen cases' writes W. de Vries, 'of appeal to Rome from the East . . .'

[12] For an extensive and deep explanation of the various differences between East and West, cultural, national etc. see the works of Steven Runciman, *The Eastern Schism*, and Philip Sherrard, *The Greek East and the Latin West* (London, Oxford University Press, 1959).

[1] W. de Vries, 'The Origin of the Eastern Patriarchates', *O.I.C.* ii (1966) pp. 65–6.

and this was the contention of Cardinal Newman as well.[2] To answer these assertions we can refer to the following statement made by B. Jackson:[3]

Cardinal Newman in his very bright and sympathetic sketch of Theodoret writes the following remarkable sentence. 'This at least he has in common with St. Chrysostom that both of them were deprived of their episcopal rank by a council, both appealed to the Holy See, and by the Holy See both were cleared and restored to their ecclesiastical dignities.' It would be difficult in the compass of so short a sentence to combine more statements so completely misleading. To say that Chrysostom and Theodoret both appealed to the 'Holy See' is as much an anachronism as to say that they appealed to the court of the Vatican or to the Dome of St. Peter's. In their day there was no Holy See, that is to say, *kat' exochen*. All sees were Holy Sees, just as all Bishops were styled Your Holiness. Rome, it is true, was the only apostolic See in the West, but it was not the only apostolic See, and whatever official precedence it could claim over Antioch, Jerusalem and Alexandria was due to its being the See of the old Imperial Capital, a precedence expressly ordered at Chalcedon to be shared with the New Rome on the Bosphorus. As to the 'appeal' we have seen what it meant in the case of Theodoret.[4]

Thanks to the new Emperor Marcian he could return to his See in the following year.[5] It meant the same in the case of Chrysostom. Cut to the quick at the cruel and brutal treatment of his friends after his banishment from Constantinople in the summer 404, he pleaded his cause in letters sent as well to Venerius of Milan and Chromatius of Aquileia as to Innocent of Rome. Innocent very properly espoused his cause, declared his deposition void, and did his best to move Honorius to persuade Arcadius to convoke a Council. The cruel story of the long martyrdom of bitter exile and the death in the lonely chapel at Comana is a terrible satire on the restoration to ecclesiastical dignities. The unwary reader of the 'Historical Sketch' might imagine the famous John of the mouth of gold brought back in triumph to Constantinople by the authority of the Pope in 404, as he had been by the enthusiasm of his flock in 403, and Arcadius and Eudoxia cowering before the power of the Holy Church like Henry IV at Canossa in

---

[2] ibid. p. 68. J. H. Newman, *Historical Sketches*, ii, 308.

[3] *A Select Library of Nicene and Post-Nicene Fathers of the Christian Church*, Second Series, vol. iii, p. 9, Note 5.

[4] *Epist.* 113. The author is referring to the appeal made by Theodoret to Pope Leo after his deposition by the Robber Synod of Ephesus in 449.

[5] cf. J. Quasten, *Patrology*, iii, p. 537.

1077. The true picture of the three years of agony which preceded the old man's passage to the better world in 407 is a painful contrast to contemplate.

This is a typical example of the so-called Eastern appeals to the Popes and the Pope's interventions in the East. But in order to create an accurate idea of the relations between East and West during the first millennium we must look at some further relevant factos.

The first serious clash between the Eastern and Western Churches occurred between those two great prelates, Photius the Patriarch of Constantinople and Nicolas, Pope of Rome, and revealed the extent of the gap which separated East from West. 'Photius was one of the most wonderful men of all the Middle Ages', writes Adrian Fortescue. 'Had he not given his name to the great schism, he would always be remembered as the greatest scholar of his time, and as, in every way, the greatest man in the Byzantine church . . .. He was a sort of universal genius, philosopher, philologist, theologian, lawyer, mathematician, natural scientist, orator, poet. His extant works fill five volumes of Migne.'[6] Pope Nicolas was no less distinguished. As a contemporary wrote of him: 'Since the time of Blessed Gregory [the Great] no one who has been raised to the Papal dignity can be compared to him. He commanded kings and tyrants as if he were lord of the world.'[7] 'Nicolas totius mundi Imperatorem se fecit.'[8]

From the controversy between these two prelates we can see clearly the distinction between East and West and the existence of two independent bodies in the Universal Church. Photius stood by the principle that 'The Churches must agree on the essential points; for the rest, the principle of Church freedom should prevail.' And in a letter sent to Pope Nicolas he declared that the West should accept

[6] Adrian Fortescue, *The Orthodox Eastern Church* (second ed., London, 1908) pp. 138–9. Fortescue follows J. B. S. Carwithen and A. Lyall, *History of the Christian Church* (London, 1856) (see J. N. Valeta, *The Letters of Patriarch Photius* (London, 1894), p. 119), and like other Roman Catholic authors such as C. Baronius and J. Hergenröther makes Photius the author of the schism. But recently Roman Catholic authors like Jugie, Grumel and especially Dvornik have re-examined the facts about the controversy between Photius and the Pope and restored the truth about the attitude of Photius towards Church unity.

[7] Regino, *Chronicon* an. 868 (*Mon. Germ. Hist., Script.* i, 579), quoted by Fortescue, op. cit., p. 142.

[8] F. Heiler, *Urkirche und Ostkirche*, p. 239. Cf. F. Dvornik, *Patriarch Photius, Father of Schism or Patron of Reunion?*, p. 24.

the decisions of the Eastern Church and *vice versa*. During the conflict between them, two Archbishops were unfrocked by Pope Nicolas (Günter of Cologne and Thiegand of Trier) and appeals were made by their supporters to Patriarch Photius. Photius, however, upheld his principle, that clergy condemned by the West should be recognized as such by the East and *vice versa*, because he held that the two Churches were equal and there was no right of appeal between them. The statements made by Western writers that Easterners appealed to the Pope are a distortion of the facts. Photius, being consistent, sent the records of the Council of 867 to the Emperor of the West, Louis II, in order to ensure their application in the West. Another episode further illustrates the independence of the Eastern Church. During the second reign of Photius, in the year 879, a Council was summoned in the Church of St. Sophia, at which 383 bishops from the East and three bishops from the West, representing the Pope, were present. The papal representatives thought that the Council was the place in which they could announce the decisions of the Pope—as we gather from the papal letters which they carried. The bishops, however, rejected these claims: they regarded the Pope as the leader of the West, and the Patriarch of Constantinople as the leader of the East. This conception they derived from the Twenty-eighth Canon of the Council of Chalcedon (451). But they did not go beyond the definition contained in that Canon. For when two bishops present at the Council, Basil of Martyroupolis, a representative of the Patriarch of Antioch, and Procopius of Caesarea in Cappadocia, asserted the superiority of the Bishop of Constantinople, this proposition was rejected on exactly the same grounds.[9] Another event at this Council was the acceptance even by the Pope's representatives of Patriarch Photius' principle that those who are excommunicated in the West should be recognized as such even in the East and *vice versa*.[10] The significance of this decision is of great importance because it shows that the two Churches in the West and in the East agreed that matters of discipline should be decided independently. Moreover, Patriarch Photius, in his willingness to settle all matters between the two Churches, and endeavouring to avoid any misunderstanding, asked Pope Nicolas, in a subsequent letter, not to accept clerics from the East without a letter of recommendation from himself.

The independence of the Eastern Church is demonstrated by another

[9] Mansi, 17A, c. 500 and 521.   [10] ibid, c. 497.

point, which Francis Dvornik, the well-known Roman Catholic scholar, has recognized. 'Never' he says, 'did a Patriarch ask a Pope in his synodal letter for confirmation of his election. The election of the Patriarchs and Bishops was regarded as a matter concerning the internal affairs of the Eastern Church and the Emperor. The Eastern Church was always very jealous in defence of its absolute independence in disciplinary matters . . .'.[11] The contention of W. de Vries that 'In the second millennium confirmation [by the Pope] came to be an appointment . . .'[12] does not correspond with the facts. We have on the contrary evidence that the Eastern Patriarchs not only refrained from asking the Pope for any confirmation of their election (except the recognition which all bishops always require from their fellow bishops to maintain communion with them), but also requested that the Popes should announce their own election to them and give them a satisfactory confession of their faith. Peter of Antioch, for example, asked Pope Leo for a profession of faith. There may be papal letters sent to the Eastern Patriarchs in which the Popes in their arrogance might say that the power of the Patriarchate itself was conferred by the Holy See: *ab eadem ipsam patriarchalem auctoriatem promanare*;[13] but the fact remains that in the East little importance was attached to such claims by Rome.

In 906 Leo VI, the Emperor of Byzantium, wanted to contract a fourth marriage with Zoe Carbopsina, by whom he had a son (Constantine Porphyrogenitus), in order to make him his lawful successor. But a fourth marriage had never been allowed in the Orthodox Church. Following the application of the Emperor a Council was convoked in Constantinople to which the Pope sent representatives.[14] In that Council, with the assistance of Pope Sergius, not only was the fourth marriage of the Emperor allowed but Patriarch Nicolas, who opposed the decision, was deposed.[15] After the death of Leo, Patriarch Nicolas was restored and in a letter to Pope Anastasius III (911–13) he

[11] F. Dvornik, *Patriarch Photius, Father of Schism or Patron of Reunion?* p. 24.

[12] W. de Vries, 'The Eastern Patriarchates and their Relationship to the power of the Pope', *O.I.C.*, ii (1966), p. 130.

[13] cf. R. de Martinis, *Juris Pontificii de Propaganda Fide*, Pars I, Vol. vi, 1 (Rome, 1894) p. 454, 2, in de Vries, 'The origin of the Eastern Patriarchates', p. 61.

[14] Migne *P.G.* cxi, 195–200. Letter of Patriarch Nicolas, No. 32, to Pope Nicholas (de quartis nuptiis perperam acceptis apud Romanos).

[15] J. Gay comments (*L'Italie méridionale et l'empire Byzantin* (Paris, 1904) p. 189) 'la vie scandaleuse [of Pope Sergius] fait une contraste étrange avec la noble et austère figure du Patriarche Byzantin Nicolas'.

condemned fourth marriages especially as applied to the Eastern Church and accused Rome of introducing its own customs to the Eastern Church by sanctioning this marriage.[16] Patriarch Nicolas, one of the great Patriarchs of Constantinople, wrote many letters to Pope John,[17] in which he emphasized that, in order to re-establish harmony between the two Churches each should recognize the autonomy of the other, and must not interfere in the other's internal affairs. Patriarch Nicolas sent two legates who were living in Rome to visit the Pope personally and let him know the Patriarch's views, which the Pope agreed to accept.[18] Yet only a few years later another Eastern Emperor, Romanus Lecapenus, wanted to make his son Theophylact, who was sixteen years old, Patriarch of Constantinople, and in order to succeed he asked the help of Pope John XI. The Pope sent four clerics to Constantinople for the purpose and they took part in the ordination and the enthronement of the boy.

From the first, the Church had always allowed a great variety of customs and usages in its different provinces. But Rome gradually tried to enforce its own ways on other parts of the Christian world. And its attempts to do this in the East gave rise to some of the worst controversies and scandals in the history of inter-church relations, and were also a contributory cause of the final separation between Catholicism and Orthodoxy.

A major difficulty arose when Pope Leo IX (1049–54) tried to introduce Roman customs into Southern Italy, which was ecclesiastically under the jurisdiction of the Patriarch of Constantinople and politically under that of the Byzantine state. The Patriarch Michael Cerularius, in retaliation, closed all the Latin monasteries and churches in Constantinople. Once more two great personalities representing two different worlds had clashed. In order to settle the dispute, which was about theological matters as well as over the question of Roman customs, Pope Leo sent to Constantinople (1054) three delegates, one of whom, Cardinal Humbert, was the leader of the movement of Cluny. The papal delegates brought letters for the Emperor and the Patriarch Michael Cerularius, whom the Romans accused of obtaining the patriarchal throne unlawfully. That was of course an

---

[16] Patriarch Nicolas, Letter No. 32; cf. also G. Every, *Misunderstandings Between East and West* (Ecumenical Studies in History, No. 4, Lutterworth Press, London, 1965) pp. 52–3.

[17] Letters 53, 54, 55, 56. Migne, *P.G.* cxi, c. 247–58.

[18] Letter 28. Migne, *P.G.* cxi, c. 175–82.

easy accusation, which had been used even against Photius, because the Romans thought that such charges would permit them to appear on the scene as arbiters of the case. Patriarch Michael, however, had good reasons for not coming into contact with the Roman representatives. He maintained that the three Roman delegates were not really the delegates of the Pope and that the papal seal was forged— the letters were abrupt in tone, whereas the Patriarch knew that the Pope was courteous.[19] Moreover, by the time the Roman delegates arrived in Constantinople Pope Leo had died and their mission was thereby nullified, although it was confirmed later. Nonetheless Cardinal Humbert and his followers went into the Church of St. Sophia on Saturday 16 July 1054 and left on the holy altar, in the presence of the Emperor and the congregation, the excommunication of the Patriarch of Constantinople and his adherents. The excommunication likened the Orthodox Church to various heretics (Simonians, Valentinians, Arians, Nicolaitans, Donatists, Severians, Manicheans, Pneumatomachians . . .) and declared that:

By the authority of the Holy and Indivisible Trinity and of that of the Apostolic See of which we are carrying out the *legatio*, by the authority of all the Orthodox Fathers of the seven Ecumenical Councils and of the whole Catholic Church, we subscribe the anathema pronounced by our Lord the most Holy Pope upon Michael and his followers if they do not reform themselves in this fashion: Anathema, maranatha, together with the Simoniacs, etc., and if they do not recant with all the heretics and with the devil and his angels, Amen, amen.

The impression created in the East by the excommunication, and even more by the words of the anathema itself, is clearly shown in the following statement by N. Glubokovsky, a Russian professor:

The formidable fact is that, usurping the divine authority over the whole Church, the Pope put himself on a level with the Holy Trinity and above the Ecumenical Councils which he himself had recognized. This hierarchic self-exaltation cut the Papacy away from the whole

---

[19] Letter of Michael to the Patriarch of Antioch, ch. 9. The Papal letter contained such expressions as 'If there be any nation anywhere in the world which arrogantly disagrees with the Roman Church, such a nation *non sit jam dicenda vel habenda ecclesia aliqua sed omnino nulla, quin potius conciliabulum haereticorum et synagoga Satanae.*' Cf. N. Glubokovsky, 'The Modern Papacy and Reunion', *C.E.*, v (1924) p. 126.

Christian East and has become an impassable barrier of division between them.[20]

Soon after, Patriarch Michael summoned a Council which condemned the Papal letter and excommunicated its author and those who accepted it.[21] The other patriarchs of the East accepted the decisions of that Council, although Peter of Antioch wrote to Michael Cerularius: 'the Latins are our brothers, and it is only ignorance that makes them deviate. We must not demand from them the same scrupulous exactitude that we demand from our own highly educated circles. It should be enough that they confess the Mystery of the Trinity and the Incarnation.' Perhaps, he suggested, they had lost the copies of the acts of the earlier councils.[22]

Yet the breach between the two Churches became a permanent one, even if it was a gradual process rather than an immediate happening. A penetrating account of the real issues between East and West is given by Sir Paul Rycaut, a seventeenth-century diplomat, who resided for a time in Smyrna:[23]

But let us not only hear what the Greeks themselves do utter in this point, but observe the words of that famous Venetian Father Paul Sarpus, who in the 25th Chapter of his history of the Inquisition, hath these pertinent and impartial words: The Eastern and Western Churches continued both in communion and Christian charity for the space of nine hundred years and more, in which time the Pope of Rome was reverenced and esteemed no less by the Greeks than by the Latins; ... ecclesiastical discipline was severely maintained in each country by the prelates of it, not arbitrarily but absolutely, according to order and canonical rigour, none putting his hand into the Government of another, but one advised the other to the observance of the Canons. In those days never did any Pope of Rome pretend to confer benefices in the dioceses of other Bishops; neither was the custom yet introduced of getting money out of others by way of Dispensation or Bulls. But as soon as the Court of Rome began to pretend that it was not subject to Canons, and that she might, according to her own discretion, alter any Order of the Fathers, Councils, and the Apostles themselves; and that she attempted, instead of the

---

[20] *C.E.* v (1924) p. 127.
[21] Mansi 19, 812 ff.   [22] S. Runciman, op. cit., p. 65.
[23] Paul Rycaut, *The present state of the Greek and Armenian Churches* (London, 1679), pp. 117–20. This book is of great importance and it seems to me that it is little known to Orthodox scholars.

ancient Primacy of the Apostolical See, to bring in an absolute dominion, not ruled by any Law, or Canon, then the division grew.
And as this division grew between the Eastern and Western Churches
for the causes aforesaid, for the same reasons were the causes of
division and separation in the Western Church itself.

It should now be clear that the schism was not caused by the East
alone as the Roman Catholics assert. It should also be remembered that
it was one of many disputes between East and West, though in this
particular instance there resulted a more permanent breaking of
intercommunion. Had the Crusades not taken place it is probable that
the Churches would have resumed their relations, even though the
latest dispute had resulted in something unusual in the history of the
two Churches, namely, mutual excommunication. Nevertheless,
attempts at a reconciliation never stopped: but since the reasons which
dictated them were more often political than ecclesiastical, they failed.
Two factors played a most important role in the moves towards
reconciliation. First, the desire of Rome to impose upon the Eastern
Church the Roman primacy, and second, the Greek fear of the Turks
who, threatening the Eastern Empire, compelled the Orthodox
Church to ask the West for help.

4. *Attempts at Unity*, 1054–1453

The history of the Church is not only a history of divisions but also
of efforts to restore unity. But alas, over all these negotiations hung the
heavy shadow of political opportunism. And they were not made
easier by the fact that Rome and Constantinople held different conceptions of Church unity. In Rome the idea of Pope Gregory VII was
dominant—that the spiritual power of the papacy was parallel to that
of the sun, and the power of kings and emperors to that of the moon.
In Constantinople, on the other hand, it was generally recognized that
the supreme doctrinal authority was an Ecumenical Council, which
could be called by the five Apostolic Patriarchs of Rome, Constantinople, Alexandria, Antioch and Jerusalem. In other words, as far as the
Roman Church was concerned, union meant the submission of the
Eastern Church to the Pope; to the Eastern Church it meant that
the Bishop of Rome should resume his place amongst the five senior
patriarchs of Christendom.[1]

[1] Runciman, op. cit., p. 58.

There were, of course, people on both sides who deplored the idea of a breach within Christendom. In 1089 Pope Urban II sent an embassy under Cardinal Rangier and Nicolas, Abbot of the Greek Monastery of Grottaferrata in Rome, with a letter to the Emperor of Byzantium, Alexius Comnenus, lifting the excommunication imposed upon him by Pope Gregory VII in 1081 and asking for the reopening of Latin Churches in the Eastern Empire. On this occasion the Patriarch of Constantinople, Nicolas II, wrote a letter to the Pope informing him that the Latin Churches were now free, but he asked the Pope to come to Constantinople to discuss the differences between the two Churches; or, if that were impossible, he would write a letter explaining these matters. At the same time the Patriarch remarked that the Pope had omitted to send the traditional letter on his accession; but he thought that this could be repaired by his personal presence or by a statement. Although there was no development of this correspondence, it is apparent that the two Churches did not at this stage consider themselves in schism.[2] There were Latin pilgrims at Constantinople and Greek ones at Rome because the common people in both East and West were not concerned about disputes and differences between their church leaders.

The Council of Bari (1098) was held because of the difficult position in which the Byzantines found themselves when faced with the threat of the Seljuk Turks. In this situation the Byzantines asked the Pope for help, and thus brought about the first Crusade. Anselm, Archbishop of Canterbury, who was in exile from England, addressed the Council and showed the same attitude to the Greeks as Peter of Antioch had showed to the Latins. He held that the difference between Eastern and Western theology was not great, and emphasized that the Greeks were fellow-Christians and not schismatics.[3]

In the year 1113 or 1114 the Archbishop of Milan, Peter Chrysolan, who was himself a Greek, was sent by Pope Paschal to Constantinople. He addressed the Emperor and the Holy Synod, and spoke to them about the differences that divided the two Churches. But the main issue—that of Papal authority—continued to keep them apart. Then, in 1120, Peter the Venerable, later Abbot of Cluny (1122–57), wrote a letter to the Patriarch of Constantinople which shows that the schism of 1054 was not considered to be final. He addressed the Patriarch as

---

[2] For details see Runciman, op. cit., pp. 60–2.

[3] Migne, *P.L.* clviii; Anselm's *Life* by Eadmer, quoted in Fortescue, op. cit., pp. 203–4.

'the great Pontiff of God at Constantinople' and he regarded Constantinople as 'the Christian city founded by Jesus Christ and the Emperor Constantine'.[4] In the year 1136 the Emperor of the West, Lothar III, sent another Anselm (who later became Bishop of Havelberg and afterwards Archbishop of Ravenna) to Constantinople, in order to conclude a political agreement with the Byzantine State. During his stay in Constantinople he took up the question of the division of the two Churches. There were public discussions in moderate terms in the Churches of St. Sophia and St. Irene in the hope of ending the schism by a general Council. In the year 1170 representatives of the anti-pope Calixtus III were sent to Constantinople to take part in a Council which was summoned by Patriarch Michael III, but because of disagreements the Council was discontinued. And, in reply to a letter from the Pope, Michael made a strong defence of the Eastern position and rejected the Petrine claims of Rome.

Pope Innocent III sent three Cardinals, in succession, to Constantinople; Peter in 1204, Benedict in 1205, and Pelagius in 1208. There they held discussions in which two theologians, the brothers John and Nicolas Messarites, took part. At this time the barbarous sack of Constantinople by the fourth Crusade had just taken place, and the Greeks did not like hearing even the name of the Latins. After the capture of Constantinople, the Greek clergy sought shelter in the Greek state of Nicaea, and Latin Patriarchs were installed in the Patriarchates of Constantinople, Alexandria and Antioch.[5]

By the express desire of a number of Greeks, a Council was summoned in the Lateran in 1215. During it the Latins gained a better knowledge of the Orthodox, and understood that they ought to make some concessions to them. The Council therefore decided to allow the Orthodox to maintain their own Church customs. 'If in some parts of the world there are different nations with different languages and Church rites, the Bishop can choose capable men who may perform the Divine Liturgy in the language and according to the rites of those people.'[6] This is in accordance with the ideas of Pope Gregory[7] and the Patriarchs of Constantinople.

---

[4] Runciman, op. cit., p. 114.

[5] cf. Runciman, op. cit., pp. 149 ff.

[6] Hefele, *Concilien-Geschichte*, v, 882, 885.

[7] A. Michael, 'Lateinische Aktenstücke . . .' in *Historisches Jahrbuch* (1940), p. 50 and F. Heiler, *Altkirchliche Autonomie und Päpstlicher Zentralismus* (1941), pp. 210–16, 227.

During the occupation of Constantinople by the Crusaders, the Greek Emperor of Nicaea needed the aid of the Pope in order to re-take Constantinople; and the Pope, since he was involved in conflict with the Emperor of the West, Frederick II, was willing to negotiate with the Eastern Church. Discussions took place at Nicaea and at Nymphaion. The interesting point in these discussions was the proposal of the Orthodox theologian Nicephorus Blemmydes who suggested the compromise formula that the procession of the Holy Spirit is 'from the Father through the Son'.

From 1261, when Constantinople was re-captured by the Greeks, until the Council of Lyons in 1274, there were more contacts between Constantinople and Rome; but all had the disadvantage of being under pressure from the Emperor, who was hoping for military help from the West.

After the outrages which the Greeks suffered from the Crusaders, they became less desirous of reunion. Nevertheless force of circumstances compelled the convocation at Lyons in 1274 of the so-called Council of Union, in which two famous Western theologians took part; St. Albert the Great, and Bonaventure, Bishop of Albano. Bonaventure felt a special sympathy with the Greeks and even changed his name to the Greek Eutyches. At this Council, although agreement was reached and the Pope, Gregory X, delivered a sermon on Luke 22: 15 'I have longed to eat this passover with you', unity was acknowledged as impractical, since the East was not willing to accept the Roman terms. All that was achieved was the securing of political assistance from the Pope. We must acknowledge that the Popes Gregory X, Innocent V and Nicolas III were willing to help the Byzantine state politically, although they knew that their terms of unity could not be accepted.

Pope Martin IV did not favour the Byzantine state, and the same attitude towards the East was shown by his successors. But a new danger arose which brought Rome and Constantinople into contact again. This was the threat of the Ottoman Turks who were continually extending their dominion in Asia Minor. Between 1333 and 1370 the Emperors of Constantinople several times approached the Pope for help, but this was only to be obtained after the reunion of the Churches. At that time the Popes were at Avignon and promised help, but none was given. The Byzantine state was in great danger, and its only hope of survival lay in Western help. In face of the Turkish threat the Emperor of Byzantium, John VIII, resumed the attempt to unify the Church and started negotiations with Pope Martin V. In 1438 Pope Eugenius IV summoned a Council at Ferrara to discuss reunion. The political preoccupations of both sides dominated the Council, for the Pope had difficulties with the anti-papal Council of Basle and the Emperor of Byzantium was threatened by the Ottoman Turks. However, there were on both sides men who hoped for reunion for its own sake. But it soon became apparent that there were great theological differences between East and West. And the Greeks had the greatest difficulty in understanding the Western scholastic approach to Christian doctrine, which had emerged as a distinctively Latin theology in contrast to that of the Patristic period which was largely Greek in nature.

In 1439 the Council was transferred from Ferrara to Florence, ostensibly because of an outbreak of the plague; the plague, however, had disappeared two months before the move to Florence, and the Easterners were greatly inconvenienced by the change. The Pope had promised to aid the Byzantine Emperor, and the Emperor pressed the Orthodox to compromise. Again the main obstacle to unity was the Roman Primacy, but eventually an ingenious formula of union was agreed upon, 'As it is contained in the decisions of the Ecumenical Councils and the sacred Canons'—*Quem ad modum etiam in gestis oecumenicorum conciliorum et in sacris canonibus continetur.*[8] Like Pope Gregory X at the so-called Council of Union in Lyons 1274, Pope Eugenius IV announced the union of the Churches with an 'element of pathos':

Shout, ye heavens, and exult, O Earth! The wall of partition has fallen, that divided the Eastern from the Western Church. Joy and harmony have returned; for Christ the cornerstone, Who has made both one, unites them with the bond of everlasting unity, and after the thick black darkness of a severance of many years' standing the brightness of a much desired unity again illuminates all. Our Mother the Church rejoices that it has been granted her to see her sons, hitherto at strife, once more living in peace. She, who sometime during the Schism wept bitter tears, may now thank God in infinite joy by reason of this fair accord. All the faithful throughout the wide earth,

---

[8] Carl Mirbt, *Quellen zur Geschichte des Papsttums und des Römischen Catholicismus*, ed. 4 (1924), p. 234. The original text was altered later, so Febronius said. See Hergenröther, *Anti-Janus* (Freiburg, 1870), pp. 118 ff. Cf. Mansi, *Concilia*, xxxi, 1031, in Cardinal Peter Gaspari, *The Catholic Catechism* (London, 1934), p. 301.

all who call themselves by the name of Christ, may bring felicitations to their Mother, the Catholic Church, and may rejoice with her.[9]

This rejoicing, however, was a little premature. The formula agreed on could be interpreted by each side in different ways. And the Orthodox at home could also hold that their representatives had submitted, under pressure, to the Papacy. As Adrian Fortescue writes:

The Council's decision was not acceptable in the East, because it was seen that the Greek representatives accepted the faith of the Roman Church in every point at once, in the hope of getting help from the Western Princes against the Turks. But, when they returned home and found that no help came, the union was soon rejected by the Byzantine Church.[10]

At a Synod in Jerusalem in 1472 the Patriarchs of Alexandria, Antioch and Jerusalem denounced the union with Rome. The Emperor, seeing that the Turks were very near to the capital, displayed a great desire to accept the decision of the Council of Ferrara–Florence, but this was unpopular in Constantinople. *Constantinople fell in 1453*; no help had been received from the West.

5. *Roman Catholic Efforts to Convert the Orthodox*

The attempts by the Roman Church to convert the Orthodox started long before the fall of Constantinople, at a time when the whole of Southern Italy was Orthodox and belonged to the Patriarchate of Constantinople. From this beginning the Roman Church extended its efforts throughout the Eastern Orthodox world, and although much was made of the fact that those who were converted were allowed to keep their own rites and customs, this was at the price of accepting the Roman primacy and Roman direction of their Church affairs—the very things which Orthodoxy had always opposed and resisted in its disputes with Rome.

[9] Karl von Hase, *Handbook to Controversy with Rome*, transl. from the 7th German ed. by A. W. Streane (London, 1906), vol. i, p. 22.

[10] A. Fortescue, op. cit., 219–20. Father Leeming is generous enough to write a long chapter in his recently published book (*The Vatican Council and Christian Unity* (London, 1965), pp. 183–201) with the title 'The debt of the West to the East'. Since the very foundation of the Christian Church is of Eastern origin, it is not surprising that the founders of the Church were able to provide for it the necessary equipment for a speculative theology. However Father Leeming is among the very few English Roman Catholics who know the Eastern Church, and he impresses upon his readers the importance of Orthodoxy.

Nor have Eastern rites and customs always been respected. According to the speeches of the Eastern 'Uniat' Fathers in the Second Vatican Council, a large number of those who agree to be united with Rome are compelled to be Latinized. In a book edited by Maximos IV Sayegh, the late Patriarch of Antioch and all the East, who was in communion with Rome (not to be confused with the lawful Patriarch of Antioch, who is Orthodox),[1] the contributors repeatedly make bitter complaints that those who are united with Rome are compelled to accept the Latin Rite.

The proselytizing activities of Roman Catholics—often carried out with powerful political support and pressure—and the lack of respect for Eastern ways of worship have carried a deep resentment against Rome among the Orthodox. Partly this is because the latter think it is a scandal to carry out missionary work among fellow-Christians, whereas in the West conversions from one church to another are not unusual. Partly it is because the Orthodox—during the Turkish occupation, for instance—have been in an extremely weak position, from a political, economic and educational point of view, and have been unable to resist the Roman advance in the East. By way of reaction many Orthodox, 'converted' to Catholicism in the past, have returned to their own Church when the political situation has changed. This happened, for instance, in Czechoslovakia,[2] Romania, the Ukraine and Russia, after the Second World War. Fr. Charles Boyer deplores that these Christians left the papal sphere.[3] It should be pointed out to him that during the war in Croatia alone, for example, one thousand Orthodox priests and bishops were exterminated by the Roman Catholics.[4]

[1] *The Eastern Churches and Catholic Unity* (London, 1963). See also the reaction of Eastern Catholics because of the elevation of Eastern (Catholic) Patriarchs to the Cardinalate, *O.I.C.* i (1965), pp. 408–11.

[2] The union with Rome, for example, of the Byzantine Christians in Czechoslovakia, dating from 1649, was brought about as a result of pressure exercised by the Austrian Government.

[3] C. Boyer, *Christian Unity and the Ecumenical Movement*, pp. 56, 57, 88, 89.

[4] Cf. official documents pertaining to the trial of Cardinal Stepinac. See also *Persecution of the Serbian Orthodox Church in Yugoslavia*, published by the Serbian Orthodox Church in the United States (Chicago, 1954). See also the recent book of Carlo Falconi, *The Silence of Pius XII*. 'On Croatia', writes Falconi, 'the most striking fact was that two Ambassadors of Pavelic to the Holy See were never reproached with the horrors perpetrated against the Orthodox Christians— forced mass conversions, pillaging of Orthodox Churches, massacres of Orthodox Bishops and priests, extermination camps. Only one man in the Roman Curia challenged the two Ambassadors of Pavelic, and that was Cardinal Tisserant, cf. *The Observer*, 16 May 1965.

The Roman hope of converting the Orthodox still dominates the minds of many modern Catholic authors. As Fr. Boyer writes:

If those separated Christians whom Pius XI called 'venerable oriental Christians' are being considered, their return to Catholic unity is so pressing that it is not rash to hope for it. The most likely thing is that some of the autocephalous Churches, or at least a few important groups of one Church, will ask to be united, without waiting for others to join them. In that case, it is more a kind of corporate reunion, in the sense that the Church which unites remains the same, except for the state of schism.[5]

Fr. M. Jugie writes similarly that 'without being untrue to themselves [the Orthodox] should renounce their false ideas, accept Catholic doctrine and so become Catholics as they are'.[6]

In 1948, after the Second World War, an Orthodox Conference, representing more or less the whole of the Orthodox Church behind the Iron Curtain, was held in Moscow. It issued the following statement which illustrates the reaction of the Orthodox Church to the proselytism of the Roman Church:

In the course of many centuries and even to the present day the Papacy has striven by means of bloody wars and all kinds of coercion to convert the Orthodox to Catholicism, either directly or through the 'Uniat Movement', for instance, the Rumanians in Transylvania in 1700, the Bulgarians in Turkey in 1859–60, and in the last war 240,000 Serbians, Albanians, Croatians, as well as Orthodox in Czechoslovakia, Poland, the Ukraine, and Byelo-Russia.[7]

It is very difficult for the Roman Church to change or abolish the machinery for making conversions amongst Orthodox people. But, from an Orthodox point of view, the settlement of the question of the so-called 'Uniat Churches' is of paramount importance for the relations of the two Churches.[8] I do not share the opinion that the 'Uniat'

---

[5] C. Boyer, op. cit., p. 88.

[6] M. Jugie, A.A., *Ou se trouve le Christianisme intégral? Essai de démonstration catholique* (Paris, 1947).

[7] *Proceedings of the Conference of the Heads of the Autocephalous Orthodox Churches Held in Moscow, July, 1948* (Y.M.C.A. Press, Paris, 1952), p. 238. For an accurate idea of the Roman Catholic attempts to convert the Russian Orthodox people see Walter Kolarz, *Religion in the Soviet Union* (1961), pp. 176–244.

[8] The origin of the 'Uniat Churches' was the decision of the Lateran Council (1215) to permit the use of various church rites, provided that the Primacy of the Pope was recognized. In the year 1576 a papal representative was appointed

Eastern Churches have a providential role in the progress towards unity between Orthodox and Romans. The Orthodox think that the 'Uniats' have betrayed the Orthodox faith, that they have exchanged Orthodoxy for the gifts of Roman missionaries and the advantages of the Western Roman Catholic powers. For this reason the abolition of the rite of the 'Uniat' Churches must be the first step if there is a sincere desire on the part of Roman Catholics to engage in dialogue with the Orthodox. As long as the Roman Church maintains all the machinery for Eastern conversions there will be very little hope of a real Roman-Orthodox dialogue.

---

in Constantinople, and seven years later the Jesuits settled there for the purpose of proselytism. A 'Uniat' Patriarchate in Antioch was established by Pope Benedict XIV. It was called Melchite ('Melchites' was the name given by the Monophysites to those who held the Orthodox faith which was the faith of the Byzantine Emperor ('Melchite' = 'Royal')); see E. J. B. Fry, 'The Melkites', E.C.Q. v (1944) pp. 331–41. The word *uniti* appeared first in Poland where, after the regulations of Pope Clement VIII (1596), the Polish Orthodox, under the pressure of the Jesuits and the Polish King Sigismund III, accepted the papal primacy and united with Rome.

Chapter II

THE ORTHODOX AND CATHOLIC CHURCH

1. *The Meaning of 'Orthodox' and 'Catholic' in the Three Churches*

The Roman justification of its own Catholicity was at one time the greater number of its adherents compared with the Orthodox and Protestants, since this, it said, was the implication of the word ' Catholic' as used in the Creed. But the criterion of Catholicity should be the quality and not the quantity. If it were the latter Arianism could have rightly claimed to be the Catholic faith, as it numbered in its time more adherents than the Catholic Church. Today Roman Catholics acknowledge that the geographical definition of Catholicity cannot be applicable;[1] they see that catholicity is a qualitative not a quantitative concept.

As Henri de Lubac writes:

The Church is Catholic not because she is spread abroad over the whole of the earth and can reckon on a large number of members. She was already Catholic on the morning of Pentecost when all her members could be contained in a small room, as she was when the Arian waves seemed on the point of swamping her, she would still be Catholic if to-morrow apostasy on a vast scale deprived her of almost all the faithful. For fundamentally Catholicity has nothing to do with geography or statistics. It is true that it should be displayed over all the earth and be manifest to all, yet its nature is not material but spiritual. Like sanctity, Catholicity is primarily an intrinsic feature of the Church.[2]

[1] See, for example, M. Schmaus, *Katholische Dogmatik*, III, i (Munich, 1958), p. 604; cf. George H. Tavard, *Two Centuries of Ecumenism*, p. 42.

[2] H. de Lubac, *Catholicism. A Study of Dogma in relation to the Corporate Destiny of Mankind* (London, 1962), p. 14.

The Anglican Church maintains that 'It is the Faith of the whole true Church of Christ, the sincere belief and profession of which makes a Catholic Church.'[3] Anglican theologians, however, while maintaining the continuity of their own Church, regard all the three great Churches, Orthodox, Roman Catholic, and Anglican, as branches of the one Church, so that the unity of the Church is not destroyed by its divisions.[4] Newman, while still an Anglican, said that Eastern Orthodoxy, Roman Catholicism and Anglo-Catholicism form the three branches, of different nature but of equal value, of the one Church. Emmanuel Amand de Mendieta says that he means 'by Catholicism a certain manner of presentation of Christian doctrine (dogma and theology), of divine worship or liturgy, and of religious and moral life; and I say that no Church, Orthodox, Roman Catholic or Anglican, has any right to claim a monopoly of that presentation'.[5]

Now the meaning of Catholicity for the Orthodox Church is demonstrated by Ignatius of Antioch who says that every local Church which has a bishop is a complete Catholic Church.[6] 'The Orthodox view is that the category of organic unity can properly be

---

[3] See John Pearson, 'Holy and Catholic' in P. E. More and F. L. Cross (edd.), *Anglicanism. The thought and practice of the Church of England, illustrated from the Religious literature of the seventeenth century* (London, 1957), pp. 35–39; cf. p. 40, the words quoted in the text, which are from William Sherlock, *A Vindication of the Doctrine of the Trinity* (1690).

[4] John Pearson, in op. cit., p. 27. '. . . even as a house built upon one foundation, though consisting of many rooms, and every room of many stones, is not yet many, but one house. Now there is but one foundation upon which the Church is built, and that is Christ: for other foundation can no man lay, than that is laid, which is Jesus Christ.' The Tractarians, nevertheless, recognized that 'the Church Catholic ideally should be one visible, undivided Society, possessing all the notes mentioned in the Creed. Unfortunately that of unity is in certain respects lacking. Yet oneness in some measure persists because of the retention of the ancient Episcopal Ministry, and the Body of doctrine handed down from the undivided Church'. P. E. Shaw, *The Early Tractarians and the Eastern Church* (1930), p. 33.

[5] *Rome and Canterbury. A Biblical and Free Catholicism.* Transl. by Coslett Quin (London, 1962), p. 237.

[6] The local communities were called Catholic, because they were identified with the Catholic Church, as they had the same faith with that, and consequently they were Orthodox. In this sense the Orthodox Church uses the word Catholic. This is the christological conception 'Where Christ is, there is also the Catholic Church' (Ignatius, *Pol. Mart.* 16. 2. Cf. Thomas Sartory, O.S.B., *The Oecumenical Movement and the Unity of the Church*, p. 219.)

applied only to a local Church, i.e. a single community united under the headship of one Bishop and possessing with him, the fullness of Sacramental life.'[7] The link which unites the local Orthodox Churches with one another and shows the unity of the whole, is the deposit of the Faith *quod ubique, quod semper, quod ab omnibus creditum est*. 'In the Orthodox view the whole Church, in all its fullness, is present in every Church action, in every one of its members, in every congregation. This interpenetration between the particular and the general, the individual and the universal is precisely the principle of "Catholicity"— of the life of each in accordance with the whole'.[8] This is the meaning of the word 'Catholic' in the sacred Creed, as Cyril of Jerusalem interpreted it,[9] and when the celebrant in the Orthodox Liturgy prays 'for the stability of the Holy Churches of God', he expresses this sense of unity, for they belong to God, and he alone unites them. Because the local Church is the very Church itself, it is not simply a part or a member of the wider universal Church. The local Church is itself the Catholic Church in time and in space.[10] But even if we took the possession of an Apostolic See as being the criterion of Catholicity, the Orthodox Church shows an impressive degree of Catholicity, having a great number of Apostolic Sees. Its territory embraces the land where Christ himself was born and lived and died. It includes bishoprics in cities of which the names are already familiar words in the New Testament, Jerusalem and Nazareth, Antioch, and many others.[11] For the Orthodox the catholicity of the Church is represented through the Apostolic succession; but the Pope as successor of the Apostles does not guarantee the Apostolicity of the whole Church. He does not decide who is to be consecrated bishop. The office of the

---

[7] A. Schmeman, ' "Unity", "Division", "Reunion" in the light of Orthodox Ecclesiology', *TH.* xxii (1951) p. 244; cf. also S. Bulgakow, 'One, Holy, Catholic and Apostolic Church', *C.E.* xii (1931), p. 98 ff.

[8] L. Zander, 'The Ecumenical Movement and the Orthodox Church', *E.R.* i (1949) p. 269. The distinction between the Greek word 'Catholic' and the Slav 'Sobornost' that the first gives a static picture of the Church, while 'Sobornost' gives a dynamic image (Villain, op. cit., p. 160, n.8) is a matter developed by the Russian émigrés and it has not acquired universal Orthodox recognition.

[9] 'It is called Catholic because it teaches generally and always all the dogmas which came to man's knowledge', *Cat.* 18.

[10] cf. Schmeman, op. cit., p. 245.

[11] cf. Cardinal Lercaro, op. cit., p. 85. 'The East, the cradle of Christianity, Jerusalem, Antioch, Salonica, Cyprus—several became the great historical Patriarchates'.

bishop stems directly from God and each bishop has, *jure divino*, an independent pastoral authority over his Church.[12]

How then can one distinguish the Orthodox Catholic Church from those Churches which are not Catholic? Firstly there is the episcopal function. Wherever there is the genuine Apostolic succession there is the Catholic Church.[13] Secondly there is acceptance of the teaching of the genuine bishops.[14] Ignatius of Antioch writes, 'Whenever the Bishop may appear, there the multitude should be. For where Christ is, there is the Catholic Church.'[15] Consequently the Catholic Church is where there is a canonical and genuine bishop, the successor of the Apostles.

The word Orthodox, which is used by almost all the writers against the Arian Bishops, can be found in the work of Theodoret:[16] 'The Catholic Church of the Orthodox in Constantinople.' But before the great schism the expression 'Orthodox Church' was used for both Eastern and Western Churches, as Roman Catholic writers themselves acknowledge.[17] Likewise the expression 'Catholic Church' was used for both Churches, Eastern and Western. Today the Orthodox and Roman Churches both claim Orthodoxy and Catholicity.

The terms 'Western' and 'Eastern' refer not to the location of the Church, but to the place where the Head of the Church is to be found. Constantinople means East and Rome means West, although the faithful are now scattered over the world. This characterization comes from the division of the Roman Empire. As the term Western or Latin does not mean that the Western Church has no claims beyond the Alps, so the term Eastern includes the Orthodox in the West. It is now evident that the division of the two Churches is not simply a geographical separation between East and West, but one between two different jurisdictions, which represent two different expressions of one and the same faith of the Catholic Church. In the light of these

[12] Cf. S. McCrea Cavert, *On the Road to Christian Unity* (New York, 1961), pp. 85–6.

[13] Irenaeus, *adv. Haer.* 3.3. Newman said it is the Apostolic Succession that safeguards the Church's Unity. 'The Apostolic Succession is necessary in order to their possessing claim of descent'. J. H. Newman, 'Catholicity of the English Church', *British Critic* (1840), p. 54.

[14] Irenaeus, *adv Haer.* 4, 26, and Hippolytus, *Refutatio omnium haeresium*, pref., Lib. i, 50–55.

[15] Ignatius, *Smyrn.* viii.

[16] *Haereticarum fabularum compendium*, 4, 12. Migne, *P.G.* lxxxiii. 433.

[17] C. Boyer, op. cit. p. 17, n. 14 and p. 33.

explanations we can determine whether a Church is Catholic or non-Catholic. According to this the three Churches, Roman, Orthodox, and Anglican are all Catholic Churches. But there is of course a difference in the interpretation of the word 'catholic' given by the three Churches. The Anglican agrees with the above interpretation.[18] The Roman identifies itself with the Catholic Church and excludes other Churches which do not recognize the Pope as the Head of the Christian Church. The Orthodox on the other hand, while claiming that it is the one true Catholic Church, puts the Faith as the main characteristic of the unity of the Church.

Having in mind what we have said, we reach the conclusion that there are two main marks of Catholicity. First there is the Apostolic origin, which all the Churches which maintain the Apostolic succession actually have, and secondly, there is the Apostolic Faith.

2. *The Claims to Catholicity in the Anglican Church*

Canon Pawley[1] writes that the Anglican Church believes itself, with the Orthodox, to have retained the Catholic doctrine of the Church to which the Roman Church has added things which were not believed '*ubique ... semper, ... ab omnibus*' ('everywhere, always, by all', Vincent of Lerins). There are strong pointers indicating that the Church of England maintains the Catholic faith. Newman in his *Apologia* shows that during the time of the Oxford Movement there was a deep spiritual demand for a re-catholicizing of the Anglican Church. The leaders of the Oxford Movement tried to make the catholic conception of the Church once more central in Anglicanism and to prove that the Anglican Church teaches the primitive ancient Faith. Later, in 1889, in the symposium *Lux Mundi*, Catholic thinkers under the leadership of Charles Gore, revealed new possibilities for the Anglo-Catholic Movement. As Visser 't Hooft writes:[2]

There is no fair observer who denies that Anglo-Catholicism has succeeded in making the Church of England aware of the 'Catholic'

[18] For the reunion between the Anglican Communion and other Churches, Anglicans give a wider interpretation of the term Catholicity. Cf. Visser 't Hooft, op. cit., p. 118.

[1] Bernard C. Pawley, 'An Anglican Views the Council', *S.C.U.* p. 117.

[2] Visser 't Hooft, ibid. pp. 28–29. A full account of Tractarians' claims of Catholicity can be found in P. E. Shaw, *The Early Tractarians and the Eastern Church* (1930), pp. 36–45.

elements of its heritage, so that today it is no longer as a hundred years ago a Protestant Church in which some reminiscences of Catholicism have survived, but rather a Catholic Church, which retains certain emphases of the Reformation.

In actual fact the Church of England is the Catholic Church of the English people. In the words of Newman written when an Anglican, 'We are the English Catholics; abroad are the Roman Catholics, some of whom are also among ourselves; elsewhere are the Greek Catholics.'[3] The Church of England is the legitimate heir of the Catholic Church in the British Isles. As Professor Florovsky says, from the Orthodox point of view the Church of England is in schism,[4] although England claims that its antiquity is greater than its connexion with Rome and that it is not in schism from the Catholic Church. From the very beginning of its existence up to the present time the Church of England has kept unbroken its continuity and the apostolic succession. It is true that there was a breach between the Church of England and the Roman Church, but the Church of England from the time of St. Augustine to Archbishop Parker was something more than two provinces of the Western Church. It was even then a national church. While the Roman Church excommunicated the *Ecclesia Anglicana*, it could not prevent this Church from working under the guidance of the Holy Spirit. As Bishop Jewel of Salisbury writes in his *Apology*, they did not plant a new Church in England but only 'renewed the old that was undoubtedly founded and used by the Apostles of Christ, and other Holy Fathers in the primitive Church.' And as Bishop Gore says:

It was saved from doing anything which would have severed its dependence upon the Catholic Church properly interpreted, and in decreeing rites and ceremonies afresh it did nothing which Catholic Tradition, again properly interpreted, has ever condemned. This is very natural, because the Christian faith, though it can adjust itself to the various needs of man, intellectual and moral and national, in each successive age, yet everywhere makes its central appeal to what is constant and unchanging. It is the existence of this common heart of man, which makes possible a Catholic religion. But in every race

---

[3] J. H. Newman, *Parochial and Plain Sermons* (new ed., London 1891), vol. iii, pp. 191–2.
[4] *H.E.M.*, p. 197.

and in every epoch the same religion receives a special development and its theology and its rites become special and distinctive, Greek or Latin or Russian or Celtic or English. And this Catholicity the Anglicans gladly recognise.[5]

And as J. L. Casserley writes:

The Reformation stands out as a genuine reformation of a pre-existing reality which was provided for and given to Anglicanism by its Anglican history. It is an episode in Anglican existence and not the beginning of Anglican existence. When Anglicans go back to the beginnings they return, like the great reformers themselves, not to the reformers, but to the Patristic Christianity of the early Church and ultimately to the Apostolic witness itself.[6]

'The repudiation of papal authority' writes Archbishop Cyril Garbett,[7] 'did not break the continued and uninterrupted work of the Church. The Church of England maintains the Catholic faith, the Holy Scripture, the Apostolic Tradition and the Sacraments of the Catholic Church.' Again, Gore writes, 'the common Creed, the common Sacraments, the sacred Ministry, all appear in the early history of the Church as having equal and undisputed authority. They were all retained and emphasised by the Church of England when it became separated from the Roman Church. These were familiar themes with Anglican Divines of the seventeenth century. The Tractarians set themselves then to make these elements of the doctrine of the visible Church—Holy, Catholic and Apostolic—current coin again in the familiar thought and speech of men.'[8] 'They did not dispute the appeal to scripture, as the final court of appeal in matters of doctrine. On the contrary, they found this appeal in all the Fathers. At no time has the Church of England lost these distinguishing marks of the Catholic Church.'[9]

[5] C. Gore, *The Anglo-Catholic Movement Today*, p. 26.

[6] J. L. Casserley, *Christian Community* (1960), p. 112.

[7] Cyril Garbett, *The Claims of the Church of England* (1960), p. 15.

[8] Gore, *The Anglo-Catholic Movement*, p. 30. 'Dr. Pusey used to be fond of declaring that the Church of England had no distinctive doctrines: that it only taught the Catholic faith as it was common to all times and parts of the Church'.

[9] Gore, op. cit., pp. 7–8; cf. especially Michael Ramsey, *Constantinople and Canterbury*, pp. 4–5.

Note to Chapter II. The Thirty-Nine Articles and their position in the Church of England

In the Church of England, as has often been said, there are no comprehensive confessional statements comparable to the *Summa Theologica* of Thomas Aquinas or to the *De Fide Orthodoxa* of John Damascene. There are two books which occupy a central place in the piety and scholarship of Anglicanism and these are: the Holy Bible and the Book of Common Prayer.[1] It is the Book of Common Prayer as a whole that the Anglican Church considers as its confession, even more than the Thirty-Nine Articles which appear in it.[2]

Since many non-Anglican writers insist that the Thirty-Nine Articles constitute the authoritative text for the teaching of the Church of England,[3] we must examine this question in detail, remembering that without a thorough knowledge of an organism like the Church of England, it is easy to come to mistaken conclusions. Certainly there is strong desire amongst many Anglicans that the Thirty-Nine Articles should be removed from the Prayer Book and we frequently encounter Anglican clergy who deny them any authority. But for a systematic and authoritative explanation of the actual character of the Thirty-Nine Articles let us first see what Bishop Gore had to say in a brief description of them.

The articles bear with them almost throughout the savour of a bygone situation. Many of them are deeply repugnant to the spirit that one may call modern or critical or liberal, even if the 'prima facie' force of their language can be legitimately weakened. The whole discussion of Justification and Predestination is antiquated and quite unenlightening, and the anti-Roman articles are so ambiguously expressed that it does not appear clearly what is being condemned. I do not think that the present terms in which the clergy subscribe to the Articles, the Prayer Book and the Ordinal, as containing, all taken together, the doctrine of the Church of England, which at the same time is scriptural doctrine, ought to present any real difficulty to us. But I find myself in agreement with a large number of those who have most to do with the interests

---

[1] Cf., for example, G. Ellison, *The Anglican Communion. Past and Future.* (The Seabury Press, Greenwich, Connecticut, 1960) pp. 17–18.

[2] J. F. Lescrauwaet, 'The Reformed Churches', *C.* vi (1965), p. 73.

[3] P. Trembelas, *The History of the Reformation in the Anglican Church* (Thessaloniki, 1956) pp. 57–67 (original in Greek).

of religion in the universities and the theological Colleges that the Articles of Religion ought to be relegated to the position of historical documents. Nor at present, at least, would it appear to be desirable to have any document other than the Nicene Creed substituted for them as the standard of doctrine to be accepted by the clergy. Of course in addition they must be able conscientiously to use the services and teach the catechism which means that they are in harmony with the doctrines implied or taught.[4]

In the writings of the great Anglican theologians it is clear that the Thirty-Nine Articles are always called 'Articles of Religion' and never 'Articles of Faith'. Archbishop Laud of Canterbury said that 'The Church of England never declared that every one of her Articles are fundamental to the Faith.'[5] Archbishop Ussher of Armagh said: 'We do not suffer any man to reject the Thirty-Nine Articles of the Church of England at his pleasure, yet neither do we look upon them as essentials of saving Faith or legacies of Christ and his Apostles.'[6] Similarly Bishop Pearson of Chester[7] said that:

The Book of Articles is not, nor is pretended to be, a complete body of Divinity, or a comprehensive explication of Christian doctrines necessary to be taught; but an enumeration of some truths, which upon and since the Reformation have been denied by some persons; who upon their denial are thought unfit to have any cure of souls in this Church or realm, because they might by their opinions either infect their flock with error, or else disturb the Church with Schism, or the realm with Sedition.

The Lambeth Conference of the Anglican Bishops in 1888 passed a resolution, which throws some light on the position of the Articles among the Churches of the Anglican Communion. The resolution is as follows:

---

[4] Gore, op. cit., p. 59. The Thirty-Nine Articles, says Bishop G. Ellison, do not pretend to be a complete statement of the Faith (op. cit., p. 17). Cf. also Gore, *Orders and Unity*, p. 201, n. 1.

[5] *A Relation of the Conference between William Laud, late Archbishop of Canterbury, and Mr. Fisher the Jesuit, by the Command of King James*, vol. ii (Oxford, 1839) p. 42.

[6] See *The Works of George Bull, Bishop of St. David's*, ed. Edward Burton, vol. ii (Oxford, 1827), pp. 211–12.

[7] *The Minor Works of John Pearson*, ed. by Edward Churton, vol. ii (Oxford, 1844), p. 215.

As regards newly-constituted Churches, especially in non-Christian lands, it should be a condition of the recognition of them as in complete intercommunion with us, and especially of their receiving from us Episcopal Succession, that we should first receive from them satisfactory evidence that they hold substantially the same doctrine as our own, and that their clergy subscribe Articles in accordance with the express statements of our own standards of doctrine and worship; but that they should not necessarily be bound to accept in their entirety the Thirty-Nine Articles of Religion.[8]

It is evident that the Thirty-Nine Articles, taken as a whole, are intended to be Articles of peace and concord. In the discussions between Orthodox and Anglicans during the 1920 Lambeth Conference, the latter said that 'the Thirty-Nine Articles are not Articles of Faith, but Articles of a practical public State's confession, as is shown by their vague character ... If you wish to learn the mind of the Church of England, study the Prayer-book and not the Thirty-nine Articles'.[9]

In the discussions with the Orthodox representatives at Lambeth Palace in 1930, the Anglicans stated that if there were any ambiguity in the Thirty-Nine Articles they were 'in all cases to be interpreted by what the Prayer Book itself said'.[10] 'We have here an application', writes Visser 't Hooft,[11] of the characteristic Catholic principle *Lex orandi, lex credendi,* which leads in practice to an increasing emphasis on the more Catholic liturgy as over against the more Protestant statement of Anglican doctrine'. However, during the Moscow Conference between Anglicans and Russian Orthodox, the impression which Dr. A. M. Ramsey, then Archbishop of York, received was this: 'Whereas in the discussions between Anglicans and other Orthodox Churches in the 1920's and 1930's there was on the Anglican side a tendency to soft-pedal the Thirty-Nine Articles, and to suggest that they did not greatly matter since they were concerned with "local" controversies and were less important than the Anglican appeal to antiquity, no trace of this unrealism is seen in the Moscow Conference. Here, the Orthodox were encouraged to deal with the Church of England as it is. On the subject of the Thirty-Nine Articles the Russians were outspoken and trenchant. Yet, even so, the Articles stood up to

---

[8] Puller, op. cit., pp. 48–9. Cf. Davidson, *The Five Lambeth Conferences,* p. 174.
[9] *C.E.* iii (1922) p. 12.
[10] *Doctrinal Report,* p. 61.
[11] op. cit., p. 40.

their onslaught with rather more success than might seem likely . . .'.[12]

After this necessarily brief interpolation we can deal with the Anglican Church in the following chapters, without it being thought that we have overlooked a document of such historical importance in Anglicanism.

In 1967 the Archbishops of Canterbury and York set up a permanent Commission on Christian Doctrine, whose first task was to re-examine the place of the Thirty-Nine Articles in Anglican tradition. The Commission was appointed by the Archbishops and consists of seventeen members representing different schools of thought in the Anglican Church. It reported in 1968 on the subject of the Articles (*Subscription and Assent to the Thirty-Nine Articles*, S.P.C.K., 1968), and has gone on to consider other subjects referred to it by the Archbishops. Its report on the Articles aroused little or no controversy and may be taken to express the mind of the Church of England on the subject.

[12] *The Moscow Conference in Retrospect* from an address by the Archbishop of York. S., Series 3, No. 23 (Summer 1958), p. 562.

Chapter III

EAST AND WEST

1. *Orthodoxy as an Issue between Rome and the Reformers*

The tragedy of Christian disunity was brought about, not only by the schisms between Rome and Constantinople, but also by the splintering of Western Christendom during the sixteenth century. The causes which gave rise to the Reformation, religious, racial and national differences, contributed to the doctrinal divisions of Western Christendom. The Latin world remained pre-eminently Catholic, while the Anglo-Saxon, Scandinavian, and most of the German countries became Protestant. Like the Monophysite Churches in the East, the Protestants regarded Christianity as something which would support and encourage all national and historical peculiarities. The result was that it became subservient to them, instead of being a unifying force which could transcend and reconcile the differences between the nations. As Berdyaev wrote: 'Christian Churches proved weak by comparison with the stormy and dynamic secular movement often of demonic character'.[1]

For Protestants and for Roman Catholics alike Orthodoxy was of great importance. It was necessary for both of them to show that they were loyal to the ancient tradition, which was maintained by the Orthodox Church. The Roman Catholic apologists insisted on complete agreement between Rome and the East. They insisted on the unbroken unity of doctrine between the two Catholic communions through the ages in spite of the schism. The Protestants on the other hand tried to show that the teaching of the Roman Church was different from that of Orthodoxy. Briefly speaking, both Romans and Protestants appealed to the Eastern Churches as a standard of Orthodoxy and Catholicity. The Anglicans especially were inclined to believe that the contribution of the Orthodox Church might be considerable,

[1] N. Berdyaev, 'The Unity of Christendom in the strife between East and West', *E.R.* i (1948), p. 12.

simply because in the Greek Church continuity with the undivided Church of the first centuries had never been broken.

After the completion of the Western divisions, the Protestants attempted to establish relations with the Patriarch of Constantinople; and there were in fact some serious efforts for unity between them and the Orthodox Church. Later on, however, because of their zeal, they started systematically to convert individual Orthodox people to their respective bodies. This Protestant proselytizing of the Orthodox can be compared with the Roman Catholic aggression against them. But just as the Orthodox Church had opposed the Roman attempts against it, so with the same vigour it repelled the Protestants. And the feelings of the Orthodox towards Protestantism up to now have been the same as towards the Romans—a resentment resulting from bitter experience. However, an exception to this is to be found in the Orthodox attitude to the Anglican Church, which has, on the whole, had a greater respect for the Eastern Church and no desire to proselytize its members.

2. Orthodox–Anglican Relations

Relations between the Orthodox and Anglican Churches began with Cyril Lucaris, one of the most celebrated prelates of the Orthodox Church, who was born in the year 1572. He became Patriarch of Alexandria, and held this position for nearly twenty years. He was then transferred to Constantinople as Ecumenical Patriarch.[1] Cyril had begun to enter into contact with both Protestants and the Church of England while he was Patriarch of Alexandria, and from there, at the invitation of Archbishop George Abbot and King James I, had sent a young monk, Metrophanes Kritopoulos, to study theology at Oxford.[2]

[1] Bibliography for Lucaris: Germanos of Thyateira, *Kyrillos Loukaris, 1572–1638* (London, 1951); Chrysostom Papadopoulos, *Kyrillos Loukaris* (2nd ed. Athens, 1939); Steven Runciman, *The Great Church in Captivity* (Cambridge 1968), Bk II, Ch. 6; G. A. Hadjiantoniou, *Protestant Patriarch* (London, 1961).

[2] During his stay in England Metrophanes Kritopoulos established a warm and sincere friendship with English prelates and politicians, especially with Thomas Goad, Chaplain to Archbishop Abbot, for whom he wrote a brief description of the Orthodox Church and its teachings. See G. Florovsky, *H.E.M.* pp. 183–187; J. Marshall, *An Eastern Patriarch in England and Germany* (London, 1925); I. Karmiris, *Metrophanes Kritopoulos* (Athens, 1937). Kritopoulos became Patriarch of Alexandria in 1636, but died in 1639. V. Stephanidis, *Ecclesiastical History* (Athens, 1959), p. 799; Colin Davey, 'Metrophanes Kritopoulos, Pioneer for Unity', *Theologia* (Athens), 1967. D. G. Ionescu, *Relaţiile Ţărilor Române cu Patriarchul din Alexandria*, Bucharest (1935), pp. 12–14. Cf. also G. Ravanis, 'Greek Students in England during the Turkish occupation', *Ekkl. Pharos* ii (1972) [in Greek].

About the same time Cyril also received a letter from Antonio de Dominis, a Roman Catholic Archbishop who had become an Anglican, together with a copy of his *De Republica Ecclesiastica*, published in 1617. De Dominis assured the Patriarch that 'in this Tractate, I strive to defend and vindicate your Oriental Churches, and that of Constantinople especially, from all Romish calumniations. I defend, moreover, the ancient rights of Patriarchs, and reduce the Bishop of Rome to his right place by taking away from him his absolute supremacy.' He concluded by begging the Patriarch to 'enter into serious consideration of uniting your Eastern Churches with this most noble and flourishing Church of England . . . and utterly abolish so inveterate a schism.'[3]

Cyril, as we noted, had been corresponding with Archbishop Abbot from 1612 onwards, and the latter took an increasing interest in the affairs of the Orthodox Church. Successive English Ambassadors in Constantinople used their influence to support and protect Cyril and his Church, and one of them, Sir Thomas Roe, became his close friend and adviser, and also helped with the arrival and installation of the Greek printing-press which Nikodemos Metaxas brought from England, though it was only in operation for a few months. In gratitude for all this, Cyril, through Sir Thomas Roe, presented to King Charles I the famous Codex Alexandrinus,[4] and, later, to Abbot's successor William Laud, an Arabic manuscript of the Pentateuch.

From these beginnings, there grew a continued desire on the part of the Anglicans to know more about the faith of the Orthodox Church. Such information they received from Christopher Angelos, a monk from the Peloponnese who resided in England, and from the Orthodox theologian George Koressios, who sent an *Apologia to the circle of wise men in England from the clergy of Constantinople*. It is also interesting to note that Archbishop Laud, in his disputation with Fisher, the Jesuit, declared that Rome, and not the Eastern Church, had separated from the Apostolic tradition.

Another illustration of the desire of the two Churches to get to know one another is that in the year 1672 John Covel, the Anglican chaplain to the English Embassy in Constantinople, at the request of several distinguished Anglican churchmen and scholars, asked the Ecumenical Patriarch to acquaint his Church with the Orthodox faith—the number of the sacraments; the Holy Eucharist; Baptism;

---

[3] More and Cross, *Anglicanism*, ibid. pp. 73–5. There is no evidence that Orthodox writers are aware of the existence of this letter.

[4] *H.E.M.*, p. 184.

the Office of the Bishop; celibacy of the clergy; the infallibility of the Church; the visible Church; the invocation of the Saints; the Veneration of their images; etc. To this petition the Patriarch replied in his 'Synodical Answer to the question, What are the sentiments of the Oriental Church of the Greek Orthodox? sent to the Lovers of the Greek Church in Britain'.[5] In 1677 with the help of Henry Compton, Bishop of London, a Church (St. Mary, Crown Street, Soho, London) was built 'For the Nation of the Greeks'.[6] At the end of the seventeenth century Gloucester Hall, Oxford, now incorporated in Worcester College, was re-founded by Dr. B. Woodroffe in 1697 in order to educate needy Greek students from the East.

At the beginning of the eighteenth century new relations developed between the Patriarchate of Alexandria and the Nonjurors through the arrival in England in 1712 of the Greek Bishop, Arsenius, Metropolitan of Thebais, who came with a letter to Queen Anne from the newly-elected Patriarch Symeon Kapasoulis. From that time relations continued, and letters were exchanged between Constantinople and the Nonjurors between 1716 and 1725. In their letters the Nonjurors said that they were willing to omit the *Filioque* clause from the Creed, that they rejected Purgatory, and accepted the sacraments, and that they proposed the term 'change' instead of transubstantiation, though they refused to reverence sacred relics and images. On this basis the Nonjurors asked to join the Orthodox Church. The Patriarchs of Constantinople, Alexandria, Antioch and Jerusalem answered that the only way for them to be accepted in the Orthodox Church was by accepting the Orthodox faith. For this purpose they sent to the Nonjurors a brief summary of the Orthodox Confession of the Patriarch of Jerusalem, Dositheos. But when the Archbishop of Canterbury, William Wake, informed the Orthodox that the Nonjurors were schismatics, relations were broken off completely.[7]

[5] I. Karmiris, *The dogmatic and symbolic Mnemeia of the Orthodox Catholic Church* Vol. ii, pp. 687–694 (in Greek). G. Williams, *The Orthodox Church of the East in the Eighteenth Century* (London, 1868), pp. xii–xiii, 67–75.

[6] Florovsky, *H.E.M.* p. 257, cf. V. T. Istavridis, *Orthodoxy and Anglicanism*, (London, 1966) p. 4.

[7] G. W. Williams, op. cit.; Tavard, *La poursuite de la catholicité* (Paris, 1965), pp. 128–9; cf. also G. Florovsky, *H.E.M.* pp. 191–3, Fortescue, op. cit., pp. 257–8; cf. also Th. Lathbury, *History of the non-Jurors, their controversies and Writings, with remarks on some of the Rubrics in the Book of Common Prayer* (London, 1845), pp. 309–11, 311–18, 343–4. J. H. Overton, *The Non-Jurors, their Lives, Principles and Writings* (London, 1902), pp. 451–66. Once again it appears that Orthodox writers have no knowledge of these last two books.

The first official declaration by the Anglican Church that they had no desire to make conversions at the expense of the Orthodox, but were only interested in developing brotherly relations between the two Churches, marked a new era in the contacts between them. This occurred in the year 1839, when the priest George Tomlinson called upon the Patriarch of Constantinople as a representative of the Archbishop of Canterbury.[8]

In the first years of the Oxford Movement there was but little talk of the relations between Anglicanism and Orthodoxy. The issue was raised, however, in 1841, when the Archbishop of Canterbury consecrated an Anglican Bishop to exercise spiritual jurisdiction over the Protestants in Jerusalem. Newman and his friends saw in this a betrayal of that common Catholic ideal, which was the bond between Anglicanism and Orthodoxy. 'This was the third blow', says Newman,' which finally shattered my faith in the Anglican Church'.[9] From the Orthodox side the Metropolitan of Moscow, Philaret (1782–1867) had encouraged good relations between Orthodox and Anglicans when he published in 1832 a book entitled *Conversation between a Seeker and a Believer*, in which he did not condemn the Churches outside the Orthodox Church. When William Palmer (1811–79), of Magdalen College, an Oxford High Churchman, made an attempt to receive Holy Communion in Moscow he was refused permission by the Russian Church on the ground that his faith was not in harmony with Orthodoxy. This impelled him to write a book which was published anonymously in Aberdeen, called *The Harmony of the Anglican Doctrine with the Eastern Catholic and Apostolic Church* (1846). The book provoked such opposition amongst Anglicans that Palmer joined the Roman Church.[10]

[8] It is surprising, however, that in 1837 the Patriarch Gregory (1835–40) betrayed a complete ignorance of the very existence of such a person as the Archbishop of Canterbury. G. K. A. Bell, *Randall Davidson*, Vol. ii, p. 1087.

[9] *Apologia Pro Vita Sua*, ch. iii (World's Classics ed., London, 1964, p. 148). For the general attitude of the Tractarians towards the Orthodox Church see P. E. Shaw, *The Early Tractarians and the Eastern Church* (London, 1930), pp. 5, 101ff., 142. See also W. F. Hook, *Reasons for Contributing towards the Support of an English Bishop in Jerusalem* (1842). Moreover see H. R. T. Brandreth 'Approaches of the Churches towards each other in the nineteenth century', *H.E.M.* pp. 288–90, 'The Jerusalem Bishopric.'

[10] Tavard, *Two Centuries of Ecumenism*, pp. 47–8; cf. also Florovsky, *H.E.M.* pp. 194–5, 198, 200. Dr. Owen Chadwick writes that 'William Palmer held strange, perhaps bizarre, ideas about the Eastern Orthodox Church; and it is clear that his particular ideas, so far as they were exceptional, are inappropriate as illustrations of any movement, even though something may often be learned about historical groups from the eccentricities which appear in their vicinity.' *The Mind of the Oxford Movement* (London, 1960), p. 30.

Finally, E. B. Pusey wrote:

Why should we direct our eyes to the Western Church alone which, even if united in itself would yet remain sadly maimed, and sadly short of the Oneness she had in her best days, if she continued severed from the Eastern?[11]

In the year 1857 an association was founded for the promotion of the unity of Christendom, with the intention of uniting 'in a bond of intercessory prayer' Roman Catholics, Greeks and Anglicans.[12]

Seven years later, in 1864, through the influence of John Mason Neale, the Eastern Churches Association was founded by the Reverend William Denton. Neale was an outstanding scholar who wrote an immense *History of the Holy Eastern Churches*, and also translated numerous Greek hymns into English, which have since become widely used in Anglican worship.[13] One of the founder-members of the Eastern Churches Association was George Williams, who published the correspondence between the Nonjurors and the Orthodox.

Theological discussions between the Orthodox and the Anglican Churches took place in the year 1870 at Ely, when the Greek Archbishop of Syros, Alexander Lycurgus, came to England. At the conference the differences between the two Churches were discussed systematically. These were divided into (a) those which should be revised, namely the *Filioque* clause in the Creed; (b) those which should be discussed, namely the number of the sacraments, the Holy Eucharist, transubstantiation, priesthood, second marriage of clergymen, the invocation of saints, prayers for the dead, the use of ikons, and the acceptance of the Seventh Ecumenical Council; and (c) those differences which can be maintained, namely, the marriage of bishops, etc.[14] After that first theological encounter between the two Churches

[11] *A letter to the Rev. R. M. Jelf* (Oxford, 1841), pp. 184 ff., in G. Florovsky, *H.E.M.*, p. 197.

[12] Tavard, *Two Centuries of Ecumenism*, pp. 44–5.

[13] cf. *Selections from the writings of John Mason Neale* (London, 1887), pp. 160ff. In 1914 the Eastern Churches Association was united with the Anglican and Eastern Orthodox Churches Union, founded in 1906, to form the Anglican and Eastern Churches Association. Between the two World Wars it offered a valuable service to the mutual understanding of the two Churches. Its well-known magazine *The Christian East* contains information and other material of great importance for the two Churches. See *Sermon at the Centenary of the Anglican and Eastern Churches Association* by Dr. A. M. Ramsey, S., Series 4, No. 11 (1964), pp. 615–17.

[14] G. Williams, *A Collection of Documents relating chiefly to the visit of Alexander, Archbishop of Syros and Tenos, to England in 1870* (London, 1876).

several other meetings took place; for example, the discussions in Bonn (1874–5) between Old Catholics, Anglicans, and Orthodox.

The Anglican Church spoke officially on the Orthodox Church during the third Lambeth Conference in 1888 when it resolved that:

This conference, rejoicing in the friendly communications which have passed between the Archbishop of Canterbury and other Anglican bishops, and the Patriarch of Constantinople and other Eastern Patriarchs and bishops, desires to express its hope that the barriers to fuller communication may be, in course of time, removed by further intercourse and extended enlightenment.

But it added:

it would be difficult for us to enter into more intimate relations with the Eastern Church so long as it retains the use of ikons, invocation of the saints and the cult of the Blessed Virgin.[15]

There was another important contact between Anglicans and Orthodox in the year 1899 when the Archbishop of Canterbury, Frederick Temple, wrote to the Ecumenical Patriarch suggesting (1) that neither Church should make conversions from the other; (2) that there should be an exchange of visits between the clergy of Constantinople and London; and (3) that mutual announcements of important events should be made in the two Churches. The Patriarch, Constantine V, gladly accepted the proposals of the Anglican Primate and appointed a special Orthodox committee to consider the differences between the two Churches, in the meetings of which the Rev. T. E. Dowling, Anglican chaplain in Constantinople, was allowed to take part. This commission asked the Anglicans: (1) What is the official teaching of the Anglican Church, where can it be found, and what is its authority? (2) What is the teaching of the Anglican Church concerning the infallibility of the Church and the Ecumenical Councils? (3) What is the Anglican teaching concerning salvation? (4) How many sacraments does the Anglican Church accept and in particular what does it teach about the sacraments of Baptism, the Eucharist, and Ordination? (5) What is the teaching of the Anglican Church concerning predestination, the Holy Spirit, and Holy Tradition? The

---

[15] R. Davidson, *The Five Lambeth Conferences, 1867–1920* (London, 1929), p. 168.

Anglican answer to the Ecumenical Patriarch can be found in the book by Bishop John Wordsworth *Some Points in Teaching of the Church of England set forth for the information of Orthodox Christians of the East*, published in London in 1900.

In the year 1907 the Ecumenical Patriarch appointed as his official representative to the Archbishop of Canterbury the Archimandrite C. Pagonis, an action which has been regarded as an indirect recognition not only of the validity of Anglican orders, but of the Church also.[16] In 1912 the Anglican and Eastern Churches Union arranged for Fr. F. W. Puller of the Society of St. John the Evangelist, Cowley, to visit St. Petersburg and give lectures on the faith of the Anglican Church.[17] And at the very time when the Synod of the Russian Church granted its sanction to a Russian branch of the Union, four Anglican Bishops—those of Wakefield, Bangor, Exeter, and Ossory— were paying a visit to Russia.[18]

The relations between Orthodoxy and Anglicanism were directed mainly towards two centres, Constantinople and Moscow.[19] Many Anglicans had successful contacts with the Great Church of Russia, but at the time when the Russian Church became free from state control and re-organized itself, a new storm arose which ended its activities. Nevertheless during the last meetings of the Synod of All Russia in 1917–18 it passed the following resolution:

The sacred Synod of the Russian Orthodox Church, gladly seeing the sincere efforts of the Old Catholics and Anglicans towards union with the Orthodox Church, bestows its benediction on the labour and efforts of those who are asking the way towards union with the above-named friendly Churches. The Council authorises the sacred Synod to organise a permanent committee with departments in Russia and abroad for the further study of Old Catholics and Anglican difficulties in the way of union and for the furtherance as much as possible of the final aim.[20]

[16] J. Kotsonis, *The Canonical view of Intercommunion with the Orthodox* (Athens, 1957), p. 194.

[17] F. W. Puller, *The Continuity of the Church of England* (3rd imp. 1913) pp. v–vi. For the business of the Anglican and Eastern Orthodox Churches Union see its *Annual Reports*, i–v (London, 1907–1914).

[18] F. W. Puller, op. cit., p. vi, cf. N. Zernov, *H.E.M.*, pp. 649–650.

[19] Apart from these two centres of Orthodoxy, the Anglicans also developed relations with other autocephalous Churches, i.e. the Churches of Serbia, Greece and Rumania. *Lambeth Conference 1920*, p. 146.

[20] *Lambeth Conference 1920*, p. 145.

In 1920, at the invitation of the Archbishop of Canterbury, Randall Davidson,[21] the Ecumenical Patriarch sent Orthodox representatives to the Lambeth Conference for the first time. Among them was the well-known Metropolitan of Didymoteichon, Philaretus Vapheidis, who, with the other members of the Orthodox delegation was welcomed by the President in full session of the Conference. The Orthodox delegates had seven meetings with the Anglicans, and the following conclusions were reached: (1) The Orthodox recognized the validity of Anglican baptism, but they considered baptism and confirmation ought to be performed at the same time. (2) The Anglicans seemed ready to recognize the decision of the seventh Ecumenical Council concerning the veneration of the holy images. (3) The Anglicans acknowledged that the *Filioque* clause in the Creed was introduced into the Creed in an irregular manner, but were unwilling to remove it. (4) The Anglicans declared that the Thirty-Nine Articles do not constitute for Anglicans 'articles of faith' but 'articles of religion', consequently they do not represent the official teaching of the Church, which is contained in the Prayer Book. (5) The Anglicans made some concessions on the doctrine of the Holy Eucharist as a sacrifice, and the use of unleavened bread and the Epiclesis. (6) The Orthodox said they would be satisfied with the terms 'Metabolê' or 'Metapoiêsis' instead of 'transubstantiation'. Both sides agreed that where there is no priest of one of the two Churches, a priest of the other can perform weddings. The Anglicans declared that they prayed for the departed and they gave a satisfactory explanation as regards the question of priesthood. There was, however, disagreement about the doctrine of the Church.[22]

In 1921 the Church of England's Eastern Churches Committee drew up thirteen 'Terms of Intercommunion suggested between the Church of England and the Churches in Communion with her and the Eastern Orthodox Church'. This document became the basis for subsequent Anglican-Orthodox discussions, and in particular for those held in 1930 and 1931. (For the text, see Appendix, pp. 253-9 below.)

'The terms of Intercommunion' published in 1923 by the Archbishop of Canterbury's Eastern Churches Committee included the problems:

[21] Letter from Archbishop of Canterbury to Patriarch of Constantinople, *C.E.* i (1920), pp. 57-58. For details of the relations between Randall Davidson and the Orthodox Church see G. K. A. Bell, *Randall Davidson, Archbishop of Canterbury* (2 vols., 1935), especially vol. ii, pp. 1087-1114.

[22] *Lambeth Conference 1920*, p. 148.

1. The Christian Faith. 2. The Canon of Holy Scripture. 3. The sufficiency of Holy Scriptures. 4. The Creed of the Church. 5. The decisions of the Council of Chalcedon concerning the Faith. 6. That no one can form another Creed. 7. The doctrine of Holy Spirit. 8. The *Filioque* clause. 9. The variety of the customs in the Church. 10. The number of the sacraments. 11. The Holy Eucharist. 12. The Holy Orders of the Church. 13. The sacred images.[23]

In the year 1927, the Fellowship of St. Alban and St. Sergius was founded, which was to become one of the chief focal points of the contacts between Orthodox and Anglicans.[24]

The Lambeth Conference of 1930 was a climax in the relations between Anglicans and Orthodox. The then Archbishop of Canterbury, Cosmo Gordon Lang, had the inspiration of inviting the Ecumenical Patriarch to appoint a general Orthodox delegation for that Conference. In his letter (29 February 1930) to the Patriarch, the Archbishop emphasized the cordial desire of the Anglican Church to come into mutual agreement and brotherhood with the Holy Orthodox Church.

The Ecumenical Patriarch, with the useful assistance of the Patriarch of Alexandria, Meletios,[25] very quickly formed the Orthodox delegation led by the Patriarch of Alexandria himself. He was the second Patriarch of Alexandria (the first was Cyril Lucaris) to have dealings with the Anglican Church. What Cyril had inaugurated Meletios consolidated. The Bishop of Gloucester, A.C. Headlam, wrote to his niece Miss P. L. Wingfield on 3 August 1930,

Meletios was very helpful. He wanted to come to terms, so he put his questions in a way that was easy to answer them. They had a good many conferences together and had a good deal of trouble with one or two of his people. The Rumanian Archbishop was inclined not to be conciliatory. The Rumanians are unlike the others—not Philo-Anglican—and are a good deal under Romanist intrigues. If we had

---

[23] V. T. Istavridis, *Orthodoxy and Anglicanism* (London, 1966), pp. 35 ff.

[24] It publishes the magazine *Sobornost* (1928–33, mimeographed, under the title *The Journal*, etc; 1934, printed under the title *Journal* etc.; 1935, printed under the title *Sobornost*; cf. N. Zernov, *H.E.M.*, pp. 662–4).

[25] Meletios Metaxakis, the celebrated Greek Orthodox Prelate: 1911–1918, Metropolitan of Kition, Cyprus; 1918–1920, Metropolitan of Athens; 1921–1923, Ecumenical Patriarch of Constantinople; 1926–1935, Patriarch of Alexandria; d. 1935. For these discussions see N. Zernov, *H.E.M.* p. 651; J. G. Lockhart, *Cosmo Gordon Lang* (London, 1949), pp. 355, 360–62; cf. also R. Jasper, *Arthur Cayley Headlam* (1960), pp. 208–210.

had one or two more days it would have been completely satisfactory.[26]

The Anglican Church, the British Government, and the press gave a warm welcome to the Patriarch on his arrival in London to lead the theological discussion with the Anglican theologians. The Archbishop of Canterbury declared in one of his addresses:

My joy is great, because His Holiness the Patriarch of Alexandria is the leader of the Orthodox delegation. I can say that in England Patriarch Meletios is the most honoured amongst the Orthodox prelates. He has worked more than any other for the stability of the already existing relations of our Churches.

The programme of the Orthodox delegation in England was full of meetings, lectures, conferences, and private discussions. It was evident that the unity of the Churches could not be established simply by discussion or conferences between theologians. For the reality of Church unity, the way must be prepared by studies, speeches, publications, in order that the laity also may be enlightened. For the unity of the Church does not come from the work and the agreement of the theologians alone, but also and equally from the agreement in spirit of the bishops and their congregations. This way is difficult, but it is the surest one. Agreement between the theologians without the psychological preparation of the laity may well come to nothing.

The 1930 Anglican-Orthodox discussions were the first official ones of this kind. A Subcommittee of the Lambeth Conference, under the Bishop of Gloucester, met with the Orthodox delegation to discuss the differences between the two Churches. The delegations were composed as follows:

Orthodox

The Pope and Patriarch of Alexandria, Meletios. The Metropolitan of Thyateira, Germanos (Ecumenical Patriarchate). The Metropolitan of Epiphaneia, Ignatius (Patriarchate of Antioch). The Archbishop of the Jordan, Timothy (Patriarchate of Jerusalem). The Bishop of Novibad, Irenaeus (Patriarchate of Serbia). The Archbishop of Bukovina, Nectarius (Patriarchate of Rumania). The Metropolitan-elect of Paphos (Church of Cyprus). The Metropolitan of Corfu, Athenagoras [the present Ecumenical Patriarch] (Church of Greece). The Archimandrite Michael Constantinides (Church of Greece). The

---

[26] R. Jasper, op. cit., p. 209.

Archimandrite, Sabbas Sovieroff (Church of Poland). The Bishop of Znepolsky, Paisios (Church of Bulgaria).

Anglicans

The Bishops of Gloucester, Atlanta, Chichester, Chicago, Dublin, Egypt and the Sudan, Fulham, Gibraltar, Guildford, Montreal, Nassau, N. Indiana, Rhode Island and W. Michigan.

During the discussions the following questions were raised by the Orthodox:

1. Are the *Terms of Intercommunion* drawn up and published under the auspices of the Archbishop's Eastern Churches Committee regarded by the Committee of the Lambeth Conference as expressing the mind of the Anglican Church, and, if not, where and in what do they diverge from that mind?
2. What is the supreme constitutional body in the Anglican Church which decides authoritatively in matters of differences in faith?
3. If a member of the Anglican Church uttered publicly opinions contrary to the Faith of the Church, what is his status in the Church, and how is it decided?
4. Does the Anglican Church agree that Holy Orders is a *mysterion* and that in its unbroken succession it is a link with the Apostles?
5. Does the Anglican Church agree that the Bread and Wine become the Body and Blood of Christ and that the rendering of the Eucharist is a spiritual sacrifice, propitiatory for the living and the dead?

The following questions were asked by the Anglicans in their turn:

1. Whether the question of the validity of Anglican orders will come before those other Branches of the Orthodox Church which have not as yet made any pronouncement on the subject and whether any further explanations are required in relation to the question.
2. Whether the Orthodox Church accepts the validity of Anglican Baptism.
3. What policy the Orthodox Church desires to follow with regard to the administration of the Sacraments by Anglican Priests when no Orthodox Priest is available and vice versa.
4. For the guidance of the Anglican Bishops in the U.S.A., what steps would be taken towards the unification of the Orthodox Church in that country.
5. Whether the Orthodox Church has examined the 'Suggested Terms' of Intercommunion published in English, Greek, and Russian.
6. Whether the Orthodox Church would agree to the appointment of a Joint Commission on Questions of Doctrine.

7. Whether the Anglican Church could help the Orthodox Church in organizing educational institutes such as, for example, High Schools in Orthodox countries.

8. What attitude the Orthodox Church would take towards the Y.M.C.A.[27]

After many private, and four official, meetings between 15 and 18 July, the following decisions were arrived at.

1. It was agreed that a Joint Commission of Orthodox and Anglicans should be appointed for the consideration of questions of Doctrine.

2. It was agreed by the Anglican Bishops that the 'Terms of Inter-communion . . .' published under the auspices of the Archbishop of Canterbury's Eastern Churches Committee in 1921 . . . are not inconsistent with the mind and doctrine of the Anglican Church.

3. It was agreed by the Orthodox Delegation that the suggested 'Terms of Intercommunion' . . . would form a useful basis for discussion with certain modifications.

4. It was stated by the Anglican Bishops that in questions of faith the authentic decision would be given in the Anglican Communion by the whole body of Bishops without, however, excluding the cooperation of clergy and laity during the discussions.

5. It was stated by the Orthodox delegation that the final authority in matters of Doctrine in the Orthodox Church lies with the whole body of Bishops in Synod, without excluding the expression of opinion by clergymen and laymen.

6. It was stated by the Anglican Bishops that in the Anglican Communion the Bishop has jurisdiction in questions of discipline through his own court in the first instance, with due provision for appeal to the Provincial Court or a similar body.

7. It was stated by the Orthodox Delegation that in the Orthodox Church spiritual cases are tried in spiritual courts, sentence being given in the case of a Bishop by a court of Bishops, in the case of other clergymen by the Bishop through his own court.

8. It was stated by the Anglican Bishops that in the Anglican Communion Ordination is not merely the appointment of a man into a particular post, but that in Ordination a special *charisma* is given to the person Ordained, proper for the Order, and that the nature of the special gift is indicated in the words of Ordination, and that in this sense Ordination is a *mysterion*.

9. It was stated by the Anglican Bishops that the Preface to the Ordinal declares 'that from the Apostles' time there have been these Orders of ministers in Christ's Church; Bishops, Priests and Deacons,' and that to

[27] Istavridis, op. cit., pp. 48–9.

preserve unbroken succession the rules regarding Ordination have been framed 'to the intent that these Orders may be continued, and reverently used and esteemed, in the Church of England.'

10. The Orthodox Delegation stated that they were satisfied with regard to the maintenance of the Apostolic Succession in the Anglican Church in so far as the Anglican Bishops have already accepted Ordination as a *mysterion*, and have declared that the Doctrine of the Anglican Church is authoritatively expressed in the Book of Common Prayer, and that the meaning of the Thirty-Nine Articles must be interpreted in accordance with the Book of Common Prayer.

11. It was stated by the Anglican Bishops that in the Sacrament of the Eucharist 'the Body and Blood of Christ are verily and indeed taken and received by the faithful in the Lord's Supper', and that 'the Body of Christ is given, taken and eaten in the Supper only after an heavenly and spiritual manner', and that after Communion the consecrated elements remaining are regarded sacramentally as the Body and Blood of Christ; further, that the Anglican Church teaches the doctrine of Eucharistic sacrifice as explained in the Answer of the Archbishops of Canterbury and York to Pope Leo XIII on Anglican Ordinations; and also that in the offering of the Eucharistic Sacrifice the Anglican Church prays 'by the merits and death of Thy Son Jesus Christ, and through faith in this blood, we and all Thy whole Church may obtain remission of our sins, and all other benefits of His passion', as including the whole company of faithful people, living and departed.

12. It was stated by the Orthodox Delegation that the explanation of Anglican Doctrine thus made with regard to the Eucharistic Sacrifice was agreeable to the Orthodox Doctrine, if an explanation were to be set out with all clearness.

13. It was stated by the Anglican Bishops that in different parts of the Anglican Communion, Anglican clergy, at the request of the Orthodox clergy, provide sacramental ministrations to Orthodox laity, who are out of reach of their own Church's ministrations; that such clergy always desire to keep the Orthodox to whom they minister faithful to the Orthodox Church and are ready to teach them the Orthodox faith and to notify Orthodox Bishops or Priests of persons thus receiving their ministration or instruction.

14. It was stated by the Orthodox Delegation that the whole question of arrangements in such circumstances is to come up for discussion at the forthcoming Synod of the whole Orthodox Church.

15. It was stated by the Orthodox Delegation that it is the practice of the whole Orthodox Church not to re-baptise after Anglican Baptism.

16. It was stated by the Orthodox Delegation that in its forthcoming Pro-Synod the Orthodox Church would probably not object to recognising the Baptism of children and their instruction from Ortho-dox books by Anglican Clergy, or to marriage or any other rites being

performed by Anglican Clergy (in case of need where no Orthodox Priest is available), provided that all persons baptised or married are properly registered as Orthodox, and their names notified as soon as possible to the competent Orthodox authority.

17. It was stated by the Orthodox Delegation with regard to the Holy Eucharist that, pending a formal decision by the whole Orthodox Church and therefore without giving the practice official sanction, for which it has no authority, it is of the opinion that the practice of the Orthodox receiving Holy Communion from Anglican Priests in case of need and where no Orthodox Priest was available, might continue, provided that an Orthodox authority did not prohibit such a practice.[28]

The Joint Doctrinal Commission referred to in paragraph 1 of this statement met the following year (October 1931) under the chairmanship of the Metropolitan of Thyateira, Germanos, and the Bishop of Gloucester (A. C. Headlam) and discussed the following questions:

1. The Christian Revelation.
2. Scripture and Tradition.
3. The Creed of the Church.
4. The Doctrine of the Holy Spirit.
5. Variety of Customs and Usages in the Church.
6. The Sacraments.

The Report of this Commission concludes with three Resolutions already agreed between Anglicans and Old Catholics; these the participants agreed to lay before the authorities of their respective Churches for consideration:

1. Each communion recognizes the catholicity and independence of the other, and maintains its own.
2. Each communion agrees to admit members of the other communion to participate in the Sacraments.
3. Intercommunion does not require from either communion the acceptance of all doctrinal opinion, sacramental devotion, or liturgical practice characteristic of the other; but implies that each believes the other to hold all the essentials of the Christian Faith.[29]

---

[28] *Lambeth Occasional Reports 1931–8* (London, S.P.C.K., 1948), Appendix III, pp. 92–4.

[29] ibid., pp. 39 ff. comprising the Report (pp. 44–59, in English and Greek), A Résumé of the Proceedings (pp. 60–84), and Appendixes (pp. 85–113, including the report of the 1930 discussions reproduced above). See also G. K. A. Bell (ed.) *Documents on Christian Unity, Third Series, 1930–48* (London, 1948), No. 157, pp. 38–43.

Owing perhaps to political conditions in 1931–9 little further of note took place in Orthodox-Anglican relations in those years. There followed the War of 1939–45 which prevented the meeting of a Lambeth Conference in 1940; so it was not until 1948 that the next Lambeth Conference 'received the Report of the Joint Doctrinal Commission appointed by the Ecumenical Patriarch and the Archbishop of Canterbury, which met in 1931'; it thanked the theologians concerned 'for their valuable work in elucidating the *Suggested Terms of Intercommunion*', and asked the Archbishop of Canterbury, in co-operation with the Ecumenical Patriarch, to appoint a further Commission, to continue the work which the original Commission had begun (Resolution 66(a)). It added in the same Resolution, section (b):

The Conference is convinced that the contribution of the Orthodox tradition is essential to the full life and witness of the Universal Church, and that a deepened understanding and fellowship between our two Communions has much to give to the healing of the nations, and especially to the growth of mutual understanding between East and West in the world today.

These words remain valid for the relations of the Anglican and Orthodox Churches since 1948. There have been many contacts of varying degrees of friendliness, but positive steps to closer relations in regard to terms of intercommunion have not been taken.

A notable example of the exchange of courtesies and meeting of personalities at the highest level was the visit of the Ecumenical Patriarch Athenagoras to Archbishop Michael Ramsey in London, in November 1967—the first visit in history of a Patriarch of Constantinople to England.

'The Archbishop of Canterbury', it was stated on his behalf, 'regards the visit of the Ecumenical Patriarch Athenagoras to England as a great step forward in Anglican-Orthodox relations, and a contribution to the whole cause of Christian Unity'. The Patriarch and the Archbishop discussed relations between the Anglican Communion and the Orthodox Churches. The *Church Times* (17 November 1967) commenting on the Patriarch's visit to London wrote enthusiastically,

It is hardly ever possible to estimate the exact significance of any one particular event during the long, hard road to Christian unity. But the visit paid to the Archbishop of Canterbury by the Ecumenical Patriarch, Athenagoras I, has certainly been one of the more momentous of the many efforts made in recent years to mark a definite advance along that road.

Fourteen hundred years of unbroken Christian history are embodied in the office held by the Archbishop's distinguished and most welcome guest. All those privileged to be presented to His All Holiness during the visit must have carried away with them the sense of having shared in a historic occasion. And they will also remember the impact, however brief, of an extraordinary personality, a Christian leader imbued with the power and charity of the Spirit. England and the Church of England are the richer for the visit of the Patriarch of the East.

In the joint communiqué the Patriarch and the Archbishop noted 'the growing interest in Orthodoxy shown by the clergy and people of the Church of England thoughout the visit'.

A Roman Catholic spokesman said that 'the Patriarch has undoubtedly cemented the bonds not only between Anglicanism and Orthodoxy, but also between Orthodoxy and English Catholicism'. He continued, 'I hope that the success of the visit will be a precedent for the visit of Pope Paul to England in the not-too-far-distant future. Pope Paul, like the Patriarch, would come as a spiritual not a temporal leader.' (*Catholic Herald*, 17 November 1967.)

Following the traditional links between Alexandria and Canterbury, Dr. Ramsey, the Archbishop of the See of St. Augustine, on 28 January 1970, sent to Nicolaos VI, Pope and Patriarch of Alexandria, an invitation to visit Lambeth from 16 to 18 May 1970.

Patriarch Nicolaos and his entourage, including the present writer, were welcomed in Lambeth with joy and greeted by the Archbishop of Canterbury 'with many thoughts of sacred history'. The Patriarch assured the Anglican Communion that he visited Lambeth 'to renew the warm and old links between the Church of Alexandria and the Anglican Communion' (*Church Times*, 8 May and 22 May 1970).

During the stay of the Patriarch of Alexandria in Lambeth informal talks took place between the two Church leaders and their assistants.

After his visit in Lambeth Patriarch Nicolaos and his entourage flew from London Airport to Edinburgh to be received by the General Assembly of the Church of Scotland and remain there as the guests of Kirk for ten days. That visit is the first in which the Church of Scotland has had an official visit from the head of any of the Eastern Orthodox Churches. (For details on both visits see Metropolitan Methodios of Aksum, 'Alexandria–Canterbury', in *Ekklesiastikos Pharos*, 52 (1970) pp. 315–326 and 'Alexandrino-Scotica' ibid., pp. 181–205, and ibid., 53 (1971), pp. 391–523.)

3. *Roman–Anglican Relations*

The Church of England—*Ecclesia Anglicana*—was originally a part
of the Western Church and in communion with the centre of Western
Christendom, Rome; but the conversion of the Britons to Christianity
was not the achievement of the Romans. According to one authority,
'the Britons were converted by Greeks, but most probably through
interpreters.'[1] If we content ourselves with the authority of Tertullian
that 'the regions of Britain, inaccessible to the Romans, were subdued
to Christ' in the second century (*Britannorum inaccessa Romanis loca,
Christo vero subdita*),[2] we must accept the opinion of those who assert
that Britain became Christian from the East, either by direct communication, or through the Churches of Gaul.[3] For example, John
Lawrence writes:

It is sometimes argued that British Christianity has a largely Eastern
origin through the pre-Augustinian Christianity which was preserved
in the Celtic Church. It is argued that the first missionaries to Britain
came from Gaul, where they were under the influence of Irenaeus, who
was an Easterner; and it is pointed out that in Ireland the study of Greek
persisted longer than elsewhere in the West. Moreover, Theodore of
Tarsus came to impart an Eastern slant to Latin Christianity in Britain
during the formative phase.

Theodore (Archbishop of Canterbury 668–90) was a Greek. 'This
great man' (Lawrence continues) 'converted what had been a missionary station into an established Church' because before him the Bishops
had been Romans; from his time they were English.[4]

Roman rites and customs which were adopted in Britain were
brought here not by the Celtic founders of Christianity in these
islands, but by the thirty-nine monks who, under the leadership of
Augustine, were sent to Britain by Pope Gregory I in 596.

It was at the Synod of Whitby, in 664, that representatives of the
Celtic Church in the north of Britain, planted by Irish missionaries,
on the one side, and of the Church in the south, planted by St. Augustine
and his followers, on the other, met to settle the differences between
them in the date of Easter and other customs; the decision went in

---

[1] W. F. Hook, *Lives of the Archbishops of Canterbury* (London, 1860), vol. i,
p. 145.

[2] Tertullian, *Adv. Judaeos*, 7.

[3] A. Neander, *History of the Church* (Edinburgh, 1849), vol. v, p. 11. Cf. also
J. Lingard, *The Antiquities of the Anglo-Saxon Church* (London, 1806), vol. i,
p. 2, n. 2.

[4] *R.E.C.*, pp. 120–1.

favour of the Roman usage, and from that date the Church in Britain was officially committed to Roman ways; and although Christians in the north hesitated, they gradually fell into line.

From the eighth century Western Europe and Britain gradually became the productive pasture-land on which the Popes fed, until in 1213 (two years before Magna Charta) the English Parliament refused to permit the King of England to pay a tax to the Pope. Puller says that since the time of Urban, the Popes made an attempt

to rob the various Chapters, Metropolitans and Provincial Synods of Western Christendom of their rights in regard to the election and confirmation of Patriarchs, Archbishops and Bishops; and by this robbing they not only increased their power, but they also absorbed vast sums of money into their own treasury; because they forced all those who were to be made Bishops to pay very heavy fees in order to obtain their appointments. Thus, for example, during the fifteenth century each Archbishop of Canterbury, and also each Archbishop of York, had to pay for his appointment ten thousand florins of gold into the papal exchequer; and the Bishops of Winchester, a very richly endowed See, had to pay as much as twelve thousand florins of gold.[5]

This extortion, linked with the great dissatisfaction with certain developments in the doctrine of the Church, and in morals and integrity, provided the first rumblings of the coming cataclysm within the Roman Church. Since Rome refused to accept the suggestion that the Christian Church was corrupt, all the warnings made no impact upon its leadership. So the smouldering discontent broke into open dissatisfaction, and the Western Church was plunged into the chaos of the Reformation. It was in the course of this general upheaval that the Church of England repudiated the authority of the Pope.[6] That happened, not because it was convenient 'but because the Scriptures, newly opened to the people, could present no warrant for the claims which the papacy was making for itself.'[7] Dr. Ellison, Bishop of Chester, gives us a convenient summary of the causes which gave rise to Anglicanism:

The Church was in a state of corruption and turpitude which it was slow to shed. It is generally recognized that, in the closing years of the

[5] Puller, op. cit. pp. 11–12.

[6] Cf. Bernard Pawley, *Looking at the Vatican Council* (S.C.M. Press, London, 1962), p. 25.

[7] G. Ellison, *The Anglican Communion*, p. 14.

Middle Ages, in almost every department the life of the Church had become debased and ineffective. The leaders had become so engrossed in the problems of territorial government that they had lost the vision of their true office. The Apostolic Spirit had been steadily disappearing from the whole corpus of the rulers of the Church. The diminished personalities of the Popes of these times are only too close a reflection of their anaemic view of their pastoral life. The worship and practice of the Church had become clogged by a mass of superstition, and an over-powering clericalism. The monastic system had largely outlived its usefulness. The constant demands of the Roman court for money payments for spiritual services had brought its name into disrepute.[8]

Apart from these negative factors, the Roman Church was an obstacle to the progress of the Church, being unable to adjust, to accommodate herself to new ways and insights, to reform herself in time, and to sweep away the corrupt accretions of centuries. 'The Papacy', it has been said, 'forced the seekers for truth to cut new channels through which their beliefs might be expressed.' Today Roman Catholics recognize the partial responsibility of their Church for the division of the sixteenth century.

This break in Anglo-Roman relations took place during the reign of King Henry VIII of England; but there were no changes in doctrine during his reign.[9]

While Mary was on the throne (1553–58) the Church of England became reconciled with the Roman See. Parliament repealed the long list of anti-papal legislation passed since 1529, and petitioned for reconciliation. Reginald Cardinal Pole, Archbishop of Canterbury and Papal Legate, convened a National Synod in 1555 for the restoration and reformation of the Church; Archbishop Cranmer and Bishops Latimer and Ridley were burned at Oxford (1555 and 1556); and during the same period about two hundred other Protestants suffered.[10] But in 1558 Mary and Cardinal Pole died, and their mission failed.[11]

During the reign of Queen Elizabeth I (1558–1603) communion between the Church of England and the Roman See was again broken. Elizabeth, the last surviving child of Henry VIII and daughter of his

---

[8] Ellison, op. cit., pp. 11–12.

[9] David Woodward, *Our Separated Brethren*, p. 12; cf. G. Tavard, *La Poursuite de la Catholicité. Étude sur la pensée anglicane* (Paris, 1965), pp. 15–35.

[10] John Foxe's famous *Book of Martyrs* recounted their sufferings and had a great influence on English views of Roman Catholicism.

[11] cf. Thomas Phillips, *Reginald Cardinal Pole. His Life* (2 vols. London, 1767). See also Martin Haile, *Life of Reginald Pole* (London, 1910).

second wife, the Protestant Ann Boleyn, was led by the most active and the most vigorous elements of the English nation to abandon the policy of her sister in religious matters and to restore the Anglican Church for the peace of the nation. The Sovereign was proclaimed by Parliament, not the Head of the Church, but simply the Supreme Governor 'in all causes ecclesiastical and temporal' (1559), and was invested with the rights which Holy Scripture was held to grant to righteous and godfearing princes. Then the Prayer Book, which had been given a decidedly Protestant character in 1552, was changed in a more Catholic direction (1559).

The Act of Uniformity of 1559 set the pattern for the English Church of the future. 'By its careful balance in preserving all that was right and good in the first sixteen centuries of Christendom, while admitting and encouraging the new learning and the appeal of personal religion for which the Reformers stood, the Elizabethan Settlement produced a synthesis which is the heart of Anglicanism.'[12]

After the Council of Trent a court was convened in Rome to try Queen Elizabeth; and in the year 1570 the Pope, Pius V, by his Bull *Regnans in excelsis*, excommunicated her and her successors and absolved all her subjects from their allegiance to her. The mission of the Spanish Armada, sent by Philip of Spain, not without Papal encouragement, against the British Isles in the year 1588, led to penal reprisals against those who remained loyal to the Pope. 'This unfortunate Bull, unrepealed, still regulates the formal attitude of the Roman Catholic Church to the Church of England.'[13] Since that time the relations of the two Churches, Roman and Anglican, have been influenced by 'the unhappy experiences of Mary's reign, the plots against Elizabeth I and James I, and the desertion of James II [which] all helped to build up a monstrous fear of Rome which centuries have not been able to dissipate'.[14]

There were no official relations between Rome and Canterbury. Although unofficially, the two Churches lived side by side until the year 1850, when Rome deliberately established in England a Roman Catholic Hierarchy in rivalry to that of the bishops of the Church of England. The effects of *Regnans in excelsis* still remained.

[12] Ellison, op. cit. p. 13. Cf. G. Tavard, 'L'Epoque Elisabethaine' in *La Poursuite de la Catholicité*, pp. 37–59.
[13] Pawley, op. cit. p. 29.
[14] J. R. H. Moorman, *A History of the Church in England* (London, 1961), p. 283.

Nevertheless the idea of a reconciliation had never been extinguished in the Church of England. In the early part of the eighteenth century an attempt was made to open negotiations with the more liberal section of the Roman Communion in France known as the Gallicans. This was the time when the Non-jurors started correspondence with the Eastern Orthodox Church.

William Wake (Archbishop of Canterbury 1716–37) had made contacts with French priests when he was a chaplain in Paris, and in 1717 correspondence between him and Dr. L. E. Du Pin of the Sorbonne was opened with some support from the Archbishop of Paris.

Wake was immensely interested in this approach, but quite determined not to compromise the Anglican Church or to allow it to be thought of as in any way inferior to the Church of Rome. For two years a considerable correspondence took place and some agreement was reached; but in 1719 the negotiations came to an end through the death of Du Pin and the complete submission of the Archbishop of Paris to pressure from Rome.[15]

The Oxford Movement gave the Church of England greater self-confidence. It was a dynamic demonstration of the self-sufficiency of Anglican theological and ecclesiastical thought, a providential event which shook the Church of England to its foundations. Those who are working for Christian unity find an abundant source of light and faith in the study of this great movement. The early relations between the Oxford Movement and Rome are shown by Tract XX (of the famous *Tracts for the Times*) by John Henry Newman, in which he wrote: 'popery must be destroyed. It cannot be reformed.' It is quite certain that Newman was at first very anti-Roman. He was convinced that the Church of Rome was corrupt, that it had introduced doctrines and practices which were not part of the traditions of the primitive Church, in which he had such deep faith, and that the Church of England had just as much claim to Catholicity as had Rome itself. Newman changed his mind, firstly because of the articles written by Wiseman suggesting that the Church of England resembled the Donatist schism, and secondly because of his consciousness that

[15] Moorman, op. cit., p. 283; cf. T. H. Lupton, *Archbishop Wake and the project of Union between the Gallican and Anglican Church* (1896). See for details Norman Sykes, 'Ecumenical Movements in Great Britain in the Seventeenth and Eighteenth Centuries', *H.E.M.* pp. 154–8.

Christ had promised that the Holy Spirit should guide the Church into all truth. The Primitive Church did not know the whole truth; this was revealed only slowly in the course of history. It was not the Primitive Church that should be taken as the model, but that Church which showed most signs of holiness, of being the true Body of Christ. From that time Newman began to look on Rome with new eyes.[16]

With his Tract XC Newman tried to support the Catholicity of the Church of England, but at the same time he was preparing the ground for his conversion to the Roman Church. Tract Ninety was published in the year 1841 under the title *Remarks on Certain Passages in the Thirty-Nine Articles*. Of these Articles Newman deals especially with the fourteen which are most anti-Roman: 'With remarkable acumen he demonstrates that what the Articles in fact do, is not to condemn the official teaching of Catholicism but certain extravagances which have grown up in the Church of Rome.'[17]

Tract Ninety caused protests in a great part of the Church of England and Newman's opponents accused him of sophistry and conscious dishonesty. Towards the end of 1844, he started to write an essay on *The Development of Christian Doctrine*, which convinced him of the lawfulness of the additions which have been made to Roman Catholic doctrine in the course of the centuries. The result is well known. On 9 October 1845 Newman became a member of the Roman Church, and later published his *Apologia pro Vita Sua* to explain the evolution of his religious thought and his decision to abandon the Church of his baptism.

One of the most interesting features of the Oxford Movement's relations with Rome was Pusey's role. He tried to restore unity between Romans and Anglicans by recalling the Catholic nature of

[16] Moorman, op. cit., pp. 344–5. Cf. Tavard, 'Le Movement d'Oxford', in *La Poursuite de la Catholicité*, pp. 175–208.

[17] Moorman, op. cit., p. 345. With Newman there were H. E. Manning, T. W. Allies, F. W. Faber, and W. Ward, who followed his example. Since that time the influence of the Roman Church has penetrated into many quarters which were previously hostile. Newman became a member of 'the folk of the Anti-Christ', as he had called the Pope. Newman's thought reminds us of St. Augustine's reasoning; 'there are so many things which with good reason keep me in the Catholic Church. The agreement of all nations and peoples kept me there; its authority first established by miracles, fed by hope, increased by charity, confirmed by its antiquity, these all keep me there.' *Contra Epistolam Funtamentalem Manichaei*, 5.

Anglicanism. He published three volumes under the title of *Eirenicon* (1865, 1869, and 1870), in which he called for more peaceful relations between Romans and Anglicans.[18] But the promulgation of the Dogma of Papal Infallibility by the first Vatican Council (1870) finally discouraged Pusey's attempts.

From then until the end of the century little actual contact between Canterbury and Rome is recorded, though a private visit to Pope Pius IX was made by Dean Stanley in the year 1863.[19]

However, the Oxford Movement made a deep impression on English society, so that some English churchpeople began to look upon Rome with much more kindly eyes. One such was Lord Halifax (1859–1934), whose highest ambition it was to assist in healing the breach between England and Rome. In the year 1894, while staying at Madeira, he made friends with a French priest, the Abbé Portal (1855–1926).[20] Lord Halifax and the Abbé succeeded in being received by Pope Leo XIII in September 1894. The outcome was the Pope's Letter *Ad Anglos* (1895), and the Encyclical *Satis Cognitum* (1896).[21] Lord Halifax and Abbé Portal had had many conversations, which they reported to the Pope and to the Archbishop of Canterbury. The English Roman Catholics did not view the *rapprochement* favourably, and did everything they could to prevent the conversations succeeding. Two years later Leo XIII, carried away by the intransigence of his *curia*, published the Bull *Apostolicae Curae*, in which he declared that 'ordinations performed according to the Anglican rite are utterly invalid and altogether void'. This, which has been described as 'one of the sharpest and most public rebuffs that the Church of Rome can ever have administered to a peaceful Christian communion', made

---

[18] Liddon, *Life of Pusey* (1898), Vol. iv, pp. 95ff., 135ff., 173ff.; cf. Tavard, *Two Centuries of Ecumenism*, pp. 46–7.

[19] A. Vidler, *The Church in an Age of Revolution* (London, 1961), p. 156.

[20] Abbé Portal had, under the pseudonym F. Dalbus, published the book *Les ordinations anglicanes* (Paris, 1894), in favour of the validity of the Anglican orders, and in December, 1895, he founded the *Anglo-Roman Review*, in Paris. Portal was convinced of the possibility of a corporate reunion between Anglicans and Romans and he encouraged collective *rapprochement* between these two bodies in order to increase their knowledge of each other. He arranged important meetings in Rome and France for this purpose.

[21] Woodward, op. cit. p. 51. Although Leo XIII condemned Anglican orders he exhorted those charged with the care of souls in the Anglican Church to continue to have 'the glory of God and the Salvation of Souls' at heart, in hope of a reconciliation, though through conversion of individuals or communities. See *Apostolicae Curae*, quoted in Tavard, *Two Centuries of Ecumenism*, p. 89.

any further conversations impossible.[22] The Anglican Bishops replied to the Bull in a learned *Responsio* defending the validity of Anglican orders.[23] However 'Rome had spoken, and the matter was closed', as the Bishop of Ripon says, quoting St. Augustine.[24] Just as St. Augustine's dictum was long disputed in the African Church, so the question of Anglican orders will remain open for discussion with the Roman Church.

After the First World War the two old friends, Lord Halifax and Abbé Portal, resumed their efforts for new contacts between their Churches. This was after the 1920 Lambeth Conference, which had made an appeal for unity to all Christian people.[25] Conversations were held at Malines in December 1921 and March 1923, between the Roman Catholics Cardinal Mercier, Mgr. Van Roey, and the Abbé Portal, and the Anglicans Dr. Armitage Robinson, Bishop W. H. Frere, and Lord Halifax. In November 1923 and May 1925 they were joined by Mgr. Batiffol and Canon Hermer, and Bishop Charles Gore and Dr. B. J. Kidd. As David Woodward writes:

The matters chosen for discussion at the first Conference, which was secret, were a memorandum, presented by Lord Halifax, and the 'Appeal', from the Lambeth Conference. The second Conference received in advance approval by Pope Pius XI, and by the two Anglican Archbishops, and a memorandum composed by the Anglican representatives was used as the text for discussion of practical measures for corporate reconciliation. The third Conference discussed three Anglican memoranda on St. Peter's position and the early interpretation of the Petrine texts of the primitive Church, and on the rejection of Papal authority in England in the sixteenth century. The fourth Conference discussed two catholic theological and historical memoranda on the relation of the Episcopate to the Papacy, and was followed by an Anglican written reply, then a memorandum by Dom Lambert Beauduin 'The English Church united not absorbed.' It suggested a

---

[22] After the condemnation of the Anglican Orders by Rome Lord Halifax wrote to Portal 'we are momentarily defeated, but God willing, His will shall be accomplished and if he permits us to be wounded, it is no dream, it is as sure as ever' (in Tavard, op. cit. p. 63).

[23] Moorman, op. cit. p. 405.

[24] cf. St. Augustine, *Sermo* 131, c. 10. 'Roma locuta, causa finita est'. See 'Canterbury and Rome: The Question of Anglican Orders. A Summary' by Norman Sykes, *H.E.M.* pp. 297–8; cf. also Moorman, ibid. p. 404 ff.

[25] *Conference of Bishops of the Anglican Communion 1920* (London, S.P.C.K., 1930), p. 133 ff.

uniate regime in England, and was followed by Gore's memorandum 'on unity with diversity' and then a Catholic written reply. After the death of Cardinal Mercier and Abbé Portal (1926) a fifth Conference was held under the presidency of Mgr. Van Roey to agree upon reports of the Conversations.[26]

The conversations were friendly and considerable agreement was reached; all present felt that the reunion of Anglicans and Roman Catholics would confer benefits on both parties; but neither side spoke with any real authority, and the atmosphere was essentially private and informal. Even so, suspicion was aroused in Rome; and after the death of Cardinal Mercier any further conversations of this kind were officially banned by the Pope.[27]

The main points on which the Anglicans and Romans expressed divergent opinions were these:

I. There was unanimous agreement on the necessity for visible Catholic unity. The Anglicans were prepared to grant that, if other obstacles to visible unity could be removed, it might be possible to recognize an historical precedence in the See of Rome. The Romans, on the other hand, insisted that the episcopate required a visible head as the centre of its unity, and it was realized that the whole question of the relation of the papacy to the episcopate was of such importance as to demand fuller consideration in the future.

II. The Roman Catholics pointed out that the Pope's theoretical right to intervene anywhere could not be surrendered; but it was not inconceivable that he might normally be content to abstain from actually exercising it in England. The Anglicans, without as yet admitting the principle of universal jurisdiction, hoped that in any case, if reunion were accomplished, the Pope might restrict himself to dealing directly with the Archbishop of Canterbury and other Metropolitans. But Archbishop Davidson informed Cardinal Mercier that he was unable to accept the Pope as sole Vicar of Christ. The terms 'spiritual leadership' and 'general superintendence' were suggested as

[26] Woodward, op. cit. pp. 51–2; Viscount Halifax, *Leo XIII and Anglican Orders*, pp. 323 ff. For the contribution of Bishop Gore to the Malines Conversations see G. L. Prestige, *Life of Charles Gore*, pp. 478–89, see also Gore's important memorandum 'On Unity in diversity' in Dr. Frere's *Recollections of Malines*. See also C. Boyer, *Christian Unity and the Ecumenical Movement*, pp. 73–81. Cf. also Tavard, *La Poursuite de la Catholicité*, pp. 235–7.

[27] Lord Halifax (ed.), *The Conversations at Malines, 1921–1925* (1930) quoted in Moorman, op. cit., p. 419.

leading more easily towards agreement; but Gore raised objections even to 'general superintendence' and preferred the words 'spiritual responsibility'.[28]

III. The Anglicans asked for the re-examination of the question of Anglican Orders, and a discussion took place on the possibility, in the event of reunion, of the retention of such characteristics of Anglicanism as the use of the vernacular in worship, the English rite, Communion in both kinds, and married clergy.

IV. It was recognized that the only solution to the question of the reunion of the two Churches was a union which did not mean the absorption of the Church of England.[29]

At the fourth of the Conversations, in May 1925, Gore read his memorandum on 'Unity in Diversity'. It was intended as a plea for the widest possible toleration of differences both in doctrine and in practice, provided that agreement could be secured about those articles of faith necessary to the Catholic Communion. There were two distinctions in matters of doctrine, which appeared to be recognized by Roman Catholic theologians. There was, first, the distinction between doctrines which were *de fide*, and those which, whatever their degree of authority, did not bind under positive penalty of heresy. There existed also another distinction, that between doctrines which were fundamental and doctrines which were not fundamental. Gore suggested the definition of 'fundamental doctrines' as 'those which have always been held and believed in the Church in substance', about which it could therefore be said that there had been no development in substance but only in terminology. This formula would cover the doctrine of God, the Atonement, the visible Catholic Church and the sacraments as real instruments of specific divine gifts, together with other matters of importance, but, clearly, from the Anglican point of view, it did not apply to those dogmas defined by the Roman Church in mediaeval or modern times, and imposed as a condition for Communion. Whether these dogmas were true or not, they rested not on historical evidence but on *a priori* inference. Here Gore asked, 'whether the idea were wholly impossible that, with a view to the corporate reconciliation of Romans and Anglicans, Rome could be

---

[28] G. L. Prestige, *Life of Charles Gore* (London, 1935), p. 482. Gore declared that he had 'not the least desire to submit to Roman Authority as an individual'; but also 'his way of conceiving of unity *in Corpore* is certainly not acceptable to Catholics' says Boyer, *Christian Unity and the Ecumenical Movement*, p. 78.

[29] For a good account of the Conversations by a modern R.C. ecumenist, see Tavard, *Two Centuries of Ecumenism*, Ch. xi, pp. 124–35.

content to require the acceptance of no further articles of faith than those which fell under the head of "fundamental"?'[30]

Although the conversations did not achieve any direct results of a practical character, 'they helped . . . to remove misunderstandings and to indicate the extent of agreement which seemed already to exist between the two Churches'.[31]

First, on the question of the sacraments the two parties came to complete agreement, which can only mean that the Anglicans accepted a formulation which was practically indistinguishable from the doctrine of transubstantiation. Secondly, on the question of the Holy Scriptures the English participants conceded that the Bible needs the interpretation of the Church before it can be acknowledged as the final standard of faith and doctrine. Finally on the question of the Papacy, which remained of course the greatest stumbling block, there was agreement up to this point: that the supremacy of the Pope should be acknowledged, but not his Infallibility. 'In fact the conversations at Malines show a considerable effort on both sides to define their respective positions and to clarify the facts of the problem. Perhaps the conversations of Malines, although called private, were still too official.'[32]

Between the end of the Malines Conversations and the death of Pope Pius XII in 1958, there was little improvement in official or semi-official Anglican–Roman relations. The Ecumenical Movement, whose progress was marked by a series of conferences of its two branches, 'Life and Work' and 'Faith and Order', at Stockholm (1925), Jerusalem (1928), Oxford (1937), and Edinburgh (1937), had full Anglican

[30] Prestige, pp. 487–8. Cf. also Visser 't Hooft, op, cit. p. 34.

[31] Visser 't Hooft, op. cit. p. 34.

[32] C. Boyer, op. cit. pp. 76, 80. See also 'Canterbury and Rome: The Malines Conversations. A Summary' by Norman Sykes, *H.E.M.* pp. 298–300. In October 1966, forty years after the end of the Malines Conversations, Cardinal Suenens and the Bishop of Winchester, Dr. Allison (representing the Archbishop of Canterbury) unveiled and dedicated at Malines a plaque of thanksgiving for the life and work of Cardinal Mercier, commemorating also the second Viscount Halifax and the others who took part with him in the Anglican-Roman Conversations there from 1921 to 1926. It is particularly interesting to note that this commemoration occurred when preparations were being made for formal conversations between the Roman and the Anglican Churches.

During the commemoration Service, a message from the Pope was read. He hailed the Conversations as a 'courageous attempt of those pioneers who sought the ways of the Lord to bring the Catholic and Anglican Churches closer together.' (*Catholic Herald*, 4 Nov. 1966).

participation, but Roman Catholics were throughout this period forbidden to take part in it.[33] Since the Orthodox Churches were still very weakly represented in it—their full participation began only at New Delhi, 1958—the movement appeared to be Anglican and Protestant, or in some Catholic eyes 'Pan-protestant', only. In England, the personal relations of William Temple (Archbishop of Canterbury, 1942–4) and George Bell (Bishop of Chichester, 1928–58) with Roman Catholic leaders were friendly, if not close, and during the war of 1939–45 the movement known as 'The Sword of the Spirit' had both Roman and Anglican membership and official support. But this was only possible because its aims were limited to moral renewal and the public life of the nation, all doctrinal or ecclesiastical questions being excluded. Roman Catholics, when present at meetings, were forbidden even to join in prayer with 'non-Catholics', and at such meetings therefore not even the 'Our Father' could be said together: later this one prayer was cautiously allowed, but nothing else. In 1948 came the inauguration of the World Council of Churches with its First Assembly at Amsterdam, but the Roman attitude to the World Council was at first extremely reserved. Such was the state of affairs on the Roman side throughout the pontificates of Pius XI and Pius XII.

Pope Pius XII was succeeded by Pope John XXIII who changed the whole spirit of the Roman Church and brought to Roman Catholics a new approach to the rest of Christendom. The See of Canterbury at that time was occupied by Dr. Geoffrey Fisher, who will go down in the history of the Church of England as the man responsible for a climax in Anglican-Roman relations. On his way back from visits to the Patriarchs of Jerusalem and Constantinople in December 1960, Dr. Fisher paid a courtesy call on the Pope. After centuries of hostility and prejudice, and in view of possible misunderstandings on both sides, this first visit since the Middle Ages of an Archbishop of Canterbury to the Pope was an act of considerable courage and statesmanship. It was regarded by the two Churches as a suitable time to start clearing away the centuries of prejudice and misunderstanding which separated the two communities.[34] It was agreed that an unofficial representative

[33] The Papal rulings, binding on Roman Catholics, concerning the Ecumenical Movement, were given in the Encyclical *Mortalium Animos* (1928), and this negative attitude remained virtually unchanged for thirty years.

[34] Pawley, op. cit. p. 16. For all the expansive good will on both sides, that meeting hardly contributed to the cause of closer relations between Anglicans and Romans.

of the Archbishops of Canterbury and York be sent to reside in Rome.[35] Subsequently it was decided that the Anglican Communion would send Observers to the Second Vatican Council and Dr. John Moorman, Bishop of Ripon, was chosen, amongst others, to attend the sessions of that Council. In March 1966 the next Archbishop of Canterbury, Dr. Michael Ramsey, paid the first official visit to the Pope on behalf of the whole Anglican Communion. On 24 March 1966, after a Service of Prayer, in which both Pope and Archbishop took active part, at the Basilica of St.-Paul-without-the-Walls, they signed a Common Declaration recording their resolution to forget the past and to promote a theological and practical dialogue between their churches. As a result of this, a Joint Preparatory Commission of representatives of the two Churches met three times in 1967, and was succeeded by the Anglican–Roman Catholic International Commission, which by the end of 1971 had also met three times, and produced 'working papers' and an Agreed Statement on Eucharistic Doctrine. These developments are treated below in chapter VIII (Sect. 3, pp. 238–241).

All these moves indicate that a new era in inter-Church relations has taken place, and point towards the reconciliation of the two Churches.

[35] ibid. p. 18.

Chapter IV

HOW THE THREE CHURCHES VIEW
ONE ANOTHER

1. *The Orthodox Church as seen by the Anglican Church*

The Church in England at the time of its foundation and for four and a half centuries afterwards was in Communion with the Orthodox Church. When the final separation between Rome and Constantinople took place, 547 years after St. Augustine came to England, the Church of England was not given an opportunity to express its opinion of the Roman attitude towards the East. The obscurity in the position of the Anglican Church towards the East is the result of the Church of England having never officially broken with Rome. The Provincial Synods of York and Canterbury did not withdraw from communion with the Church of Rome. What the Church of England did was to say that 'the Bishop of Rome hath no greater jurisdiction given to him in Holy Scripture by God in this Kingdom of England than any other foreign Bishop'.[1] But the actual breach of Communion was brought about by the act of Pope Paul III and by the Bull *Regnans in Excelsis* of Pope Pius V (1570). The Church of England from its foundation to King Henry I (1135) was an independent Church and the Popes interfered very little with it. Therefore its position is very peculiar with regard to the East, because just as it never withdrew from Communion with Rome, neither did the Anglican Church ever withdraw formally from communion with the Orthodox Church. What makes the Communion of Orthodox and Anglicans difficult now is the confusion prevailing in the Orthodox view of the rise of Anglicanism. On the contrary, Anglicans believe that their Church has never been separated from the undivided Catholic Church. This

[1] Richard W. Dixon, *History of the Church of England from the Abolition of the Roman Jurisdiction* (2nd ed., London, 1884), Vol. i, pp. 227, 238.

belief is clearly stated in the appeal of Archbishop Cranmer, who said, in 1556, when under Queen Mary Tudor he was charged with heresy: As touching my doctrine, it was never in my mind to teach contrary to the Word of God and the Catholic Church of Christ according to the exposition of the most Holy and learned Fathers and martyrs. I only mean and judge as they have meant and judged. I may err, but heretic I cannot be, inasmuch as I am ready to follow the judgement of the Word of God and of the Holy Catholic Church, using the words that they used, and none other, and keeping their interpretation.[2]

Implicit in this declaration that the Anglican Church has never broken away from the Undivided Church is the supposition that it is not separated from the faith of the Orthodox Church. And since the Orthodox Church made no claims of jurisdiction over the Anglican Church the latter never condemned the doctrine or the practice of the Orthodox Church. On the contrary, since the time of the Reformation the view has been held in the Church of England that in the East the Catholic faith has remained intact. For instance Alexander Knox (d. 1831) and his disciple Bishop Jebb, 'taught that the Greek Church represented the original body of Christendom; that the Church of England perpetuated the Greek tradition; and that since she represented this tradition rather than the Latin, she should seek an understanding of, and an approach to the Churches of East'.[3] Again, A. C. Headlam wrote that 'the Eastern Church professes to be the only true Church, both Catholic and Orthodox'[4]—though it is still

[2] ibid., p. 502.

[3] cf. *Remains of Alexander Knox*, Vols. i–iv, especially vols. iii, pp. 210, 211, and iv. See also *Thirty years Correspondence between John Jebb and Alexander Knox*, ed. by Charles Forster, Vol. i; cf. moreover Tavard, *La Poursuite de la Catholicité*, pp. 177–180.

[4] cf. A. C. Headlam, *The Teaching of the Russian Church* (London, 1897), p. 1. This does not mean that all the Anglicans admit Headlam's opinion, as the quotations from Mascall show. In these we can see the German tendency, which dominates Western Roman and Protestant scholarship, 'to characterize Orthodoxy on the basis of modern and contemporary documents.' Such was, for example, the case of Wilhelm Gass, who in his book, *Symbolik der Griechischen Kirche* (1872), in which he emphatically wrote that 'the modern Greek Church is not identical with the Ancient Church, and has widely departed or deviated from the early foundations'. Opposed to Gass was Ferdinand Kattenbusch in an article 'Kritische Studien zur Symbolik im Anschluss an einige neuere Werke' in *Theologische Studien und Kritiken*, Jahrg. 51 (1878), pp. 94–121, and in his book *Lehrbuch der Vergleichenden Confessions-Kunde. Erster Band: Prolegomena und Erster Teil: Die Orthodoxe Anatolische Kirche* (Freiburg i/Br. 1892), who maintained that 'in order to grasp the genuine spirit of Orthodoxy one has to go

one thing to assume a common faith, and another to discover whether this is really so, or to seek to re-establish intercommunion. E. L. Mascall suggests that

when we do approach Orthodoxy, whether in historic Byzantium or present-day Europe . . . we shall be faced with much the same task as when we approach the Churches of the West, namely the task of disentangling the authentic Christian norm from its accidental, and largely falsifying, accompaniments. For Orthodoxy no more than Western Christianity has been free from these embarrassments. Greek theology for the last few centuries has very largely been based upon Latin scholasticism, often of a very decadent type, with slight modifications about the Papacy, the epiclesis and the *Filioque*, and has more recently shown a readiness to accept somewhat excessively and uncritically the biblical theories of German liberal Protestantism. Russian Orthodoxy . . . has been quite as much influenced by German mysticism and idealism as by the genuine Orthodox tradition.[5]

He also refers to the report *Catholicity* which spoke of 'the excessive dependence of the Byzantine Church upon the civil power and . . . the fact that it remained outside the main stream of European history, thus missing the Renaissance and the Reformation and the whole of the great scientific movement of the modern world.'[6]

Some Anglicans have considered that the practice and teaching of the Orthodox Church provides a convenient touchstone for deciding what things may find a place within a national branch of the Catholic Church without tending towards papalism. Others have been interested in the Orthodox Church because of their hostility to Rome. It is also true that many Anglicans have been as hostile to Orthodoxy as to Rome, and have shared the doubts expressed by the Lambeth Conference of 1888: 'it would be difficult for us to enter into more intimate relations with that Church so long as it retains the use of icons, the invocation of Saints, and the cultus of the Blessed Virgin'.[7]

---

back to the Fathers, to St. Athanasius, the Cappadocians, and indeed to Pseudo-Dionysius, rather than to Mogila or Dositheus', who wrote occasional polemical books addressed primarily to the problems of the Western Controversy between Rome and the Reformers. Cf. G. Florovsky, *The Ethos of the Orthodox Church*, pp. 182–3.

[5] *The Recovery of Unity. A Theological Approach.* (1958), p. 62–3.

[6] ibid., p. 61. See also B. Leeming, 'An Anglo-Catholic on "The Recovery of Unity" *E.C.Q.* xii (1958), pp. 265–6.

[7] R. Davidson, *The Five Lambeth Conferences 1867–1920* (London, 1929), pp. 168–9. (See above, p. 40).

But according to the 'Branch Theory', developed by Newman and his followers, Anglicans say that the Catholic Church consists of three branches, growing from one trunk, the Eastern Orthodox, the Roman and the Anglican.[8] So Fr. Puller, lecturing at St. Petersburg in 1912, said that the Anglicans think of themselves as forming a part of the same Holy Catholic and Apostolic Church of which the Russian is another part; 'and we are therefore accustomed', he said 'to regard the Holy Church of Russia and all the Holy Orthodox Churches of the East, as Churches which are sisters of the Holy Church of England'. And although 'the faithful members of the English Church love the Russian Church, they do not know so much about her as they would wish to know. And perhaps it is the same with you here.'[9]

It is significant that in the Church of England the Greek Fathers have been read and honoured to a degree unusual in the West. And the Anglican appeal to the traditions of the undivided Church has generated a similar attitude to that of the Orthodox Church towards them. 'Whereas in the East', said Dr. Ramsey at the University of Athens in 1962, 'the Holy Tradition had remained in essence the same, in the West the Tradition had been complicated in the Middles Ages.'[10] Dr. Ramsey has also written:[11]

The Church of England is debtor both to East and to West, and to the unity which once belonged to them. As regards the East, she has striven to recognise the debt in two ways. One way is by recovering within herself the true inheritance of Eastern theology, and a long line of the greatest Anglican teachers have found inspiration in the Greek Fathers; Thorndike, Maurice, Wescott, Gore are among them.

And elsewhere Dr. Ramsey says that a Westerner discovers from coming into touch with the East three things: (1) He discovers a

[8] A full description of the Branch Theory can be found in Newman's works; see especially J. H. Newman, Introduction to [Deacon] William Palmer's *Notes of a Visit to the Russian Church in the years 1840, 1841* (1882) pp. v–vii, 'through the division each party to it loses some spiritual treasure, and none perfectly represents the balance of truth, so that this balance of truth is not presented to the world at all'. William Temple quoted these words to describe the divided Churches in his inaugural sermon at the second Conference on Faith and Order August, 1937. See the Orthodox answer in *E.R.* iv (1949) pp. 434–43; cf. Tavard, *La Poursuite de la Catholicité*, pp. 185 ff.

[9] Puller, op. cit. p. 2.

[10] *Constantinople and Canterbury*, p. 2.

[11] *The Church of England and the Eastern Orthodox Church* (London, S.P.C.K., 1946), pp. 7–8.

vivid realization of the centrality of the Resurrection in Christianity; (2) he discovers also how the worship of the Eastern Church is filled with the lifting up of earth to heaven; and (3) he sees the Eastern realization of the Communion of Saints.

Professor Hodges, who is very much involved in the relations of Orthodoxy and Anglicanism, writes that:

in the Eastern Orthodox world, the Apostolic faith has lived on substantially unaffected by either Papal or Protestant innovations. It presents to us the faith and life of the undivided Church, not as a historical memory but as a present fact; it shows us the meaning of the non-Papal Catholicism, not as a theoretical possibility but as an actuality.[12]

Professor Hodges continues:

I am not idealising the Orthodox Church as it now exists, or saying that its day to day life at the present time is necessarily healthier or more vigorous than ours in the West. I should hesitate to say such a thing even if I had had the opportunity (as I have not) of seeing Orthodoxy at close quarters in a country where it is at home. The Orthodox world presumably has its good and bad spots, as has the West, and all of us, East and West, live an ambiguous life which partly exemplifies our faith and partly betrays it. Such is the condition of human existence, including even Christian existence in this world. I am not now speaking on this empirical level. I am speaking on the level of doctrine, and saying that the Orthodox Faith, to which the Orthodox Fathers bear witness and of which the Orthodox Church is the abiding custodian, is the Christian Faith in its true and essential form, to which we all aspire and by which we are all judged. Nor does this mean that all Orthodox theologians are individually wiser or sounder than their Western colleagues. It is a question of principles, not of persons, and the wind of spirit, bringing the gifts of wisdom and understanding, blows where it will.[13]

2. *The Orthodox Church as seen by the Roman Church*

After the Schism between Constantinople and Rome, the Roman Church tended to work on the assumption that there was no Church in the East, but only scattered Christians. Although this contention may be dismissed as a polemic exaggeration, Rome interpreted

---

[12] H. A. Hodges, *Anglicanism and Orthodoxy*, p. 39.
[13] op. cit., p. 47.

Christian universality as universality of the West. The situation was changed by Pope Pius IX and his successors, who although they issued documents inviting the Orthodox to return to the Roman Church, emphasized that there is no great gap between the two Churches.

The Roman Church now tends to believe that the Orthodox Church keeps intact the same Catholic faith as itself. What separates Orthodoxy from Catholicism is merely historical and national. Orthodoxy, according to Roman Catholics, is really a chip off the Roman block, detached from the golden mountain but still made of the same gold. Owing to the schism and to the contingencies of history—the invasions of the Crusades and then of Islam—Orthodoxy 'withdrew from history' (they say) at the end of the tenth century, 'whose convictions and mentality it has carefully preserved, but in a sterile way'.[1] This view is demonstrated by Encyclical Letters of the Popes, and from the position of those Orthodox who are united with Rome but maintain more or less the Orthodox teaching and tradition (Uniate Churches). If Orthodoxy were to recognize the Roman Primacy in the fuller sense, it could be in full communion with Rome. 'Our Orthodox brothers are not separated from us by a very wide gulf', said Leo XIII (*non ingenti discrimine seiunguntur*, Encyclical *Praeclara gratulationis*). 'Their attachment to the great mysteries of the Faith, their eucharistic liturgy, their belief in the infallibility of the Church, their veneration for the Mother of God and for the Saints, as well as the attitude of their best theologians and the radical changes in political conditions, all inspire me with the confidence that the end of the schism is no longer very far away.'[2] According to the Roman Church, the Orthodox Church is in schism. If the Orthodox Church will recognize the Pope as the head of the Church and the successor of Peter, it will maintain all its privileges and customs and nothing is to be changed in its constitution.[3] Similarly, the union of these churches is very easy, provided that the East will recognize the leadership of the West and come to the Roman court. The Roman Church admits that both Churches have the same faith in different forms of expression. According to Roman Catholic ecumenists, for example, the problem of

---

[1] O. Clément, 'A misunderstanding at Rhodes?' *E.R.* xii (1960), p. 224.

[2] C. Boyer, 'An Ecumenical Testimony', *E.E.* p. 17, and G. Thils, 'Ecumenism', *E.E.* pp. 174–5.

[3] *Osservatore Romano*, 13 May 1956, and *Herder Korrespondenz*, July 1956, p. 450 ff.

the Procession of the Holy Spirit is merely a divergence in point of view. This opinion is by no means unanimously acceptable to all Roman Catholic authors. 'It is logical from the Roman point of view that the Orthodox Church, as a "schism", must have her distinctive, schismatic features, and cannot be "identical" with the Catholic Church of old, even in its Eastern version.' Such were the opinions of M. Jugie, Th. Spacil, etc.[4]

Cardinal Bea expresses a modern Roman view when he writes:

The Oriental Church still preserves unbroken the succession of Bishops from the Apostles and, along with that valid sacraments, above all the Holy Eucharist. The Liturgy of the Mass is the centre of their religious life, is considered the true sacrifice atoning for the living and the dead, and is celebrated with great solemnity. In doctrine the Orientals retain the ancient apostolic and patristic tradition, and differ from the faith of the Latin Church only in a few points, particularly in their denial of the dogmas defined by Councils since the separation, such as the primacy and infallibility of the Pope. Although they have not accepted the definitions of the Immaculate Conception and Assumption, devotion to Our Lady remains strong amongst them and these dogmas are found in their liturgical books and generally admitted by their members.[5]

'The Church of Constantinople', he says elsewhere,[6] 'maintained the true faith, therefore she took the name Orthodox, i.e. of the true doctrine.' Particularly with regard to administration, W. de Vries writes that 'throughout the first ten centuries Rome never claimed to have been granted its preferred position of jurisdiction as an explicit privilege. The Popes recognise the powers of the Patriarchs of Alexandria and Antioch as being derived in each case from ancient custom and the Canons, especially Canon 6 of the Council of Nicaea, which in turn justifies its action with reference to legitimate custom.'[7] In accordance with these customs the Patriarchs and Bishops of the East

[4] cf. Florovsky, *The Ethos of the Orthodox Church*, p. 185. See also the article of T. O. Reilly, 'Apostolicity' in the *Catholic Encyclopaedia*, from which it would appear that Roman Catholics think that the Eastern Orthodox by withdrawing from the See of Rome have lost the Apostolic succession. K. Adam, on the other hand, accepts that the Eastern Orthodox, in view of their valid episcopal ordinations, preserved the Apostolic succession; cf. his *Spirit of Catholicism*, p. 190.

[5] Augustin Cardinal Bea, *The Unity of Christians*, ed. Bernard Leeming, S.J. (London, Geoffrey Chapman, 1963), pp. 27 ff. Cf. also A. Cardinal Bea, *The Way to Unity after the Council* (London, G. Chapman, 1967), p. 138.

[6] op. cit., p. 40.   [7] *Die Entstehung der Patriarchate*, pp. 346 ff.

are freely elected, the liturgy and canonical legislation are regulated independently, and the discipline of the clergy and the people is managed without the Pope's interference.[8]

H. J. Schultz gives a fresh account of the attitude of Roman Catholicism towards the Orthodox Church. He concludes his chapter 'Autonomy of the Patriarchates' thus:

Especially because of the development of the liturgical rites in the several Patriarchates, even to-day the patriarchal structure in the whole Christian East is regarded as just as untouchable as the rite itself. Patriarchate and liturgy are considered the pillars of their tradition.[9] Every abridgement of the ancient patriarchal rights, such as occurred from 1000 A.D. onwards in the case of those united with Rome, is therefore felt as a violation of the original tradition and shocks all Eastern Christians as much as would an interference with their liturgy.[10]

It is true that today Roman Catholic authors like Schultz, W. de Vries, who are mentioned above, and Gommenginer[11] show, from a Roman Catholic point of view, that the Orthodox are really *incorporated* in the undivided Church of Christ. This is because the withdrawal from Communion (which happened between Rome and the Orthodox) is a sign of loss of membership in the Church only if and when it has been decreed because of open heresy or apostasy, or for schism and rebellion against the authority of the Church. Another voice, that of Orest Kéramé,[12] asks:

Is the average Catholic prepared to accept the Orthodox for what they are, namely the Catholicism of the East?

Father Leeming writes that:

The concept of the Church's catholicity and apostolicity must include the Eastern Churches, which are so closely united to us in doctrine, outlook and spirituality; and for the fulness of catholicity and apostolicity

---

[8] W. de Vries, op. cit., pp. 348 ff., 356 ff., quoted in Hans Joachim Schultz, 'The Dialogue with Orthodox', *C.* iv (1965), p. 69.

[9] Cf. Archbishop J. Tawil, 'Die Ostkirche gestern und heute' in *Die Stimme der Ostkirche* (Freiburg, 1962), pp. 11–12.

[10] Schultz, 'The Dialogue with the Orthodox', ibid. p. 69.

[11] 'Bedeutet die Excommunikation Verlust der Kirchemitgliedschaft?' in *Zeitschrift für Katholische Theologie*, 73 (1951), pp. 1–17.

[12] 'Einheit mit der Orthodoxie?' in *Una Sancta*, 17 (1962) pp. 197–224, and *Concilium*, iv (1965), p. 73.

union with the Orthodox, and indeed with all separated Christian brethren, is a clear postulate. I repeat: the assumption must not be made that the Catholic Church is the Church of the West. To make that assumption and act upon it by exclusive attention only to the Western tradition is to impoverish, or even deny, the very idea of the Church's catholicity.[13]

The Second Vatican Council in the Decree on Ecumenism included a special consideration of the Eastern Churches.[14] The Decree acknowledges that

for many centuries the Churches of the East and West followed their own path yet were linked in the fellowship of brothers, in faith and sacramental life. By common consent, the Roman See was in control should disagreements over faith of discipline arise between them. [sic] Among other important matters, the sacred Synod takes pleasure in reminding all men that many particular local churches are flourishing in the East, including the Patriarchal Churches which hold the leading position, and several of them boast an Apostolic origin. From that time onwards, there has prevailed among the Eastern Christians a concern and care for the preservation of the family relationship in the fellowship of faith and charity that should exist in local churches, for they are sisters; it still prevails in our day. There is, likewise, no ignoring the fact that, from the beginning, the churches of the East have been in possession of a treasury from which the Western Church has borrowed heavily in the way of liturgical practice, spiritual tradition and juridical organisation. Nor must it be considered unimportant that the fundamental dogmas of Christian belief; the Trinity and the Word of God made flesh of the Virgin Mary, were defined in the East. The preservation of this belief has cost and still costs that Church much suffering. The Apostolic heritage has had various forms of modified acceptance; from the very beginning of the Church, it has had a different development in various places as a result of variety of character and living conditions. With the failure of mutual understanding and charity, not

---

[13] *The Vatican Council and Christian Unity*. A Commentary on the Decree on Ecumenism of the Second Vatican Council, together with a translation of the text (London, 1965), p. 159.

[14] Decree *De Oecumenismo*, edition pubd. by the Catholic Truth Society (London, 1964), pp. 22–26 (quoted by kind permission). See also the English text in *The Decree on Ecumenism of the Second Vatican Council*. A New Translation by the Secretariat for Promoting Christian Unity, with a Commentary by Thomas F. Stransky, C.S.P. (Paulist Press, New York, 1965), pp. 69–77. See also Bernard Leeming, *The Vatican Council and Christian Unity*, pp. 12–15. [Italics in this quotation are the present author's.]

to mention external causes, all this has given divisions their chance. For this reason, the sacred Synod calls upon all men to give due consideration to the special character of the birth and development of the Churches of the East and to the character of the relations which existed between them and Rome before the separation; *they must be correct in their appraisal of these matters*. The exhortation is especially directed to men who make it their aim to further the restoration of full communion which is desired between the Eastern Churches and the Catholic Church. If these points are carefully kept in mind, it will make a supreme contribution to the proposed dialogue. Everyone is familiar with the great love which Eastern Churches put into the performance of the sacred liturgy, especially the celebration of the Eucharist, the Church's lifespring and pledge of the glory that is to come. That is where the faithful join their bishop and, through the Son, the Word made flesh, who has suffered and entered his glory, with the outpouring of the Holy Spirit, have access to God the Father and attain fellowship with the Blessed Trinity, for they are made 'to share the divine nature' (2 Peter 1:4). The celebration of the Lord's Eucharist in the individual churches builds up the Church of God and makes it grow, while the practice of concelebration makes their fellowship manifest.

In the worship of the liturgy Eastern Churches extol Mary, ever a virgin, with hymns of great beauty. It was, after all, the Ecumenical Synod at Ephesus that made the solemn proclamation of Mary as the most holy Mother of God, to secure for Christ an appropriate and true recognition as Son of God and Son of Man, as the Scriptures show him. They also, in the liturgy, sing the praises of many other Saints, including the Fathers of the Universal Church.

These churches, for all their separation, are in possession of true sacraments, notably the priesthood and the Eucharist, by virtue of the Apostolic Succession. This possession of theirs keeps them connected to us by the closest degree of kinship. Given appropriate circumstances therefore, and the approval of ecclesiastical authority, some sharing in sacred rites (*Communicatio in Sacris*) is not only possible but advisable.

In the East one finds, moreover, a wealth of spiritual traditions formed chiefly by monasticism. Monastic spirituality has had a flourishing existence in the East ever since the glorious days of the Fathers. It has spread to the West from the East and has been the source and wellspring of the formation of the religious life among the Latins, and has repeatedly been a force of re-invigoration. This is the reason why Catholics are earnestly recommended to have frequent recourse to the spiritual treasury of the Eastern Fathers; it catches a man up entirely in Divine contemplation.

Recognition, respect, preservation and encouragement—everyone must know the importance of the attitude with regard to the liturgical and spiritual heritage of Eastern Christians, if a loyal guard is to be kept on the fullness of the Christian tradition and the reconciliation of Eastern and Western Christians is to be accomplished.

Furthermore, the Churches of the East had, from earliest times, always followed their own rules which had the authorisation of the Fathers, the Synods, and Ecumenical Synods at that. Variety in practice and custom is no obstacle to the Church's unity; on the contrary, it is an embellishment and it makes no slight contribution to the fulfilment of her mission (cf. *supra*). The sacred Synod, therefore, hopes to remove all doubt with the announcement that the Churches of the East, with the requirements of the unity of the whole Church in mind, *have every opportunity to govern themselves by their own rules* which are, after all, more suited to the mentality of their faithful and better adapted to securing the good of their souls. Thorough-going observance of this traditional principle—it has not always been maintained—is one of the essential preliminary conditions for reunion.

What has already been said about legitimate variety we are pleased to apply to differences in theological expressions of doctrine. When revealed truth is explored there is a difference to be seen in the methods and approaches of the East and the West to the understanding and statement of Divinity. It is not surprising that perception of revealed mystery on the one side is occasionally more penetrating than the other, and set in a better light. Consequently it must be admitted that, in such cases, the theological expressions which differ are often complementary *rather than contradictory*. As far as the genuine theological traditions of Eastern Christians are concerned they are admittedly remarkably well rooted in the sacred Scriptures, they find their support and their expression in the life of the liturgy, they draw sustenance from the living traditions of the Apostles and from the writings of the Eastern Fathers and spiritual writers, their tendency is towards the right ordering of life or, rather, to the full contemplation of Christian truth.

This sacred Synod thanks God that many Eastern children of the Catholic Church who keep guard over their inheritance and desire to live it with greater freedom from fault, with greater fullness, are now living in full communion with their brethren who support the tradition of the West. It declares that the whole of this heritage, spiritual and liturgical, disciplinary and theological, in its varying traditions, is relevant to the fully Catholic and Apostolic character of the Church.

After thorough scrutiny of these points, the sacred Synod repeats the statement of past Councils and Roman Pontiffs: if fellowship and unity are to be restored, 'no burden should be imposed beyond those which cannot be avoided' (Acts 15:28). It eagerly desires that, from now on, every effort be directed towards the gradual achievement of unity, in the different institutions and forms of the Church's life, chiefly by prayer and brotherly dialogue on the subjects of doctrine and the requirements of the pastoral office, to which our age gives increased urgency. In the same way, it brings to the notice of the faithful and the Pastors of the Catholic Church their ties of kinship with men who have left the East and are spending their lives far from their homeland. It is hoping thereby for an increase in brotherly co-operation with them, in a spirit of charity from which every breath of faction and rivalry is excluded. If this work is promoted wholeheartedly, the sacred Synod hopes that, with the removal of the wall dividing the Western from the Eastern Church, one single building will, at long last, come into existence, firmly based on its cornerstone, Christ Jesus, who will make them both one. (Cf. Council of Florence, sess. vi (1439), Definition *Laetentur caeli*: Mansi 31, 1026 E.)

The above quotation from a decree of the Second Vatican Council requires special consideration. In it the Fathers of the Roman Church diligently avoid condemnation of the Eastern Church. Not only this, but they admit that the Latin Church has profited greatly from the Eastern spiritual treasury. When they speak about separation, they say that the break took place between East and West, instead of the traditional Roman contention that the Eastern Church broke off communion with Rome. What the Eastern Church rejects completely is the statement of the Council Fathers that 'by common consent, the Roman See was in control should disagreement over faith or discipline arise between' the Eastern Churches. Here lies a fundamental difference of interpretation of the several contacts between East and West, which divides Western and Eastern thought.[15] Another point which needs special emphasis is that the Council Fathers do not ask the Easterners to come back to Rome, but they hope 'that, with the removal of the wall dividing the Western from the Eastern Church, one single building will, at long last, come into existence, firmly based on its cornerstone, Christ Jesus, who will make them both one.' This statement reveals a change for the better in the traditional attitude of the Roman Church towards the East.[16]

Unfortunately this Decree of the Vatican Council does not fully satisfy the Orthodox. First of all the Orthodox Church, in Orthodox eyes, is not separated from Rome in the sense in which the Council understands the 'separated brethren'. Secondly, the Orthodox Church

[15] Cf. Francis Dvornik, *Byzance et la Primauté Romaine* (Paris, Editions du Cerf, Unam Sanctam (49), 1964), p. 152.
[16] W. de Vries, 'Communicatio in Sacris', *C.*, iv (1965), p. 12.

4

is treated together with the 'Uniates', whom in any case the Orthodox regard as betrayers of Eastern Christendom. In other words, the Orthodox Church is one of a number of Churches which are separated from Rome. In this the Orthodox Church desired deeper understanding from the Vatican Council. However, we can say that the present Decree on Ecumenism as it stands marks a tremendous improvement in the attitude of the Roman Church towards the East, when one considers the real attempts which have since been made to interpret the Decree in a manner which gives great satisfaction to the Orthodox. An example of this is the article by Cardinal Giacomo Lercaro, to which we will refer again.[17] Cardinal Lercaro emphazises that the Orthodox Churches have their own heritage and they must be known and respected. Another commentary on the Decree on Ecumenism, made by Fr. Thomas F. Stransky, C.S.P., a member of the Vatican Secretariat for Promoting Christian Unity, tends to acknowledge an ecclesial equality between Orthodoxy and Roman Catholicism. Likewise Cardinal Jaeger in his book *A Stand on Ecumenism* stresses the strong interest of the Council Fathers in the Orthodoxy and Catholicity of the Eastern Orthodox Churches.

There is another example of great importance indicating the new attitude of the Roman Church towards the Orthodox, which W. de Vries[18] describes as follows:

We witnessed the most recent case of liturgical services in common with non-Catholics on the occasion of the trip of the reigning Pope, Paul VI, to the Holy Land in January, 1964, and of his meeting with Patriarch Athenagoras of Constantinople. The Pope gave the Patriarch a Chalice for the Holy Sacrifice. In doing this he was acknowledging the Eucharistic celebration of the separated Eastern Christians as in itself good, and paid no attention to the view that the separated churches do not celebrate the Holy Sacrifice legitimately. Many stricter moralists had previously declared this to be absolutely inadmissable. Now that the Pope himself has admitted it, no one will henceforth have the hardiness to maintain the contrary.

Cardinal Lercaro, Archbishop of Bologna, said that this symbolic gesture in offering a chalice to each of the Eastern Patriarchs he met at Jerusalem is of great theological significance. One does not offer a chalice to those heads of Churches whose Eucharistic celebrations one thinks to be illegitimate . . . is not this an eloquent confirmation of the

[17] *C.* i (1965), pp. 83–91.
[18] 'Communicatio in Sacris', *C.* iv (1965), p. 21.

text of *De Oecumenismo*, which affirms that by the celebration of the Eucharist the Orthodox Churches are built up in the One Church of God?[19] A great impression was made on the third Pan-Orthodox Conference (Rhodes 1964) by the humble and brotherly tone of Pope Paul's Message:

Your Excellencies and dearly beloved Brethren in Christ. It is from the bottom of our heart that we send you our fraternal greetings. While your brothers of the Roman Catholic Church, gathered in Council, are asking themselves about the way to follow ever more faithfully the designs of God for His Church in this time, so rich in possibilities and at the same time so full of trials and temptations, you are preparing also to turn to the same problems in order to respond always better to the Lord's will.

Fully aware of the importance of your venerable assembly, we fervently pray for the light of the Holy Spirit upon it.

Rest assured that we ourselves, with the Council gathered together now, and the whole Catholic Church, watch the progress of your labours with the greatest interest, associating them in fervent prayer with those going on at present near the tomb of the Apostle Peter, in full confidence that the grace of the Lord will the more richly be with both because a common charity has inspired this common prayer.

We keep in mind the recommendations of the Apostle Paul: 'Bear one another's burdens; it is thus that you will fulfil the law of Christ.' We dare to count on the fruits of your prayers, your Excellencies and beloved brethren in Christ, that the Lord will grant us the grace necessary to the faithful accomplishment of the work to which the mysterious design of His Providence has called us.

May the All-holy Mother of God, to whom we pray and whom we honour with the same fervour, intercede for us that we grow ever in the love of her Son our one Saviour and Lord. May charity nourished at the table of the Lord make us daily more eager for 'the Unity of the Spirit in the Bond of Peace'. Eph. 4:3.

From the Vatican, 29th October 1964   PAULUS PP. VI
                                             Bishop of Rome.[20]

A very important statement on the Orthodox Church was also made by Pope Paul at Castelgandolfo on 2 August 1967. He said: 'The East is teacher. It teaches us how the faithful are called upon to

[19] Cf. *O.I.C.* i (1965), p. 187.

[20] G. Dejaifve, 'The Third Pan-Orthodox Conference in Rhodes', *O.I.C.* i (1965), pp. 140 ff.; cf. also J. Karmiris, 'The Third Pan-Orthodox Conference in Rhodes', *Eccl.* 41 (1964), pp. 608–69.

speculate on the revealed truth, that is, to the formulation of a theology which we may call scientific . . .'.

It remains to examine the Orthodox representation in the World Council of Churches. The Roman Catholics recognize that by participation in the World Council the Orthodox Church defends the Catholic Faith, and 'whatever may have happened in the distant past, Catholicism must recognize Orthodoxy for the courage and constancy of its doctrinal witness. The fidelity of the Orthodox to the ancient tradition is a precious guarantee of ecumenical relations in the future.'[21] 'In a particular sense we also felt thankful to the Orthodox delegation' (in Evanston), writes Eva-Maria Jung,[22] 'because it was due to them alone that the Catholic voice was heard in the "Ecumene". Their two statements signified a unanimous witness to our common Catholic Tradition and a challenge to the Protestant Churches to re-evaluate their position in the light of this tradition.' Another view on this is that 'the Orthodox Church does not seem capable of standing the strain alone (owing to its lack of an appropriate theology and administration). Sooner or later', continues Clément, 'it looks as if it will have to apply for fraternal aid to Rome, and to theological "science" perfected by Rome; it will have to take stock of itself and of its own adhesion to Catholicity' [Roman, of course].[23]

3. *The Roman Church as seen by the Orthodox Church*

It is fundamental that the teaching of the Orthodox Church concerning the Roman Primacy is identical with that of the ancient Church. The Great Fathers, especially Gregory of Nazianzus, taught that the Roman Church provided the rule of faith: '*Manifestum namque indicium est non esse rectae fidei omnem qui in fide Gregorio non concordat.*'[1]

According to Gregory of Nazianzus the relations amongst the Bishops of the Christian Church were to reflect the relations between the Apostles, i.e. relations of equality and 'orderliness and moderation'

[21] Tavard, *Two Centuries of Ecumenism*, p. 210.
[22] 'Roman Catholic impressions of the Evanston Assembly', *E.R.* vii (1955) p. 118; cf. also 'What can Western Churches learn from Eastern Churches: The Contribution of Eastern Orthodoxy to European Culture', *E.R.* xi (1959), pp. 321–22.
[23] O. Clément, 'A misunderstanding at Rhodes?' op. cit. p. 225.
[1] Rufinus, *Orationes*, in Otto Bardenhewer, *Geschichte der Altkirchlichen Literatur* (Freiburg, 1923), iii, p. 163.

which excluded 'love of ruling'. Gregory asks 'Who among the disciples of Our Lord went up with him to the mountain for prayer? Peter and James and John. Who were present just before his passion? These three.'[2] In another homily[3] he says 'Although I honour Peter, I am not only Petrine; I also honour Paul but I am not only Pauline. I do not accept the distinction made by men, in those matters which have been made by God.' The Orthodox therefore are unable to admit '*Primatus Petri*', '*Ecclesia Petri*' and '*Ubi Petrus, ibi Ecclesia*'. On the contrary Gregory[4] extols Paul and calls him Apostle and Preacher of the Nations and Protector of the Jews, as having the care of all the Churches, the first after Christ, as standing between God and humanity.[5]

It is remarkable, says E. Michaud, that in his Epistles, Gregory of Nazianzus writes that

although nature had not given two Suns, nevertheless we have two Romes, which radiate like lamps to all the universe. The New Rome [Constantinople] shines in the East, and the Old Rome shines in the West. But both are equal.[6]

Following the witness of the great Fathers of the Church, such as Gregory, Basil, John Chrysostom, Athanasius and others, the Orthodox Church admits that the Church of Rome is one amongst the many Apostolic Churches of Christ.[7] Accepting the decisions of the Universal Councils, it regards the Roman Church as earlier than Constantinople, but Constantinople as equal to it—Rome is older, not pre-eminent.

The Orthodox Church through the centuries made strong efforts to maintain unity with her sister Church of Rome. In fact it is a mark of the unity of the Church during the first centuries that many of the Western Fathers are included amongst the Fathers of the whole Church, that amongst the Popes there were Greeks, and that amongst the Saints of the Eastern Church are many of the Popes. Unfortunately

[2] Migne, *P.G.* xxxvi, 193.

[3] ibid. 301.

[4] ibid. xxxv, 461.

[5] Cf. E. Michaud, 'Ecclésiologie de St. Grégoire de Nazianze' in *Revue Internationale de Theologie*, xii (1904), p. 570.

[6] Migne, *P.G.* xxxvii, 1068. Michaud, ibid. p. 571.

[7] Tertullian, *De praescriptione haereticorum*, 36, where the Roman Church is merely put on a par with other Churches founded by Apostles. It was, however, the only such foundation in the West.

the Orthodox Church later suffered from physical attack by the Western Church's Crusades and from spiritual attacks through its proselytizing activities. There is a deep feeling in the Orthodox Church that the Roman Church is imperialistic, aggressive, and lacking in Christian charity. It regards Rome as being poisoned by egoism, derived from the favourable political circumstances in which it found itself. Moreover, it regards the Roman Church as a legalistic theocracy which has been maintained by the Curia since the Middle Ages. It believes that a bureaucratic system prevails in Rome serving only the hegemony of Rome.

The Orthodox Church believes that the establishment of the Roman Primacy has changed the ancient teaching of the Roman Church so that today there is a great gap which separates it from the Eastern Catholic Church. Rome is not the touchstone of right faith any more.[8] Although the Eastern Church recognizes the validity of the Roman sacraments and the Apostolic succession of its priesthood, it has not expressed officially its final decision on the position of the Roman Church in the whole Christian Church. It does, however, think that the Roman Church lies between schism and heresy. The Eastern Church has avoided a decision on this matter because of the pre-dominant desire of Orthodoxy not to increase the gap between the two Churches. The new dogmas of the Roman Church have caused much surprise in the ecclesiastical and theological circles of the Ortho-dox Church, which is fully convinced that the Popes, by the new dogmas, offered such a striking proof of their fallibility and such lack of respect or charity towards the East, that the latter could not but lodge a protest against dogmatic definitions so rash, inopportune and contrary to the ecumenical spirit. For a fuller discussion of this see the section concerning Mariology in Chapter VI. Dr. N. Zernov, sum-marizing the Orthodox attitude towards Christian Churches separated from it, writes:

[8] There was a formidable decision on the Roman Church made in Moscow in the year 1948, during the celebration of the 500 years of the autocephalous [self-governing] existence of the Russian Church. After the celebrations the delegates examined the relations between Orthodoxy and Roman Catholicism, and declared 'the Conference condemns the Papacy and all the new Roman Doctrines, by which Rome has corrupted the New Testament's teaching of Jesus Christ; the Conference moreover condemns all the bloody wars made by the Popes in order to convert the Orthodox to Roman Catholicism.' *Actes de la Conférence des Chefs et des Representants des Eglises Autocephales, 8–18 juillet 1948* vol. i (Moscow, 1950), pp. 94–291. See also especially vol. ii (Moscow, 1952), pp. 440–4.

But, if Eastern theologians are still disputing among themselves on this important issue, the general behaviour of the Orthodox in regard to separated Christians follows a distinct line which adheres faithfully to the practice of the undivided Church. According to this, Christians who have left the communion of the one Church are treated in various ways, for their alienation is not of the same degree of gravity . . . . Orthodox Theologians are still in search of doctrinal formulas which will solve the contradictions between the belief in one Catholic Church and the existence of schisms, heresies, and animosity among its members . . . .[9]

The Orthodox Church ascribes to Rome the primary responsibility for the theological controversies during the Middle Ages which caused the divisions in the Western Church. 'Is it not characteristic', says Clément, 'that after the schism in the eleventh century the Eastern Church was marked by a free prophetic spirit which (where necessary) reformed the Church from within; whereas in the West throughout the Middle Ages more and more heresies arose claiming freedom in the name of the Holy Spirit?'[10]

In view of all this the Orthodox Church considers that it alone continues to be the One, Catholic, and Apostolic Church, which has come down to our days without innovations or changes directly from the college of the Apostles. There has been no final decision as to the position of the Roman Church and unless it will accept the common faith which both East and West inherited, Orthodoxy cannot continue to regard it as the Catholic Church of the West. The Orthodox Church has not clung rigidly to the positions of the first ten centuries; it has not 'withdrawn from history'. It suffered from the impact of history and experienced humiliation and persecution. 'Despite its inadequacies and apparent failures, in the deepest sense Orthodoxy has perhaps responded all the same to the challenges of history.'[11]

Yet though this is the semi-official attitude of Orthodox churchmen and theologians, there is still a great affection for all the talents and greatness of the Roman Church. 'The Orthodox Church is neither "Roman" nor "anti-Roman". We are merely "anti-papist" ' writes Professor A. Kartaschoff.[12]

We can understand the situation better if we realize that amongst the Roman Catholic hierarchy and writers we can find many friends of the Orthodox Church, but amongst the Orthodox there is hardly a

[9] N. Zernov, H.E.M., pp. 672–73.
[10] O. Clément, op. cit., p. 226.
[11] ibid.
[12] 'Orthodox Theology and the Ecumenical Movement', E.R. viii (1955), p. 34.

person who is not *prejudiced against Rome*. There was, for instance, a storm in the Church of Greece at the idea of a *rapprochement* between Orthodoxy and Rome. It is not without significance that the late Archbishop Chrysostom of Athens declared that 'as long as I am alive there will be no contacts with Rome'. This attitude is understandable, for a lot of problems have been created by the Roman Church, because predecessors of the present Pope showed arrogance and indifference towards the Orthodox Church in Greece; for example, Pope Pius XII refused to send representatives to the 1900th celebration of St. Paul's arrival in Greece. Another great hindrance to the relations between the Church of Greece and Rome is the existence in Athens of a handful of Catholics of the 'Greek Rite' who do propaganda for the Roman Primacy, misleading the simple and ignorant Orthodox people.[13]

We should also note that the message sent by the third Pan-Orthodox Conference to Pope Paul in 1964, though cordial, is to some extent reserved. And its references to 'honouring one another' and 'awaiting the accomplishment of the will of our Lord Jesus Christ for his Church' indicate the determination of the Orthodox to preserve that independence of mind which they have always felt to be threatened by the Papal claims to universal jurisdiction. The message reads as follows:

His Holiness the Pope of Rome Paul VI, Vatican City.
We who are gathered together in a Pan-Orthodox Conference on the Pauline Island of Rhodes have received with great joy the very agreeable message of Your Venerable Holiness. In sincerity we appreciate the words of love and peace in the same and only Lord which you have had the kindness to address to us on your own behalf and on behalf of the Second Vatican Council and the whole Roman Catholic Church.

Unanimously we express our warm thanks to your Holiness. In the same spirit and in the hope that the Lord who has redeemed His Church by His own blood will, through the intercession of the most Holy Mother of God, grant comfort and strength to you and to us to rejoice in the good fellowship of Christ, we salute you in the peace and Love of our Lord.

'Persevering in prayer' and 'honouring one another', we follow the path of the Counsels of God, while awaiting the accomplishment of the Will of our Lord Jesus Christ for his Church, because He is faithful for ever.[14]

[13] See the strong protest in *Soter* (Athens) vi (1965) p. 729.
[14] J. Karmiris, 'The third Pan-Orthodox Conference in Rhodes', *Eccl.* 41 (1964), pp. 610–11.

Courage was therefore shown by the Patriarch Athenagoras when, amidst all this hostility towards Rome, he declared that Constantinople and Rome are 'the two sister Churches.'[15]

4. The Roman Church as seen by the Anglican Church

Much of the Anglican writing concerning the Roman Church can be found in the works of the seventeenth-century Anglican divines. John Cosin (1594–1672), speaking of the agreements and disagreements between Anglicans and Romans, says that the Bishop of Rome could be acknowledged to be the Patriarch of the West, but not by divine right.[1] William Laud (1573–1645), says: 'The Roman patriarch, by ecclesiastical constitutions, might perhaps have a primacy of order'; but he is equal to the other patriarchs.[2] Isaac Barrow (1630–77), on the other hand, says that there is not one Canon of the Catholic Church directly declaring the authority of the Pope; nor any mention made of him, except thrice [twice] accidentally; once upon occasion of declaring the authority of the Alexandrine Bishop, the other upon occasion of assigning to the Bishop of Constantinople the second place of honour, and equal privileges with him.'[3] Elsewhere Barrow says that the order fixed among the great Sees of the Christian Church followed the greatness, splendour and opulency of the cities. Amongst the other Anglican Divines, John Bramhall (1594–1663), Gilbert Burnet (1643–1715) and George Hickes (1642–1715) plainly deny any universal authority of the Pope.[4] James Ussher is reputed to have called the Pope 'Antichrist',[5] and, although he denied the authorship of this remark, it remains as an indication of Anglican feelings towards Rome during the seventeenth century. Marco Antonio de Dominis (the former Roman Catholic Archbishop of Spalato who from 1617 to 1622 was in the Church of England) calls the Pope 'Pharaoh' and 'Antichrist'.[6]

The Roman Church did a great deal towards establishing Christianity firmly in England. It sent St. Augustine, who with his missionaries converted the south-east of England. The Church of England was

---

[15] *Apostolos Andreas* (Istanbul), 11 Dec. 1963.
[1] P. E. More–F. L. Cross, *Anglicanism* (London, 1957), p. 55.
[2] op. cit., p. 57.
[3] op. cit., pp. 61, cf. p. 65.
[4] op. cit., pp. 65–9.
[5] op. cit., p. 69.
[6] op. cit., p. 74.

united with Rome until the Reformation. St. Gregory, Pope of Rome, has always been regarded as the Apostle and founder of the Church of England. The Anglican Church, says Puller,[7] recognizes that 'the Local Roman Church, over which St. Gregory presided as being its Bishop, is our Mother Church, for which we should naturally wish to feel a filial reverence and gratitude'. But in later times the Popes became tyrannical, so that this filial feeling has in fact almost disappeared. However, when Anglicans speak about the foundation of their Church they like to acknowledge that the Roman Church in the time of Pope Gregory was a loving Mother.

Amongst the Tractarians the Church of Rome was recognized as a true Church. Some of them were attracted by the great Church of the West, others and especially William Palmer (of Worcester College, Oxford) said that Rome is 'an unsound and corrupt Branch of the Christian Church' or that 'the Church of Rome is a corrupt Church, but still a part of the Church of Christ in spite of its glaring imperfections'.[8] In favour of Rome were W. G. Ward,[9] Froude,[10] Pusey, and Newman. Keble maintained neutrality towards Rome.[11] More recently, Archbishop Garbett wrote that the Church of England, in accepting the spiritual supremacy of the Pope, acknowledged advantages in the existence of a higher spiritual power. But since the Reformation, the promulgation of the decree of Papal infallibility has further widened the breach with Rome.[12]

Like Villain, Garbett[13] thinks that the Church of England is inspired

[7] Puller, op. cit., pp. 3–4, cf. also Cyril Garbett, *The Claims of the Church of England*, p. 23. A different view has been expressed, however, for example: 'Great Britain owes much more than most are willing to acknowledge to the Eastern Church. Rome may have been the stepmother of the Church of England, *but assuredly the Orthodox East was her mother.*' A. Lowndes, *Vindication of Anglican Orders*, Vol. ii, p. 545.

[8] Cf. William Palmer, *Treatise on the Church of Christ*, 3rd. ed., vol. I, Part I, chapter xi; H. P. Liddon, *Life of Pusey*, ii, 295; see also F. Oakeley, *Historical Notes on the Tractarian Movement* (1865), p. 36 ff.

[9] Wilfrid Ward, *W. G. Ward and the Oxford Movement*.

[10] Froude's *Remains*, Part I, vol. i (1838), pp. 306–8.

[11] John Keble, *Letters of Spiritual Counsel*, ed. by R. F. Wilson (1870), pp. 78–9.

[12] Garbett, op. cit., pp. 18–19. The Tractarians generally rejected the supreme authority of the Pope. They accepted a primacy, but not his authority over his brethren.

[13] Op. cit., p. 34. See Villain, *Unity*, pp. 137–8: 'The Platonic characteristic of the Caroline Divines (Lancelot Andrewes, Jeremy Taylor, William Laud, Simon Wilson [*sic*], John Donne, to mention only the most important) comes from the fact that they draw largely on the Greek Fathers'.

more often and more directly by Platonic philosophy, and especially the Eastern Fathers of the Church.

The new doctrinal definitions of the Roman Church[14] are thought by Anglicans to be innovations, which are not grounded on Scripture nor on the tradition of the Early Church. On this point E. L. Mascall insists that modern Christianity must go back to its origins. The claim, characteristic of his book,[15] is that both Byzantium and Rome, as well as the Reformation, have been unfaithful to the ancient Tradition. The dialogue between the Churches should be based on Patristic thought. On Roman Catholic Ecclesiology, Mascall says 'Rome must abandon juridical ecclesiology and make it sacramental'.

It is indisputable, as Anglicans admit, that the Roman Church represents half of Christendom and that for long it was characterized by strong discipline and uniformity. It still has great boldness in proclaiming what it considers to be the Gospel and is unwilling to compromise on what seem to it to be essential truths. The zeal and sacrifice which it consecrates to the service of the one Lord in every corner of the world are well-known. Anglicans believe, however, that they must raise their positive protest against the methods of the Roman Church in interpreting truth.

5. The Anglican Church as seen by the Orthodox Church

As we try to see the Anglican Church with Orthodox eyes we must remember that clear-cut definitions are ruled out in advance where Anglicanism is concerned. Judged by the principles of the Orthodox Church, the Church of England had the right to proclaim itself self-governing and autonomous, provided that there were certain canonical principles, which in fact there were. The old Church of England went on without any breach in either its legal or its spiritual continuity. It continued to profess the Catholic faith, which was once for all delivered to the Saints. It preserved without any break the Apostolic Succession of its Ministry,[1] although 'many Anglicans maintain

---

[14] 'The Immaculate Conception of Mary', wrote Gore in *The Anglo-Catholic Movement Today* (1925), p. 31, 'is a (supposed) fact of history which has no basis in historical evidence at all'. Similarly, the dogma of the Papal supremacy and infallibility is plainly contrary to the facts of history. It was never part of the Eastern tradition of the Church.

[15] *The Recovery of Unity*, p. 232.

[1] C. Garbett, op. cit., p. 15, 17, 55.

Apostolic succession primarily as a symbol and Bond of Unity.'[2] Some Anglican theologians have considered Episcopacy to be not only of the *Bene esse* of the Church, but part of its *esse*, as Canon Richardson says.[3] Consequently Orthodox theologians, influenced by the writings of Anglicans like Gore[4] and A. M. Ramsey,[5] have accepted that the Church of England means by Apostolic succession 'that grace is bestowed by our Lord, through the action of His whole Church. But certain actions in this work of grace are confined to Bishops, whereby the truth is taught that every local group or Church depends on the one life of the one Body.'[6] We find a similar opinion to that of Archbishop Ramsey in G. W. Broomfield's book *Revelation and Reunion*, in which he writes: 'there seems to me to have been a general principle implicit in Apostolic practice, and underlying the evolution of Church order. This was that appointments to the official ministry are the business of those who themselves have received authority to make such appointments.'[7] As Archbishop Ramsey has written recently:

Our Church has two aspects: On the one hand we claim to be a Church possessing Catholic Tradition and continuity from the ancient Church, and our Catholic Tradition and continuity includes the belief in the real Presence of Christ in the Blessed Sacrament; the order of Episcopacy and the Priesthood, including the Power of a priestly absolution. We possess various institutions belonging to Catholic Christendom like monastic orders for men and women. Our Anglican Tradition has another aspect as well. We are a Church which has been through the Reformation, and values many experiences derived from the Reformation, for instance, the Open Bible: great importance is attached

---

[2] *The Second World Conference on Faith and Order* (*1938*), p. 246. Such was the opinion of the Archbishop of Canterbury, Randall Davidson, cf. H. D'Espine, 'The Apostolic Succession as an Ecumenical issue. A Protestant View', *E.R.* iv (1952), pp. 154–155, and of William Temple, cf. F. A. Iremonger, *William Temple, Archbishop of Canterbury, His Life and Letters* (1948), p. 586.

[3] C. C. Richardson, *The Sacrament of Reunion* (1940). See G. K. A. Bell, *Christian Unity: The Anglican Position*. Olaus Petri Lectures at Upsala University, October, 1946 (London, 1948), pp. 23–31. Appendix: Extracts from Anglican Writers on Episcopacy.

[4] *The Ministry of the Christian Church*, pp. 65–109.

[5] *The Gospel and the Catholic Church*, pp. 81–6, 216.

[6] Cf. also Daniel Jenkins, in *The Nature of Catholicity* (1942), p. 54. Jenkins endorses Ramsey's opinion, although he thinks that such a claim comes with a shock of surprise to many modern Protestants.

[7] G. W. Broomfield, *Revelation and Reunion* (1942), p. 185.

to the authority of the Holy Scriptures, and to personal conviction and conversion through the work of the Holy Spirit.[8]

What we have said about the Orthodox attitude towards Rome applies to some extent also to the Orthodox attitude towards Anglicanism. The Orthodox belief that their Church is the one Holy, Catholic, and Apostolic Church on earth, gives the impression that Orthodox theology is even more exclusive than Roman Catholic. But the Orthodox Church has shown some recognition of the sacraments of other churches. For instance, her practice of receiving converts from Rome or Anglicanism by Chrismation without Re-baptism (though this has *not* always been the case in the past) 'is a clear indication that the sacramental limits of the Church do not coincide with its ceremonial boundaries'.[9]

Orthodox theologians are divided as regards the character of the Anglican Church. Some see it from the exaggerated point of view which divides it into three parties, commonly known as High Church, Low Church, Broad Church. It is this idea that leads many, not only Orthodox, but Roman Catholics also, to think that the Church of England is a sort of confederation of three separated Churches, each with its own liturgy, its own doctrinal formularies and its own separate hierarchy. This is completely mistaken. Dr. Ramsey says that

though there is High Church and Low Church, it is all the time One Church with a single life, and all the members of the Church of England share together in the Creeds, Holy Scriptures, the Sacraments, the rule of the Bishops and the Liturgy; so do not think of High Church and Low Church as utterly separate factions but as two aspects of the life of a Church which is all the time one.[10]

Some Orthodox theologians judge the Church of England from the Thirty-Nine Articles alone, which prevents them from having a true appreciation of this Church from an Orthodox point of view.[11] The Articles bear little relation to the present life of the Church, but are polemical principles long ago established. The Articles do not represent

[8] *Catholic Herald*, 17 Sept. 1965; cf. Gore, *The Anglo-Catholic Movement*, p. 7.
[9] N. Zernov, *H.E.M.*, p. 673.   [10] *Catholic Herald*, loc. cit.
[11] Such was the attitude of the Russian Orthodox Church during the Russo-Anglican discussions in Moscow, July 1956; cf. H. M. Waddams, *Anglo-Russian Theological Conference*, pp. 64–65. Cf. also *Conferinţa Română Orthodoxă–Anglicană ţinută la Bucureşti 7–8 junie 1935 si Călătoria I.P.S. Patriarchului D. D. Dr Miron în Anglia 28 junie–7 julie 1936*. Bucharest, 1938.

the whole Faith of this Church. In these matters the Orthodox attitude towards the Anglican Church sometimes tends to be ill-informed.[12] When the Anglican Church and its tradition is more fully understood by the Orthodox, I am sure it will be recognized that Anglicanism represents a genuine spirit of Orthodoxy so developed as to be understood by modern thought. Anglicanism is not a Protestant Church, but a reformed Catholic Church, which maintains its unity with the tradition of the ancient undivided Church.

Professor Comnenos, in his book on Anglican orders, wrote that 'very many of the lay and clerical members of the Anglican Church are inclined to be Orthodox in mind and would gladly enter into union with Orthodoxy, or otherwise fully communicate with it, if the non-recognition of their Priesthood did not stand before them as an insurmountable obstacle.'[13] A leading Orthodox personality, Germanos, Archbishop of Thyateira, speaking at the Gloucester Diocesan Conference on 1 June 1923, said that 'the Orthodox Church has always considered the venerable Anglican Church as a branch, in many particulars, in continuous succession with the Ancient Church'.[14] By a branch, Archbishop Germanos meant not one of the parts of Catholicism, according to the Branch Theory, but a Church especially representing the Catholic Church in England. Similarly Professor Bulgakov writes that 'Anglicanism in its tendency towards the restoration of the Ancient Church, as a reaction to Protestantism, is already becoming more and more Orthodox, and this process is naturally a way to its reunion with historic Orthodoxy.'[15]

6. The Anglican Church as seen by the Roman Church

Following the Dictionnaire de Théologie Catholique (Article 'Anglicanisme'), we observe that the Church of England is regarded by Roman Catholics as 'admitting every doctrine which can be called Christian;

---

[12] e.g. Trembelas, The History of the Reformation in the Anglican Church, p. 124.

[13] P. Comnenos, 'Anglican Ordinations', C.E. ii (1921), p. 113.

[14] C.E. v (1924), p. 128.

[15] S. Bulgakov, 'One, Holy, Catholic and Apostolic', C.E. xii (1931), pp. 95–6. I do not ignore the Letter of Khomyakov to W. Palmer, where the Russian Orthodox thinker defines Anglicanism: 'It is a narrow ledge of dubious terra firma, beaten by the waves of Romanism and Protestantism, and crumbling on both sides into the mighty waters': quoted in W. J. Birkbeck, Russia and the English Church, pp. 102–3. But this extreme idea on Anglicanism has never found acceptance amongst Orthodox theologians.

it rejects, however, on the one side Socinianism and on the other what it calls the corruption of Rome, and yet we can find within it both Socinians and those who hold all Roman doctrine.'

Newman, nearly twenty years after he had left the Church of England, writes in his *Apologia pro Vita Sua:*[1]

It [the Church of England] may be a great creation, though it be not divine, and this is how I judge it . . . And, as to its possession of an episcopal succession from the time of the Apostles, well, *it may have it,* [our italics] and, if the Holy See ever so decide, I will believe it, as being the decision of a higher judgement than my own. . . . the Church of England has been the instrument of Providence in conferring great benefits on me; had I been born in Dissent, perhaps I should never have been baptized; had I been born an English Presbyterian, perhaps I should never have known our Lord's divinity; had I not come to Oxford, perhaps I should never have heard of the visible Church, or of Tradition, or other Catholic doctrines. As I have received so much good from the Anglican Establishment itself, can I have the heart, or rather the want of charity, considering that it does for so many others, what it has done for me, to wish to see it overthrown? I have no such wish while it is what it is, and while we are so small a body. Not for its own sake, but for the sake of the many congregations to which it ministers, I will do nothing against it.[2]

In one of his *Lectures on Anglican Difficulties* (delivered in 1850 and referred to in the passage of the *Apologia* just cited),[3] Newman says to the 'Children of the Movement of 1833' that 'whatever was the case with others, their duty at least was to become Catholics, since Catholicism was the real scope and issue of that Movement'.

The repudiation of the validity of Anglican orders by the Pope (1896) declared that the Church of England is in a position which prevents it, according to Roman Catholicism, from administering the Sacraments validly. Nevertheless, there are Roman Catholics who see the Anglican Church as the legitimate heir of the Ancient English Church. This is the opinion of a French Roman Catholic who says that the Anglican Church is the descendant of the *Ecclesia Anglicana* of

[1] *Apologia* (1st ed., 1864, repr. Fontana Books, Collins, London 1959), Appendix 3. (Fontana ed. pp. 325–31). In the 2nd ed., 1865, the substance of this Appendix appears as Note E (ed. M. J. Svaglic, Oxford, 1967, pp. 296–8).

[2] Fontana ed., pp. 327–8; ed. Svaglic, pp. 296–7.

[3] Fontana ed., p. 330; omitted from the 1865 and later eds. but see footnote in Svaglic's ed. p. 205.

the Middle Ages, and the latter, moulded from the start by the thought of St. Augustine and Plato, differed considerably from the Church on the Continent. Not only was it never on familiar terms with Thomism and Aristotelianism; it should also be remembered that at the end of the thirteenth century its Bishops even went so far as to condemn St. Thomas Aquinas. In the sixteenth century, prevented by the Schism from taking part in the Council of Trent, it had to reform itself through its own efforts. This is 'Catholic' but isolationist tradition.[4]

As the Roman Church shows a kind of charity towards all Christians, so it does the same towards Anglicanism. Cardinal Bea, referring to the visit of Dr. Fisher to the Pope, call him 'Anglican Archbishop of Canterbury and Primate of all England'. According to Cardinal Bea, Anglicans are brothers separated from the Catholic faith; because of their separation they do not constitute the Church of England and they do not adhere to the Catholic faith.[5] This view can be found in the Encyclical letter of Pope Pius XII (*Mediator Dei*). According to this Encyclical those who are baptized validly 'are in the mystical body and become by common life members of Christ the Priest'. Admittedly Cardinal Bea says that the Encyclical letter *Ad Petri Cathedram* describes those who are baptized as children of the Holy Mother Church, which feels for them great love, 'a love full of deep sorrow and grief, and of a heartfelt affliction, because of the separation which prevents them enjoying so many privileges and rights, and makes them lose so many graces'.[6] It is the duty of the mother, says Cardinal Bea, not to cease to be the child's mother nor he the fruit of her womb, even if the child does not know and hence does not recognize his mother. Since this Mother is identified with the Roman Church which the Romans believe is the only true Church, it is the children's duty to follow it.

It is noticeable that Cardinal Bea nowhere uses the term '*Church* of England', but always calls it 'Anglicanism' or 'the Anglican Communion'. On the contrary Pope Paul in his sermon on Holy Thursday, 1964, said 'Greetings and Peace to the whole Anglican Church'.[7]

Similarly, the Roman Catholic Cardinal Jaeger[8] expresses very sympathetic opinions about the Anglican Church. Although in his

---

[4] 'Spiritual Approaches to Anglicanism', in M. Villain, *Unity*, p. 135.
[5] *The Unity of Christians*, p. 66.
[6] op. cit., p. 67.
[7] Leeming, *The Vatican Council and Christian Unity*, p. 279.
[8] Jaeger, *The Ecumenical Council*, p. 152.

book there are some mistakes concerning the causes which gave rise to the Reformation in England and the various views and tendencies within the Church of England, his attitude towards Anglicanism is of great importance. He, for instance, emphasizes that 'it would be incorrect to describe the Anglicans simply as Protestants. The Anglican Church is, in fact, along with the Lutheran and Calvinist, a special type of reformed Christianty'; and also that

the Anglican Reformation retained, more than the Lutheran and Calvinist, positive elements of the Tradition of the Old Church, and so Anglicanism is closer to the Roman Catholic position. Thus the Anglicans held more firmly than all the other reformed confessions to the Councils of the first millennium and the doctrine of the Fathers. They preserved a pronounced sense of the visible unity of the Church and upheld a structure of the Church based on the episcopate. In general, their theology discountenanced an unrestricted application of the principle of the free interpretation of Scripture, since it paid regard to the Tradition of the early Church. In addition, Anglicanism retained more of the Liturgical riches of the Old Church and many forms of its public worship.

Moreover there are other Roman Catholics who believe that present-day Anglo-Catholic theology has restored the concept of tradition as a norm of faith. In this sense it is certainly 'Catholic'. It is not based solely on Scripture, but mainly on the witness of the past centuries, particularly the patristic age, and that of the Catholic Liturgies, both Latin and Byzantine.[9]

The Second Vatican Council does not deal at length with the Anglican Church, which it includes among the many Communions in the West separated at the Reformation from the Roman See; in chapter III of the Decree on Ecumenism it is stated that 'The Anglican Communion has a special place among those which continue to retain, in part, Catholic traditions and structure'.[10] In the past Rome has never

---

[9] Tavard, *Two Centuries of Ecumenism*, p. 213.

[10] *Decree on Ecumenism* (Catholic Truth Society), p. 21. On this point Canon B. Pawley observes that 'although Cardinal Bea had said that he hoped that there would be somewhere in the drafts "explanations of the dogmas which have been obstacles between Romans and Anglicans", the only explanation offered was one showing that the infallibility of the Pope (even then only under carefully defined circumstances) concerned his office, and not his person.' B. Pawley, 'The First two Sessions of the Second Vatican Council through Anglican Eyes', *E.E.*, p. 106.

accepted the Catholicity of the Church of England and it regarded it as not only schismatic but also heretical.[11] Now the Roman Catholic Church recognizes that, in the Ecumenical Movement, Anglicanism is to be distinguished from Protestantism. In the decree *De Ecumenismo*, Anglicanism is placed where it is owing to a desire to avoid the reaction of other communions, which might be offended; originally in the draft decree the phrase was 'pre-eminent among those communities in which Catholic traditions and structures partly continue'.[12]

It will be seen from the above that the Roman Catholic view of Anglicanism has considerably changed in emphasis and tone, if not in its formal basis. It remains true on Roman Catholic principles that Anglicans, being outside the Papal Communion, would in any case be in schism, and that, unlike the Orthodox, they have not even a valid ministry and sacraments (apart from Baptism) having lost the Apostolic succession at the Reformation. But instead of the negative aspects being stressed, together with the aberrations (as they appear from a traditional Roman viewpoint) of some Anglican theology and practice, Roman Catholics increasingly pay attention to, and emphasize, those things in Anglicanism, including Baptism, and the elements of Catholic tradition, which it shares with the Catholic Church as a whole. Moreover, Anglican practice in such matters as the vernacular liturgy, non-fasting communion, and even a married clergy, can no longer be used by Roman Catholics as a reproach and cited as symptoms of departure from Catholic norms, since the Roman Church itself has moved, or is tending to move, in the same direction. Even the matters which once seemed finally decided, like the invalidity of Anglican Orders, are now being re-opened to discussion in Roman Catholic circles, albeit unofficially and privately. To this important subject we turn in the next chapter.

[11] W. Visser 't Hooft, *Anglo-Catholicism and Orthodoxy*, p. 134.
[12] Jaeger, *A Stand on Ecumenism*, pp. 128–9.

Chapter V

ANGLICAN ORDERS

1. The Roman Catholic view

On the accession of Queen Elizabeth I the See of Canterbury was vacant through the death of Cardinal Pole: Matthew Parker became Archbishop of Canterbury and through him the whole episcopal succession of the Church of England derived, although later, through Laud, the English episcopate received also consecrations in the Irish and Italian successions. Nevertheless, if Parker had never been consecrated, this would be a severe blow to the argument that in the Church of England the episcopal succession of the ancient and medieval Church was preserved. Roman Catholics for a long time believed that Parker's so-called consecration was a myth, that is, that he never had even the form of consecration. (He was said, in a story first put out in 1604, to have been appointed at a meeting of bishops at the Nag's Head tavern in London.)[1] The opinion that Parker was never consecrated was however refuted by the findings of the Roman Catholic historians, Le Courayer, Lingard,[2] E. Estcourt[3] and P. Gasparri.[4] The *Dictionnaire*

[1] This story was accepted by A. Champney, *De Vocatione ministrorum* (Douai, 1614), p. 497; to this Pierre François Le Courayer replied with *A defence of the Validity of the English Ordinations* (pp. 42 ff). It is very important to note that Courayer, in defending Anglican Ordinations, introduced an opinion similar to that of some Orthodox theologians. 'He does not question that they are without the Pale of the Catholic Church; and it is only with reference to the case either of Anglican Clergymen individually, or of the Anglican Church as a body, returning to the bosom of the Church of Rome, that the question assumes a more practical aspect'. See the Editor's Introduction to the new edition (Oxford 1884), p. lxiv.

[2] *Histoire d'Angleterre* (Paris, 1846), vol. ii, pp. 444 and 636.

[3] *The Question of Anglican Ordinations Discussed* (1873), p. 154: 'It is however very unfortunate that the Nag's-Head story was ever seriously put forward; for it is so absurd on the face of it that it has led to the suspicion of Catholic theologians not being sincere in the objections they make to Anglican Orders.'

[4] *Tractatus canonicus de sacr. ord.*, vol. ii (1893), p. 279, and 'De la valeur des ordinations anglicanes' in the *Revue Anglo-romaine*, vol. i, p. 481.

de Theologie Catholique[5] regards the idea that Parker was not consecrated as a slander. The consecration of Parker unquestionably took place in the Chapel of Lambeth Palace on Sunday 17 December 1559, in the morning between 5 and 6 a.m.[6] Today even Roman Catholics accept that the Bishops who consecrated him were canonically consecrated.[7]

There are two points connected with Canon Law which according to Roman Catholics make Anglican Ordinations non-canonical. These are, first, that Parker had been consecrated by bishops who were expelled from their sees; and secondly, that Parker had been ordained priest by the Edwardian Rite, which itself was illegal, having been abolished by Mary. There are two further related points: first, whether the Edwardian Rite can be regarded in 'form' and 'matter', as a Sacramental ordination; and second, whether the first bishops who used the Edwardian Rite had the real intention of doing what the Church had always done in Ordination.

The Bull *Apostolicae curae* of Pope Leo XIII, 2 September 1896, is based on these two latter points.

A Greek liturgiologist, Professor Trembelas, criticizes the Roman Catholic objections to the validity of Anglican orders.[8] He makes the following points:

1. As regards the assertion of the Bull, that the 'Form' of the sacramental rite should expressly indicate that it is Priesthood which is given, and should furthermore define this Priesthood exactly, Professor Trembelas says that such an attitude to the Form of the Sacrament, which the Bull demands, can be found nowhere,

---

[5] Vol. xi, 1156.

[6] The consecration of Parker is evidenced by the Journal of his life, which was found after his death among his papers. Amongst these there are these remarkable words: '17. Decembr. Ann. 1559. CONSECRATUS sum in Archiepiscopum Cantuarien. Heu! Heu! Domine deus, in quae tempora servasti me?' *Life of Parker* by Strype, Appendix, p. 15, in P. F. Le Courayer, op. cit., p. 42.

[7] A. Boudinhon, *De la Validité des ordinations anglicanes* (Paris, 1895), cited in *Dict. Catholique*, col. 1159; F. Dalbus, *Les Ordinations anglicanes* (Paris, 1894), pp. 15–16; L. Duchesne, 'Les ordinations anglicanes par Dalbus' in the *Bulletin critique*, 15 July 1894.

[8] P. Trembelas, 'The Validity of Anglican Orders and the objections of the Roman Catholic Church', in *Theologia*, xxvi (1955), pp. 337–74. See also Arthur Lowndes, *Vindication of Anglican Orders* (New York, vols. 1–2, 1897–1900), and Courayer, op. cit. These works broadly refuted the Latins' objections to the validity of Anglican Orders. See also *Leo XIII and Anglican Orders* by Viscount Halifax (London, 1912).

neither in the old rites, nor even in the Form of the Sacrament of Baptism, which Our Lord established.[9]

2. As regards the 'matter', Professor Trembelas shows that in the Latin Church itself there were repeated changes in the 'matter' of Ordination, so that we cannot be sure what, in fact, constitutes the 'matter' of this Sacrament, even in Latin Ordinations.[10]

The objection that the 'matter' (the laying-on of hands) is separated from the 'form' (Preface, Prayers)—in other words that the time between is too long—is completely groundless.[11] The words which accompany the laying-on of hands, according to Anglican ordinance, are sufficient, Professor Trembelas holds, to make the ordination valid.[12]

Professor Trembelas accepts the explanations given by Francis Mason in his work *Consecration of the Bishops in the Church of England* (1613), written under the supervision of the Archbishop of Canterbury, George Abbot, and in the answer (1897) to the Bull of Leo XIII of the two Archbishops of Canterbury and York.[13] He therefore finds the sacrificial character of Anglican Ordinations to be satisfactory.

The terminology used in Consecration of Bishops in the Church of England gives precision to the whole ceremony. It is entitled 'The Form of Ordaining or Consecrating of an Archbishop or Bishop' and afterwards it is specifically stated that the candidate is offered to be 'ordained and consecrated to be Bishop'. This terminology is in agreement with the Roman Catholic rite.[14]

We now reach another point in the Bull of Leo, that the bishops who ordained Parker did not have the necessary intention, viz. to ordain him in the way that the Church had always performed ordination. The purpose of the English reformers was to maintain in the Church of England the practice of the Primitive Church; this explains that their intention was really to do what the Church teaches[15] and for this reason in the Anglican rite of ordination there are no heretical points.

The Anglican position on this matter is clearly stated by E. J. Bicknell—that in the Church of England it is made abundantly clear

---

[9] P. Trembelas, op. cit., p. 354; cf. Courayer, op. cit., pp. 93–105.
[10] Trembelas, p. 356.
[11] ibid., pp. 355–58.
[12] ibid., p. 358.
[13] ibid., p. 364.
[14] ibid., p. 365.
[15] Preface to Prayer Book of 1549.

that the intention of the rite is to confer the orders which our Lord instituted and the Apostles conferred. Its purpose is shown by the use of the language of the New Testament throughout the ordinal. It means its orders to be those of the New Testament. 'The Roman arguments', he says, 'rest upon two great assumptions. First that Rome is at all times infallible, and therefore its teaching at any time about the meaning of priesthood must be accepted without question. Secondly, that Rome has a divine right to implicit and universal obedience, and therefore any change in the form of service without its consent shows a contumacious spirit. Neither of these assumptions can be granted; and without them the whole argument collapses.'[16]

All this bears witness to the fact that Catholic elements predominated in the Church of England and the continuity of priesthood was maintained even in the use of the new Anglican rite of ordination.[17] Then what are the real causes of the rejection of the validity of the Anglican orders by Pope Leo XIII? This rejection was a matter of expediency. As Archbishop Chrysostomos Papadopoulos writes, the question of the validity of Anglican orders was brought up by the movement of Lord Halifax to promote a scheme of re-union of the Church of England with Rome.[18] Lord Halifax co-operated with the French Lazarist Abbé E. F. Portal, who under the pseudonym F. Dalbus published the book *Les ordinations anglicanes* (Paris, 1894), in favour of the validity of the Anglican orders, which was regarded by Rome as the first step towards the union of the two Churches. Portal visited London and Rome and had the impression that recognition would be given. Lord Halifax, who visited the Pope, after Portal, had the same hopes. In addition to this, the commission which was set up by the Vatican in order to study this question included people who had already expressed approval of the validity of Anglican orders. They

---

[16] Bicknell, *Theological Introduction to the Thirty-nine Articles*, p. 341.

[17] Trembelas, op. cit. p. 372.

[18] Chrysostomos Papadopoulos, Archbishop of Athens, *The question of the validity of the Anglican Ordinations* transl. by J. A. L. Douglas (London, Faith Press, 1931), pp. 8–9. Cardinal Vaughan 'regarded the movement at first with impatience, and later with unconcealed dislike': cf. J. G. Snead-Cox, *Life of Cardinal Vaughan*, vol. ii, p. 142, and Abbot Gasquet, *Leaves from My Diary*, p. 59, in *Leo XIII and Anglican Orders*, pp. 383–4. Lord Halifax says on Cardinal Vaughan's attitude 'I say it with regret: the whole of Cardinal Vaughan's conduct, as I think the correspondence makes sufficiently clear, was unworthy of him', op. cit. p. 386.

were Duchesne and Gasparri.[19] Apparently the Pope was favourably inclined towards a solution of this question, but the Roman Archbishop of Westminster, Herbert Vaughan, indicated to the Pope that such a solution would be harmful to the restored Roman Catholic hierarchy in England. Also it was thought that the condemnation of Anglican Orders would lead to a greater number of converts from Anglicanism to Roman Catholicism. Therefore, at the last moment, the Pope changed his mind.[20]

This action of the Roman Church, Professor Trembelas adds, resulted in inconsistency; for whilst it rejects the validity of Anglican orders, it recognizes the validity of the Holy Eucharist celebrated by clergy who are thought by the Latins to be without priesthood. The truth is that the Roman Church does not recognize the validity of the Holy Eucharist celebrated by clergy who are not validly ordained; but, as Bulgakoff rightly observed,[21] the potential validity of the sacraments and consequently the validity of the Holy Eucharist, depends on the validity of ordination. To agree that Anglican orders are without validity implies agreement that none of the sacraments (except perhaps Baptism) performed by such celebrants is valid. Rejecting the validity of Anglican orders and accepting that of the other sacraments in the Church of England leaves only one solution; that for the celebration of any of the sacraments, even of the Eucharist, it is not necessary to have a celebrant in Holy Orders. It is true that the Roman Catholic Church teaches that heretic or unbeliever, Jew or Gentile, can validly perform the sacrament of Baptism. If this is

[19] The members of the Commission were Dom Aidan Gasquet, Canon Moyes, Father David Fleming, O.F.M., who opposed validity, and Bishop Gasparri, Abbé Duchesne and Father de Augustinis, S.J., who favoured validity. Two other members were added later, Father Scannell and Father Calasanzio de Lleveneras, O.F.M.C.: Tavard, *Two Centuries of Ecumenism*, p. 61, n. 5. Cf. G. K. A. Bell, *Christian Unity: The Anglican Position* (London, 1948), pp. 67–71 and Viscount Halifax, *Leo XIII and Anglican Orders*, pp. 217–71. Gasparri had earlier published another treatise, *De sacra Ordinatione*, where he was against the validity of the Anglican orders.

[20] See J. J. Hughes, 'The Papal Condemnation of Anglican Orders', in *Journal of Ecumenical Studies*, vol. iv, no. 2 (Temple University, Philadelphia, 1967). See also J. J. Hughes, *Absolutely Null and Utterly Void* (London, 1968), and further, *Ampleforth Journal*, vol. lxxiii (1968), parts i, ii, iii. (J. J. Hughes, a former Episcopalian, is now a Roman Catholic priest.)

[21] See translation by W. J. Birkbeck in the Church Historical Society series (1899) under the title 'The question of Anglican Orders'.

true of Baptism, it must be true of the Eucharist also, says Trembelas. He then asks why there is so great a discussion on the validity of the Anglican orders, as long as a simple layman who may be a heretic can validly celebrate the sacraments.[22] Here lies a point of misunderstanding regarding the validity of the Sacraments performed by the Anglicans. The famous Bull *Apostolicae Curae* (1896) not only declared Anglican Orders to be invalid but, by implication, other Anglican sacraments also. That is, both sides in the controversy agreed in the traditional Catholic view that valid sacraments depend on a valid ministry. Only one who is validly consecrated a bishop, they held, can consecrate other bishops, or ordain priests or deacons; only a bishop (or, in Roman usage, a priest commissioned by him) can administer Confirmation; only validly ordained priests can celebrate the Eucharist or give sacramental Absolution. In this context Baptism, Marriage, and Holy Unction were hardly in question; but, if the Church of England had no valid Orders, the laity would have been deprived of the sacraments of Confirmation, Holy Communion, and Absolution, which Anglicans felt to be vital for the life of the Church.

On this basis, an *impasse* was reached between the Roman and the Anglican points of view which is still unresolved. Perhaps, however, the way to its solution will be found through a thorough-going re-examination of the whole question of the Ministry and Sacraments in the life of the Church. Despite movements of opinion in several quarters, nothing like general agreement on such a re-examination has yet begun to emerge.

After Dr. Ramsey's visit to Rome in 1966, however, Cardinal Heenan, Archbishop of Westminster, revealed that he had indicated to the Holy See his willingness to have the whole question of the validity of Anglican Orders re-examined by a commission of historians, not necessarily confined to Roman Catholics. But, he added, there was a difficulty that if the commission concluded that Anglican Orders were not valid from the Roman Catholic point of view, the wound might be opened afresh and might prove a new cause of strife. He said that there is no reason why they should not want to recognize the validity of Anglican Orders. 'If the Commission found from the evidence that the Anglican clergyman is offering a true Mass, in our

[22] Trembelas, p. 374. See also *Church of England Newspaper*, 25 Mar. 1966, p. 16. The recognition of the validity of Anglican orders was advocated at the same time by many Roman Catholic authors: cf. *Revue Catholique des Églises*, Nos. 1, 2, 4, pp. 47, 114, 244.

sense, we should not object. If the investigation could be carried out without raising false hopes and without the danger that it might be a fresh cause of strife, we would be willing for that Commission to be set up.'

Recently there have been further signs that the question of Anglican Orders may be reconsidered by the Roman Catholic Church. Bishop Helmsing of Kansas City-St. Joseph, the Roman Catholic co-chairman of the Anglican/Roman Catholic Joint Preparatory Commission[23] has said:

The possibility of the Catholic Church taking another look at the validity of Anglican Orders is a question which must be faced in the perspective of the belief of both Churches at the present time, in contrast to the historical and juridical perspectives in which it had been faced in the past. There is a change in the understanding of the Eucharist, and of the role of the minister of the Eucharist.

He added:

There is hope that it may be possible to re-open this question in a perspective somewhat different than that obtaining in the past.[24]

In this connection, it is interesting to note a significant pronouncement concerning Anglican orders made by the well known Dutch theologian H. W. Van der Pol of Nijmegen University, who described as 'obsolete' the usual Catholic arguments against the validity of the Anglican orders. Speaking at an eight-day conference for Catholic and Anglican Students organized by the Unitas movement at Culemborg, Holland, he said that, many Canon lawyers in Holland, Belgium and Germany denied today that the *Apostolicae Curae* was 'an infallible utterance'. The Church of England had made a great contribution to Christian unity. In their Ecumenical efforts Anglicans always mentioned the problems of episcopacy and the Sacraments.[25]

2. *The Orthodox view*

The question of Orthodox recognition of Anglican Orders was first raised in the nineteenth century. But it was not until the twentieth

[23] The names of the twenty-five members of this Joint Commision—twelve Roman Catholics and thirteen Anglicans—were published in the *Tablet*, 15 July, 1967, p. 783. See also pp. 238–41, below.

[24] *Church Times*, 8 Sept. 1967, p. 24; and *Tablet*, 9 Sept. 1967, p. 949.

[25] *Catholic Herald*, 2 Sept. 1966.

century, and so after the Papal Bull *Apostolicae Curae* of 1896, that individual Orthodox Churches made official pronouncements on the question. The first to do this was the Oecumenical Patriarchate which in 1922 decided to accept their validity.[1] In 1923 the Patriarchate of Jerusalem[2] and the Church of Cyprus[3] followed the example of Constantinople. In 1930 the Patriarchate of Alexandria[4] and in 1936, the Church of Rumania[5] followed suit. The Church of Greece decided in 1939 that this question should be considered by the whole Orthodox Church.[6]

A negative decision was taken by the Russian Church and others taking part in the Conference at Moscow in the year 1948.[7] This decision was based primarily on a consideration of the Thirty-Nine Articles, but these, as we have shown in the Note to Chapter II (pp. 30–33, above), are not a complete exposition of Anglican doctrine.

The Moscow conference concluded that the question of Anglican Orders must be examined in relation to the further question of agreement in matters of faith. It therefore asked that the Church of England should declare authoritatively what its faith is. It was not content with the repeated declarations by Anglicans that they believe the Catholic faith as it was maintained by the Early Church, that they accept Scripture, Tradition, and the Sacraments, and that they appeal to the Fathers.

However, there are some facts which must be taken into consideration, to put this decision into perspective. The Moscow Conference, which of course was an Orthodox assembly, had not been prepared canonically. The delegates were invited to Moscow to take part in the celebrations of the fifth centenary of the independence of the Russian Church, and although there was good Orthodox representation, it had

---

[1] *Ekklesiastiki Aletheia*, 42 (1922), 327, 343; *C.E.* xii (1931) pp. 13–14; G. K. A. Bell, *Documents on Christian Unity: First Series*, pp. 93–6.

[2] *Nea Sion*, 18 (1923), 127–128; *Ekkl. Aletheia*, 43 (1923), 96; see also *C.E.* iv (1923), p. 121; Bell, op. cit., pp. 97–8.

[3] *Apostolos Varnavas*, 5 (1923), 261–262; see also *C.E.* iv (1923), p. 122; Bell, op. cit., pp. 98–9.

[4] *C.E.* xii (1931), pp. 1–3; Bell, op. cit., *Third Series*, p. 38.

[5] *Orthodoxia*, xi (1936), 282–284; *Eccl.* 14 (1936), 188; Bell, op. cit., *Third Series*, p. 49.

[6] *Eccl.* 17 (1939), 315 and *The Validity of the Anglican Orders* (Athens, 1939); Bell, op. cit., *Third Series*, pp. 50–1.

[7] *Actes de la Conference des Chefs et des Representants des Eglises Orthodoxes Autocephales, 8–18 juillet 1948*, vol. ii (Moscow, 1952), pp. 445–7.

no great authority for its decisions. There were representatives, for example, of the Church of Rumania which had already in 1936 recognized Anglican Orders. Likewise, the representatives of the Church of Antioch, who also represented the Church of Alexandria, were not canonically authorized by the Holy Synod of the Patriarchate of Alexandria to take part in the Conference, but only by the Patriarch himself, who had not understood exactly what was intended at that conference. The representatives of the Ecumenical Patriarchate and the Church of Greece, although they were there for the celebrations, did not take part in the conference at all. The representatives of Poland, Albania, and Czechoslovakia were not the legitimate representatives of their respective churches, but bishops who were installed there after the war by the Russian Church. It is clear, without apportioning blame, that the decision of the Moscow Conference was not based on adequate study, nor does it possess canonical authority.

It should be emphasized that the Orthodox approach the question of the validity of Anglican Orders from a standpoint different from that of the Roman Church. This can best be considered by answering the following two questions: How should a priesthood outside the Orthodox Church be regarded? And how should its clergy who join the Orthodox Church be received?

As regards the second question, according to the Patriarchate of Alexandria (see later in this chapter), priests ordained by Anglican Bishops who are converted to Orthodoxy should not be re-ordained. The question is not a theological one, but one of Canon Law, and the principle of 'Economy' is applied. Metropolitan Antony came to the conclusion that 'Anglicans may be admitted by the "third rite" (penance only) especially in view of the sincere and humble aspiration of many of them to be united with our Holy Church'.[8]

Yet not all the Orthodox Churches have agreed with this conclusion. At the time of writing their different decisions have meant in practice different ways of exercising 'Economy' in individual cases. All are agreed, however, that a final decision on the matter can only be taken by the Orthodox Church as a whole through an Oecumenical Synod or pro-Synod. It should also be pointed out that the recognitions so far made by different Orthodox Churches are conditional rather than absolute. They must be seen within the context of the conversion of individual Anglican clergy to Orthodoxy, or of the

---

[8] *C.E.* viii (1927), p. 69.

eventual corporate re-union of the Anglican and Orthodox Churches, *not* as final judgments on the status of Anglican Orders or the approval of mutual intercommunion now.

How should a priesthood outside the Orthodox Church be regarded? To answer this we must first look at the Orthodox view of the Sacraments, their outward form and inner meaning, and the intention of those who celebrate them.

Scripture and Tradition together show their outward form and inner content, and agree with the well-known definition of the Sacraments, as composed of something natural and supernatural, visible and invisible, a sign and a grace, or, in other words, the union of Divine Grace with the ceremony performed by the priest.[9] The second factor, the intention, in Orthodox eyes means the intention of the Church—not of the celebrant priest—as the necessary factor in the due administration of the Sacrament. On this point it is clear that the Church of England in both its ancient and revised ordinals considers that it is continuing the three-fold ministry of the Apostolic Church, as can be seen from the Preface to the Ordinal in the Book of Common Prayer. Similarly, the words at the laying on of hands 'Receive the Holy Ghost for the office and work of a Priest' and 'of a Bishop', the examination which each undergoes before God and in the presence of the congregation, the question by which the call to the Ministry is tested, and the fact that the work of each particular order in the Church is extolled and commended, all show the intention of the English Church in its Ordinal to remain faithful to the New Testament and the primitive Church. But the Orthodox Church teaches that every sacrament performed outside the Orthodox Church is invalid unless a decision otherwise has been made by 'Economy', taking many other factors into consideration. Therefore Anglican orders cannot be accepted as valid by the Orthodox Church simply because the apostolic succession has been upheld. Bulgakov[10] maintained that so far as the outward historical and canonical criteria go, the apostolic succession has not been broken in the Anglican Church and that Anglican orders are capable of being pronounced valid. But the question should not be decided simply by the outward criteria. Likewise Sokolov held that by itself the outward maintenance of the apostolic succession was insufficient to satisfy the Orthodox criteria for the validity of Anglican

[9] Androutsos, *The Validity of the Anglican Ordinations*, p. 28.
[10] A.J. Bulgakov, *Concerning the Canonicity and Authenticity of the Anglican Hierarchy from the Orthodox Standpoint.* (transl. W. J. Birkbeck, S.P.C.K., 1899)

Orders.[11] Androutsos enunciated four points on which the whole Anglican episcopate must collectively give satisfactory answers before the Orthodox could deem the Anglican Orders to be acceptable by Economy: Does the Anglican Church accept the seven Sacraments? What is its teaching in regard to confession and absolution? What is its faith in regard to the Real Presence and the Eucharistic Sacrifice? Does it regard the dogmatic decisions of the seven Ecumenical Councils as incontrovertible?

Archbishop Chrysostomos Papadopoulos gave a favourable answer to these questions.[12] 'In general then the Ministers of the Church according to the Anglican Ordinal, are presented as the immediate successors of the Apostles, Pastors and Teachers whom God Himself consecrated', and who are called to this Ministry and 'Almighty God Himself accepts and takes them into the Ministry of His Church' and 'the Holy Spirit calls them to this work'. In all that the Church of England does in ordination, she shows that she accepts priesthood as a Ministry established by God. She does not specifically name priesthood as a sacrament in the ordination rite, but in it are found all the characteristics of a sacrament. Thus the question could be solved not theologically but canonically and in this way the Orthodox Church could recognize the validity of her orders.

Let us now go back to the year 1922, when after long study,[13] the Ecumenical Patriarch and his Synod recognized Anglican Orders.

---

[11] V. A. Sokolov, *An Enquiry into the Hierarchy of the Anglican Church.* A translation of the most relevant passages appears in Riley, *Birkbeck and the Eastern Church* (S.P.C.K., 1917) pp. 280–291. W. J. Birkbeck, a British journalist, was sent in the year 1888 by the Archbishop of Canterbury to the celebrations of the commemoration of St. Vladimir in Russia. The impression made by Orthodoxy on Birkbeck was so deep that he decided to give his life to the cause of Anglo-Orthodox friendship. He became a close friend of the procurator of the Russian Synod, Pobiedonostseff, as well as of Tsar Nicholas himself, and remained active for many years as a constant agent of friendship between the two Churches.

[12] *The Validity of Anglican Ordinations* (1931), p. 14.

[13] Encyclical on Anglican Ordinations from the Ecumenical Patriarch to the Presidents of the Orthodox Churches, *C.E.* iii (1922), pp. 113–16. See also Letter of the Ecumenical Patriarch to the Archbishop of Canterbury, ibid., pp. 111–13. These are also published in Bell, *Documents on Christian Unity, First Series,* pp. 93–6. A negative attitude towards the validity of the Anglican Orders is shown by J. Malinovsky in his 'Dogmatic Theology', *Sergiev Posad,* iv (1909), pp. 344 ff. A full summary of Russian literature on Anglican Ordinations can be found in a recently published treatise of Professor Voronov in *Theological Studies* (pubd. by the Patriarchate of Moscow), iii (1964), pp. 64–114.

The decisions of the Ecumenical Patriarchate took note:

1. That the ordination of Matthew Parker as Archbishop of Canterbury by four bishops is a fact established by history.
2. That, in this ordination and those subsequent to it, there are found in their fullness those orthodox and indispensable visible and sensible elements of valid episcopal ordination—namely, the laying on of hands, and the *Epiclesis* of the All-Holy Spirit, and also the purpose to transmit the Charisma of the Episcopal Ministry.
3. That the orthodox theologians who have scientifically examined the question have almost unanimously come to the same conclusions, and have declared themselves as accepting the validity of Anglican ordinations.
4. That the practice in the Church affords no indication that the Orthodox Church has ever officially treated the validity of Anglican Orders as in doubt in such a way as would point to the re-ordination of the Anglican Clergy being regarded as required in the case of the Union of the two Churches.
5. That expressing this general mind of the Orthodox Church the Most Holy Patriarchs at different periods, and other Hierarchs of the East, when writing to the Archbishops of the Anglican Church have been used to address them as 'Most Reverend Brother in Christ', thus giving them a brotherly salutation.

Our Holy Synod, therefore, came to a decision accepting the validity of the Anglican priesthood, and has determined that its conclusion should be announced to the other Holy Orthodox Churches in order that opportunity might be given them also to express their opinion, so that through the decisions of the parts the mind of the whole Orthodox world on this question might be known.[14]

When the 1930 Lambeth Conference had clarified the Anglican attitude to the Apostolic Succession and the Sacraments of Holy Communion and Ordination, the Church of Alexandria expressed its decision recognizing Anglican Orders by a letter sent to the Archbishop of Canterbury, Cosmo Lang, as follows:

Inasmuch as the Lambeth Conference approved the declarations of the Anglican bishops as a genuine account of the teaching and practice of the Church of England and the Churches in communion with it, the Holy Synod welcomes them as a notable step towards the union of the two churches. And since in these declarations, which were endorsed by the Lambeth Conference, complete and satisfying assurance is found

[14] *C.E.* xii (1931), p. 13; cf. also *E.C.Q.* i (1936), pp. 55, 56.

as to the Apostolic succession,[15] as to a real reception of the Lord's Body and Blood, as to the Eucharist being *Thysia Hilasterios* (propitiatory sacrifice), and as to Ordination being a *Mysterion*, the Church of Alexandria withdraws its precautionary negative to the acceptance of the validity of Anglican ordinations and, adhering to the decision of the Ecumenical Patriarchate of July 28th 1922, pronounces that if priests, ordained by Anglican bishops, accede to Orthodoxy, they should not be re-ordained, as persons baptised by Anglicans are not re-baptised . . . .[16]

The difficulty for a final solution is not so much the historical question as to whether the Anglican hierarchy rightly claims to stand in the line of Apostolic Succession, but the dogmatic question whether its teaching on Apostolic Succession is fully Orthodox, for if it is not, the teaching would invalidate the act of consecration. For this reason some Orthodox theologians ask that, in order to enable the Orthodox Church to recognize the sacramental character of Anglican Orders, there should be a definite doctrinal statement on priesthood from the Anglican side, which would be official Anglican teaching, and which would give affirmative answers to the questions which the Orthodox ask. Such questions are outlined by J. A. Douglas[17] as follows: 'What do you think of yourselves? Do you account yourselves to be the successors of the Apostles? Do you believe yourselves to have the power, office and function of ruling the Church and safeguarding the Deposit of Faith? Are you Bishops in the sense in which we believe our Bishops to be Bishops? Is your conception of the Priesthood, of the Eucharist and of the Sacraments essentially the same as our conception? Only say so and we are ready to accept your Orders as valid.' From this conclusion we see that the Orthodox view of Anglican Orders depends on how the principle of Economy is applied. And this depends on doctrinal agreement between the churches. The recognition of orders must come before any further acts of reunion.

[15] As E. J. Bicknell has written, 'Our claim in the Church of England to-day is that we possess the historic ministry of the Catholic Church, coming down in historical descent from the Apostles. We lay stress on it for several reasons. (i) It is a visible and concrete link with the Church of the past . . . It is a pledge that there has been no breach of continuity in the Church's life . . . (ii) It is the ministry not of a local Church but of the whole Catholic Church . . . (iii) . . . The succession is the guarantee of valid ministrations . . .' (op. cit. pp. 330–1).

[16] G. K. A. Bell, op. cit. *Third Series*, p. 38.

[17] In his preface to the English translation of C. Papadopoulos, *The Validity of Anglican Ordinations*, p. xxix.

If Anglican Orders were recognized by the whole Orthodox Church this would lead to 'Economic intercommunion', that is to say, an intercommunion in special circumstances—the second phase through which the process towards reunion between the two Churches must go.

The question therefore from an Orthodox point of view is not so much the technical one of the validity of Orders, but the problem whether Orthodoxy and Anglicanism will in the future stand for the same truths of faith and life, and whether the spiritual life of these Churches leads them to a common conception of the faith.[18]

Bibliography for Chapter V

(A) *The Roman Catholic view on Anglican Ordinations*

Decisions were made on the question of the Anglican orders by the Popes Julius III, in his Bull *Breve de Facultatibus* (8 March 1554), Paul IV, in his Bull *Praeclare datissimi* (20 June 1555) and Brief *Regimini Universalis* (30 October 1555) and Leo XIII, in his Bull *Apostolicae Curae* (13 September 1896). For a complete bibliography on this Bull see A. J. C. Allen, 'On the Bull *Apostolicae Curae*' in *Revue Internationale de Théologie* (Berne), 1897, No. 19, p. 22, and the reply of the Anglican Bishops, *Responsio Archiepiscoporum Angliae ad Litteras apostolicas Leonis Papae XIII de Ordinationibus Anglicanis*, London, 1897.

Boundinhon, A. *De la Validité des Ordinations Anglicanes*. Paris, 1895.

Bevenot, Maurice, S. J. *Are They Priests? The Nature of Anglican Orders*. Catholic Truth Society, London, 1959.

Clark, F. *Anglican Orders and Defect of Intention*. London, 1956.

— *Eucharistic Sacrifice and the Reformation*. London, 1960.

Courayer, Pierre Fr. Le. *A Dissertation on the Validity of the Ordinations of the English, and of the Succession of the Bishops of the Anglican Church; with the Proofs Establishing the Facts Advanced in this Work*. First published in Latin, 1723; English Edition, Oxford, 1844.

Dalbus, F. (pseud.) *Les Ordinations Anglicanes*. Arras, 1894.

Denny, E. *Anglican Orders and Jurisdiction*. London, 1893.

Dix, G. *The Question of Anglican Orders*. Revised edition, London, 1956.

Duchesne, L. '*Les Ordinations Anglicanes* par Dalbus' in the *Bulletin Critique*, 15 July 1894. Duchesne's article quotes Dalbus's table.

Estcourt, E. E. *The Question of Anglican Ordinations Discussed* with an Appendix of original documents and Facsimiles. London, 1873.

Gasparri, P. *De la Valeur des Ordinations Anglicanes*. Paris, 1895.

Haddan, A. W. *Apostolic Succession in the Church of England*. London, 1869.

[18] Visser 't Hooft, op. cit. pp. 123, 126, 127.

Hughes, J. J. *Absolutely Null and Utterly Void*. London, 1968.

Lacey, T. A. and E. Denny, *De Hierarchia Anglicana, Dissertatio Apologetica*, London, 1895.

Lowndes, A. *Vindication of Anglican Orders*. New York, 2 vols. 1897–1900.

Marchal, L. 'Ordinations Anglicanes' in *Dict. de Theologie Catholique* (ed. Vacant et Mangénot), Vol. xi, col. 1155.

Messenger, C. E. *The Reformation, the Mass and the Priesthood*. Vols. i–ii. London, 1937.

Papadopoulos, Chrys. *The Question of the Validity of the Anglican Ordinations*. Trans. by J. A. Douglas. London, Faith Press, 1931: First Part: the Latin View.

Quien, M. Le. *Nullité des Ordinations Anglicanes*. Paris, 1725.

Responsio Archiepiscoporum Angliae ad Litteras Apostolicas Leonis Papae XIII de Ordinationibus Anglicanis, London, 1897. It was translated and published in Greek by Longmans and Co., in 1897. Trans. by J. Gennadios, Greek Ambassador in London. (This answer of the Archbishops of England to the Pope is sufficient from an Anglican point of view to indicate the Anglican view on the Validity of its ordinations. For this reason any special treatment here of the question from an Anglican viewpoint is unnecessary.)

Trembelas, P. The Validity of the Anglican Ordinations and the objections against them by the Roman Catholic Church. *Theologia* xxvi (1955), pp. 337–74.

Vaughan, H. Cardinal Archbishop, and Catholic Bishops of the Province of Westminster, *Vindication of the Bull 'Apostolicae Curae'*. London, 1898.

Verdin, G. 'Les ordinations anglicanes au tribunal de l'ancienne Église Catholique', in *Internationale Kirchliche Zeitschrift* (Berne), 11 (1921), No. 4, pp. 209 ff.

(B) *The Orthodox View on Anglican Ordinations*

Alivizatos, H. 'The Validity of the Priesthood of the Anglican Church', *Ecclesia* (Athens) xvii (1939), pp. 237 ff. (In Greek).

Alivazatos, H. S., and R. C. Mortimer, *Dispensation in Theory and Practice with Special Reference to the Anglican Churches*. London, 1944.

Androutsos, Ch. *The Validity of the English Ordinations from an Orthodox Point of View*. Translated by F. W. Groves. London, 1909.

Bratsiotis, P. *Orthodox and Anglicans, 1918–1930*. Athens, 1931 (in Greek)

— 'The Anglican Ordinations from an Orthodox Point of View', *Ecclesia* xvii (1939) pp. 274–290. 2nd edition, 1966. (In Greek)

Bulgakov, A. J. *Concerning the Canonicity and Authenticity of the Anglican Hierarchy from the Orthodox Standpoint.* Translated by W. J. Birkbeck. London, 1899.

Cerensky, V. A. *On the Question of the Authenticity of Anglican Ordinations.* Kazan, 1897. (In Russian)

Comnenos, P. 'The Question of the Validity of the Anglican Ordinations', *C.E.* ii (1921), pp. 107–16.

— 'Constantinople and Anglican Ordinations', *C.E*, iii (1922), pp. 100–117.

Cotsonis, J. *Intercommunion.* Athens, 1957. (In Greek).

— *Concerning the Validity of the Priesthood of the Anglicans.* Athens, 1958. (Engl. trans. of articles in *Greek Orthodox Theological Review*, iii (1957), iv (1958).) See also *TH.* 1957, pp. 354–375, and 532–549.

Damalas, N. *The Relations between the Anglican and Orthodox Churches.* London, 1867. (In Greek).

Dionysios of Bryoula, 'General Review of the Question of Anglican Ordinations' in *Ekklesiastiki Aletheia* (Constantinople), xvii (1922), 31–34. (In Greek)

Dyovouniotis, C. *The Questions of the Unity between the Orthodox and Anglican Churches and of the Anglican Ordinations.* Alexandria, 1932. (In Greek)

— *About the Unity of the Anglican Church with the Orthodox* (Athens, 1932). (In Greek)

Every, E. 'The Eastern Orthodox Churches and Anglican Ordinations'. *E.C.Q.* vii (1948), pp. 543–552.

Hardy, E. *Orthodox Statements on Anglican Orders*, New York, 1946.

Helioupolis, Gennadios of. 'The Validity of the Anglican Ordinations', *Orthodoxia* (Istanbul), 13 (1928). (In Greek)

Gill, J. 'The Orthodox Church of Greece and Anglican Orders'. *E.C.Q.*, iv (1940), pp. 163–168.

Istravridis, V. *Orthodoxy and Anglicanism.* Published by the Anglican and Eastern Churches Association. See Greek *Orthodox Theological Review*, 5 (1959).

— *Orthodoxy and Anglicanism.* Translated by Colin Davey. London, 1966. (See pp. 121–31).

Karmiris, J. 'Papacy and Anglican Ordinations', *Nea Sion* (Jerusalem) 1952. (In Greek).

Malminovsky, J. 'Orthodox Dogmatic Theology', *Sergiev Posad*, iv (1909), p. 344 ff. (In Russian).

Papadopoulos, C. *The Question of the Validity of Anglican Ordinations.* Translated by J. A. Douglas. London, 1931.

Rozdjenstenstvensky, A. *Does the Anglican Church Accept the Three Degrees of the Sacred Ministry?* Koutais, 1901. (In Russian)

— 'On the Question of the Validity of the Anglican Hierarchy' in the Magazine *Viera Slovo* 1903, Vols. 11 and 12. (In Russian)

Sokolov, J. P. 'On the Authenticity of the Anglican Hierarchy', *Christian Reading* (Theological Academy of St. Petersburg), xciii (1902), pp. 153 ff. (In Russian)

Sokolov, V. A. *An Enquiry into the Hierarchy of the Anglican Church.* (A translation of the most relevant passages is in Athelstan Riley, *Birkbeck and the Russian Church*, i (1917), pp. 280–291.)

Trembelas, P. 'A Note on the Validity of the Anglican Ordinations', *Eccl.* xvii (1939), p. 291. (In Greek)

Voronov, L. A. 'Anglican Priesthood in Russian Theological Science', *Theological Studies* (published by the Patriarchate of Moscow), iii (1964), pp. 64–144.

Zernov, N. *Orthodox Encounter.* London, 1961. (See pp. 188–9)

PART TWO

Chapter VI

THE CHURCH

1. Ecclesiology

The Church has the authority to decide the articles of belief to which the faithful must adhere. It is also the life of 'a people made one with the unity of the Father and the Son and the Holy Spirit'.[1] It is 'a society equipped with hierarchical organs, the Mystical Body of Christ, an assembly to command attention, a spiritual growth'.[2]

Both Orthodox and Roman Catholic theologians agree, however, that no full doctrinal definition of the Church has been made by an Oecumenical Council. And even the Council of Trent avoided making such a definition. This is why ecclesiology in both Churches is drawn primarily from Biblical and Patristic sources. But we should note that both in the Fathers and in later writers, the differing political and ecclesiastical circumstances in East and West led to different approaches to, and statements of, the doctrine of the Church. Where there was an absence of controversy, theologians could be content with selected quotations from the Bible and its interpreters, to emphasize this or that truth about the Mystical Body of Christ. But where there was division or schism, they were forced to set one interpretation against another, in order to clarify the difference between orthodoxy and heresy.

Orthodox ecclesiology uses as its primary source Cyril of Jerusalem's *Catechetical Decrees*, in which the Church is described as a spiritual

---

[1] Second Vatican Council, Constitution *On the Church*, 4; cf. Lorenz Cardinal Jaeger, *A Stand on Ecumenism. The Council's Decree* (transl. by Hilda Graef, Geoffrey Chapman, 1965), pp. 179–180. 'In this way the Universal Church is clearly a people made one with the unity of the Father and the Son and the Holy Spirit' (Cyprian, Augustine, and John of Damascus).

[2] Second Vatican Council, Constitution *On the Church*, 8; Jaeger, op. cit., pp. 183–5. The Slavophils said that 'the Church is the great *organism*, not merely an external institution, but the great body—the Mystical Body of Christ, the great stream of the life of Grace which shall embrace everyone and everything'; cf. N. Von Arseniev, 'The Slavophil Doctrine of the Church', *C.E.* ix (1928), p. 132.

society which God called into existence to replace the Jewish Church.[3] Cyril also uses other 'time-honoured commonplaces', as J. N. D. Kelly puts it, to describe the Church and its life, but we must note in his writings 'the absence of any discussion either of its hierarchical structure, so prominent in Cyprian a full century before, or of the relation between the outward, empirical society and the invisible community of the elect—a theme which was later to absorb Augustine'.[4]

But Roman Catholic ecclesiology was developed out of controversy, though it shared with the East the basic doctrine of the Church as the Mystical Body of Christ, the 'fullness of him who filleth all in all'. (Eph. 1.23). It was the Donatist controversy, and the Donatist insistence on a purely spiritual church, which led Augustine to formulate *his* teaching on the subject. It was the conciliar movement, and the controversies about juridical and institutional problems, that were largely responsible for the changed concept of the Church in the Middle Ages. And in the sixteenth century theological controversy on the nature of the Church was obviously conditioned by the extreme spiritualistic position taken by the Reformers. In the twentieth century a truer picture of the Church has been restored by the Encyclical *Mystici Corporis* of Pius XII which lays down that fundamentally the Church consists of all the faithful.[5]

Although Anglicans give different answers to the most fundamental questions about the Church, nevertheless they would all agree that the Church is the Body of Christ. They distinguish, however, between the ideal Church and the actual Church, and because of this they emphasize the constant need to test the tradition of the Church against the Bible. This is in contrast to the Orthodox belief that the Church, because it is infallible, possesses a tradition that is true and authoritative in itself.

For Anglicans the Church is a symbol of divine life, rather than the

---

[3] *Catech.* 18, 22–28.

[4] J. N. D. Kelly, *Early Christian Doctrines*, pp. 401–5.

[5] P. Mikat, 'Collaboration between Clergy and Laity', *Concilium*, ix (1965) pp. 34–5. 'The Visible Society and the Mystical Body of Christ are not two things, but one only, the compound of a human and a divine element', but the Visible Church and the Mystical Body were certainly identical, though not in the same formal respect. 'The Church as a Visible Society is co-extensive only with its historical dimension, while the Mystical Body is co-extensive with the workings of Christ's grace, and this is part of the mystery'; cf. Raniero La Valle, *Coraggio del Concilio* (Brescia, 1964), p. 41; cited in Jaeger, *A Stand on Ecumenism*, p. 183.

divine life itself. It is a society founded and constituted by an invisible Head in whom all its vitality resides. Christ is its life, its hope, the secret of that revival and restoration of which, because of the fallibility of its human element, it stands in permanent need. 'The Church must therefore continually turn in penitence to its Lord, that it may be cleaned from its blemishes.'[6]

For the Roman Catholics, the Church is an institution which was founded immediately and personally by the true and historic Christ during his earthly life, *per ipsum verum atque historicum Christum, cum apud nos degeret, proxime ac directo institutam*. This is the meaning of the words of Pope Pius XII in his Encyclical when speaking of the temporal foundation of the Church: 'The Divine Redeemer began to build the mystical Temple of his Church when He was preaching and giving His Commandments: He completed it when He hung in glory on the cross; He manifested and promulgated it by the visible mission of the Paraclete, the Holy Spirit, upon his disciples.'

There is complete agreement between Orthodox and Romans about the sacramental character of the Church. The mission of the Church is the redemption of the world by the incorporation of men into the Body of Christ. This is achieved through the Holy Spirit, who was sent to the Church once for all at Pentecost.

According to the Orthodox Church the means of the transmission of the divine gifts is a charismatic power, which was transmitted from the Apostles to their successors right down to the present time by the laying on of hands. This transmission is expressed in the permanent Apostolic Succession, which is 'one of the essential marks of the Church'. It is the mysterious bond which secures the unity of the Church. The same teaching is found in the Roman Church with one difference: in the Orthodox Church Apostolic succession is a charismatic principle but in the Roman Church it is Church Law which makes that Church a juridical organism rather than a charismatic one. The Anglican Church equally believes that the fulfilment of the Church's mission in the world is through the Apostolic Ministry. This Ministry is perpetuated through those whom the Apostles appointed

---

[6] John A. F. Gregg, *The Universal Church in God's Design*, Amsterdam Assembly Series, Vol. i, p. 58; cf. L. Hodgson, in *The Nature of the Church: Papers presented to the Theological Commission of the World Conference on Faith and Order*, ed. by R. Newton Flew (London, 1952), p. 145.

to be their colleagues and successors, and it developed into the graded hierarchy of Bishops, Priests and Deacons.[7]

Dr. W. A. Visser 't Hooft writes that, 'Orthodoxy says, *in ecclesia salus*, but refrains from saying *extra ecclesiam nulla salus*.' But this is not quite the case. An extreme view, such as that of the Russian Archbishop, Anthony of Kharkov, would argue that there is 'no spiritual reality, no grace, outside the Orthodox Church ... It makes no difference whether the non-Orthodox have or have not "right beliefs". Purity of doctrine would not incorporate them in the Church. What is of importance is actual membership in the Orthodox Church.'[8] The Orthodox delegation at the Lambeth Conference of 1920, however, spoke more tolerantly when they said: 'We found it necessary to make it clear that our Church has not yet, like the Western Church, made a public pronouncement regarding the possibility of the salvation of Christians outside its bosom, but that, as was to be expected, it does not accept those who do not belong to it as forming part of the Church in the true and proper sense of that word.'[9] Visser 't Hooft is therefore correct when he goes on to say that Orthodoxy 'rejects the relativistic position of those who would consider all Churches as equally valid expressions of the one invisible Church, and the intolerant attitude of those who deny the right of any but their own Church to call themselves Churches of Christ.'[10]

In the decree *On Ecumenism*, the Second Vatican Council spoke of the nature of Christian bodies outside the Roman Church. It went so far as to say, 'For the Spirit of Christ has not refrained from using them as means of salvation which derive their efficacy from the very fullness of grace and truth entrusted to the Catholic

---

[7] Hodgson, op. cit., p. 141. John Jewel, Bishop of Salisbury 1560–71, denied essential elements of the Church. First he 'denied the existence and indeed the need of a visible institutional counterpart of the Church Catholic', and secondly he did not believe that the test of Catholicity lay in the Apostolic Succession. He believed rather in the theory of doctrinal succession. 'The Catholicity of the Church was to be measured only by the degree of its conformity to the teachings of the early Church, the Church of the Apostles and the Fathers'; cf. W. M. Southgate, *John Jewel and the Problem of Doctrinal authority* (Harvard University Press, 1962), pp. 193–201.

[8] Florovsky, *H.E.M.*, p. 214.

[9] G. K. A. Bell, *Documents on Christian Unity, First Series 1920–4* (London, 1924), p. 63.

[10] 't Hooft, op. cit., pp. 106–7.

Church.'[11] But the whole text assumed without argument that when the Creed spoke of 'the Catholic Church' it meant 'the Roman Church' as now understood, and none other. 'On these slender foundations' wrote an Anglican observer at the Vatican Council, commenting on the draft decree, 'it was hoped to rebuild the dilapidated and divided Church of God.' According to Article 14 of the Decree *On Ecumenism*, as it is interpreted by Jaeger, 'all baptized persons would be truly incorporated in the Church permanently and irrevocably but baptism alone is insufficient for a full and perfect sharing in the blessing and privileges of the Church'.[12]

Looking at the text *On the Church* of the Second Vatican Council we see that under the head of papal infallibility, primacy, universal jurisdiction and so on, it repeats

dogmatically and uncritically the conciliar teaching about the papacy, quoting familiar biblical texts . . . What was difficult for the observers was the total lack of reference under this head to the huge corpus of writings which now exist, questioning and claiming to disprove, first of all, the biblical arguments on which the papal claims are alleged to be based, and then the reasons subsequently given for the extension of them. . . . But if there were to be footnotes, and if there were to be 'explanation', it would have been better if they had shown some elementary knowledge at least of the existence of other schools of thought, and of other interpretations of Holy Scripture.[13]

Although from an Orthodox and Anglican point of view the decree *De Ecclesia* is unsatisfactory, a fact acknowledged even by some Roman Catholics, such as Hans Küng, the well-known progressive theologian,[14] the Church was described by the Vatican Council, not only as a Community established in this world, visible and hierarchically ordered, but also as the house of God, 'the Temple and tabernacle of God, his people, his flock, his vine, his field, his city . . .',[15] which 'indicate a turning away from the juridical, triumphalist, clericalist idea of the Church belonging to the counter-Reformation, and a growing trend towards the scriptural idea of the Church'.[16]

[11] *On Ecumenism*, 3 (trans. in *Vatican II on Ecumenism*, ed. Michael Adams, Sceptre Books, Dublin & Chicago 1966).

[12] Bernard Pawley, 'An Anglican Views the Council', in *S.C.U.*, p. 118; cf. also his article in *E.E.* pp. 102–103; cf. Jaeger, op. cit., pp. 184–5.

[13] B. Pawley, 'An Anglican Views the Council', p. 117.

[14] Hans Küng, *The Changing Church*, p. 27.

[15] *Council Speeches of Vatican II*, p. 25.

[16] H. Küng, op. cit., p. 28.

Hans Küng summarizes the ecclesiology of Vatican II as follows:

1. The Church was seen as the eschatological people of God of the New Covenant, to which all, laity and those who bear office, belong;
2. The preaching of the word of God and the celebration of Baptism and Eucharist are constitutive of the Church, which thus exists essentially as the local Church, the Community;
3. The sinfulness of the Church in this world, and hence her constant dependence upon God's forgiveness;
4. The charismatic, pneumatic structure of the Church in the New Testament, built not only on the Apostles but on the prophets, in which the Holy Spirit is given to all Christians, and each individual Christian has his particular spiritual gift, his special charisma for the building up of the Community;
5. The sharing of each individual Christian in the Universal priesthood of the faithful, who form, all together, a royal prophetic and priestly people and are all, without exception, called to evangelical perfection and holiness;
6. The function of office in the Church as selfless, brotherly service towards the individual Christian and the whole great people of God, in which all are brothers under one Lord:
7. The special importance of prophets and teachers (theologians) alongside the Apostles and their successors;
8. The brotherly association of the Bishops, who form a College, together with the Pope, in a common, corporate responsibility for the whole Church;
9. The theological significance of sacramental episcopal consecration, by which an individual is accepted into the College of Bishops and receives his authority from Christ;
10. The rightfulness of the priesthood, and the association of Bishops and priests together in one single service of the Church;
11. The restoration of the permanent diaconate, on the model of the early Church;
12. The necessity of multiplicity and freedom within the one Church and the meaning of different traditions, especially those of both West and East, as manifesting the Church's Catholicity;
13. The missionary structure not only of the 'missionary Church', but of the Church as a whole, and the special relation of the Church to the poor;
14. The Church's service to the world and care for men of other religions;
15. The positive aspect of a separation of Church and State.[17]

[17] Küng, op. cit., pp. 28–30.

Needless to say, Küng's interpretation of the ecclesiology of Vatican II is an attempt to reconcile Roman ecclesiology with that of the Orthodox. But his eighth point—'the Bishops, who form a College, together with the Pope'—is only acceptable to Orthodoxy if this means that the Pope is 'primus inter pares' as member and chairman of the College of Bishops. It is *not* acceptable if it means the Bishops together with a Pope who retains all his privileges of infallibility and jurisdiction—as recent events have shown is still the case.

2. *The Church visible and invisible*

From the Reformation onwards the doctrine of the Church became the central point of controversy between the Churches, and the source of most of their differences. They disagreed, however, not about the scriptural and patristic descriptions of the Church as founded by God himself, as the Bride of Christ, as the pillar and ground of the truth, as One, Holy, Catholic, and Apostolic; but over how to answer the question: Which Church to-day can rightly claim to be the true Church?

Many Protestants followed the teaching of Luther in making a distinction between the visible and invisible Church in this world. By this they meant that although many visibly claim to be members of the Church, only some—the invisible company of the elect—really are such. And who these are only God knows. This doctrine was an attempt to answer their Roman Catholic critics, who asserted that in separating themselves from the Papacy they were outside the true Church. No, they replied, we are certain that God knows who his true followers are, and that your corrupt Church cannot justify its exclusive claims to be the only Church. As Luther puts it, the Creed says 'I believe in one Holy Church', not 'I see one Holy Church'.

But this distinction cannot be maintained.[1] For although Fathers such as Origen, Jerome, and Augustine, agreed that the Church contains both false and true members, and that the latter constitute the *corpus Christi verum*, they still see the Church as a visible community with external marks which distinguish it from heretical and schismatic bodies. Furthermore, we have no evidence that St. Paul regarded membership of the universal *ecclesia* as invisible and exclusively spiritual, shared only by a limited number of the members of the

[1] cf. R. Rothe, *Anfänge der Christlichen Kirche* (1837) referred to in Gore's *The Holy Spirit and the Church*, p. 32; cf. F. J. A. Hort, *The Christian Ecclesia* (London, 1897), p. 169.

external *ecclesia*, namely, those whom God had chosen out of the great mass of mankind and predestined to life, or those whose faith in Christ was a genuine and true faith.[2]

The Church is made up of the laity and the clergy who have the Apostolic succession. It includes both saints and sinners. It is visible, because its founder, Jesus Christ, became flesh and grew up a man, because the faith is acknowledged outwardly, and because the Sacraments, although they communicate invisible grace, are visible signs. Moreover, the hierarchy was introduced through a canonical and historical Apostolic Succession, another visible sign. On these matters the Orthodox and Roman Churches agree.

Clement of Alexandria claimed that the Church is a visible society, plain for all to see, and that it is spotless and without the slightest blemish. Origen says that the Church is an organized community, 'the congregation of Christian people' or the assembly of believers.[3] The Church seems to him a sort of world-wide republic, with its own laws and constitutions, or, in the well-known phrase 'the city of God'.[4]

The idea of the visible Church and its unity has been prominent in the East since the time of Victor of Rome (A.D. 190) when, having attempted to excommunicate the Churches of Asia for keeping Easter after their own reckoning, he was reproved by Irenaeus for introducing into the Church the idea that a rigid uniformity, rather than a common faith, was the bond of union.[5] In the West, however, Cyprian's conception of the Church was dominant. Although he regarded the Church as a spiritual entity, he approached it with a practical and legalistic attitude, 'owing much to analogies borrowed from Roman Law and conditioned by the problems created by the Novatianist schism'.[6] Setting out to show that the Church ought to be one, he declared that in fact it was one and accordingly identified the one Church with Rome. After him came Augustine, who attributed to the Pope a pastoral and teaching authority extending over the whole Church, but was by no means prepared to ascribe to the Bishop of Rome, in his capacity as successor of St. Peter, a sovereign and infallible doctrinal *magisterium*.[7]

[2] Gore, *The Holy Spirit and the Church*, pp. 32–33.

[3] *Homily in Ezech*. I, ii, *in Exod*. 9, iii.

[4] *In Ios*. 8, 7.

[5] Eusebius, *Hist. Eccl.* v. 23–24.

[6] J. N. D. Kelly, op. cit., p. 204.

[7] It should be noted that Augustine, like Cyprian, regarded the African Church as independent of Rome.

Yet although the Roman Church emphasizes the hierarchical system more strongly than the Orthodox do, both teach that inner union with our Lord is realized most fully within the visible Church, and that for this reason Christians should not be separated from it.[8] And although the Romans stress the teaching *magisterium* of the Pope and the bishops, while the Orthodox see the episcopate as the representatives of the people in matters of doctrine, and, as the Encyclical Letter of the Eastern Patriarchs of 1848 declared, the whole Body of the Church as the Guardian of the true faith,[9] both Churches assert that it is in the visible Church that true teaching is maintained, and in its sacraments that the power of atonement is found and Divine Grace mediated. This is the positive reason why both Churches claim that those who are inside the visible Church are saved, while 'extra ecclesiam nulla salus'.[10]

Orthodox and Roman alike teach that those who are outside the visible and true Church but believe in Christ can be called Christians, in so far as they acknowledge faith in the divine and human person of Christ. But in order that these Christians may be members of the Church they must have been joined to the visible Church of Christ. An assembly of people who believe in Christ cannot automatically claim to be the Church of Christ. The Church of Christ is that which was founded by Christ himself, which maintains the whole of his teaching, and which keeps the essential characteristics of the Church according to the creed, unity in faith, worship and administration.[11]

[8] Professor Francis Grivec is mistaken in denying this in his article, 'The Church the Body of Christ and the Conciliar idea', *E.C.Q.*, i (1936) pp. 30–1.

[9] See E. Every, 'Khomiakoff and the Encyclical of the Eastern Patriarchs in 1848', *S.* Series 3, No. 3 (1948) pp. 102–4. N. van Arseniev, 'The Slavophil Doctrine of the Church', *C.E.* ix (1928), pp. 132 ff. It should be noted that the Slavophils and some Roman Catholics have misunderstood this Encyclical, which did not say that the consensus of the faithful can correct the errors of the hierarchy.

[10] Patristic teaching often says that we can obtain everything outside the Church except salvation. 'Extra Ecclesiam totum habere potest, praeter salutem', Augustine, *Serm. ad Caesariensis Eccl. plebem.* 'He who has not the Church for his Mother, cannot have God for his Father', Cyprian, *De cath. ecc. unit.* 6: 'Habere non potest Deum patrem qui Ecclesiam non habet matrem.' 'Dost thou believe'—so runs the Baptismal interrogation in St. Cyprian's day—'in the remission of sins and eternal life through the Holy Church?' *Epist.* 69, 7; *Epist.* 70, 2. See also Gore, *The Ministry of the Christian Church*, pp. 16 ff.

[11] Gore, *The Ministry of the Christian Church*, pp. 11 ff. From a Roman Catholic point of view the visible unity of the Church is perfectly realized only under

These characteristics distinguish the Church of Christ from the other Christian communities. This is why the Church, as the guardian of the faith, never recognized a heresy or a schism as possessing parallel powers of salvation. *Ubi Ecclesia ibi est Spiritus Dei* was the unanimous teaching of the Fathers of the Church. In this sense the Church has been compared with the Ark of Noah, implying that there is no life and salvation outside it. The Orthodox and Roman Churches mean by the visible Church the Church which constitutes one body organized under the bishops and has the same faith,[12] though the Roman Church appears to have elevated obedience to an infallible Pope into a fundamental principle of the visible Church.

Anglican theologians also affirm that the Church is a visible society. For instance, Richard Hooker (1554–1600) wrote

By the Church . . . we understand no other than only the visible Church. For preservation of Christianity there is not anything more needful, than that such as are of the visible Church have mutual fellowship and society one with another. In which consideration, as the main

---

three conditions: 1. Agreement in the same objective content of the Faith; 2. Membership in an hierarchically organized Body of the Church; 3. A share in the communion of the same sacraments, especially of the Eucharist. The visible Church is constituted by the elements of faith, hierarchy, and sacraments as means of Grace; the visibility of the Church is something different from the visibility of the State and 'we too, firmly believe and unreservedly confess that outside this Church there is no salvation nor remission of sin', Boniface VIII, Bull *Unam Sanctam*, 1302; Gasparri, *Cath. Cat.* p. 304; see also Decree for the Jacobites of Florence and Bull *Cantate Domino*, 1441; Gasparri, op. cit., 307. But Pius IX (Encycl. *Quanto conficiamur*, 1863, to the Bishops of Italy) said that 'those who labour under invincible ignorance of our Holy religion, yet keep the precepts of the law of nature graven by God in all men's hearts, who are prepared to obey God, and who lead an honourable and upright life, are able, by the powerful workings of God's light and grace, to attain eternal life.' *Acta Pii IX*, I. iii. 613.

[12] From an Orthodox point of view the visible unity of the Church is defined by the fundamental doctrine of the Orthodox Church that as Christ is the unique Saviour of Mankind (Acts 4:12) in the same sense the Church is the one single source of the Sacraments, the unique Ark of Salvation. So that any departure from the teaching of the Church is called heresy, any separation from the lawful authorities is called schism. Both constitute rebellion against the Divine authority of the Church and exclude men from the Communion of the Holy Spirit. According to Prof. Androutsos the frontiers of the Church cannot be extended beyond the frontiers of the Orthodox Catholic Church even when the validity of the Sacraments which are performed outside the Church, is recognized.

body of the sea being one, yet within divers precincts hath divers names, so the Catholic Church is in like sort divided into a number of distinct societies, every of which is termed a Church within itself. In this sense the Church is always a visible society of men.[13]

And Richard Church (1815–90), a follower and historian of the Oxford Movement, argued that

It is only by becoming embodied in the undoubting conditions of a society, by being, as it were, assimilated with its mind and motives—that is to say, with living human minds and wills—and performing all its actions, that ideas have reality, and possess power, and become more than dry and lifeless thoughts.[14]

But there is a proper sense in which the Church can be described as both visible and invisible. And that is when we see it as both human and divine. For Our Lord, its Head, is invisible, and so is the Divine Grace which sanctifies it. And our union with our Lord, through faith, is a spiritual and unseen experience. On this point also the three Churches, Roman, Orthodox, and Anglican agree. As the sixteenth century Anglican divine, Richard Field, put it: 'Hence it cometh that we say there is a visible and invisible Church, not meaning to make two distinct Churches, as our adversaries falsely and maliciously charge us.'[15] Similarly Tertullian said that the Church on earth is an outpost of a celestial society,[16] and Clement of Alexandria that the Church on earth is the image of the heavenly one.[17] Bicknell reminds us that the Church consists not only of the Church militant here on earth, but also of the faithful who are at rest.[18] And the Council of Trent defined the Church as embracing both the Church triumphant (the glorified departed) and the Church militant here on earth (containing good and evil) in a fellowship which is one as regards the profession of belief and the sacraments, and only differs in the degree to which the life conforms to the profession.

[13] More and Cross, *Anglicanism*, p. 41. Also in H. Bettenson, *Documents of the Christian Church* (ed. 2., paperback, 1967), p. 302.

[14] R. W. Church, *The Christian Church* (Oxford House Papers, No. xvii) pp. 4–5. Cf. C. Gore, *The Ministry of the Christian Church*, pp. 9–11.

[15] Richard Field, in More and Cross, ibid.

[16] Tertullian, *De Bapt.* 15, 'Una ecclesia in caelis'.

[17] *Strom.* iv, 8, 66. The souls of the faithful departed are not cut off from the Church, which even now is the Kingdom of Christ; cf. Augustine, *De Civitate Dei* xx, ix, 2, *P.L.* xli, 674.

[18] Op. cit., p. 237.

The invisible unity of the Church, which is always essentially present, is manifest in the visible historical unity and, as Möhler says, the invisible Church emerges from the visible Church, the second being the source of the first because it is constituted by the incarnate Christ and the Holy Spirit. 'The Church is one, both visible (militant) and invisible (triumphant).'[19] The visible and invisible Church together constitute the one Church of Christ. Their unity is a 'given' fact, based on the person and work of the one Christ.[20]

The two Churches, Roman and Orthodox, also agree that the Church, through its authority as the treasury of divine grace, is infallible, though they have a different view of the *magisterium*. This is yet another point which lies behind their common affirmation that only those who are members of the visible Church will be certain of salvation.

3. *Holy Scripture and Holy Tradition*

Romans and Orthodox unanimously teach that there are two sources of Christian doctrine, Holy Scripture and Holy Tradition.[1] Tradition is the unwritten teaching which came down to later generations of Christians from the Apostles, and which is found in the writings of the Fathers and the practices of the Church. But Tradition and Scripture do not exist in isolation from each other. Both Irenaeus and Tertullian remind us that Christ himself is the ultimate source of Christian doctrine, the Word by whom the Father is revealed, and that he entrusted his revelation to his apostles, through whom alone knowledge of it could be obtained.[2] 'Church, Bible, and Tradition are in an unbroken unity', writes Professor Bratsiotis.[3] And Bicknell adds that

[19] H. Alivizatos, in Flew (ed.), *The Nature of the Church*, p. 45.

[20] The Second Vatican Council defined the unity of the visible and invisible Church as follows. The Church has two aspects, the vital-mysterious and the structural-social and both form 'a single reality, the compound of a human and a divine element': 'so the Church, while being life in the triune God, is at the same time the visible sacrament of this saving unity (*De Ecclesia*, 9c), the sacrament or instrumental sign of intimate union with God and of unity for the whole human race'. (Theodore Jeménez Urresti, 'The Ontology of Communion and Collegial Structures in Church,' *C*. viii (1965), p. 5; cf. Jaeger, *A Stand on Ecumenism*, pp. 27–28.)

[1] B. Vellas, 'The Authority of the Bible according to the teaching of the Orthodox Eastern Church,' *TH*. xxii (1951) pp. 602 ff, 608 ff.

[2] Irenaeus, *Haer*. 3; Tertullian, *De Praeser. Haer*. 13.

[3] P. Bratsiotis, 'The Authority of the Bible from an Orthodox point of View', *TH*. xxxiii (1952), p. 508.

we must never forget that the Church existed and was at work in the world for many years before any single book of the New Testament was composed. These books were written by members of the Church for members of the Church. They presuppose a certain knowledge in those who read them, based upon oral instruction . . . . So today Scripture cannot be our earliest teacher. It is the Church that points us to the Bible as differing from all other books and that gives us that elementary instruction by word and example in the Christian life without which the Bible would be largely unmeaning.'[4]

The Orthodox would agree that Tradition is prior to Scripture. But they would not agree with the Roman Church's exaltation of Tradition above Scripture as the central principle in matters of doctrine and practice. They would see this as the outcome of a parallel exaltation of ecclesiastical authority in an external and legalistic way, and would agree with the sixteenth-century Reformers that it was this attitude which was responsible for the abuses in the Western Church.

In the Orthodox Church true tradition is based on two things: the Liturgy of the primitive Christian Church and the teaching of the Fathers who interpreted Holy Scripture. 'Tradition in the Orthodox Church', says Professor Florovsky, 'is as the Church itself, the union of divine and human reality. But its human elements, its concrete expressions in dogma or in Liturgy, do not remain human. They are so changed that they become divine in themselves.' He continues:

When divine truth is pronounced and expressed in the human tongue, the very words are transfigured. . . . These words become sacred . . . this signifies that in the adequate expression of a Divine Truth certain words, i.e. definite conceptions and ideas or a definite train of thought, have been eternalized and stabilized. . . . The uninterrupted continuity of revelation in the Church not only interprets but also completes the revelation contained in the Scriptures. For there is much truth which has been disclosed to the Church by the Holy Spirit, which cannot be found in, or proved from, the contents of the Bible. While nothing in Tradition can contradict the biblical revelation, the Scriptures are not sufficient. Although the Ecumenical Councils represent adequate and therefore unchangeable formulations of divine truth, they do not exhaust the contents of Tradition, for there is a great deal of tradition which is essential to the Church, but which is as yet unformulated. Tradition is more than formulated dogma, for the mystical life of the

---

[4] Bicknell, op. cit., pp. 128–129. See also Gore, *The Holy Spirit and the Church*, p. 166, note 1, and pp. 171–2; also *Belief in Christ*, p. 86.

Church is more than its explicit expressions. Some of the most central orthodox beliefs have never been formulated, for instance Mariology, the doctrine of the Saints and eschatology, but it would be impossible to maintain that these do not therefore belong to Orthodox tradition.[5]

At the Second Vatican Council there were some Fathers who argued that there is only one source of revelation, but that it is apprehended in two forms or kinds, namely Holy Scripture and Tradition. This corresponds to the Anglican position. Today it is commonly agreed by Romans and Orthodox that, as W. M. Horton puts it, 'traditions contrary to Scripture cannot be sound traditions'.[6] Horton goes on to say that 'One of the two "permitted opinions" among Roman Catholics is that tradition is not (as other Catholics say) a parallel source of divine truth, separate from the Scriptures, but simply the authorized churchly interpretation of the Scriptures in their wholeness.'

That Holy Tradition is to be used to throw light on the interpretation of the Holy Scriptures, and that it must never contradict the Scriptures, is maintained by Orthodox, Anglicans and some modern Roman Catholic theologians. It must, however, be emphasized also that the Orthodox Church agrees with the Council of Trent on the question of the material insufficiency of Scripture. Orthodox and Roman alike teach that there are truths in Tradition which are not contained in Scripture, for example, the validity of baptism by heretics, and the justification of infant baptism. In this way Tradition complements the contents of Scripture. Moreover, Tradition, though it is an interpretation of Scripture, is not only this, for the whole deposit of faith was committed by Christ to the Church which infallibly guards and preserves it through the unbroken succession of the episcopate, as the Orthodox say, or of the *magisterium* as the Romans affirm, though both really mean the same thing. Therefore, according to Roman Catholicism and Orthodoxy, Holy Scripture and Holy Tradition are two sources of revelation of equal value. Nevertheless the Fathers of the Church frequently declare the sufficiency of Holy Scriptures (a position maintained by the Anglican Church). For example Clement of Alexandria said that it is the Bible which, when interpreted by the Church, is the source of Christian teaching.[7] Athanasius affirms that

[5] George Florovsky, 'The Holy Spirit in Revelation', *C.E.* viii (1932), p. 60.
[6] Walter Marshall Horton, *Christian Theology: An Ecumenical Approach* (1955) p. 49.
[7] Migne, *P.G.* ix, 532; cf. Origen, *Cont. Cels.* iii, 15, 15–20; *De Princ.* 3. 6. 6.

'the Holy and inspired Scriptures are fully sufficient for the proclamation of the truth'.[8] Cyril of Alexandria wrote: 'with regard to
the divine and saving mysteries of faith no doctrine, however trivial,
may be taught without the backing of the Divine Scriptures. For our
saving faith derives its force not from capricious reasonings, but from
what may be proved out of the Bible.'[9] John Chrysostom bade his
congregation look to no other teacher than the oracles of God;
everything was straightforward and clear in the Bible, and the sum
of necessary knowledge could be extracted from it.[10] Augustine likewise declared that 'Holy Scripture has paramount authority',[11] and
Vincent of Lerins said that the Scriptural Canon was 'sufficient, and
more than sufficient, for all purposes'.[12]

However, in 1931 the Joint Anglican–Orthodox Doctrinal Commission declared that

Everything necessary for salvation can be founded upon Holy Scripture
as completed, explained, interpreted and understood in the Holy
Tradition by the guidance of the Holy Spirit residing in the Church.
By Holy Tradition we mean the truths which came down from Our
Lord and the Apostles through the Fathers, which are confessed unanimously and continuously in the Undivided Church, and are taught
by the Church under the guidance of the Holy Spirit.[13]

'This view of Tradition' writes Visser 't Hooft,[14] 'is perhaps illogical
in that it seems to suggest at the same time that the Scriptures by
themselves are altogether sufficient, and that they are only sufficient
if combined with Tradition.' It represents, however (he argues), the
reality of Anglican faith which has both a great reverence for the
authority of the Bible and a strong sense of the scriptural reality of
Tradition, as God's way of leading the Church. The Church must
look backwards as well as forwards. It must check itself by comparing
its teaching and liturgy with that of the primitive Church. The main

[8] *Cont. Gent.*, i.; cf. *De Syn.* 6.

[9] *Cat.* 4. 17.

[10] Migne, *P.G.* lxi. 361, 485.

[11] *De Civ. Dei*, xi, 3.

[12] Gore, *The Holy Spirit and the Church*, pp. 173, 197. Vincent of Lerins,
Adversus profanas omnium novitates haereticorum commonitorium, 2.

[13] *Joint Doctrinal Report*, p. 12; cf. J. P. Mackey, *The Modern Theology of
Tradition* (London, 1962) pp. 187, 188; cf. also G. L. Prestige, *Fathers and Heretics*
(London, 1940) pp. 21, 24.

[14] Visser 't Hooft, op. cit. p. 49-50.

emphasis of the Church is on the Tradition of the undivided Church, that is to say, the Tradition which existed before the breaking up of Christendom into Eastern and Western, Orthodox, Roman or Protestant. Such innovations in Church life as have been made by the Roman Catholic Church, either at the Council of Trent or at the first Council of the Vatican, or by other Churches at the time of the Reformation, have no authority for the Orthodox, for they do not correspond to the imperative norm of all tradition: *Quod semper, quod ubique, quod ab omnibus creditum est, hoc est vere proprieque Catholicum*.[15]

According to Orthodox teaching the criterion of genuine and true Tradition is its Apostolic origin.[16] By contrast the Roman Church is continually creating tradition 'which in fact pays no real attention either to the silence of scripture, or to the actual facts about the Tradition in its earlier stages'.[17]

Who is the authentic interpreter of the sources of Revelation? According to the Orthodox Church the infallible Word of God, which is necessary for salvation, should be communicated by infallible and authentic means. Such an authentic judge and guardian is the Church, which is represented by the Ecumenical Councils and the Fathers of the Church. 'These wise thoughts,' writes Villain,[18] 'enable us to appreciate the peaceful beauty of a continuity of life which was not broken by the crisis of the Reformation, but on the contrary remained uniform and faithful to avoid the precipitation of such a crisis.' The Roman Church, however, answers the question differently. Following the teaching of Irenaeus and Tertullian that the apostolically founded sees could be relied upon to have preserved the Apostles' witness in its purity, it regarded itself as in a special sense the appointed custodian and mouthpiece of the Apostolic Tradition.[19]

If the Church is the superior judge and guardian of the validity of Holy Scripture and Holy Tradition, then the question arises: who guarantees the authenticity of the Church—the Church which defines

---

[15] Vincent of Lerins, *Commonitorium* (*P.L.* l, 640.)

[16] B. Vellas, op. cit., p. 611.

[17] (*Sensus Fidei*); Gore, *The Holy Spirit and the Church*, pp. 196–7.

[18] *Unity*, p. 157.

[19] When Irenaeus assigns a special importance to the Roman Church in maintaining the tradition, it is because its pre-eminence brought Christian men from all parts of the world to it, so that tradition there was not merely local but ecumenical, because the tradition was there maintained by men from all parts. This is the undoubted meaning of the famous phrase (Iren. *c. Haer.* iii. 3); cf. Gore, *Roman Catholic Claims*, pp. 97–8.

the Scriptures and confirms the Tradition? This question is very important, because it poses the problem of the relation of the Church to the sources of revelation. The answer is that our Saviour has promised that he will remain with the Church until the end of the World and that he will send the Holy Spirit to guide it into all truth. And that he has kept his promise by infallibly guiding and inspiring the Ecumenical Councils, whose decisions are therefore seen as the authentic teaching of the Church. On this both the Orthodox and Roman Churches agree. There is a difference, however. In the Orthodox Church final authority does not rest entirely with the hierarchy but with the whole body of the faithful (although the episcopate does bear the dominical commission to teach, and as such possesses infallibility). For though a synod of bishops may claim ecumenical status and infallibility, their decisions need to be accepted by the whole Church, as those of the Council of Florence, for instance, were not. In the Roman Church a bishop must accept the authority of the 'Supreme Pontiff' in order to partake of the *magisterium*, or teaching function of the Church.[20]

A Roman Catholic has written:

The authoritative interpretation [of Tradition] in the Anglican Church may be found in the Fathers of the early centuries and the doctrinal decisions of the first Ecumenical Councils. The Ecumenical Creeds have a place in the Liturgy, although the so-called Athanasian Creed is not obligatory.[21] In England the *Ecclesia Anglicana* has wanted to hold on to the Tradition of the early Church more consciously and explicitly than have the continental Churches and has desired to limit itself to the expurgation of what it considered to be late-Mediaeval deformations.[22]

But Bicknell writes that 'what our Lord promised to his Church was not infallibility, but an infallible guide, the Holy Spirit.'[23] J. P. Mackey retorts: 'It sounds rather weak to say that the Church has an infallible guide but it is not itself infallible. For what good is an infallible guide who does not guide infallibly?'[24] Yet Bicknell, in his caution, is typical of the Anglican approach to authority, for he continues:

---

[20] J. P. Mackey, *The Modern Theology of Tradition*, p. 198.

[21] This is an error. The use of the Athanasian Creed is directed by the Book of Common Prayer for the major feasts of the Church's year.

[22] J. F. Lescrauwaet, 'The Reformed Churches', *C*. vi (1965), p. 73.

[23] Bicknell, op. cit., p. 273.

[24] J. P. Mackey, op. cit., p. 190.

The guidance of the Holy Spirit is not irresistible: it is not a substitute for intellectual or moral effort. The Church may through sinfulness miss or reject it. Just because the Church is not perfectly holy, therefore she is not perfectly responsive to her infallible Guide. Thus even a decision that is issued by a general council is not infallible. The more general the council and the wider the acceptance of its decision, the more it represents the deliberate and considered opinion of the Church and the greater the authority with which it comes to us. But general councils are not an automatic machinery for turning out infallible utterances.

4. The Primacy in the Universal Church

Orthodoxy does not deny to the Holy and Apostolic See of Rome a Primacy of honour, together with the right (under certain conditions) to hear appeals from all parts of Christendom. Note that we have used the word 'primacy', not 'supremacy'. Orthodox regard the Pope as the bishop 'who presides in love', to use a phrase of Saint Ignatius: Rome's mistake—so Orthodox believe—has been to turn this primacy or 'presidency of love' into a supremacy of external power and jurisdiction.

This primacy which Rome enjoys takes its origins from three factors. First, Rome was the city where Saint Peter and Saint Paul were martyred, and where Peter was bishop. The Orthodox Church acknowledges Peter as the first among the Apostles: it does not forget the celebrated 'Petrine texts' in the Gospels . . . although Orthodox theologians do not understand these texts in quite the same way as modern Roman Catholic commentators. . . . Secondly, the see of Rome also owed its primacy to the position occupied by the city of Rome in the Empire. . . . Thirdly, although there were occasions when Popes fell into heresy, on the whole during the first eight centuries of the Church's history the Roman see was noted for the purity of its faith. . . . Because the see of Rome had in practice taught the faith with an outstanding loyalty to the truth, it was above all to Rome that men appealed for guidance in the early centuries of the Church. But . . . the primacy assigned to Rome does not overthrow the essential equality of the bishops. The Pope is the first bishop in the Church—but he is the *first among equals*.[1]

It cannot be too strongly emphasized that the dispute between Rome and Orthodoxy about the Papal Primacy is basically a dispute about the *universal supremacy of jurisdiction* which Rome has claimed, the

---

[1] Timothy Ware, *The Orthodox Church* (1963), pp. 35–6.

corollary of which is her further claim to be the *principium radix et origo* of the unity of the Church. It should also be pointed out that in this dispute Rome has concentrated her defence on the 'Petrine claims', whereas Orthodoxy has based her argument on the claim that the ecclesiastical importance of a see is dependent on its civil importance as a capital city, in other words, when the capital of the Empire was moved to Constantinople—'New Rome'—the Bishop of Constantinople could claim a position of importance and privilege equal to that of the Bishop of 'Old Rome', and second to him in honour. This claim was accepted and endorsed by the third canon of the Council of Constantinople in 381, and the twenty-eighth canon of the Council of Chalcedon in 451, though this latter was not accepted at the time in the West.

It was when Rome insisted on its own view of its jurisdiction that the division with Constantinople occurred. After the division new Rome continued to enjoy the privileges granted to it by the Ecumenical Councils. This primacy of the Ecumenical Patriarch of Constantinople, 'well established as it is in the Orthodox Tradition is a constant and essential element of the Church's structure',[2] assuring the *Koinonia* of the Churches.

A more accurate exposition of the status of the Ecumenical Patriarch within the Orthodox Church was given by a prominent Russian Prelate, the Metropolitan of Kiev, Antony Khrapovitsky, in a message to the statesmen assembled at the Lausanne Conference (December 1922–January 1923):[3]

According to the doctrine of Christ's Church as expressed in the decisions of the seven Ecumenical Councils, the See of Constantinople is not only one of the Ecclesiastical Provinces but is considered as a constant element of the Orthodox Church in all its fullness, as an authority linked not only with its own diocese but likewise with the whole Orthodox Church throughout the world. This is why since the fifth century the Patriarch of Constantinople as Bishop of the New Rome was recognized by the Ecumenical Councils as the equal in power and honour of the Bishop of Old Rome (Canon II of the second Ecumenical Council and Canons XXVIII and XXXVI of the fourth Ecumenical Council). And what is especially important, it was

[2] Elia Melia, *P.A.*, pp. 111 ff.

[3] Not of course the Lausanne Conference on Faith and Order (1927) but the political conference which led to the Treaty of Lausanne after the First World War.

recognized that he had the right to receive the appeals of Bishops who were not satisfied with the decisions of regional councils (Canon XVII of the fourth Ecumenical Council). In this latter sense the Patriarch of Constantinople is, in the eyes of Orthodox Christians in every country, the supreme Judge.

The traditional description of the Primacy of the Patriarch of Constantinople is that of *Primus inter pares*; but this Primacy does not possess an immediate universal jurisdiction outside its own territory, nor the privilege of infallibility. The authority of the Patriarch of Constantinople is *ex officio* and safeguards the unity of the Orthodox Catholic Church, and as the late Bishop of Ochrida, Nicolai Velimirovič, put it: 'The Ecumenical Patriarchate is the natural and necessary centre of Orthodoxy.'[4] In the Orthodox Church episcopal authority is exercised both locally and ecumenically, but the Primacy of the Ecumenical Patriarch includes the *ex officio* privilege of exercising power to initiate certain matters at the level of the whole Church. This privilege implies that the Ecumenical Patriarch is invested with the highest authority as the centre of the unity of the Church.[5]

Thus the Primacy of the Patriarch of Constantinople has an ecclesiastical justification. The Primacy of the Bishop of Rome, however, to use the words of Fr. Yves Congar,

from the eleventh century onwards ... borrowed much from the vocabulary, insignia, ceremonial, style, and ideology of the imperial court. These factors sometimes go back to pagan days and even by way of the Hellenistic monarchy of Alexander, to the Persian paganism of the fourth century B.C. Even the title curia assumed by the papal administration was borrowed from the secular vocabulary and, at the time, there were those who did not fail to point this out.[6]

The primacy of the Ecumenical Patriarch of Constantinople derives from the twenty-eighth Canon of the fourth Ecumenical Council.

This Canon was voluntarily accepted as agreed by the Eastern Bishops in spite of the objections raised by the Papal legates on the ground of the boldly interpolated sixth Nicaean Canon: *Romana ecclesia semper habuit primatum*. Although this falsification was again put forth by

---

[4] *C.E.* ii (1921), p. 73.
[5] A. W. Kartashoff, 'The Reunion of Orthodoxy' in *Tserkovni Vestnik*, 5–6 (1956), pp. 4–12.
[6] *P.A.*, pp. 141–2.

Rome in Carthage forty years later, it was documentally disproved and the matter remained as before. The twenty-eighth Canon of Chalcedon has always remained, and still remains, a binding, active norm in the Eastern Church, notwithstanding the systematic and unremitting opposition of the Papacy, which was obviously not recognized there as the supreme resort in the Church of Christ.[7]

The Orthodox Church, agreeing with St. John Chrysostom and Gregory of Nazianzus, adheres to the belief that Jesus Christ, in his words in Matthew 16:18, by no means intended to say that his Catholic Church would be built on the apostle Peter only. The keys, as that symbol of authority for the government of the Kingdom of God, were bestowed by him afterwards (without symbolic phraseology), upon the apostles collectively.[8] Likewise the foundation of the Church does not exclude the other apostles.[9] Ecclesiastical tradition also disagrees about the implication of the word 'rock' for in some texts Christ himself is regarded as the head and cornerstone, beside which none other can be laid.[10] So some Fathers regard Our Lord himself as this rock on which the Church is built; while others say that it was St. Peter's faith in Christ as the Son of the living God.[11] Cyril of Alexandria refers to the rock[12] as Christ himself, apprehended by faith.[13] Epiphanius[14] and Theodoret[15] see it as the symbol of St. Peter's faith. Likewise St. Augustine[16] and St. Cyprian[17] maintain that 'the other Apostles were what Peter had been, because they had rights of honour and of authority equal to his'. Cyril of Alexandria, in his sermon on John 21:15–17[18] says that these words meant no more than the formal restoration of Peter's pastoral functions as an apostle after his denial of the Lord, the variant between 'lambs' and 'sheep' merely following the customary Hebrew style of poetic or solemn diction.

[7] N. Glubokovsky, *C.E.* v (1924), pp. 162–3.
[8] Matt. 28:18–19.
[9] Eph. 2:19–22.
[10] 1 Cor. 3:11; 10:4.
[11] Matt. 16:16.
[12] On Matt. 16:18.
[13] Migne, *P.G.* lxx. 444, 940.
[14] *C. Haer.* 59. 7.
[15] *Quaest. in Exod. interr.* 68.
[16] On 1 Cor. 10:4.
[17] *De Eccles. Unit.* 4.
[18] *P.G.* lxxiv. 749.

The same is true of the admonition to establish his brethren[19] which Chrysostom[20] and Basil[21] interpret as illustrating a general truth of God's dealing with men, namely that restoration after sin is possible on condition of repentance. The Roman interpretation that the repeated 'Feed my lambs', and the variation 'Feed my sheep', indicate the two constituent elements of the Church, the laity and the clergy, is a particularly rabbinical argument, for it suggests that the apostles themselves are the sheep, and that the pastoral office or the government of the whole Church, was committed to St. Peter. But when the apostles strove among themselves for pre-eminence, Christ did not then confer this primacy upon one of them to put an end to the strife, but said that none among them is to rule as lords of this world rule;[22] no one is to call himself master.[23] The greatest among them will be he who renders to the others the greatest services.[24]

In view of all this it is the doctrine of the Orthodox Church that Christ alone is Head of the Church. There is no visible head, for Christ committed the unity of the Church to his apostles collectively. And while we may acknowledge the historical merits of the Papacy in securing the unity of the Church, we must point out that it has also had the opposite effect. The whole controversy is neatly contained in the words of Pope Boniface in his Bull *Unam Sanctam* of 1302. 'Of this one and only Church there is one body and one head . . . namely Christ'. With this both Orthodox and Romans agree. But he goes on to say: 'and Christ's vicar is Peter, and Peter's successor, for the Lord said to Peter himself, "Feed my sheep".'[25] And here Orthodox and Romans part company.

In the Anglican Church a similar opinion to that held by the Orthodox is maintained. W. M. Southgate says of Bishop Jewel of Salisbury (1522–71) that although he 'was convinced that unlimited claims could not be substantiated by the history of the Bishop of Rome in the early centuries of the Church, he did not distort the history of the early Church in order to make his case. He readily admitted that "the Bishop of Rome had an estimation, and a credit, and a prerogative

---

[19] Luke 22:32.
[20] On Matt. 16:18.
[21] *Hon. de hum.* 4.
[22] Mark 10:42–3; Luke 22:25–6.
[23] Matt. 23:8 ff.
[24] Matt. 20:27; Mark 10:44.
[25] Bettenson, *Documents of the Christian Church* (ed. 2, paperback, 1967), p. 115.

before others". Specifically, he "had the first place" of the four Patriarchs, both in Council and out of Council, and therefore the greatest authority and direction of matters in all assemblies.'[26] Jewel developed this subject in vast detail and pointed out that the early prerogative of the See of Rome was not *de jure divino*. Southgate says that Jewel was most careful in this point. The respect which men like St. Augustine accorded the See was not due to any divinity in the See or its holder but was derived from simple historical causes, the antiquity of the See, the glory of its martyrs, and the position of Rome as the Imperial seat. Most important of all was the purity of religion . . . preserved there for a long time without spot. Doctrine was not dependent upon the Church for its validity; rather the possession of sound doctrine lent authority to the Church. Because the teachings of the Apostles at the beginning were exactly observed in Rome without corruption the Church was then held in reverence and estimation above others. But now, since the Church of Rome has lost its purity of doctrine it can no longer command men's respect.[27] Gore, too, accepted the Orthodox view when he wrote

We Anglicans have always appealed . . . specially to the formal utterances of Eastern Councils reckoned as ecumenical—the third canon of Constantinople and the twenty-eighth of Chalcedon. Romans reply that the latter—the most explicit—canon was not accepted by Rome and that the Easterns must therefore have admitted that it was not valid. But this is not the case. Whatever polite and conciliatory language they thought it wise to use to the powerful pontiff at Rome, the canon remained in their eyes valid, and was explicitly reaffirmed in the Council 'in Trullo' (Canon xxxvi).[28]

5. The Ecumenical Councils

From the fourth to the seventh centuries the great Ecumenical Councils were *de jure* and, in effect, *de facto* the highest authority in the Church, and they were gradually given an infallibility which has been recognized ever since. In fact the fourth Ecumenical Council explicitly began this process when it declared: 'We will permit neither ourselves

---

[26] Southgate, op. cit., p. 125.

[27] ibid, p. 127.

[28] C. Gore, *The Holy Spirit and the Church*, pp. 203, 207; *Roman Catholic Claims*, p. 102; cf. E. L. Mascall, *The Recovery of Unity*, pp. 197–210. Mascall accepts the Primacy of Peter, but he rejects the absolute supremacy in governing the Church.

nor others to overstep even by so much as a syllable what our fathers at Nicaea determined, mindful of the saying, "Remove not the landmarks which thy fathers have set".' Gregory the Great said, 'I esteem them [the Councils] as I do the four Gospels.' The Ecumenical Councils, when lifted above the turmoil of factions and clothed in the glory of antiquity, presented themselves to posterity with this authority, and the same authority descended in due course upon each of the later representative assemblies of the whole Church.

St. Cyprian was the first who sought to throw a supernatural lustre over the Councils. Together with the African Bishops he upheld the Councils over against the assertions of Rome: 'This is our pleasure, in accordance with the prompting of the Holy Spirit, and the Lord who has exhorted us thereto through many visions.' St. Augustine said that the Councils held in individual provinces should give way without any demur to the larger Councils, whose members come from the whole Christian world. Gregory of Nazianzus, however, appears to have had no great opinion of the Councils, for, he said 'I have come to the conclusion, if I am to write truly, that I shun every assembly of bishops, for I have never seen a good end come of any Council, because, so far from bringing about a diminution of evil, they have rather augmented it.'

Roman Catholics have attempted to argue that the authority of the Papacy is superior to that of a council, or that it was Papal approval of a Council's decisions that made them authoritative. But this is not historically accurate. Certainly the Pope's representatives were present at most of the Councils, and presided over the fourth and sixth. Certainly Papal representation was required if a Council was to be truly 'Ecumenical', and Papal approval if its decisions were to have the authority of the Universal Church. But this does not establish the Roman argument. For, as N. Glubokovsky writes,

It is true that in the West various kinds of *reservatio mentalis* were in use from very old times, and that the Popes tried to place themselves above the Councils, but they were, all the same, compelled to submit to them as in the case of the Trullan Council. Even such a Papistic coryphaeus as Leo I was compelled to 'coordinate' with the Council of Chalcedon, although the latter was convened against his wishes .... But generally, the Popes, through their legates, used to take an active part in the Ecumenical Councils, although the Councils were not convened by the Popes and though they were not always convened in accordance with their wishes, though certainly they never played a part in the Papal consultative apparatus and though there were cases when the Councils were called together notwithstanding the Papal declaration that the convening was unnecessary. The Councils were the independent and the supreme legislative, juridical, and doctrinal tribunal of the saving Church, *ecclesia salvifica*, of Christ for teaching and administration.[1]

The German theologian Karl von Hase (1800–90), who has been called 'the Nestor of modern scientific theology', explains that during the religious conflicts of the fourth century, which disturbed the Eastern Church especially,

the Bishops of Rome, without themselves taking a very enthusiastic share, almost always had the intelligence and the good fortune to take that side which, according to the natural development of dogma, must carry the day, and by this means their reputation and their powers of perception as guardians of the pure faith were much enhanced. Also the Bishops who spoke the Latin tongue and who had neither special interest nor personal knowledge in these contentions, generally followed the Pope as the sole Bishop of Apostolic institution in the West. Therefore it follows that the agreement of the Bishop of Rome (with the whole bulk of the Church of the Western Empire) was very valuable to the Eastern Bishops, and was sought by party leaders in Greece with adulation and laudation, not as an infallible person, but still with the recognition that the Church at Rome had never fallen away from the pure Apostolic faith.

What the Easterns had recognized regarding the right faith maintained by Rome, was understood as a historical fact, not as a dogmatic necessity. This explanation was given by the Greek Emperor at the Council of Florence: 'What one of the Fathers uttered in a complimentary vein in a letter to the Pope must not for this reason be at once inferred to be a right and prerogative.'[2] 'Generally', writes Archbishop Jaeger, 'a Council's decrees were confirmed by the Pope by being signed by his representative in his name. There was no dichotomy between Pope and Council. The latter met in union with the Pope who was united with the bishops by virtue of his office as Peter's successor.

---

[1] N. Glubokovsky, 'Papal Rome and the Orthodox East', *C.E.* v (1924), p. 165. A 'Papistic coryphaeus' presumably means 'an outstanding spokesman for the Papacy'. (*Koryphaios*, from *koryphē*, head, is applied to the leader of the chorus in Greek drama, who speaks on their behalf.)

[2] Karl von Hase, op. cit., vol. ii, pp. 260–261.

The Pope actually participated through his legates.'[3] But there was no idea of such a primacy amongst the non-Roman fathers of the Ecumenical Councils. There was no Patriarch of the undivided Church in East and West to whom was awarded the prerogative to confirm, or reject, or veto, or change, the findings and the decision of the Fathers reached, after the invocation of the Holy Spirit, in Ecumenical Councils. If the Pope really thought that he was the head of the whole Church then necessarily his legates should have presided over all the Councils, not only the fourth and sixth. But we know that in the first Ecumenical Council there was no president; in the second there were Gregory of Constantinople and his successor, Nectarius; in the third St. Cyril of Alexandria; and in the fifth and seventh the Patriarchs of Constantinople.

In the fourth Ecumenical Council we can see the attitude of the Eastern Church towards the Papal claims. The twenty-eighth Canon of this Council gives the same prerogatives as the Pope possessed to the Patriarch of Constantinople also. Even the 'Tome' of St. Leo on questions of faith was not accepted until after an examination of the passages of scripture involved, while he and his successors protested in vain against the decision to allow the equality of the Patriarch of Constantinople.[4] Moreover, a Roman Catholic authority tells us that at the time of the fourth Ecumenical Council the Romans knew very little about the situation in the East, and they cared only for their own dignity,[5] while an Anglican suggests that their objection to the twenty-eighth Canon of the Council was due to this ignorance.[6]

Of the third Council Archbishop Jaeger writes: 'Pope and Council acted together, for speaking in Pope Celestine's name, the Roman Priest Philippus told the Council Fathers at Ephesus, "The members have united themselves with the head, for yourselves are well aware that the Holy Apostle Peter is the faith and the head of all the Apostles." '[7]

[3] L. Jaeger, *The Ecumenical Council*, p. 6. Bishop Jewel wrote that in the early years the Bishop of Rome 'had no authority neither to summon Councils, nor to be president or chief in Councils, nor to ratify and confirm the decrees of Councils, more than any other of the four Patriarchs'. In those times the decrees of the Councils could stand in force, 'although the Pope mislike them and allow them not'; Cf. Southgate, op. cit., p. 130.

[4] Karl von Hase, op. cit., vol. i, p. 260.

[5] A. Pichler, *Geschichte der Kirchlichen Trennung zwischen dem Orient und Occident* (Munich, 1864–5), vol. ii., p. 636.

[6] G. Every, *The Byzantine Patriarchate*, p. 22.

[7] Jaeger, *The Ecumenical Council*, op. cit., p. 6.

The Orthodox Church, however, has a different interpretation of what Philippus said at Ephesus, namely that he spoke on behalf of his master, but that the Council Fathers paid no attention to his words, and went on to unfrock Nestorius. The Council and St. Cyril thus did not acknowledge themselves to be the instruments of Pope Celestine. On the contrary the Pope himself agreed to the decision of the Council. That agreement is regarded by the Romans as approval— an interpretation which the Orthodox dispute.

At the second Ecumenical Council the superiority of Council to Pope was even more clearly shown, for the question of succession in Antioch was settled contrary to the wish of the Bishop of Rome, when Flavian was elected to succeed Meletius, and not Paulinus who was the Pope's candidate. Moreover, Maximus the Cynic who was supported by Rome as successor to Gregory of Nazianzus was also opposed by that Council.

There is a dispute not only about the authority which convokes, and confirms the decisions of, an Ecumenical Council, but also on the number of Ecumenical Councils which the Church recognizes as authoritative. There are, however, certain Councils which have gradually obtained unconditional recognition in the opinion of the whole Church. Others, although convened as Ecumenical, have been rejected by their contemporaries, or by subsequent generations. In the first Ecumenical Councils only a small number of Western bishops were present, while at the Councils held in the Middle Ages in the West the Orthodox bishops of the East were not represented, except on the few occasions when a reconciliation with the Eastern Church was attempted. These later Councils were merely assemblies of the Pope's advisers, as a rule summoned only to learn and carry out his wishes. So the Orthodox Church recognizes as Ecumenical only the first seven Councils, in which the whole Church took part. The Anglican Church has made no final authoritative ruling about the Councils, though it generally recognizes the first four which defined the three 'Catholic Creeds'. Some Anglicans would agree with Bishop Gore's opinion that the fifth 'did not add anything to the theological definition of Ephesus . . . and the sixth Council . . . added nothing to the work of the second and fourth Councils . . .' while the claim of the seventh 'to be called ecumenical has been seriously disputed . . . but not convincingly . . . and I do not think its con-clusions need be rejected on the ground that they are unscriptural'.[8]

[8] *The Holy Spirit and the Church*, pp. 291–2.

Other Anglicans, however, remaining suspicious of the superstition to which the veneration of ikons and relics may give rise, would be unwilling to accept the decisions of the seventh Council, though not necessarily in the derogatory words of Bishop Jewel: 'Read this second Nicene Council throughout, if thou be able. Thou wilt say, there was never any assembly of Christian Bishops so vain, so peevish, so wicked, so blasphemous, so unworthy in all respects to be called a Council.'[9]

It should be added that in 1930 the Anglicans in discussion with the Orthodox delegates to the Lambeth Conference gave the impression of a greater readiness to accept the canons of the Seventh Ecumenical Council.[10]

In the Roman Catholic Church there is no official list of the Councils which the Roman Church recognizes as Ecumenical.[11] Francis Dvornik, for instances, writes that

the eighth Ecumenical Council of the Roman Church owes the honour of being counted as such to a singular mistake on the part of Roman canonists of the eleventh century, who found the Acts of this Council in the Lateran archives and were delighted to read amongst them a decision forbidding the laity to interfere with the election of Bishops. They were so delighted with this discovery that they not only forgot that this Synod had been cancelled, but promoted it to be one of the greatest Councils of Christianity.[12]

There was during the Middle Ages the idea that Councils in which the Greeks (the Eastern Church) had not participated could not be accepted as Ecumenical.[13] So that though Daniel-Rops comes to the conclusion that the second Vatican Council will bear the number twenty-two, this is not a result of historical demonstration.[14]

From a theoretical point of view there is no great difference amongst Orthodox and Romans regarding the authority of the Councils,

[9] Southgate, op. cit., pp. 130–2.

[10] *Lambeth Occasional Reports*, pp. 111.

[11] Henri Daniel-Rops, *The Second Vatican Council*. The story behind the Ecumenical Council of Pope John XXIII. Translated by Alastair Guinan (London, 1962), p. 25.

[12] Dvornik, *The Patriarch Photius*, p. 21.

[13] Cf. *Acta et decreta Synodi cleri romano-catholici provinciae Ultrajectensis*, mense Septembri (1763), p. 656. (*Ultrajectensis* = of Utrecht.)

[14] *The Second Vatican Council*, p. 27.

because their authority is that of the Church.[15] The decisions of the
Councils are conditioned by the circumstances of the time, and, as
St. Augustine says, 'those earlier Councils themselves are often cor-
rected by the later, if in the course of experience that which was
closed is opened up, and that which was hidden brought to light'.
This spirit makes intelligible the decision of the fifth Ecumenical
Council held in Constantinople in 553, when the views of two Fathers
of the Church, long dead, which at the fourth Ecumenical Council had
been expressly recognized as orthodox, were condemned.

Orthodox agree with Anglicans that the authority of the Church
is never identified with the person of a bishop or of the Pope. They
cannot accept the assumption of the Romans that in the Councils there
is a dialogue of faith between the Pope on the one hand and the
bishops together with their faithful on the other.[16] If the bishops
together with their faithful represent the totality of the Church, whom
does the Pope represent? Obviously he represents Christ or Peter.
Some Roman Catholics have gone further, saying that 'the Church
is the mystical body of the Pope, nay that the Pope is the Church'[17]
and by applying the passages in Ephesians 5 about the marital relationship of husband and wife, take it 'as an automatic conclusion that the
Body of the Church must be subject to the head'.[18] This is incompatible with both the history and the nature of the Church, and
therefore the Orthodox cannot agree with this view. This distinction,
which became more apparent in the Second Vatican Council, makes
the dialogue between Romans and Orthodox more difficult. So it
must be repeated once again that the twelve apostles are not to be
regarded as one plus eleven. After the first Pentecost, when the Church
was founded, we do not see one plus eleven, but a unity, the apostles
and elders, in agreement with the whole Church.[19]

The Ecumenical Councils, according to the Orthodox, have no
authority *ex sese*, or of themselves, but only when they express the
truth which exists in the Church as a whole. And the decisions of a
Council in order to be Ecumenical must be accepted by the whole
Church, which alone possesses the infallible prerogative to speak *ex
cathedra*.

[15] P. Franzen, 'The authority of the Councils', *P.A.* p. 43; cf. also H. Alivisatos,
'The Proposed Ecumenical Council and Reunion', *E.R.* xii (1959), pp. 1–10.

[16] P. Franzen, ibid., p. 50.

[17] A. Weiler, 'Church Authority and Government in the Middle Ages', *C.*
vii (1965) p. 68, and especially the footnote 24 on p. 70.

[18] ibid., pp. 68 and 71, n. 25.   [19] Acts 15:22, 23, 25, and 28.

In the West since 1870, however, this authority has been transferred to the Pope of Rome *ex sese, non autem ex consensu ecclesiae*. It would be superfluous, as Metropolitan Athenagoras says, to point out that this dogma has produced a kind of theological havoc everywhere.[20] Since the Vatican Council of 1870 when the Pope's supremacy over the Council was accepted, the significance of an Ecumenical Council was reduced to no more than that of an advisory body to the Pope. For this reason it was possible for non-Roman Catholics to be present at the second Vatican Council as Observers; in other words their presence did not commit the Pope to any obligation or responsibility, since he alone had the right of final decision. In the Orthodox Church, although priests and laymen can take part in a Council, it is only the participant bishops who make the decisions. And it would be impossible for anyone outside the Orthodox Church to attend such a Council.[21]

6. Church Authority

The difference between the Orthodox and the Roman Churches on the matter of authority can be found in two works by J. A. Möhler (1796–1838), a Roman Catholic historian and theologian. In his book *Die Einheit* he stresses the Orthodox view[1] but in his later work *Symbolik* he presents the Roman Catholic view.[2]

It is in the last chapter of the *Einheit*, entitled 'Die Einheit in Primas', that Möhler expresses opinions which show a more Orthodox conception of Church authority. This is not surprising since he based his argument on patristic sources.

I doubted for a long time whether the primacy is essential to the Catholic Church. Indeed, I was inclined to deny it, because the organic union of all the parts in a single entity was, apparently, achieved in the

---

[20] Metropolitan Athenagoras, 'Tradition and Traditions', *St. Vladimir's Seminary Quarterly*, vii (1963) p. 112.

[21] H. Alivisatos, 'The Proposed Ecumenical Council and Reunion', loc. cit., p. 5.

[1] J. A. Möhler, *Die Einheit in der Kirche oder das Prinzip des Katholizismus dargestellt in Geiste der Kirchenväter der drei ersten Jahrhunderte* (Mainz, 1825).

[2] J. A. Möhler, *Symbolism, or exposition of the Doctrinal Differences between Catholics and Protestants, as evidenced by their symbolic writings* (London, 1843). Karl von Hase, however, says that Möhler in his *Symbolik*, originally published in 1832, sets forth a somewhat fantastic system of theology, *Handbook to the Controversy with Rome*, English translation by A. W. Streane (1906), I, p. 11, n. 2.

unity of the whole episcopate, as we demonstrated above. Again it is clear that the history of the first three centuries is not rich enough in documents, which could dissipate all our doubts in this respect. Nevertheless close examination of the Epistles of St. Peter and the study of history, as well as serious meditation on ecclesiastical organization, finally persuaded me to accept this idea.[3]

According to Möhler, ecclesiastical authority is necessary because human weakness needs the support of the Church as an institution. And though the Church's mystical life is above and beyond canon law, the weakening of it has led to a corresponding increase and development of canonical regulations and external forms of religious observance. The Papacy remains, therefore, as a necessary sign and living centre of the unity of the visible Church, for it is only through their unity with the Pope that the bishops and the faithful can comprehend and realize the unity of the Church as a whole.

Yet, Möhler also says,

incarnate love is both the essence of the Church's life and the inner substance of the ministry of every Bishop in his diocese. It finds expression in the interior movement of the faithful towards unity with their Bishop, and in his corresponding attitude to them, to establish and preserve them in purity and strength. The Church itself is a fellowship of reconciliation, between man and God, and between man and man, through the atoning work of Christ. And their love for Him unites them both with Him and with each other. This is the inner essence of the Catholic Church. And the episcopate, the institution of the Church, is the external manifestation of this essence, not the essence itself. It is necessary to insist always on this difference. The external unity of the episcopate is merely an emanation from this inner unity.[4]

This idea, which we can also find in the writings of Ignatius of Antioch, reflects the Orthodox point of view and constitutes the fundamental principle of a bishop's authority in the Orthodox Church.

The fact that you have a young bishop [says Ignatius] should not be a pretext for excessive familiarity. It is the power of God the Father which you must reverence to the full in him. Such, I know, is the way your holy presbyters believe. They have never taken advantage of his

---

[3] Möhler, *Die Einheit*, p. 171.
[4] ibid., p. 163.

obvious youth. Inspired by the wisdom of God himself, they are subject to their bishop, or rather not so much to him as to the Father of Jesus Christ, to the universal bishop. It is therefore out of respect for this God who loves us, that our obedience must be free from all pretence, for, if we deceive the bishop whom we see, it is to the bishop whom we do not see that we are trying to lie. In such cases it is not with the flesh that we are involved, but with God who knows the things that are hidden.[5]

This is the basis of the primatial authority in the Orthodox Church, which expresses 'the practical need of ecclesiastical life by the force of which the life was gradually centralized: first, in the metropolitans (from the third century), and then the patriarchates (from the fourth and fifth centuries), with the result that the authority of the Metropolitans and Patriarchs in their areas was continually and gradually strengthened in proportion to the assimilation of the people to Christian culture'.[6]

The following description of Church authority from an Orthodox point of view was given by Visser 't Hooft:

There is no authority apart from or outside the Church itself. No one can say 'L'Eglise, c'est moi'. No standard or authority can be invented which transcends the Church itself, for if there were such a standard, the Church would not be the infallible channel of divine life in the world. The authority of the Church is self-evident. The Church is the Church. It is a sign of lack of faith in the Church if one wants to go beyond this tautology.[7]

This conception was first elaborated by Khomyakov and later by Sergius Bulgakov,[8] and there are Orthodox theologians, especially in

[5] *Magnes.* 3; see also *Smyrn.* 8, 1.

[6] Metropolitan Antony of Kiev, *C.E.* v (1924), p. 25.

[7] Visser 't Hooft, op. cit. p. 100.

[8] 'Does Orthodoxy possess an outward authority of Dogmatic infallibility?' *C.E.* vii (1926), pp. 12–24. Fr. Bulgakov developed and systematized this idea in his book *The Orthodox Church* (London, 1935). Bulgakov's ideas are analysed by Reinhard Slenczka, *Ostkirche und Oekumene, Die Einheit der Kirche als dogmatischen Problem in der neueren ostkirchlichen Theologie* (Göttingen, 1962), pp. 149–170, 'Die Lehre von der Kirche bei Sergiy Bulgakov.' See also 'The Unity, disunity and reunion of the Church according to Khomyakov', ibid. pp. 61–73. Slenczka says that it is not certain that Möhler had any influence on Khomyakov's ecclesiology; ibid., p. 62.

the USA,[9] who share it and argue that the Orthodox Church does not claim to possess any infallible and permanent criterion of Faith or a special charisma of doctrine similar to papal infallibility. 'There are not, there cannot be, external organs or methods of testifying to the internal evidence of the Church', wrote Bulgakov.[10] But this is not fully in line with Orthodox tradition. For although indeed the whole Body of the Church is considered in Orthodoxy to be infallible, the supreme external authority in the Orthodox Church still lies in the Ecumenical Councils, 'whose ecumenicity must be recognized and witnessed by the conscience of the whole Church. In other words the decisive criterion of an Ecumenical Council is the recognition of its decrees by the whole Church, which is therefore in fact the sole authority in Orthodoxy.' (It would be more correct to say the final, rather than the sole, authority.) It is apparent that 'the Universal Church cannot err, inasmuch as it is governed by the Holy Spirit, which is a spirit of the truth.' One thing however is not clearly formulated in Orthodoxy. How can the whole Church approve or disapprove the decisions of the Ecumenical Councils? There is only one solution to this question. Approval means no protestations and no schisms. When the congregations show dissatisfaction the decision is not a universal one, and the Council does not express the faith of the Church. This idea, however, could call into question the decisions of the fourth Ecumenical Council, which were not accepted by a great part of Eastern Christendom. Yet 'the Ecumenical Council', writes Professor Bratsiotis, 'continues to be the supreme administrative authority in the Orthodox Church, but until it becomes possible for such a Council to assemble, the Church as a whole may and should be administered by extra, periodical general councils in which the whole Orthodox Church is represented.'[11] It is not only the supreme administrative authority, but also the doctrinal authority, as the Patriarchal and Synodal Encyclical of the Church of Constantinople, in the time of Anthimos VII, of August 1895 (in reference to the

[9] Cf. J. Meyendorff, *The Orthodox Church*, transl. from the French by John Chapin (Darton, Longman and Todd, London, 1962), p. 226.

[10] Bulgakov, *The Orthodox Church*, p. 89.

[11] P. Bratsiotis, 'The Fundamental Principles and main Characteristics of the Orthodox Church', *Orthodoxy. A Faith and Order Dialogue*. (Paper No. 30, World Council of Churches, Geneva, 1960), pp. 14, 15. Was it not the Councils which defined the Christian Doctrine?: 'all dogmatic questions are decided by the Councils alone'; cf. N. Glubokovsky, 'The Modern Papacy and the Reunion of the Orthodox East with the Roman Catholic West', *C.E.* v (1924), p. 125.

Encyclical Letter of Leo XIII of 20 June 1894) definitely stated: 'Seven Holy Ecumenical Councils being called together in the Holy Spirit for the explanation of the true teaching of the faith against the heretics, have universal and eternal significance in the Church of Christ'. The Ecumenical Councils, says the late Professor Glubokovsky, are for us Orthodox the only supreme authority in the Church. Their importance lies not only in their decisions but also in that they were invested with the authority of the whole of Christendom.

We can find an exposition of the Roman view of ecclesiastical authority in Möhler's other book, *Symbolik:*[12]

The episcopacy, the continuation of the Apostleship, is accordingly revered as a Divine institution: no less so, and even, on that very account, the Pope, who is the centre of unity, and the head of the episcopacy. If the episcopacy is to form a corporation, outwardly as well as inwardly bound together, in order to unite all believers into one harmonious life, which the Catholic Church so urgently requires, it stands in need of a centre, whereby all may be held together and firmly connected. . . . Without a visible head the whole view, which the Catholic Church takes of herself as a visible society representing the place of Christ, would have been lost, or rather, never would have occurred to her. In a visible Church, a visible head is necessarily included.

This idea of Church authority, which is a moderate one, could not be completely rejected from an Orthodox point of view. Such an idea, which is the synthesis of the conceptions of the Church held by Khomyakov and Möhler, had been expressed by a prominent Orthodox prelate, the late Metropolitan of Kiev, Antony Khrapovitsky, when he said:

We admit for the future the conception of a single personal supremacy in the Church in consonance with the broadest preservation of the conciliar principle, and on the condition that the supremacy does not pretend to be based on such invented traditions as the above [the Apostle Peter as chief over all the Apostles, the succession of the Popes to the

---

[12] Möhler, *Symbolism*, Vol. ii, pp. 73 ff. This is based upon the St. Thomas's formula (*Summa Theol.*) according to which the unity of the Church is brought about not only through association of the Church's members among themselves, but also through the subordination of all members to the one Head, Christ, whose exclusive Vicarius is the Pope; cf. Anton Weiler, 'Church Authority and Government in the Middle Ages; A Bibliographical Survey', *C.* VII (1965), p. 66.

fulness of his pretended authority etc.] but only on the practical need of ecclesiastical life.[13]

It should be emphasized that Rome does teach that the authority of the Church is limited (and with this Orthodox and Anglicans agree), in that the Church is not invested with any authority to reveal or to decree new doctrines which are not to be found in the Holy Scriptures and the Apostolic tradition. Romans would argue, however, following Cardinal Newman's *Essay on the Development of Christian Doctrine*,[14] that there are no *new* dogmas, but rather the proclamation or formulation as the official teaching of the Church of doctrines which have hitherto lain hidden but implicit in the Scriptures and the life of the Church. Yet Anglicans and Orthodox would dispute not the *general* truth of this argument—which applies, of course, to the decisions of the Ecumenical Councils—but of the particular dogmas proclaimed in recent years by Rome on the strength of the argument. For, as Bicknell wrote, 'we claim to test the development of Roman doctrine and see whether it is healthy and whether indeed from its nature it is not inconsistent with the Christian faith.'[15] Furthermore, if, as the Orthodox would argue, it is the whole Church that guarantees the right formulation of Christian dogmas, then those proclaimed by Rome alone are not *prima facie* authoritative for the whole Church, least of all for those Orthodox or Anglicans who took no part in the deliberations which led to their proclamation. On the contrary, precisely because they were proclaimed by Rome alone, they are liable to be erroneous.

A new examination of the primacy in the Church would not result in the universal acceptance of the Roman primacy on Roman terms, but would possibly bridge the differences between the three Churches. The crucial point is the proclamation by the Roman Church that the Pope has ordinary, immediate, and truly episcopal jurisdiction over the whole Church without any restrictions or limitations. As opposed to this, the Orthodox hold that all the bishops of the Church are equal to each other and participate in the Ecumenical Council by virtue of their personal authority received at their consecration, together

---

[13] *C.E.* v (1924), p. 25; cf. also p. 124; cf. also *Church Times*, 28 Dec. 1923.

[14] Published in 1845 almost immediately after his reception into the Roman Church.

[15] Bicknell, op. cit. p. 258. Cf. Gore, *Roman Catholic Claims* (10th ed., 1909), p. 39.

constituting the supreme authority of the Church. We Orthodox cannot imagine an Ecumenical Council in which a Pope sits on a throne, separate from the other bishops. And for us the words of St. Gregory the Great show a spirit alien to the Christian truth when he said, 'My honour is the honour of the Universal Church. My honour is the strength and unity of my brethren. I am truly honoured when the honour due to every individual amongst them is not withheld.'[16] In this respect Dr. Visser 't Hooft is right in saying that in the Orthodox Church no one can say 'I am the Church', because it is the episcopate as a whole which represents the Church.

In the Anglican Church authoritative doctrinal teaching is that which commands the respect and assent of Anglicans. In other words there is a continuing search for the truth and its interpretation, within certain broadly-defined limits, rather than the categorical statement of dogma laid down by an infallible authority. Anglicans revere Scripture and tradition, the decisions of Councils and the writings of the Fathers. But they are also freer, and readier, than Romans or Orthodox, to re-interpret the past in order to explain their faith to their contemporaries; and although this may at times lay them open to the charge of holding a limited, or one-sided, or 'watered-down' doctrinal position, their freedom makes possible both the recovery of insights or emphases that have been lost or distorted, and also, over the whole spectrum of Anglicanism, a variety of doctrinal interpretation which can enrich a Church which believes it would be diminished by a too rigid uniformity.

On the specific question of Ecumenical Councils, F. W. Puller wrote that 'the great Divines of the Church of England have been accustomed to teach that their dogmatic decisions are irreformable, that is to say, incapable of being altered in substance.'[17] Bishop E. C. S. Gibson stated plainly that 'when decisions win their way to universal acceptance, there we have the needful guarantee that the Council has faithfully reflected the mind of the Universal Church, and we may well be content to believe that the Council has not erred. But the inerrancy of a Council can never be guaranteed at the moment. The test of the value of a Council is its after-reception by the Church.'[18]

---

[16] Migne, *P.L.* lxxvii, 933; cf. Gasparri, *Catechism*, p. 302.

[17] F. W. Puller, *The Continuity of the Church of England* (3rd ed., 1913), pp. 29–30.

[18] Cf. also Forbes, *On the Articles* (3rd ed., 1878), p. 299, cited in Puller, op. cit., p. 30, n. 1.

In spite of the freedom prevailing in the Anglican Church it nevertheless shows the religious genius and the courage, the patience and the self-discipline, 'to accept the demands of our faith, not because we are told we must do so, but because we believe such things to be true. Here is the true genius of Anglicanism and it is very precious.'[19]

By contrast, totalitarian authority and ecclesiastical infallibility are both alien to Anglicanism, which attributes infallibility to God alone, and not to his Church.[20] It would be wrong, however, to describe the Anglican Church as without authority of any kind. 'To affix such a label can be profoundly misleading', writes Dewi Morgan.[21] For freedom, as well as authority, is the aim of this Church. In this respect Anglicanism resembles Orthodoxy in distinguishing between those things which are necessary to salvation and those things which are peculiar to the particular Churches. This is the principle of St. Augustine and the Patriarch Photius. And contemporary Anglican theologians still claim that basically they follow the teaching of the undivided Church 'as it was given to the Apostles and worked out by the Fathers.'[22]

During the 1930 Lambeth Conference the Orthodox delegates asked the Anglicans to declare where, in any matter, the highest authority of the Church lay. The answer was that 'this Anglican Communion is a commonwealth of Churches without a central constitution. It is a federation without a federal government. It has come into existence without a deliberate federal policy. They [the Churches] are, in the idiom of our Fathers, particular or National Churches, and they repudiate any idea of a central authority other than a Council of Bishops.'[23] It is true nevertheless, as Bishop Ellison says, that the Lambeth Conferences carry immense weight not only for Anglicans but for many outside the Anglican Communion. They do so because their decisions are reached freely and are commended to the good-will of Christians by the volume of prayer, scholarship, and experience upon which they are built. The Lambeth Conference typifies the spirit of Anglicanism, its theory of authority and its method of working.[24] Anglicans, however, in no way regard the Lambeth Conference as an Ecumenical Council.

[19] Ellison, *The Anglican Communion*, p. 84.
[20] W. Temple, *Essays in Christian Politics* (1927), p. 205.
[21] D. Morgan, *Agenda for Anglicans*, p. 15.
[22] J. Moorman, op. cit., p. 31.
[23] Lambeth Conference 1930, *Report*, pp. 28, 29.
[24] Ellison, *The Anglican Communion*, pp. 83–4.

The Orthodox Church gives great emphasis to the local Church, because it is the manifestation of the whole Church. Every bishop in the Orthodox Church is equivalent to the Pope. As the nature of the Church is sacramental, the local Churches form one community, which is the mystical body whose head is Christ. The bishop is the 'ikon' of Christ, but Christ is always the one and only Lord. The bishop of a local Church is a bishop of the Catholic Church and every local Church is not merely a part of the whole Catholic Church but is in itself *the* Catholic Church, because it is in communion with all the other local Churches. In order to understand the authority of the local Churches in Orthodoxy we must identify them with the Christian communities of the primitive Church. Fr. Congar says correctly that 'the Orthodox Church maintains the ancient liturgies, in which the unity of the bishop with his community is expressed. There we cannot find "I" distinct from "we", because the celebrant, either bishop or priest, speaks in the name of all.' The Orthodox Church honours not only St. Ignatius of Antioch who was an Easterner, but also St. Cyprian who was a Westerner and who said: 'The Church is the people united to its pontiff and the flock abiding with its shepherd. This will make you see that the bishop is in the Church and the Church is the bishop.'[25]

In the Second Vatican Council there was an attempt made by several Conciliar Fathers to restore the authority of the local Church, which had been ignored by the theory of the Roman Primacy. Orthodox and Anglicans feel a degree of satisfaction at seeing in the Roman Church the restoration of the importance of the local Church which in the past was common to all. 'Our statement,' says the Auxiliary Bishop of Fulda, Edward Schick,[26] 'would lack a fundamental aspect if it did not consider the Church in the full sense, that is the Universal Church represented by local Churches. The local Church is not a certain administrative "division" of the Church, but it is a true representation and manifestation of the Universal Church.'

Möhler gives the following definition of the infallibility of the Church:

The dogmatic decrees of the episcopacy are infallible; for it represents the Universal Church, and one doctrine of faith, falsely explained by it, would render the whole a prey to error. Hence, as the institution which Christ hath established for the preservation and the explanation of His

[25] 'The historical development of authority in the Church', *P.A.* pp. 125, 126.
[26] *Council Speeches of Vatican II*, pp. 22–24.

doctrines is subject in this its function to no error; so the organ, through which the Church speaks, is also exempt from error.[27]

But the First Vatican Council subsequently invested the Pope of Rome with infallibility, when he speaks *ex cathedra*. This is of course a figurative expression, because this infallibility is limited to what the Pope, after careful weighing and deliberation, lays down with regard to faith and morals. In this case he has always to summon the high dignitaries of the Church and the learned theologians as advisers and use all human methods in order to decide on important questions. In this spirit it can be argued that the Pope is infallible because he is expressing the infallibility of the Church, not a personal infallibility. There were Popes who were not only fallible, but even heretics. The attempts by Roman Catholics to explain away the heretical letters of Honorius are based on the argument that the Pope is infallible only when he proclaims *ex cathedra*, as a teacher. Von Hase, a German Protestant, says: 'The Pope does not first, like the Delphic priestess on the tripod, seat himself on the chair of St. Peter, if he desires to pronounce his decisions with the highest authority.' Of course the Roman teaching stresses other principles, e.g. that the infallibility of the Pope was instituted by Christ in the words of St. Peter: 'I made supplication for thee, that thy faith fail not: and do thou, when once thou hast turned again, stablish thy brethren' (Luke 22:32).[28]

Some Orthodox theologians have asserted that the Church is infallible because it contains the truth and not because it expresses the truth correctly, and they define the Church in terms which are applicable only to the Church triumphant in heaven and not to the Church militant, thus disregarding its institutional and juridical realities. This is most marked in the writings of Khomyakov, who defines the Church only by the inward grace of the Holy Spirit, because he 'will not have it in any way whatever subjected to an earthly or institutional law.'[29] Yet these Orthodox should acknowledge

[27] Möhler, *Symbolism*, Vol. ii, pp. 77–78.

[28] K. von Hase, op. cit., i, p. 253.

[29] Congar, *Divided Christendom* (London, 1939) p. 217. This is acknowledged by Florovsky who says that the common interpretation of Möhler and Khomyakov leads to the 'overemphasis of the pneumatological aspect of the Church.' Cf. R. Slenczka, op. cit., p. 121. Slenczka's book is of paramount importance since it is written by a person who appears to know the Slavonic and Greek theological and Church literature. He gives the most authoritative exposition of the true Orthodox conception of the Church of any theologian of the last hundred years.

that 'so long as we are in our pilgrimage and sinners we are subject to the regime of the Church militant, terrestrial and institutional.'[30] They acknowledge, too, that, as the late Archbishop of Athens, Chrysostom, declared: 'the fact that the Church is the instrument through which the faithful are to attain salvation implies directly the visibility of the Church. If the Church is to be a fellowship of human beings, it must of necessity be a visible fellowship; it can have no existence as a community unless it has external marks by which it can be recognized.'[31] Another Orthodox prelate, Stephan, the late Archbishop of Sofia, emphasized the institutional aspect of the Church, when he wrote that

the whole Church of Christ, which comprises all the separate Churches, is subject to all the bishops, while the centre of the spiritual power of the Church is the Ecumenical Councils. . . . These Councils were the supreme authority in matters of faith, and all separate Churches, pastors, and believers were required to obey them. At these Councils, representatives of the separate Churches were always bishops or their deputies. This superior court, in uniting all the bishops who were subject to it in respect to ecclesiastical teaching, ministry and government, preserves the unity of the universal Church of Christ, with Christ as its only Head, and it also preserves the religious doctrine expressed in the inviolable Apostles' Creed.[32]

Between Rome and Orthodoxy there does exist something which could be described as a bridge. For if the Romans would proclaim with greater emphasis that the Church is the manifestation of the Holy Spirit, the mystical body of Christ, the fellowship of mutual love in the communion of the Holy Spirit, and if the Orthodox would realize that the Church is not only the divine life, but the institution which maintains, proclaims, and sets forth the heavenly reality, then there could be agreement. In other words Orthodox theology should be more human and ecclesiological and Roman theology more spiritual. The authority of the Church could then be described as the co-operation of the divine and human elements. In fact these two Churches over-emphasize one of the two aspects of the Church. The Orthodox

[30] Congar, ibid.
[31] 'The Nature of the Church', by Chrysostom, Metropolitan of Athens, *C.E.* viii (1927), p. 141.
[32] 'Fundamental Conditions for the unification of the Christian Churches,' by Stephan, Archbishop of Sofia, *C.E.* viii (1927), pp. 136, 137, 138.

give more stress to the pneumatology of the Church whereas the Romans overstress the institutional structure of the Church. They appear to represent two different worlds. They are in fact complementary.

7. The Government of the Church

In order to discuss the administration of the Roman Church we must understand its fundamental theory concerning the unity of the Church under the successor of Peter as the Vicar of Christ, the head of the Church who is *ex cathedra* infallible. The theory however does not correspond to the facts.

St. Irenaeus spoke of the Roman Church with great affection[1] because of its greatness, its antiquity, its foundation by the Apostles Peter and Paul, and above all because it represented Christendom in miniature. Speaking on the testimony of tradition Irenaeus says that the identity of oral tradition with the original revelation is guaranteed by the unbroken succession of bishops in the great sees (not only the Roman see) going back lineally to the apostles.[2] Moreover Irenaeus has a further testimony that the Church is the home of the Holy Spirit, and all the bishops of the Church are in his view spirit-endowed men who have been given 'an infallible charisma of truth'.[3] However such expressions as 'presidency of love' (Ignatius), the 'more powerful principality' founded on Peter and Paul (Irenaeus), and 'principal Church' (Cyprian) do not exactly correspond to the understanding of the Petrine succession as this was probably held in Rome itself.[4]

To begin with it must be admitted that in effect it is not the Pope who governs the Church, but the Roman Curia. This is the collective term for all the ecclesiastical offices through which the Pope, endowed with the *plenitudo potestatis* (the plenitude of the power of his primacy) governs the Church. The Roman Curia is a product of historical development, of which the main characteristic is a gradual centralization. This, however, does not mean that the Pope had not this plenitude of power from the beginning of the Church; as successor of Peter and the Vicar of Christ on earth he possessed it, according to

[1] *Haer.* 3. 3, 2.

[2] *Haer.* 3 ff.

[3] 'cum episcopatus successione charisma veritatis certum secundum placitum Patris acceperunt', *Haer.* 3. 24. 1 and 4 ff.

[4] H. Marot, O.S.B. 'The Primacy and the decentralization of the Early Church', *C.* vii (1965) p. 10; cf. J. McCue, 'Roman Primacy and development of Dogma,' in *Theological Studies* xxv (1964), pp. 161–196.

Roman teaching, from the beginning. During the first centuries the Popes interfered only in special circumstances in the administration of the Church. They 'gave only at the request of the bishops the decisions out of which the rules of Canon Law later developed, but, in our days the power of the bishops became limited by this process, so that matters by nature of particular importance and moment came by right of law under the jurisdiction and the active and permanent control of the central papal power'.[5] At the beginning the Pope himself chose his assistants, but as time passed the Curia became responsible for finding the persons who should undertake various offices.

Sacramentally, the Pope is a bishop, a member of the episcopal order. In dignity, as bishop of an important see, Rome, he is archbishop and metropolitan of that province, and primate or chief metropolitan of that country, Italy. He may also be considered as Patriarch of the West, which has only one patriarchal see, Rome, in contrast to the four Eastern Patriarchates. But none of these things gives the Pope the unique position which he now occupies. It is as an administrator that the Pope stands above all other prelates and church officers in a way that no other bishop does. The Roman Curia with its congregations, tribunals, and offices (nineteen in all) forms the structure of the central government of the Roman Catholic Church. The Curia together with the Pope constitutes what the *Corpus Juris Canonici* calls the Holy See.[6]

While the Roman Church is monarchical and authoritarian, the structure of the Orthodox Church is hierarchical and conciliar. The Orthodox Church admits that each particular Church, in both the East and the West, is self-governing, and that they were so in the time of the undivided Church. Neither the Bishop of Rome nor the Bishop of Constantinople has the right to interfere outside his own proper jurisdiction. On important questions which need the sanction of the Universal Church an appeal should be made to an Ecumenical Council, which alone is the supreme tribunal. The bishops are independent of each other, and each entirely free within his own bounds, obeying only the synodal decrees, sitting as equals in synods. None of them can claim monarchical rights over the universal Church. St. Cyprian said: 'For we desire not to use compulsion towards anyone or to lay down a law, since each bishop possesses his own liberty in

---

[5] H. Scharp, *How the Catholic Church is governed* (Nelson, 1960), p. 16.

[6] For a good description of how the Roman Curia operates see Peter Canisius van Lierde, *The Holy See at Work; How the Catholic Church is governed*, transl. by James Tucek (Robert Hale, London, 1963), pp. 44–162.

the government of the Church, and is accountable for his actions only to the Lord.' The Orthodox Church maintains the appearance of the primitive Church which was a vast diffusion of local congregations, each leading its separate life, having its own constitutional structure and officers, and each called a Church. Those who held this view of the Church were deeply conscious that each of the communities constituted the universal Church, under the leadership of Christ.[7] This is apparent at the time of the martyrdom of Polycarp of Smyrna, when his Church sent letters to all communities composing the Holy Catholic Church. Dionysius, Bishop of Corinth, an outstanding writer of the second century,[8] corresponded with the Romans, the Lacedaemonians, the Athenians, the Nicomedians, with the Church sojourning in Amastris, together with the Churches in Pontus. He wrote also to Cnossus (Crete). These letters of Dionysius of Corinth were held in universal esteem, not because the Church of Corinth was founded by St. Paul and St. Peter and others among the apostles,[9] but because Dionysius expressed the Christian spirit of mutual love in the fellowship of the Holy Ghost. According to Ignatius of Antioch the Roman Church was among the multiplicity of local bodies making up the Catholic Church: Rome 'has the primacy in the place of the region of the Romans' and moreover 'a primacy of love', which by no means implies jurisdiction over the Church Universal.[10]

In the decisions of the second and third Ecumenical Councils the government of the whole Church was defined in terms of the Bishop of Rome, the Bishop of Constantinople, the Pope of Alexandria, the Bishop of Antioch, the President of the Church of Cyprus, and the Bishop of Jerusalem. Rome recognizes the three so-called Petrine sees, Rome, Alexandria, and Antioch, as 'units' in the strict sense of the word. 'The Popes had certain reservations about the claims of Constantinople and Jerusalem because these were based on the law laid down by the Council of Chalcedon . . . but in practice, the Popes recognized the Patriarchates of Constantinople and Jerusalem, albeit

[7] Ignatius, *Eph.* 17. 1.

[8] 170 A.D., Eusebius, *Hist. eccl.* 4. 23.

[9] M. Fouyas, 'The Cephas party in the Church of Corinth.' A paper delivered at the Third [Oxford] International Congress on New Testament Studies (Manchester, 1965), pp. 3–4.

[10] Ignatius, *Rom.* (inscr.); cf. J. N. D. Kelly, *Early Christian Doctrines*, p. 191. Some have translated the expression 'primacy of love' rather forcedly, writes Kelly, as meaning 'presiding over the love-community', i.e. over the Universal Church.

reluctantly.'[11] The Popes do not, however, recognize a pentarchy of the five Patriarchs, as it is accepted in the East. According to Theodore of Studios the five Patriarchs are in a very special way the successors of the apostles. The Bishop of Rome occupies the first see, the second place belongs to Constantinople and then follow the Patriarchs of Alexandria, Antioch, and Jerusalem. Since the schism between East and West the Patriarch of Constantinople has been regarded in the East as having inherited the Roman Primacy. This is why the Orthodox are always ready to restore the Roman primacy, provided Orthodoxy be restored in Rome. 'These are the five peaks of the Church authority, and it is their judgement which must decide on divine dogmas.'[12]

In the course of time the Bishop of Rome became the sole leader of Christianity in the West, whereas in the East by the expansion of Christianity more new local Churches were founded, which either by Councils or by the Bishop of Constantinople (by virtue of his right as being the bishop of the Mother Church in the East) were proclaimed independent but united to one another in faith. Although they are divided administratively for practical reasons they really form one Church, the Orthodox Catholic Church. As in the West the Pope convenes Western councils, so in the East the Patriarch of Constantinople convokes the Pan-Orthodox Councils and presides personally or by representatives. The difference between the Patriarch and the Pope is this: practically and theoretically the Patriarch must, before deciding to convoke a Council, obtain the agreement of the local Churches, whereas the Pope in principle has the right to summon a Council without any previous agreement with the Roman officials, although in practice he always does obtain prior agreement with the most important departments of the Church. The decisions of these Councils are binding on the Patriarch, but who can deny that at times the same kind of things happen in the East as happen under the Pope? In both the East and the West, the first bishop always has the chance to impose his will. The Patriarch of Constantinople, who officially is the Archbishop of Constantinople, and Ecumenical Patriarch, is the head of the Orthodox Catholic Church and is recognized as such by the Anglican Church, the Monophysite Churches and the Old Catholic Church. Recently, His Holiness Pope Paul VI in his official correspondence with Patriarch Athenagoras I used the title of 'Ecumenical

[11] W. de Vries, S. J., 'The College of Patriarchs', C. viii (1965) p. 35.
[12] W. de Vries, ibid. p. 39.

Patriarch of Constantinople,' which implies recognition of his prerogatives. It is to be hoped that this is not just a technical or courteous expression by the Pope, for the Ecumenical Patriarch accepts Pope Paul as his senior brother in Christ.

The whole Orthodox Church is linked with the Great Church of Constantinople, not because Constantinople is the centre of the Orthodox Church *jure divino*, but because it had enlarged Christendom by the conversion of north-east Europe. When these new Churches were able to look after their own affairs and became self-contained, the Mother Church offered them their freedom and they became *autocephalous*, with heads who are metropolitans or archbishops or Patriarchs. Unity in faith rather than unity in organization is the ultimate bond uniting the Orthodox Churches. The Church of Constantinople, without a centralized control, and despite the varied nationalities, languages, and customs of its adherents, has achieved a splendid uniformity in liturgical, devotional, and canonical forms. Every local Church, by virtue of the decisions of the Universal Councils, can have its own constitution and administrative system. All Orthodox Churches maintain the conciliar or synodical system of government, which is based on the example of the first Council of Jerusalem held by the apostles and has developed from that pattern. 'Hence this ecclesiastical tradition presents itself as the continuation and extension of the Apostolic Tradition.'[13] The provincial council, which was well established and formally organized by the fourth century, is an institution which has lasted up to our own time in the shape of the annual synods of the Patriarchates and the Autocephalous Churches in the East. Apart from the Provincial Synods, history shows two other kinds of synod: councils, described as *topical*, whose canonical legislation came to be accepted equally in the East and in the West, and the synods of the Great Patriarchates, the privileges of which had been clearly fixed by the four Ecumenical Councils. These Patriarchates are Rome, Constantinople, Alexandria, Antioch and Jerusalem. This kind of administration remained the most representative and lasting form of the collegial structure of the Eastern Hierarchy.[14]

Let us come back once again to the Roman Church. Until the twelfth century the cardinals were those who shared, with the Roman Councils, authority in the Church. The Councils, however, were summoned only once a year on the anniversary of the Pope's coronation, and

---

[13] J. Hajjar, 'The Synod in the Eastern Church', *C*. viii (1965) pp. 30–34.
[14] J. Hajjar, ibid. pp. 31, 32.

because it was necessary to decide on urgent problems between Councils, the cardinals (who resided permanently in Rome)[15] greatly increased their power. Until the twelfth century all the cardinals were Italians. Since then the constitution of the College of Cardinals has been changed by the elevation of non-Italians, but until now the Italian cardinals have always been in the majority, and although the Council of Trent decided that cardinals should be chosen from the entire Catholic world, since the end of the fourteenth century, with one exception, an Italian cardinal has regularly been elected Pope. So the decrees of the Council of Trent, which sought to universalize the supreme senate of the Church, have been ignored. The number of cardinals in the Roman Church traditionally reached seventy, modelled on the seventy elders who were the counsellors of Moses, while in the East the number of bishops in the synods has usually been twelve after the model of the twelve apostles of our Lord. Today the number of cardinals has been increased and the number seventy is apparently no longer significant. In the East the number of the members of the synods of the Orthodox Churches also varies, with the exception of the Ecumenical Patriarchate and the Church of Greece, which have permanent synods made up of twelve members and the president, who is always the Primate of the Autocephalous Church. As the members of the College of Cardinals form commissions to set up offices and authorities to deal with special business, so do the members of the local councils in the Orthodox Church. In the Roman Church ever since Sixtus V, who increased the number of the cardinals, there has been a long and hard struggle which has been decided in favour of the Pope and of the monarchical system; and this has decisively determined the form and position which the College of Cardinals has today.[16]

During the Second Vatican Council many hopes were raised that an international synod of bishops would be established in Rome, to govern the Roman Church together with the Pope. At the beginning of the fourth session of the Council the Pope announced his decision to establish this international synod for consultation and collaboration in matters of central government. The Pope told the Council Fathers

[15] The Latin word *cardinalis* is an adjective derived from the noun *cardo*, meaning the hinge of a door. It was used in the Church in very early times, but it was Pope Pius V, in the year 1567, who forbade the use of the title *cardinal* everywhere except in Rome; cf. H. Scharp, op. cit., p. 20 ff; cf. also P. C. Van Lierde, op. cit., pp. 39 ff.

[16] For this whole subject see Van Lierde, *The Holy See at Work*, cited in note 6 of this section, p. 151.

that he intended by this move to give them further proof of his confidence and brotherly esteem. He carefully drew attention to the point that his announcement had been in accordance with the wishes of the Council. Furthermore he avoided any suggestion that this body of bishops would be aimed against the power of the Roman Curia, but he showed his awareness of what was uppermost in the minds of the supporters of an episcopal senate when he added that 'in a special way' it could be of use in the Roman Curia's day-to-day work. In the minds of many observers, this decision of the Pope was regarded as an abandonment of the Roman monarchical system and its replacement by a democratic and more conciliar administrative system. In fact, however, despite what the Pope said about this Council, the real result will be to strengthen the Pope's own hand. At times when the Curia is proving obstructive or slow, he will be able to call in the bishops to redress the balance. The most important point about this innovation in the administrative system is that the episcopal synod (composed of bishops to be chosen largely by the episcopal conferences) must be approved by the Pope, and is convened by him for consultation and collaboration, when this seems opportune.

This synod may be described as a central ecclesiastical organization representing the entire Roman Catholic episcopate. The principal features of it follow these lines: I. Its function is to provide advice and counsel. It may be given deliberative power in special circumstances by the Pope. It assures authentic information at the centre of the Church, and facilitates agreement in dogmatic essentials and procedures. II. Its special ends are to provide mutual information and advice. The synod is directly responsible to the Pope, who convokes it when he deems it opportune, names the place of meeting, confirms the election of members, determines matters for discussion, and sends out the necessary documents for study. The Pope presides either in person or through a representative. III. The synod can be convoked in three ways, but when convoked in ordinary session its members are: (a) patriarchs, major archbishops and metropolitans; (b) bishops chosen by national and international conferences of bishops; (c) members of religious orders elected by the Roman Council of Superiors General; (d) cardinals in charge of various organs of the Roman Curia.

The rules are not fully detailed, since several questions remain unanswered. What are to be the relations of the synod to the Roman Curia? It was said that the Senate (Lower House) will help to prevent clashes between the existing curial congregations and the post-Conciliar institutions which will be set up to interpret and codify the Council's decrees. According to people who observe the business of the Vatican the establishment of the Senate, in which the world's bishops and the heads of the Curia will both be represented, provides a clearing-house where divisions of opinion will be bridged and decisions taken. One thing which will be incompatible with non-Catholic and especially Orthodox practice is that the organization will be two-chambered, the Senate being the Lower House and the College of the Cardinals the Upper. The crucial point is that the cardinals will continue to be regarded as the governing body of the Church. It is not without significance that the pro-curial Italian press interpreting the *motu proprio* think that the Senate will be the servant of the Curia, as well as of the Pope.[17]

On 15 August 1967, Pope Paul by his statement 'Regimini Ecclesiae Universalis'[18] announced the re-organization of the Roman Curia. Yet this Apostolic Constitution leaves the Roman Curia with its power as before. The Pope acted with restraint, without offending those in charge, without provoking resistance in the Roman offices. There was no change at all in the structure of the Roman Curia. It is a simple re-organization of the central administration of the Roman Church, which still remains in the hands of the Curia.

In an interesting article by Fr. Gregory Baum, O.S.A., we see that

it will take many years before the Catholic Church will enter fully into a collegial way of government. It will be a slow progress. It will eventually lead to a new interpretation of Papal primacy, one which insists above all on the Pope's supreme authority to moderate a collegial episcopate. Already Pope Paul has repeatedly referred to himself as 'Moderator'. While the process of acquiring a more collegial form of government will be slow, it will be faster than many people think.[19]

From an Anglican point of view, the Archbishop of Canterbury, Dr. Ramsey, has said:

Anglicans welcome very greatly the emphasis put recently by the Vatican Council upon the collegiality of bishops to balance the particular position of the Pope himself. That is a development, not an alteration of

---

[17] *Catholic Herald*, 24 Sept. 1965. (By kind permission of the Editor.)
[18] *Osservatore Romano*, 19 Aug. 1967.
[19] *Catholic Herald*, 1 Oct. 1965.

doctrine, which may help us to find ourselves nearer to each other. It is no use planning for final goals unless meanwhile we get on with these matters which affect practical attitudes and co-operation, which is a thing that can begin already.[20]

The setting-up of this episcopal senate affects, it would seem, the Pope's relationship with the Roman Catholic episcopate, but this is a purely Roman matter. How has the Council affected the relation of the Pope and the whole Roman Church with other bodies of Christians? For this we must look at another of the Council's decrees, that on Ecumenism. This decree does not treat the Eastern Churches directly. The commentators on it say, for example:

In the Western Church, as a rule, jurisdiction is formally conferred by the Pope. But this is not essential in all places and under all circumstances. Jurisdiction may also be conferred through legitimate right of custom which has not been specifically revoked, or through some other sort of ecclesiastical privilege. Such was the case in the first centuries of Christianity, and still is even today in the Catholic Eastern Churches, as is expressly stated in Article 9 of the decree concerning these Churches. This helps provide a solution to the difficult problems of the jurisdiction of Eastern bishops who are not in full communion with the Apostolic Roman See.[21]

This Article does not provide a solution to the problem of Church government in the event of a union between Rome and the Eastern Churches. It is, however, the beginning of a recognition of Eastern facts. Another voice confirming the idea that the Eastern hierarchical structure will be maintained in a united Christian Church comes from Germany, from Cardinal Döpfner, Archbishop of Munich. He said, as reported in *The Tablet* of London, that

the patriarchal structure of the Eastern Churches in communion with Rome was described as a stimulating exemplar for the whole Church, but this did not mean that the patriarchal structure should be introduced into the Latin Church now, although it could provide many, perhaps as yet unsuspected, possibilities for future development. For the present the bishops' conferences, whose role has been so stressed by the Council, offered the starting point for an autonomy similar to that which existed in the patriarchal structure with its strong emphasis on

[20] ibid., 17 Sept. 1965.
[21] Jaeger, *A Stand on Ecumenism*, pp. 193–4.

collegiality. A fundamental conviction of Vatican II was that national peculiarities together with the desirability of independence and responsibility for individual ecclesiastical areas, demands a relaxation of an all too rigid centralization.[22]

There are some Orthodox who think that episcopal collegiality will make the Pope's position more acceptable to the Orthodox mind, and unity between Orthodox and Romans much more realistic than it appears today.[23]

The administrative system of the Anglican Churches could in general terms be regarded as similar to the Orthodox one. The Archbishop of Canterbury is the Primate of all England and the *primus inter pares* among the bishops of the Anglican Communion, which is made up of a number of independent Churches covering almost the whole world. As in the Orthodox Church, the methods of selecting bishops vary. What links the members of the Anglican Communion is the same as in the Orthodox Churches: it is the one faith. This bond has been given more precise expression in what has come to be known as the 'Lambeth Quadrilateral'—so called because the Lambeth Conference of 1888 put forward four points which they believed could be the basis for the unity of all Christian people.[24] Like the government of the Orthodox Churches, the government of the Anglican Communion, as a whole and in its several parts, can appear to be as variable and unpredictable as some of its ceremonial worship. But, broadly speaking, the Anglican administrative system is conciliar. There is a strong tradition of freedom and representation in Church affairs and in most areas the laity play a considerable part in its councils.

In considering the Anglican Communion a distinction must be drawn between the Church of England in the strict sense and the other Anglican Churches. Historically the origin of both is the two provinces of Canterbury (which for centuries included Wales) and York, and it is these two which (without Wales) now comprise the Church of England. This is the Established Church, having a legal status and relationship to the English Crown; for the Sovereign must be a member of it, is its titular head, and is crowned by the Archbishop of

---

[22] *The Tablet*, 5 Feb. 1966, pp. 171–2.

[23] Such was the opinion of Professor H. Alivizatos, *To Vima* (Athens), 9 and 11 Jan., 1966.

[24] These were: (i) the Scriptures; (ii) the Apostles' and Nicene Creeds; (iii) the two 'dominical' sacraments of Baptism and the Eucharist; (iv) the historic episcopate.

Canterbury. It is also related to Parliament, which has ultimate control over the status of the Church and Church bodies, down to the individual parish, as legal corporations. While the Church receives no subsidy from state funds, its right to hold endowments and other property is thus guaranteed. The appointment of bishops of the Established Church, of deans of cathedrals, and of certain parish priests where the patronage belongs to the Crown, is in the power of the state. Parliament, however, delegated nearly all its legislative functions affecting the Church to the former Church Assembly, set up in 1921, and replaced from 1970 by the General Synod. To this extent control of the Church is synodical; the General Synod includes the diocesan bishops, representative clergy, and lay people. In each diocese there is a Diocesan Synod, comprising clergy and lay people under the presidency of the bishop. A feature of the Established Church of England, not shared by the rest of the Anglican Communion, is that every incumbent or parish priest enjoys the so-called 'parson's freehold', which means that he is not appointed by the laity and cannot be removed from office except, in very rare cases, for misconduct. He is obliged to consult with representatives of the laity in a parochial church council, but they have no power over him, and he is therefore in a position to take an independent stand in matters concerning his ministry, subject to the canon law of the Church.

The other Churches of the Anglican Communion comprise the episcopal Churches in Scotland, Ireland, and Wales (since 1912 detached from the Province of Canterbury) and the principal English-speaking countries, the U.S.A., Canada, Australia, and New Zealand, together with the local Anglican Churches in regions of Africa, the Middle East, the Indian sub-continent, South East Asia, Japan, and elsewhere. All these Churches are entirely independent of the civil power and are self-governing through their synods or other assemblies, except for a few dioceses not yet grouped in any province but related directly to the Archbishop of Canterbury. These other Anglican provinces and national Churches are, in Orthodox terms, 'autocephalous', and their government is 'conciliar' or 'synodical', not by delegation from the state, but by the association of bishops together in council, and the joining with them of representatives of the clergy and, usually, the laity. The powers possessed by the clergy and laity are often quite considerable, but in matters of doctrine and Church order certain vital subjects may be reserved to the bishops. Bishops are generally chosen by some form of election involving the episcopate, the clergy, and the consent of the laity. Parish priests may be chosen by various methods, and when appointed do not possess any 'freehold' as in the Established Church. In so far as the laity have influence in the appointment and pay of their parish clergy, in areas where the Church is rooted in the local community, lay opinion may count for much. In areas which are missionary in character, the clergy will be more dependent on the bishop or on the diocese as a whole.

The Lambeth Conference is summoned every ten years at the invitation of the Archbishop of Canterbury. It is an episcopal conference, only bishops being members, and every diocesan bishop in the Anglican Communion is invited. On some occasions it has been limited to diocesan bishops, but in 1968 suffragan and assistant bishops (of whom there are a considerable number in some Anglican Churches, especially where dioceses are large and populous) were also invited. In 1968, following the example of the Second Vatican Council, observers from non-Anglican Churches attended by invitation and there were also a number of experts, priests and lay people, in attendance as consultants, corresponding roughly to the *periti* at Vatican II. Every Lambeth Conference has made statements and suggestions about the unity of the Church and the relation of the Anglican Communion with the other Churches. It deals with the practical problems of the Church and gives advice on current questions for the whole Anglican Communion. The Conference has no power to enforce its resolutions, but there is a friendly and brotherly spirit governing the exchange of ideas and experience.

A body of archbishops and bishops, called a consultative body, arranges the agenda of the Lambeth Conference, and this body since 1948 has been linked with the Advisory Council for Missionary Strategy, which also is composed of archbishops and metropolitans. The last Lambeth Conference decided to establish a permanent executive secretary.

The Lambeth Conference consists only of the bishops of the Anglican Communion. But the Church gives a considerable role to the laity and for this reason it was thought desirable to have a gathering with a wider representation. The assembly which resulted was called the Anglican Congress and included bishops, priests, and lay people. Up to now three such congresses have been held: the first in London in 1908, the second in Minneapolis, U.S.A., in 1954, and the third in Toronto, Canada, in 1961.[25] Each Congress, however, has been a separate organization, convened quite unofficially, though with the

[25] *The Anglican Communion* (Church Information Office, 1962). See also *Lambeth Conference 1930 Report*, p. 153.

approval of the Archbishop of Canterbury and other metropolitans. There is no firm expectation, as with the Lambeth Conference, that another such congress will be convened at any particular date. To a certain extent the Assemblies of the World Council of Churches now provide a similar meeting-ground.

As Dewi Morgan acknowledges, the Anglican system resembles that of the Orthodox Church. He writes: 'This is not an Anglican invention. It is shared by other Churches and, notably, by the great body of Orthodox Christians.'[26] It is inspired by the primitive Christian Church, as Archbishop Philip Carrington says: 'It was in such a way that the greater apostolic centres of Christianity acquired, in primitive times, a position of influence and prestige. The Anglican system reflects the condition of the primitive Church itself.'[27]

In the Book of Revelation[28] we read of seven churches of Asia— Ephesus, Smyrna, Pergamon, Thyatira, Sardis, Philadelphia, and Laodicea. Each has its peculiar characteristics of spiritual health or spiritual defect—Ephesus with its labour and patience and intolerance of evil, Smyrna with its works and tribulation and poverty, Pergamon with its faith, Thyatira which suffered Jezebel, Laodicea the lukewarm, and so on. Yet none of these seven was subordinate to any other, and each received its individual message from the Lord through his Apostle. (Ephesus, it may be noted, which was the largest city and had been the centre of St. Paul's ministry, is mentioned first; but besides its good points it is reproached for some falling away from its first love.) In some such way, the various independent or autocephalous Churches of the Anglican Communion and the Orthodox Church form a kind of pattern or mosaic, differing in size and differing in their qualities, but all fitting together in their relationship to Christ and his Apostles.

The characteristic of Anglican administration is an emphasis on Church order. 'In the Anglican view,' writes Molland,[29] 'it is just as vital for the Church to have a right order as it is to have the right doctrine. This attitude becomes apparent in the ecumenical discussions of the present day in which Anglicans strongly advocate certain principles of Church order. The watchword "faith and order" is a typically Anglican formulation.'

[26] op. cit. p. 35.
[27] *Anglican Congress Report* (1954, Minneapolis), p. 45.
[28] Rev. 1–2.
[29] *Christendom*, p. 165.

8. *Mariology*

On 8 December 1854 Pope Pius IX surprised the Christian world by his Bull *Ineffabilis Deus* which proclaimed the dogma of the Immaculate Conception of the Mother of God, and on 1 November 1950 Pope Pius XII in his Bull *Munificentissimus Deus* proclaimed a new dogma of the Bodily Assumption of the Mother of God. Consequently all Roman Catholics must believe and confess that faith in these two dogmas is necessary for salvation.[1]

The Church of England through its archbishops hastened to answer Pope Pius XII and expressed regret that the Roman Catholic Church had chosen by this act to increase dogmatic differences in Christendom and thereby gravely injured the growth of understanding between Christians based on a common possession of the fundamental truths of the Gospel.[2]

Is there really so sharp a difference between the Churches on Mariology, or is this a reaction against the Roman Catholic definition?

The theological position of the Orthodox Church lies between the over-estimation of the position of the Mother of God in the Roman Church, and the under-estimation of her by the Protestants. The Orthodox Church, following the teaching of the Fathers and the decision of the Ecumenical Councils, honours the Mother of God and sanctions her invocation as the Mediator above all the saints; it accepts her as 'the most favoured one ... God's blessing is on her above all women' (Luke 1:28, 42), but it rejects the two Papal Dogmas as they are not based on Holy Scripture and the genuine sacred tradition of the ancient Church, which are the sources of all Orthodox dogmas.

---

[1] For an outside observer, nothing is more striking in the Roman Church than the part played by the Mother of God in the development of the faithful and in the thought of a number of theologians. The Marian Movement started in France in the twelfth century; it was made popular through the instrumentality of a local Festival of the Immaculate Conception, 8 December, and opposed by St. Bernard of Clairvaux (*Epist.* 174 and *Can. Lugd.*). The Dominicans opposed belief in the Immaculate Conception. But Duns Scotus and the Franciscans introduced the doctrine and since it has spread to many other countries, the Church had to find an adequate doctrinal basis for this development of devotion to Mary. In 1921 Cardinal Mercier set in motion a number of studies on the concept of mediation. But it is since 1926 that the number of studies of the whole subject has rapidly increased.

[2] Archbishop Fisher's Lambeth Declaration (in *New York Herald Tribune* etc.) 18 Aug. 1950.

St. John Damascene for example says 'Let us adore God alone . . . to Him let us offer the worship of *latreia* as to God who is of His very nature adorable; so, too, the Holy Mother of God, not indeed as God, but as God's Mother according to the flesh'.[3] The Orthodox, Roman Catholic, and Anglican Churches all accept the scriptural teaching, found in the early chapters of St. Matthew's and St. Luke's Gospels, that at the time of the conception of Jesus in her womb by the power of the Holy Spirit, Mary remained a virgin, and her child had no human father. For example, the Anglican form of the Collect for Christmas Day expresses the common belief of the Church in saying that God gave us his 'only-begotten Son to take our nature upon him and . . . to be born of a pure Virgin.' Some Anglicans, it is true, would point out that mention of Mary's virginity is found only in two places in two of the four Gospels, and not in the rest of the New Testament, and, without denying Christ's divine Sonship and his perfect humanity when he 'took our nature upon him', they would say that Joseph may have been his father. This however would be a private view only, repudiated by the majority of Anglicans and never accepted by the Church corporately.[4] The Orthodox and Roman Catholic belief, besides this, includes the view that Mary was 'ever virgin', and had no other children. Anglicanism however is not committed to this, which seems to many Anglicans to go beyond the teaching of Scripture, in which 'the brethren of Jesus' are spoken of, and in which the perpetual virginity of Mary is never asserted. But this does not affect the scriptural doctrine of the Virgin Birth of Christ.

The Immaculate Conception of Mary (though sometimes confused by outsiders with the above doctrines) is quite different. It asserts that at her conception in her mother's womb, Mary was specially exempted by God from the inheritance of original sin to which, as a human being, she would otherwise have been subject. It was as if, for her, the Fall had not taken place. To this, Orthodox and Anglicans would reply that such a dogma cannot be proved by Scripture or tradition and moreover contradicts the doctrine, taught by the whole Church, that the consequences of the Fall affect the whole human race, so that all stand in need of redemption.[5]

---

[3] *De Imaginibus*, ii. 5; *P.G.* xciv, 1358.

[4] Cf. the Report *Doctrine in the Church of England* (1938), p. 82.

[5] Cf. Rom. 5:12–21. It is known that 'the development of an explicit doctrine of the Immaculate Conception originated in the Pelagian denial of original sin, a denial which forced Latin theology to consider the nature of original sin, and

Of course the Roman Church in the Council of Trent decreed that only the Mother of God, by a special privilege from God, is without original sin (*'nisi ex speciali Dei privilegio quemadmodum de Beata Virgine tenet Ecclesia'*). And the Orthodox Church teaches that the Mother of God is relatively, and by God's grace, sinless.[6] But among the ancient Fathers only St. Augustine appears to accept the Mother of God as sinless: *'Excepta sancta virgine Maria, de qua propter honorem domini, nullam prorsus, cum de peccatis agitur, haberi volo quaestionem'*.[7] This passage in St. Augustine is not quite clear and it seems to imply that although he with a modest reverence avoided the consequences of his assertion in respect to the Holy Virgin, he by no means necessarily considered her to be free from original sin.[8]

The difference between Roman Catholics and Orthodox on Mariology may not be very great and it could be bridged, because there are in the Orthodox Church the pious intuitions of the faithful which refuse to allow any sin, even original sin, to be mentioned in connection with the immaculate Virgin. The Orthodox Megalynarion, chanted by the choir after the *epiklesis* in the Divine Liturgy of the Orthodox Church, shows the honour and praise and the devotion of the Orthodox Church to Our Lady. The priest sings: 'Especially our most holy, most pure and most blessed and glorious Lady, Mary ever-virgin and Mother of God.' The choir respond: 'It is very meet to bless thee, the ever-blessed and most pure Virgin and Mother of our God. Thee that art more honourable than the cherubim and incomparable, more glorious than the seraphim, that without spot of sin, didst bear God, the Word; and thee verily the Mother of God we magnify.'

Would it not be possible for the three Churches to reach agreement on the doctrine of the Mother of God? Orthodox theologians must examine the problem on the ground of patristic teaching and the living faith of the Orthodox Church, because, in fact, many Orthodox theologians follow the Roman Catholics on this subject, although for the time being Orthodox theology as such rejects the papal dogma because it is based on pious opinions, poetic hymns and exaggerations,

---

hence to formulate more explicitly the relation between nature and grace, in a way which Orthodox theology was not forced to do'. B. Leeming, 'Orthodox-Catholic Relations', *R.E.C.*, p. 42.

[6] Trembelas, *Dogmatic*, vol. ii, 213–15.

[7] *De natura et gratia*, c. 42.

[8] Von Hase, op. cit. vol. ii, p. 135.

which do not belong to the essence of the doctrine. The Orthodox Church rejects all the mediaeval sources or traditions on the Virgin Mary which have their roots in apocryphal writings.[9]

The Second Vatican Council in the constitution *de Ecclesia*,[10] as well as providing an extensive explanation of the Roman Catholic view on the position of the Virgin Mary in the Church, also keeps the door open for further discussions with other Christians. In the introduction, for example, the Council says that is has no intention of proposing the doctrine of Mary in its fullness, or of closing the discussion on questions which the labour of theologians has not yet fully illuminated. Moreover it 'strongly urges theologians and preachers of the divine word to be careful in their consideration of the Mother of God's unique dignity, to refrain as much from falsehood by way of superlatives as from narrow-mindedness.' In addition, the Council asks theologians to develop the study of sacred Scripture, the Fathers and Doctors and the liturgiologists of the Church, and warns them to be careful to exclude from their writings and their behaviour anything which might lead separated brethren, or others, into error over the Church's true teaching.

Apart from the unanimous declaration of the archbishops of the Church of England on the new dogma of the Assumption (*Munificentissimus*, 1 November 1950), the Church of England is very careful to refrain from all exaggerations, but it does not lack its devotees to the Virgin Mary.[11] 'Rightly and properly,' writes Bishop Ellison

we offer the deepest devotion and honour to the lowly maiden, who because of her purity and obedience was found meet for the high privilege of being Christ's mother. Our calendar gives prominent place to those feast days which commemorate incidents in her life. The honour paid to her has undoubtedly brought much spiritual and moral advantage to Christians. But we are bound to mark that in the Scriptures there is a profound reticence in all the references to Our Lady. The person whom we might have expected to have occupied a place second

[9] Karmiris, *The New Dogma* (Athens, 1951), p. 9. (In Greek.)

[10] *Dogmatic Constitution on the Church* (Catholic Truth Society), Chapter viii, pp. 77–8. 'By bringing Our Lady within the scope of the Church militant, it saved her blessed name and figure from the impious hands of those who seem ever determined to make a semi-celestial personage of her'. This means that a new attempt was made 'to bring devotion to Our Lady within a compass, in which many others would be prepared to recognize a common heritage'. B. Pawley, 'An Anglican views the Council', *S.C.U.*, p. 120.

[11] E. Amand de Mendieta, *Rome and Canterbury*, p. 184.

only to Our Lord Himself is mentioned only on rare occasions. May we not assume that this reticence was a consequence of the wish of the Blessed Virgin Mary herself? The Anglican Communion inherits and respects the reticence shown in Scripture, and though not a whit less eager than others to honour the pure and humble maid, yet refuses to speculate about her, or to raise to the status of dogma those incidents about the Virgin that can of their very nature be only legendary.[12]

Gore is more explicit on Mary's position in the Church:

Inasmuch as the facts of Mary's sinless conception were demonstratively not part of the original faith, and are not witnessed to in the New Testament, they can never become a legitimate part of the dogmatic furniture of the Church.[13]

'There is no progress on this matter,' Bishop J. R. H. Moorman said after the Conference at Huntercombe between Romans and Anglicans (30 August to 3 September 1967). The Bishop added: 'Anglicans are anxious to know the minimum that is required of those in communion with Rome.'

It would seem a fair summary to say that while the dogma of the Immaculate Conception (with which that on the Bodily Assumption can be bracketed) stands as a considerable obstacle to progress, which is at present blocked by it, nevertheless the hope of advance towards better mutual understanding in the future need not be given up.

9. The Laity in the Church

The evidence we have about the role of the laity in the early Church derives mainly from the New Testament, and shows not only that they were seen as 'the peculiar people of God' and 'a royal priesthood' with a divine commission to bring salvation to the whole world, but that every single member of the Christian community had his part to play, in accordance with the gifts he possessed, in the life and work of the Church.[1]

The functions of laymen in the ancient Church have been fully studied by Roman Catholics and, more recently, by the Orthodox. In the Roman Catholic Church this subject was examined seriously

---

[12] G. Ellison, op. cit. pp. 77–8.
[13] Gore, *Orders and Unity*, pp. 197–8.
[1] I Peter 2:9, Rev. 1:6, I Cor. 12:4–30, etc.

with the purpose of reducing the disproportionate clerical emphasis
which had developed from the mediaeval period onwards. Investi-
gating the question in a dogmatic-historical way and with a good deal
of reference to recent papal pronouncements, they express the hope
that the former position of laymen in the Roman Church would be
restored.

On this subject there is official agreement amongst the three Churches
that the members of the early Church saw themselves as the people of
God, who were understood to have entered into the priestly kingdom
by baptism. The position of the laymen in both Roman and Orthodox
Churches remains in theory the same as was taught by the Fathers.[2] 'I
have said all this', says St. John Chrysostom, 'in order that each one
of the laity also may keep his attention aware, that we may understand
that we are all one body, having such difference amongst ourselves, as
members with members; and may not throw the whole upon the
priest; but ourselves also so care for the whole Church, as for a body
common to us.'[3] Both East and West have inherited the same tradition
of the role of the laity; but in the West the number of clerics and
monks during the Middle Ages and until the beginning of this century
was sufficient to supply clergy not only for the parishes, but also for
education, missions, etc., so that there was no room for the work of
laymen, and the division between clergy and laity became wider. It is
true that the Roman Church, although it admits the importance of the
lay elements in the Church, has always shown reserve towards them.
For a long time the Church has been considered as a juridical corporation or organization which was exclusively represented by the
clerical hierarchy. This turned the layman too easily into a mere
object of pastoral care.[4] But a pastoral letter from the Italian bishops on
'The Priesthood of all Believers', which appeared in *Osservatore*

[2] 'Although Councils have always been meetings of bishops in the sense that
final authority has always lain in their hands, history proves that priests and even
laymen have not been absent from them'; cf. Peter Fransen, S.J., 'The Authority
of the Councils', *P.A.* p. 59. From a Roman Catholic point of view laymen
have been present at Councils, the one exception being the Council of the Vatican
in 1870. There is no dogmatic obstacle to their presence.

[3] Chrysostom *In II Cor. hom.* xviii, 3. For a comprehensive study of what
exactly were the layman's rights and duties, liturgical, constitutional, disciplinary,
eleemosynary and evangelical, in the period before Constantine, see the work of
George Hunston Williams, 'The role of layman in the Ancient Church' in
Greek Byzantine Studies (Cambridge, Mass., 1958), Vol. i, p. 21 ff.

[4] P. Mikat, 'Collaboration between clergy and laity,' *C.* ix (1965), p. 34.

Romano in 1960,[5] discussing the subject in theological detail, and clarifying matters of scriptural exegesis, patristic teaching, liturgy, dogma and Papal pronouncements, insists on the paramount importance of the doctrine of the priesthood of all believers for the sanctification of the people, their participation in the eucharist, and the Church's apostolate. This pastoral letter warns priests to avoid, in their dealings with the laity, all undue emphasis on their own authority, and admonishes them to work with them in a spirit of love and respect, to be prudent in moderating rash suggestions, to give every attention to all reasonable proposals, to furnish religious and ethical incentives, and appeal constantly to personal initiative and responsibility. Finally the bishops warn their clergy 'not to interfere in specialized fields where they have no right to give directives, since decision there must be left to the free choice of the individual.'[6]

The Roman Church emphasizes the superiority of the sacramental character of the Church in order to avoid the secularization of thought and practice. And in another pastoral letter the Italian bishops urge a thorough study of ecclesiology on the lines of the encyclicals *Mystici corporis* and *Mediator Dei* 'which will carry us beyond the external and legal aspect of the Church to an understanding of the great mystery of her indispensable role of mediator between God and the souls of men, and of the sublime nature of her spiritual mission in human history. It will show up the enormity of the error of those who think they are working for the Kingdom of God, while cutting themselves off from community with the Church and the hierarchy which guides her.'[7]

Although the Italian bishops do not diminish the role of the laity in the Church—'at all times lay people were the Church's strength and pride, and were accorded the lofty functions of a true priesthood under the authoritative guidance of the hierarchy'[8]—it is obvious that they are trying to make a clear distinction between the hierarchical priesthood and the royal priesthood of all believers. The Orthodox would also agree that it is a fundamental error to promote a theology of the laity by minimizing the distinction between the two kinds of

---

[5] 14 April 1960.

[6] Quoted in Jaeger, *The Ecumenical Council*, pp. 113–14.

[7] *Osservatore Romano*, 15 April 1960, p. 2; Jaeger, *The Ecumenical Council*, p. 111.

[8] 'Laicismo', *Osservatore Romano*, 16 April 1960. 'The view of the Church on the mystical Body of Christ has never been wholly forgotten in Catholic theology, but there have been periods when it was pushed into the background'; cf. P. Mikat, op. cit. p. 34.

priesthood, the general and that of the ordained priests. As the constitution *On the Church* says,

> though they differ from one another in essence and not only in degree,
> the common priesthood of the faithful and the ministerial or hierarchical priesthood are none the less interrelated: a call to either of them is a
> participation in the one priesthood of Christ. . . . The fact that the laity,
> too, have an active part in the royal priesthood shows that it is a constitutive element of the unity of all the faithful, whether ordained or not,
> and shows their collaboration as a common interaction of the various
> members of one body.[9]

In the New Testament we read that 'within our community God has
appointed first Apostles, secondly prophets, thirdly teachers', and
after that those with other gifts (1 Cor. 12:28). This distinction between
those possessing different gifts and functions begins in Scripture and the
tradition of the Church, and indicates the spiritual authority attached
to office-bearers in the Christian community, an authority which
came to be given in particular to those who, as bishop, priest, and
deacon, exercised the three-fold ministry in the Church. But differences of function do not diminish the unity of the body as a whole.
Gregory of Nazianzus says of clergy and laity: 'The first governs and
takes the chair. The second is led and directed.' But this distinction
does not make a division between the leader and his followers, nor
does it make the clergy a separate group. St. Augustine declares that
all Christians are priests, because they are members of the one priest:
'Omnes sacerdotes, quoniam membra sunt unius sacerdotis'.[10]

Having in mind the teaching of the Latin Fathers and the Papal
Encyclical Letters, we can say that Orthodox, Anglican, and Roman
Churches are in agreement that the laity are also priests, but that they
are not entitled to celebrate the sacraments,[11] this being reserved for
those whose special duty it is to do so. 'The fact, however,' writes
Pope Pius XII,

---

[9] Quoted by P. Mikat, op. cit., p. 35.

[10] *De Civit. Dei*, 1.20, c. 70.

[11] With the partial exceptions of Baptism, which is normally given by a
bishop, priest, or deacon, but may be administered by a lay person in case of
need, and of Matrimony, in which baptized persons marry each other by their
mutual vows; *the presence of* a priest is desirable but not essential to Christian
marriage.

that the faithful participate in the eucharistic sacrifice, does not mean
that they also are endowed with priestly power. It is very necessary that
you make this quite clear to your flocks. For there are today, venerable
brethren, those who, approximating to errors long since condemned,
teach that in the New Testament by the word 'priesthood' is meant
only the priesthood which applies to all who have been baptized and
hold that the command by which Christ gave power to His Apostles at
the last supper to do that He Himself had done, applies directly to the
entire Christian Church, and that thence, and thence only, arises the
hierarchical priesthood. Hence they assert that the people are possessed
of a true priestly power, and that the priest only acts in virtue of an
office committed to him by the community. Wherefore they look on
the Eucharistic Sacrifice as a 'concelebration' in the literal meaning of
that term, and consider it more fitting that priests should 'concelebrate'
with the people present than that they should offer the sacrifice
privately when the people are absent. . . . We deem it necessary to recall that the priest acts for the people only because he represents Jesus
Christ, who is head of all His members and offers Himself in their
stead. Hence he goes to the altar as the minister of Christ, inferior to
Christ, but superior to the people. The people, on the other hand, since
they in no sense represent the Divine Redeemer and are not a mediator
between themselves and God, can in no way possess the sacerdotal
power. However, it must also be said that the faithful do offer the
Divine Victim, though in a different sense.[12]

However we have evidence that in the early Church sacraments
could in case of necessity be administered by laymen. 'Where the
clergy are not at hand,' says Tertullian, 'thou mayest thyself make the
offering and baptize, and art thine own priest.'[13] Frumentius, the Apostle
of Ethiopia, while yet a layman founded the Church there, and
performed the sacred liturgical service. And St. Augustine relates
that, in a shipwreck, when a layman and a catechumen were clinging
to the same plank, the layman baptized the catechumen, and the
newly baptized pronounced the absolution over the former, and thus
they both met their drowning with good courage.

[12] *Mediator Dei*. Cf. *The Papal Encyclicals in their Historical context. The teaching
of the Popes*, ed. by Anne Fremantle (New American Library, 1956), p. 28. See
also Gregory Naz., Migne, *P.G.* xxxvi, 185 and xxxv, 409; St. John Chrys.,
Migne, *P.G.* lxi, 527–528, and lxii, 87, also lii, 784 and l, 654; St. Augustine,
De Civit. Dei, Migne, *P.L.* xli, 676; Leo the Great, *Sermo iv*, Migne, *P.L.* liv, 148.
[13] *Exhort. cast.* 7.

There are, of course, exceptions to the general rule. But they do indicate a principle which the encyclical *Mediator Dei* denied, namely that the Eucharist is properly described as a 'concelebration' by priest and people together. This is supported by the Fathers and especially St. John Chrysostom and St. Augustine, who say that worship is offered by the whole mystical body of Christ by means of the priesthood of the whole body and the special priesthood of the clergy.[14]

The role of the layman has been emphatically stressed by the Second Vatican Council. He is recognized as the real missioner, the person who brings the Church to the world and the world to the Church. It is in his ordinary work and life that the Christian message is preached to those who do not know it, and it is his experience in the world which must be brought back into the Church in order to give deeper insights into its role and mission. The opinion of many Roman Catholics is that institutions must be devised which will enable the layman to exercise his function. For if he is to have responsibilities in the world, he must also have the rights which go with those responsibilities.[15]

It was in the Second Vatican Council plainly the intention to bring the laity fully into the life of the Church, and to break down the psychological barrier which has often caused the laity to make a separate compartment of their religion, to think of themselves as excellent Catholics if they fulfilled the specific requirements of the Church. . . . while they had not felt that Catholic doctrine brought any special imperatives with it.[16]

It was 'the first time a Council ever submitted a document specifically on the laity as an *ordo* within the Church.'[17] This was an inevitable result of co-operation with other Christians.[18]

How then can we reconcile these two kinds of priesthood? Are there in fact two priesthoods? The answer must be to affirm that as with the ordination of bishops, priests, and deacons there is only one priesthood and ministry but three 'offices', so with regard to clergy and laity there remains the one priesthood of Christ in which men

---

[14] *Hom. 3 in II Cor.* and *De Civitate Dei* xx. 10.
[15] P. Mikat, op. cit., pp. 35–6.
[16] 'The Post-Conciliar Era', *The Tablet*, 1 Jan. 1966.
[17] Jaeger, *A Stand on Ecumenism*, pp. 197–9.
[18] Decree *De Ecumenismo*, Articles 12, 22, 23, 36.

share in differing degrees according to their status and function in the Church.[19]

To sum up, in the Roman Church in the past the laity were excluded from the three domains of the Church: Liturgy, Church Government, and Teaching. But recently attempts have been made to reconsider this question.[20]

Addressing the laity during the Third World Congress of the Lay Apostolate, which took place in Rome (11 to 18 October 1967), the Pope stressed the fundamental principles of the Church concerning the laity.[21] There is a very important doctrine of the laity in the Church, which must be seriously maintained: 'The Church has given to the layman, a member of the mysterious visible society of the faithful, her solemn recognition . . . . She has recognized him as incorporated in Christ and as a sharer in the priestly, prophetic, royal function of Christ Himself.' Then the Pope referred to the ideals and efforts of the

[19] Y. M. T. Congar, *Jalons pour une théologie de Laicat* (Paris, 1953), p. 223. 'Ecclesia docens' (the teachers—the hierarchy) and the 'Ecclesia discens' (the learners—the laity). The layman is no longer, according to the formula of Leo XIII, 'he who, in the Church, obeys and honours the clergy' (cf. Leo XIII, Letter to Mgr. Meignan, Archbishop of Tours): 'It is established and manifest that there are in the Church two orders by nature distinct: the pastors and the flock, that is to say, the leaders and the people. To the first order belongs the function of teaching, of governing, of directing men's lives, of imposing rules on them; the other has the duty of being submissive to the former; of obeying, of executing orders, and of rendering it honour.' (17 Dec. 1888, cited in *The Laity, a collection of Pontifical Teachings*, edited by the Monks of Solesmes (Paris, Desclée et Cie, 1956) par. 142, 106.) Contrast nearly eighty years later, Christian Duquoc, O.P., 'The Believer and Christian Existence in History', *C.* ix (1965) p. 71, 72. n. 3. The layman is entitled, writes C. Duquoc, 'not only to receive the sacraments and to hear the authentic word of God, but also to contribute his views in the formulation of Church policy. This new position held by the layman, his awareness of his rights in the Church, has been and still is the source of a great number of movements unifying the laity to witness to the inspired testimony of the Christian in the world' (ibid. p. 66).

[20] In the Second Vatican Council there was an appreciation of the part played by laymen in the Church. Especially Emile Joseph de Smedt, Bishop of Bruges, Belgium (cf. *Speeches of Vatican II*, pp. 25–28) explains the part of laymen in the Church as priest, prophet and king. Nevertheless the position of laymen in that speech does not allow for the participation of a layman in the teaching of the Church and in its administration. This is similar to the Orthodox position, but not quite the same. In Orthodoxy laymen are much more active in the Church. The Orthodox repudiate the distinction between the *Ecclesia docens* and the *Ecclesia discens*.

[21] *The Tablet*, 7 Oct. to 21 Oct. 1967, and *Catholic Herald*, 13 Oct. 1967.

lay apostolate, quoting the dogmatic constitution of the Church, *Lumen Gentium*, 3. The most important point of the Pope's address was when he raised the hypothetical objection that, since the tasks of the apostolate were so vast, there should be in the future two parallel hierarchies in the Church, two organizations existing side by side. The Pope answered this point:

This however would be to forget the structure of the Church; as Christ Himself willed it to be, including diversity of ministries. Certainly the idea of the people of God, filled with grace and gifts, marching towards salvation, presents a magnificent spectacle. But does it follow that the people of God are their own interpreters of God's Word and ministers of His grace? Can they evolve religious teachings and directives, selecting from the faith which the Church professes with authority? Or can they boldly turn aside from tradition, and emancipate themselves from the magisterium? The absurdity of these suppositions suffices to show the lack of foundation for the objection. The decree on the apostolate of the laity was careful to recall that 'Christ conferred on the Apostles and their successors the duty of teaching, sanctifying and ruling in His name and power.' Indeed, no one can take it amiss that the normal instrumental cause of the divine designs is the hierarchy, or that in the Church, efficacy is proportional to one's adherence to those whom Christ 'has made guardians, to feed the Church of the Lord' (Acts 20:28). Anyone who attempts to act without the hierarchy, or against it, in the field of the Father of the family, could be compared to the branch which atrophies because it is no longer connected with the stem which provides its sap. As history has shown, such a one would be only a trickle of water, cutting itself off from the great main-stream, and ending miserably by sinking into the sands.

By these words the Pope is maintaining that there is a distinction between the priest and the layman. But because of the insufficiency of the number of clergy in many parts of the world, the laity should take over more and more duties which do not necessitate the priestly character.

These last words of the Pope suggest that, in the past, it was the great numbers of clergy which made the Roman Church appear to be hierocratic. In doctrine she accepts, like the Orthodox, the participation of the laity in various responsibilities, where priesthood is not essential.

In the Orthodox Church, parishes are governed by a council of laymen under the chairmanship of the priest, and laymen can take part in the councils of both dioceses and patriarchates. They can also be present as advisers, but without a vote, in Ecumenical and Local Councils, and there are a large number of laymen among the theologians, preachers, and catechists of the Orthodox Church.

In the Anglican Church[22] laymen have a position similar to that in the Orthodox Church, but they play a greater part in the diocesan and national councils of the Church, though there are fewer 'lay theologians' in universities and theological colleges. In recent years the shortage of clergy has led to increasing participation by the laity in the life and work of Anglican parishes, and the 'Liturgical Movement' has given expression in worship to their now more normal functions as partners with the clergy in the ministry of the Church. It need hardly be added that in the Orthodox and Anglican Churches the laity receive both the bread and the wine at the Eucharist—yet this liturgical detail is an important indication of the different attitudes of the clergy to the laity over the centuries in the Roman and the other two Churches.

[22] Garbett, *The Claims of the Church of England*, p. 106. In common with other Churches there has been in the Church of England a considerable development, since the Second World War, of what may be called 'the lay movement'. This movement emphasizes the strategic importance of laymen and women in the mission of the Church in an increasingly technical world. Some tension is becoming apparent between this lay 'secular' movement and the 'ecclesiastical' structures of Church life. See, for example, the journal *Parish and People*, organ of the movement of that name, and the book *Laymen's Church by* Bishop John Robinson and others (London, 1963). The periodical *New Christian* was associated with radical opinions and often with a distinctively lay viewpoint.

Chapter VII

THE SACRAMENTS: THE TEACHING OF
THE THREE CHURCHES BRIEFLY COMPARED

1. *Preliminary Notes*

By the word Sacrament is understood an outward sign of a particular form of union with the Church, instituted by Christ, which gives grace to those who receive it rightly. Two parts are clearly required in the Orthodox, Roman, and Anglican Churches for the accomplishment of every Sacrament: the outward part, made up of words and acts by which the divine grace is transmitted to the recipient; and the intention of the Church which administers the Sacrament. The Roman Church has subdivided the visible sign in Aristotelian terms, into matter and form (*materia* and *forma*) after St. Augustine, who analysed them into *elementum* and *verbum*, which combined make up the visible word, the visible form or the 'form of piety'. This conception, which is not alien to the Orthodox, thus requires three parts for the accomplishment of the Sacraments: (i) *Materia:* water in Baptism, bread and wine in the Holy Eucharist, oil in Unction (and Chrism) etc. (ii) *Forma:* this includes the action of the celebrant—who must normally be of the necessary order in the Church: a duly ordained priest for the Eucharist, a bishop for Ordination, but any lay person, in case of need, for Baptism. This includes both essential actions, such as taking the bread and cup into his hands in the Eucharist, pouring water over, or immersing, the person baptized, laying on of hands in Ordination, and also the speaking of the essential words such as 'I baptize thee in the name of the Father, the Son, and the Holy Spirit' in Baptism. If any of these formal conditions is lacking, the sacrament is invalid, or at least doubtful. (iii) *Intentio:* the inward intention or mental determination of the persons concerned to 'do what the Church does', that is to confer the sacrament in question,[1] as will be explained below. Until

---

[1] About the intention see Hugh of St. Victor (*Summa sententiarum*, tr. v, cap. 9, and tr. vi, cap 4, and *De Sacramentis* Lib. ii, p. vi, cap. 13), who first used this term; cf. Gasparri, *Catechism*, p. 152, and Mansi, xxxi, 1054.

the thirteenth century the Roman Church was using the terms *elementum* and *verbum*, taken, as we have seen, from a passage of St. Augustine.[2] Since that time the terms 'matter', and 'form' have been preferred.[3] The term *materia* means the action and *forma* means the whole ceremony (actions and words).

The intention of the Church, that is to say, the living essence of the sacramental forms, the intention appropriate to the sacrament, is an essential element for the maintenance of the Sacrament—the intention of the Church not of the celebrant minister—because the intention of the Church is a necessary factor of the Sacrament so far as it is manifested externally. The moral quality of the celebrant minister in no way affects the Sacrament provided that he genuinely intends to do what the Church does, and does not act in mere jest or blasphemous mockery. Again here the teaching of St. Augustine dominates: 'fear not the adulterer nor the drunkard, since I look for the Holy Dove by whom I am told, "This [the Holy Spirit] is He who is there conferring Baptism." The intention of the minister to perform outwardly what the Church does, *serio non joco agens*, is necessary in Orthodox, Roman and Anglican doctrine.[4] The Roman Catholic scholastics divide the intention of the celebrant into outward, inward (actual and virtual) and habitual (an act of the will to do what God wants), but the Orthodox and Anglicans admit that the complete outward intention is sufficient. All three Churches admit that in the Sacraments the minister acts not as an individual but as the organ of the Church, since God's promises are made not to him individually but to the Church as a whole. Therefore their fulfilment is not affected by his personal lack of faith.[5]

Nevertheless the words of Gregory the Great, who rejected baptism by heretics *quia baptisma non fuit quod in errore positi in sanctae Trinitatis nomine perceperunt*, show that the mere outward act cannot perform the Sacraments. The Roman Church, accepting the principle that even a Jew or a pagan is capable of performing valid baptism in case of necessity, appears to contradict this doctrine of intention by placing

[2] *In Joan. Evang.* xv, tract. lxxx, 3.

[3] The reply of Pope Innocent III *ad Thoriam Archiepiscoporum Nidrosiensem* is clear 'in baptism two things are always necessary and required, namely, the words and the element', *Decretales Gregorii* IX, iii, xlii, 5, cf. Gasparri, *Catechism*, p. 361.

[4] Trembelas, *Dogmatic*, Vol. iii, pp. 35 ff., and Council of Trent, sess. vii, can. ii; cf. also *Doctrine in the Church of England*, pp. 135–6.

[5] Regarding Anglican teaching on this point see Bicknell, op. cit., p. 366.

too much value on the outward act. Pope Nicolas I (858–67) considered valid the baptisms which a Jew of his time had administered among the Bulgarians for payment, and Innocent IV did the same for a baptism conferred by an actual Saracen, although the Saracen had no knowledge at all what the Church was. But Alexander VIII (1689–91) maintained that baptisms were invalid when performed by a priest who did not intend to do what the Church intends, even though the external rite be satisfactory. For this reason a Protestant says: 'Catholicism cannot escape from the fluctuations between these two points of view. The resolution at Trent inclines certainly to the second of these (*intentio interna*), but declares itself on the side of the first (*intentio externa*).'[6] From an Orthodox point of view only a member of the Church 'having the intention appropriate to the Sacrament' performs it. It is performed by a priest alone and in case of absolute necessity by a layman, provided he be an Orthodox Catholic and holds the intention appropriate to Holy Baptism.[7]

2. The Essence of the Sacraments

All the three Churches teach that the power, called divine grace, which derives from the Cross and which saves man, does not only operate directly on the inward man, but is also linked with visible things or ceremonies. This is because man is a reasoning entity. These signs do not merely symbolize the operation of the divine grace which is given, but are its means and instruments. They are not bare symbols, but pledges and seals of grace. The teaching of St. Augustine is that the sacraments are visible signs which transmit invisible grace, signs which are instruments of the divine grace, signs which distinguish believers from unbelievers.[1] This is the teaching of Anglicanism, Orthodoxy, and Roman Catholicism, although in the past several attempts were made to show points of disagreement on this subject between the three Churches. Newman's *Lectures on Justification* (1838), uphold the doctrine that the Sacraments are means of justification. This was the general doctrine of the Tractarians. The Churches in accepting the sacraments admit that the divine grace in the sacraments is of divine institution, *ex divina institutione*, i.e. by the Founder of the

---

[6] Hase, Vol. ii, p. 162. This distinction is not in use today.

[7] Androutsos, *The validity of the Anglican Ordinations*, pp. 24–5.

[1] *Conc. Trid.* sess. VII, can. 5; cf. B. Leeming, *Principles of Sacramental Theology*, second ed. (1960), p. 226.

sacraments, Jesus Christ. The doctrine that the sacraments act—in the traditional phrase—*ex opere operato* is agreed by both Western and Eastern Churches. The Augsburg Confession, however (Art. xiii), rejected the doctrine that the Sacraments justify *ex opere operato*, apart from Faith. Nevertheless, it is not certain that those who reject the phrase have always understood it in the same sense as those who accept it. The Reformation based its attack on the teaching of Duns Scotus that 'the Sacraments confer grace by means of the *opus operatum*, so that on the occasion of it an inward good impulse is not required, but it is enough that the recipient interposes no bar in the shape of a mortal sin'. But Bellarmine says that the effectiveness of the Sacrament *ex opere operato* denotes only this, that the grace is imparted by virtue of the sacramental act itself ordained by God to that end, not by virtue of the merit of the minister or the recipient, while nevertheless good will, faith, and repentance are needful as dispositions in the case of adults. The Council of Trent[2] insists on the effectiveness *ex opere operato*. In the Church of England there are some who reject the *ex opere operato*, but Pusey said that the doctrine that sacraments confer grace *ex opere operato* 'contains nothing which our Church, as well as the Lutheran, does not equally hold'.[3] The Sacraments are held to be necessary to all men for salvation in so far as they are available. It is common ground between East and West that God is in no way limited if in any particular case the sacraments are not in fact available: those who are prevented by circumstances from participating in the sacraments cannot thereby be excluded from God's saving grace, if they have the right inward disposition. Thus those who desire baptism, but by accident or persecution die unbaptized, are undoubtedly in the same position as those who have actually received it. A slight difference between Rome and the East, however, has been thought to arise in cases where a person deliberately rejects participation in a sacrament; it has been held that this is a bar to divine grace: *non defectus sed contemptus sacramenti damnat* ('not the lack of the sacrament, but the scorning of it, brings damnation'). Humanly speaking such rejection of the sacrament by human free will would seem to bring its own consequence, but since there is no evidence in the sources of revelation on this point we must beware of any positive assertion.[4]

[2] *Conc. Trid.* ibid., Can. 8.

[3] Quoted by B. Leeming, op. cit., p. 87.

[4] B. Leeming, op. cit., pp. 5–10; cf. Androutsos, *Dogmatic*, p. 299, and Trembelas, *Dogmatic*, vol. iii, pp. 30, 31; cf. also *Doctrine in the Church of England*, p. 130.

3. *The Rites of the Celebration and the Number of the Sacraments*

It is universally agreed that each Church has the right to use its own form of words—prayers, thanksgivings, praises, exhortation to the people, and so on—and its own traditional actions in the administration of the sacraments. Technically these are known as the *rite* (the words) and the *ceremonial* (the actions) respectively. (It is understood, of course, that the essential matter and form of the sacrament, as already explained at the outset, are preserved.) But the setting of words and actions, by which the essence of the sacrament is surrounded, has always varied from church to church and from the beginning there was in this no uniformity, but all the varying rites and ceremonies express one and the same faith. On this matter Professor Trembelas writes:[1]

if it was necessary for Orthodox Priests to celebrate the Holy Eucharist some of them according to the Apostolic Constitutions, others according to the rite of Serapion of Thmuis, and others according to the ancient anaphora of Hippolytus, the sacrament would be equally and in all of them sanctified.

The Orthodox and Roman Churches understand the Sacraments to be seven: Baptism, Confirmation (or Chrismation), Eucharist, Penance, Ordination, Marriage and Holy Unction. In these two Churches, the Sacraments are divided into those which are irrevocable (that is, can neither be cancelled nor repeated) and those which can be repeated: Baptism, Confirmation and Ordination are not repeatable. The Sacraments are also not all of the same value and consequently not of equal necessity. Holy Eucharist, Chrismation, and Baptism are obligatory. St. John Chrysostom said: 'By the water we are regenerated, by the flesh and blood of the Lord we are nourished' (*In Joh. Hom.* 84). The Anglican Church accepts two of these sacraments only as 'Sacraments of the Gospel' which are 'generally necessary for salvation', Baptism and the Eucharist.[2] Nevertheless, in the Book of Common Prayer it provides for Confirmation by a bishop, which should be received by all baptized persons before they are admitted to Holy Communion, and for the solemnization of Marriage on a lifelong basis ('till death us

---

[1] *Dogmatic*, Vol. iii, p. 37.

[2] Book of Common Prayer, Catechism: 'Q. How many Sacraments hath Christ ordained in his Church? *A.* Two only, as generally necessary to salvation that is to say, Baptism, and the Supper of the Lord'.

do part') in the name of the Holy Trinity. In the Ordinal it provides for the conferring of Holy Orders and Episcopal Consecration, by episcopal laying-on of hands, and regards episcopal ordination as necessary and unrepeatable.[3] These three ordinances clearly have a sacramental character. In the service for the Visitation of the Sick the Church of England provides for the Priest to give Absolution, after hearing the sick person's confession, in a form which is clearly sacramental,[4] and it encourages those who are not sick in body, but troubled in conscience, to seek the same absolution from a priest before receiving Holy Communion. Unction of the Sick is not provided in the Prayer Book but was revived by the Tractarians and is now permitted 'using . . . oil consecrated by the Bishop'.[5] The Church of England thus accepts these five rites as lawful channels of the divine grace, with firm and permanent positions in the life of the Church. Indeed, in the Report of Commission on Christian Doctrine in the Church of England[6] we observe that these other five are included among the Sacraments. Most Anglicans would agree with the words of Emile Cammaerts in a book entitled *Difficulties; Questions on Religion with Answers by prominent Churchmen* (1949), that the other sacraments besides Holy Eucharist and Baptism,

were added in course of time to celebrate those solemn moments in life when great promises are made or binding pledges given in the presence of God. The Reformation brought a reaction among the non-Catholic Churches, prompted partly by the abuses of the Church of Rome, and partly by a desire to return to a simpler form of worship inspired more directly by the Scriptures and the example of the early Church. That is why our Catechism declares there are only two sacraments necessary to salvation.[7]

Bishop Gore in an appended note comes to the conclusion that we must maintain the pre-eminence of Baptism, completed in Confirmation, and the Eucharist, and place Ordination next to them; the other three, though they fail to correspond to the stricter definition,

[3] Preface to the Ordinal, and Canon C.1. of the revised *Canons of the Church of England* (1964/69).
[4] 'Our Lord Jesus Christ, who hath left power to his Church to absolve all sinners who truly repent and believe in him, of his great mercy forgive thee thine offences; And by his power committed to me, I absolve thee from all thy sins, In the Name of the Father, and of the Son, and of the Holy Ghost. Amen.'
[5] Op. cit., Canon B. 37.
[6] *Doctrine in the Church of England*, p. 186.
[7] Op. cit., pp. 113–14.

may well be admitted as Sacraments. 'Thus was made up the list of the Seven Sacraments by which the life of the Christian was surrounded from the cradle to the grave.'[8] But when the Anglican speaks of the sacrament as the 'outward and visible sign of an inward and spiritual grace' he means something different from what the Orthodox mean when they say 'Mysterion'. And in this lies the difference between the two mentalities, Anglican and Orthodox. The Anglicans separate the outward and the inward, the visible and the spiritual, the Orthodox tend to see these as an inseparable unity.

4. *The Validity of the Sacraments outside the One True Church*

In the Orthodox Church the principle of Basil the Great is maintained—that of *Economy*. According to Orthodoxy the dogma that 'outside the true Church there is no salvation' predominates. Under the principle of *Economy*, the Orthodox Church considers that, as the Church, it possesses authority over the Sacraments, being able to adapt them according to the circumstances and from being invalid make them valid. Obviously this principle could never be invoked if it clashed with fundamental grounds of the faith,[1] but this still leaves a proper scope for its application. This conception of *Economy* has not been authoritatively defined, but historically is accepted as having been the practice of the Church, in that one and the same sacrament is seen to have been sometimes valid and sometimes invalid. In principle, however, the Orthodox Church does not recognize sacraments administered outside itself; for the acceptance of non-Orthodox sacraments involves the recognition of a Church outside the Orthodox Catholic Church. It is apparent that the Orthodox Church places greater importance on the connection between right faith and right sacraments than does the West.[2]

In the Roman Church the doctrine of St. Augustine is dominant—that those who are in a state of 'invincible ignorance' (*ignorantia invincibilis*) of the true religion are not themselves responsible for their separation from the true Church. Consequently, baptism given

[8] *The Holy Spirit and the Church*, p. 149.
[1] *Report of the Joint Doctrinal Commission* appointed by the Ecumenical Patriarch and the Archbishop of Canterbury for Consultation on the points of agreement and difference between the Anglican and the Orthodox Churches, in 1932 (London, 1932), p. 63.
[2] *Joint Doctrinal Report*, pp. 62–63.

in sincerity by those outside the Church is to be accepted. As Pope Pius IX wrote, '... no person who is baptized in the name of the Father and of the Son and of the Holy Ghost yet in a heretical or schismatical body ought to repeat that sacrament if he returns to the Catholic Church'.[3] Accordingly Bellarmine, on the basis of the resolution at Trent[4] recognized that in the administration of the Sacraments 'it is not necessary to desire to do that which the Roman Church does, but what the true Church does wherever it may be'. This is said with reference to Sacraments in general. There have been exceptions, as when ordinations carried out by Novatian were not considered valid. On the other hand marriages celebrated by Protestants are regarded by Rome as valid, because this sacrament is administered by the parties themselves in their marriage-vows to each other. But, even if limited to Baptism alone, this doctrine seems to justify the Protestant conception of the ideal Church, which is not limited to the Roman, or any other actual institutional Church. This institutional Roman conception concerning the recognition of baptisms administered outside itself, is however counteracted by another Roman view which says that although heretical baptism is valid, nevertheless full membership of the Church is not thereby acquired. In any case this view implies that the Roman Church recognizes that the Catholic Church, the true Church, is wider than the Roman.

To the Anglican Church the sacraments performed by Orthodox and Roman Catholics are valid, although from an Anglican point of view there is a reluctance to define 'valid' and 'invalid' sacraments; it is rather a question of adherence to general rules laid down by competent authority for their due administration. Irregularity of administration may be either justifiable or unjustifiable, but all the sacraments, even those which are unjustifiably irregular, are valid provided that the appointed conditions constituting the sacrament itself are fulfilled,[5] and Professor Greenslade agrees that 'it is admitted

---

[3] Pope Pius IX, 1854; cf. *P.L.* lxv, 692 and Gasparri, op. cit., p. 364. According to St. Augustine, 'Heretics have Sacraments outside the Church, but they do not profit by them, but when they return to the union of fraternal charity, the Sacrament which they possessed outside unity, then begins to profit them, which, received in schism, could not profit them'. *De Bapt. contra Donat*, 1, 12, 18. In the Orthodox Church no consideration of sacrament performed outside the Church is undertaken in the abstract, but only in actual cases of persons so baptized or ordained who are about to return to the Church.

[4] Sess. VII, Canon 4.

[5] *Doctrine in the Church of England*, p. 132.

that God's grace has worked through many an irregular ministry,
where exercised in good faith'.[6]

5. Baptism

The teaching of the three Churches is that Baptism constitutes the
entrance of man into the Christian Church and therefore is the pre-
requisite for receiving the other sacraments. The Orthodox and
Roman Churches teach that in Baptism there is a complete washing,
regeneration, and purification of the baptized person, although the
'old man' remains. No less explicit is the teaching of the Church of
England: 'There is', says the Report *Doctrine in the Church of England*,
'in the New Testament a constant paradox in the expression of the
status of Christians; they are described as washed, sanctified, victorious,
seated with Christ in heavenly places, but are also bidden to walk
worthily of their vocation, and there is full recognition that the evil
powers of "the world" or of "the old Adam" are still active with them.
Each side of the paradox is the expression of reality, and neither must
be sacrificed to the other.' It adds that 'in consequence Baptism, even
infant baptism, is a means of deliverance from the domination of
influences which pre-dispose to sin, and in that sense it is a means of
deliverance from "Original Sin" '.[1]

In the Orthodox Church only Baptism performed by clergymen is
valid, except in case of extreme urgency when it is permissible for
Orthodox laymen to baptize. The Roman Church permits, in case of
necessity, not only lay people, men and women, but even pagans and
heretics, to baptize, provided they observe the form laid down by the
Church and intend to do what the Church does.[2] Similarly 'the
Church of England has followed Western tradition in accepting as
valid baptism performed by unbaptized persons.'[3] In the Orthodox
Church the threefold immersion of the man in the water is considered
necessary; insistence on *immersion* in accordance with the etymological
meaning of the word 'baptize', 'to dip', and with the passage in the
Epistle to the Romans in which Baptism is considered to represent the

---

[6] Schism in the Early Church (London, 1953), p. 181.

[1] *Doctrine in the Church of England*, p. 137.

[2] Council of Florence, Decree for the Armenians (1439); Mansi *Concilia* xxxi,
1059, in Gasparri, *Catechism*, p. 360.

[3] *Doctrine in the Church of England*, p. 133.

three days' burial of our Lord.[4] Pope Pelagius speaks of the triple immersion as a command of our Lord, and in the thirteenth century baptism by immersion still prevailed in the West as is shown by the fonts preserved in some of the most ancient churches in Italy. This difference in the performance of baptism became a point of disagreement between Orthodox and Latins, in the seventeenth and eighteenth centuries, when the Orthodox held the opinion that the Latin baptism was invalid, because the Roman Church had introduced the performance of baptism by sprinkling or affusion instead of immersion, though Roman baptism is now recognized by the Orthodox. The Anglican Church follows in the sacrament the practice of the Roman Church. Although in the 1662 Prayer Book the rubric commands that the child should be 'dipped' into the water, it permits 'pouring' of water over him, if he is considered too weak for this, and this 'pouring' is now common Anglican practice. The Orthodox rite is maintained by the Oriental Churches, Armenians, Copts, and Abyssinians. According to Orthodox teaching the operation of Divine Grace is entrusted to God; for this reason the Orthodox Priest performs the sacrament saying 'The servant of God so-and-so is baptized in the name of the Father, of the Son, and of the Holy Ghost', whereas the Roman and Anglican Priests say 'I baptize . . .' Thus the forms used in the Orthodox and Roman rites are substantially the same, though they differ slightly in some points of detail.

6. *Confirmation*

The Orthodox and Roman Churches accept confirmation as a sacrament. In the early Church, the bishops were the normal ministers of both Baptism and Confirmation. Today this is retained in Confirmation by the Roman and Anglican Churches, while in the Orthodox Church the ancient rite is maintained through the Holy Chrism, which has been especially blessed by the Bishop. Confirmation may also be administered by a priest in the Roman Church, in special cases, with the authority of the Holy See. The Orthodox Church teaches that Chrism and Baptism belong together and should be performed at one and the same time, because Baptism, Confirmation and Holy

[4] Rom. 6: 3–4. '. . . so many of us as were baptized into Jesus Christ were baptized into his death. Therefore we are buried with him by baptism into death . . ..'

Communion constitute an inseparable whole, 'which ought to be conferred on each new Christian as such, whether child or adult'.[1] The only case in which in the Orthodox Church Confirmation is performed apart from Baptism is when a non-Orthodox is reconciled with the Orthodox Church. This is analogous with the reception of heretics as ordered by Pope Stephen I, i.e. after an imposition of hands in penance. The Anglican Church at least re-established that admission to Holy Communion was restricted to those who had been confirmed or were 'ready and desirous to be confirmed', whereas modern Roman practice admits children to Communion before they are confirmed.[2] Among Anglicans there is no unanimous agreement about the character of Confirmation. The dominant opinion is that the 'Seal of the Spirit' is impressed by a ceremony, subsequent to Baptism, 'such as an anointing, the imposition of hands, or the signing with the cross'. According to this opinion 'without Confirmation a man who has only been Baptized lacks, in ways expressed differently by different writers, something which is needful to make him a "full Christian" '. The other opinion, following in the older tradition, holds that the Seal of the Holy Spirit is impressed by Baptism in Water.[3] The Anglican Church would recognize Chrism as a pious and traditional custom, but administers confirmation by laying on of hands rather than by anointing, since the former is the Scriptural practice in regard to the gift of the Holy Spirit.[4] In the Orthodox Church, however, confirmation is given by anointing (Holy Chrism) and there is no laying on of hands. It is only in Roman, and occasionally in Anglican, practice that the two are combined. In regard to the age of Confirmation also, practice differs in that in the Orthodox Church Confirmation (Chrism) is given to infants immediately after baptism. Anglican and Roman scholars recognize that historically Baptism was originally always followed by Confirmation at the earliest possible moment. Nevertheless in pastoral practice both Anglican and Roman Churches require a child, before being confirmed, to receive some instruction and be capable of at least a childish understanding of the Faith, whether this be at the age of seven upwards, as in Roman

[1] J. Meyendorff, *The Orthodox Church*, p. 73.

[2] Bicknell, op. cit., p. 380, and n. 2.

[3] B. Leeming, *Principles of Sacramental Theology*, pp. 167–223.

[4] Especially in Acts 8, narrating how the Apostles Peter and John came from Jerusalem and laid hands upon those in Samaria who had been baptized by Philip, so that 'they received the Holy Ghost'. Cf. *The Prayer Book as Proposed in 1928*, Alternative Order of Confirmation.

practice, or only from the age of twelve, as usually in Anglicanism.
The Anglican tradition is substantially that expressed by Gore when he
writes: 'Confirmation, which is the necessary prelude to Communion,
is in a very special sense the Sacrament of conscious and deliberate
membership.'[5] The Orthodox cite Canon xlviii of the Council of
Laodicea, which states that those baptized must be anointed with
'heavenly Chrism and be partakers of the Kingdom of Christ'. The
form in use in the Roman Church is 'I sign thee with the sign of the
Cross and I confirm thee with the Chrism of salvation, in the name of
the Father, and of the Son and of the Holy Ghost. Amen.' The form
in the Orthodox Church is merely 'The seal of the Gift of the Holy
Ghost. Amen.' But despite these differences, the three Churches are
not divided by any deep disagreements on the essential nature of
Confirmation.

7. The Eucharist

Roman and Orthodox teach that by the words spoken in the Holy
Eucharist the species of bread and wine are changed into the Body and
Blood of Christ, so that although these species have the outward
qualities of bread and wine, essentially they are the Body and Blood
of Christ.[1] An immense quantity of writing and discussion has been
devoted, since the Middle Ages, and especially in the Reformation
period, to controversial questions about the interpretation of the words
'This is my Body' and 'This is my Blood' in regard to the bread and
wine in the Eucharist. Nevertheless, as far as Anglican and Orthodox
belief is concerned, we find that modern Anglican writer, Bicknell,[2]
explains that there is no real difference between the Orthodox and
Anglican views, because while Anglicanism does not deny in any way
the Real Presence of Christ, it rules out any carnal view of it. The

---

[5] Gore, *Orders and Unity*, p. 71.

[1] 'Do not, then, look on it as mere bread and wine, for it is the Body and
Blood of Christ according to the Lord's own declaration; your senses may
suggest to you the former, but your faith renders you firm and secure. Judge
not by the taste but by the faith, put away hesitation and be certain that ye have
been honoured with the gift of the Body and Blood of Christ'. Cyril of Jerusalem,
Catecheses xxii (Migne *P.G.* xxxiii, 1098 ff). Similarly St. John of Damascus,
De Fide Orthodoxa, iv, 13, *P.G.* xciv, 1143 ff and St. John Chrysostom, *Hom.*
lxxxii, 4 *in Mat.* (*P.G.* lviii, 743). Cf. Council of Trent, sess. xiii, in Gasparri,
op. cit., pp. 379–380.

[2] Bicknell, op. cit., p. 400.

opposition to such a phrase as 'real presence', he says,[3] is due in the main to the fear that it means presence in space and involves materialistic ideas. The manner of this presence[4] and its relation to the outward elements, he says, we cannot define, except in so far as we reject certain attempts of our imagination to picture it. In general, Anglicans refuse to define where definition is impossible. They prefer to quote the words of Scripture, appealing to such a text as 1 Corinthians 10:16: 'The cup of blessing which we bless, is it not the communion (partaking) of the blood of Christ? The bread which we break, is it not the communion of the body of Christ?' 'It is wise', says a typical Anglican, Bishop Ellison, 'in matters of controversy to confine ourselves to the words of Scripture, and let them speak to us with the authority they possess'.[5] He adds

On the one hand we deny the doctrine of Transubstantiation, or the changing of the substance of bread and wine, because this cannot be proved from Holy Scripture, and it overthrows the nature of a sacrament. On the other hand we deny that the Holy Communion is merely a bare commemoration of the death of Christ, or merely a sign of the love that Christians ought to have among themselves one to another. That is Zwinglianism. Between those limits we do not seek to define or to require subscription. Rather we repeat the words of Christ and in the Catechism state the fact that the Body and Blood of Christ are verily and indeed taken.[6]

'Orthodox Theologians', writes Visser 't Hooft,[7]

do not adhere to the Roman Catholic doctrine of transubstantiation. Their objection against this doctrine is based on the fact that it is at once too explicit (if the Sacraments are truly mysteries, their character cannot be explained in such logical definitions as are given in Roman doctrine) and too materialistic. For the whole basis of Orthodox thought is that 'transubstantiation' of human and earthly reality is not of a physical but of a metaphysical nature. The change in the Sacrament is real, but it does not consist in a change of the visible matter itself, but rather in a unification of the visible matter with the divine reality.

---

[3] ibid., p. 324.
[4] ibid., p. 395.
[5] G. Ellison, op. cit., p. 77.
[6] ibid., p. 78.
[7] Visser 't Hooft, op. cit., p. 92.

This is not quite accurate, because the Orthodox Church does not reject the word 'Transubstantiation', but it does not attach to it the materialistic meaning which is given by the Latins. The Orthodox Church uses the word 'Transubstantiation' not to define the *manner* in which the bread and wine are changed into the Body and the Blood of the Lord, but only to insist on the fact that the Bread truly, really, and substantially becomes the very Body of the Lord and the wine the very Blood of the Lord. In this sense it is interpreted by St. John of Damascus.[8] In the same manner the majority of the Orthodox theologians used, for the idea of Transubstantiation, a Greek term drawn from the teaching of the ancient Greek Fathers; the terms used include *Metousiōsis, Metabolē, Tropē, Metapoiēsis,* etc., or the Slavonic *Presushchestvlenie,* equivalent of the Greek *Metousiōsis.* The Slavonic word *Sushchestvo* corresponds not to *substantia,* but to *ousia* (*essentia*). The difference between Orthodox and Romans is this: the latter used this word to mean the special theory according to which the change is made, but the Orthodox used it to mean the fact of the change, according to the Patristic conception.[9]

According to Orthodoxy 'Transubstantiation' takes place at the invocation of the Holy Spirit in the words 'And make this Bread the Precious Body of Christ'—and to this the ancient rituals of Rome and Gaul agree. According to the Roman Church the change takes place when the words of our Lord are said: 'Take, eat: This is My Body'. Through the centuries the Orthodox have raised a number of questions about Latin practices with respect to Eucharist as, for example, the use by the Latins of unleavened bread (although the Roman Church has always held that the essential material is bread, whether leavened or unleavened), the reception of Holy Communion under one kind, and so on. Regarding the communion of infants, the Orthodox Church continues the example of the ancient Church in giving them the Holy Communion, whereas the Roman and Anglican Churches reject infant Communion because it is believed that communicants should

[8] *The Holy and Immaculate Mysteries,* Cap. xiii, 7; see also the Orthodox Councils, of Jerusalem in 1672 and of Constantinople in 1727.

[9] J. Douglas, *The relations of the Anglicans with the Eastern Orthodox* (London, 1921), pp. 76–7. M. Jugie, 'Le mot *transubstantiatio* chez les Grecs avant et après 1629', in *Echos d'Orient* 10 (1907), pp. 5 ff and 65 ff. From an Orthodox point of view see I. Karmiris, *The Dogmatic and Symbolic Mnemeia of the Orthodox Catholic Church,* Vol. ii, Athens 1953, pp. 773–83, and Serge Bolshakoff, *The Doctrine of the Unity of the Church in the works of Khomyakov and Möhler,* pp. 161–2.

be able, in the Scriptural words, to 'discern the Lord's body' (1 Cor. 11:29), that is, to have some conscious participation in the sacrament, which clearly infants cannot do.

Anglicans and Orthodox teach that Holy Communion should be given in both kinds; in the Roman Church (from the 11th century) the laity have communicated only in one kind. Pope Gelasius (492-6) said:

We learn that some, taking only their share of the Sacred Body, hold back from the Cup of the Sacred Blood. These persons, since they are scared by some superstition, I know not what, must in any case receive the complete Sacrament, or be altogether excluded from it, since a severance of the Holy thing which is one and the same, cannot take place without great sacrilege.[10]

Thomas Aquinas considers the withholding of the Cup as usual only in certain Churches, and justifies it by the doctrine of 'Concomitance', i.e. that in both the Body and the Blood the whole virtue of the Sacrament is contained. The Council of Trent[11] restricted the Cup to the celebrant, and it added that in the early days of the Christian Church the Cup was not usually given to the laity.

In the Anglican Church the Holy Eucharist is recognized by many of the clergy and laity as the climax of Christian worship, the most sacred act in the worship of the Church. It is valued as having been instituted by our Lord himself and its consecration is believed to have a very real effect, 'since the consecrated elements are by the Will of God now charged with a new spiritual significance and purpose, being the Sacrament of the Body and Blood of Christ'.[12] It is recognized that the Sacrament is the regular spiritual food for the believer, and it is thought normal that he should be given opportunity to communicate weekly or even daily.

Controversy has sometimes occurred in Anglicanism regarding any portions of the consecrated elements which remain after Communion, particularly about the deliberate 'reservation' of these for the communion of the sick or for any other purpose. The Prayer Book of 1662 directs that these should be 'reverently' consumed before the priest

[10] Hase, ibid., vol. ii, p. 286.
[11] Sess. xxi, Canons 2 and 3.
[12] This is a quotation from a statement on Eucharistic doctrine published in 1931 and signed by more than 200 clergymen of all shades of opinion in the Church of England, in Visser 't Hooft, op. cit., p. 53.

leaves the altar at the end of the service. The proposed Prayer Book of 1928 would have permitted 'reservation', and this was one of the points in it considered most controversial at the time. But, although rejected by Parliament and thus prevented from having any legal force, this Prayer Book certainly represented the mind of the Church of England in doctrinal matters. Both it and the Report *Doctrine in the Church of England* clearly regard the consecrated elements as being—permanently and not merely for the purpose of communion—'sacramentally the Body and Blood of Jesus Christ'.[13] Anglican practice in this testifies to Anglican belief, in contrast to that of those Protestant bodies who believe that any bread and wine remaining from the service, not required for communion, may be treated as ordinary unconsecrated materials. But the Anglican Church does not accept 'Transubstantiation' as a dogma or indeed as a true opinion.[14] To sum up the teaching of the Church of England on the Real Presence in the Holy Eucharist: we may record here the catena of quotations from the formularies of the Church of England brought together by Pusey:[15] She teaches, he says, that

'Sacraments ordained by Christ Himself' are means 'whereby God doth work invisibly in us'; 'means whereby we receive the inward part or thing signified' by 'the outward and visible sign'; and that they are 'pledges to assure us thereof'. (These passages are quoted from the 25th Article and from the Catechism.) She teaches that 'the inward part or thing signified in the Sacrament of the Lord's Supper is the Body and Blood of Christ, which are verily and indeed taken and received by the faithful in the Lord's Supper'. (This is quoted from the Catechism.) She teaches that 'Almighty God, our Heavenly Father, hath given His Son our Saviour Jesus Christ to be our spiritual Food and sustenance in that Holy Sacrament' and that this is 'a Divine thing to those who receive it worthily'. (These passages are from the first warning Exhortation of the celebration of the Holy Communion.) She teaches that then 'we spiritually eat the Flesh of Christ and drink His Blood; then we dwell in Christ and Christ in us, we are one with Christ and Christ with us'. (This is from the Longer Exhortation at the time of the Celebration of the Communion.) She teaches that we 'come' there 'to the

---

[13] Joint Doctrinal Report, p. 53.

[14] C. Gore, *The Holy Spirit in the Church*, p. 300, n. 1; cf. also *Doctrine in the Church of England*, pp. 168–9 and 172–8.

[15] *The Real Presence of the Body and Blood of our Lord Jesus Christ. The Doctrine of the English Church* (1869), pp. 234–7.

Body and Blood of Christ'. (This is quoted from St. Basil in the Second Part of the Homily concerning the Sacrament.) She teaches that we 'receive His Blessed Body and Blood under the Form of Bread and Wine'. (This is from the notice at the end of the first Book of Homilies.) She teaches that 'at His Table we', if we be faithful, 'receive not only the outward Sacrament but the Spiritual *thing* also; not the figure only but the truth; not the shadow only, but the Body'. 'Spiritual Food, nourishment of our Soul, a heavenly refection, an invisible meat, a ghostly substance'; that 'Christ' is our 'refection and meat'; that that Body and Blood are present there; for 'in the Supper of the Lord, there is no vain ceremony, no bare sign, no untrue figure of a *thing absent*'. (These passages are from the first part of the Homily concerning the Sacrament.) She teaches that 'the Bread' which 'is Blessed' or 'consecrated' with our Lord's Words, 'This is My Body', 'is the Communion of partaking of the Body of Christ'; that the Cup of Wine which 'is blessed' or 'consecrated' with His Words, 'This is My Blood of the New Testament', 'is to such as rightly, worthily and with faith receive the same', 'the Communion or partaking of the Blood of Christ'. (These passages from the rubric immediately following the words of administration, and from the 28th Article.) She teaches that, if we receive rightly 'we *so* eat the Flesh of Jesus Christ, the Son of God, and drink His Blood, that our sinful bodies are made clean by His Body, and our Souls washed through His most Precious Blood'. (This is from the Prayer of Humble Access in the Eucharistic Liturgy.) She teaches that if we receive rightly we are made 'partakers of His most Precious Body and Blood' and so 'partakers of Christ'. (These passages are from the Prayer of Consecration and the 29th Article.) She teaches that 'God Himself vouchsafes to feed those, who duly receive these Holy Mysteries, with the spiritual Food of the most Precious Body and Blood of His Son our Saviour Jesus Christ'. (This is from the Second Thanksgiving after Communion.) She teaches that 'the Body and Blood' of Christ which were 'given' and 'shed' for us; when received by us, do, if we persevere, 'preserve our bodies and souls unto everlasting life'. (This is from the words of administration.) She teaches that they are 'a salve of immortality and a sovereign pre-servative against death'; 'a deifical Communion', 'the pledge of eternal health, the defence of faith, the hope of the resurrection', 'the Food of immortality, the healthful grace, the conservatory to life everlasting'. (These passages are from the first Part of the Homily concerning the Sacrament.)[16]

---

[16] Puller, op. cit., pp. 56–8, quotes this evidence of the official teaching of the Church of England on the Subject of the Holy Eucharist collected out of its authorized formularies by Dr. Pusey.

The decision of the second Vatican Council to permit Holy Communion in both kinds, although in itself satisfying the Orthodox and Anglicans who maintain the ancient tradition of communion in both kinds, does not go far enough, because only certain people are included, namely, new priests at their ordination, abbesses at their solemn blessing, nuns receiving the consecration of virgins, adult converts being received into the Church, people celebrating their marriage or marking a jubilee of their wedding or religious profession, and deacons and subdeacons at a High Mass or Pontifical Mass. Priests gathered for a large meeting where they cannot say Mass individually or in concelebration, brothers at a concelebrated Mass in a religious House are also included. In a letter sent to each parish the Roman Bishops of England and Wales said that for the time being the Host dipped in the Precious Blood could be given at Mass on the above occasions. This method is known as *Intinctio*. Later, however, they intend to let communicants drink directly from the chalice, through a silver tube or from a spoon. The letter explains that both the Body and the Blood of Christ are present under the appearance of bread alone. The permission for distributing both species is given in these special cases so that 'the sacred sign of the Eucharistic banquet is more clearly seen'.

By the new instruction which the Pope issued on May 1967, *Eucharisticum Mysterium*, he has brought Roman Catholic teaching nearer to the Orthodox position. Among the changes ordered to emphasize the communal nature of the Eucharist are these: Communion may now be received under both kinds on many more occasions, which comes very near to the Orthodox practice. The tabernacle should, as far as possible, be placed in a special chapel of its own, and not in the centre of the Church. This change moves away from the Orthodox custom, which places it towards the back of the Holy Altar. Concelebration, where several priests offer Mass together, is to be encouraged. In the Orthodox Church concelebration is a regular practice. The main theme of *Eucharisticum Mysterium* is one which the Orthodox can fully support, namely that the Eucharist was instituted, not only for the union of the individual with Christ, but also for the union of all Christians among themselves.

According to the Orthodox and Roman Churches the Holy Eucharist is a Sacrament and at the same time a sacrifice offered to obtain mercy for those in life and in death, which will continue until the last judgement. The question arises of how often such a sacrifice may be repeated. In the Roman Church more than one sacrifice by the same Priest and on the same altar can be performed on the same day, but in the Orthodox Church only one can be performed. Bicknell says that it is not true that the Church of England denies Eucharistic sacrifice, but it does repudiate any form of corrupt teaching which makes the Eucharist in any sense a repetition of a sacrifice once for all offered on Calvary.[17]

8. *Priesthood*

In the Roman and Orthodox Churches, Priesthood is regarded as a Sacrament according to Holy Scripture and the tradition of the Church. In both these churches, and in the Anglican Church, there is a threefold ministry of Bishops, Priests, and Deacons, and these are Holy Orders, any other traditional ranks below that of Deacon, such as Subdeacon and Acolyte, being Minor Orders. But 'Priesthood' may also be understood in a general sense in which it is shared by all bishops as well as by the most numerous order of the ministry, that of priests. For the normal life of the Church, this ministry (of bishops and priests) is essential, deacons and others being assistants to this ministry. The question sometimes at issue between Orthodox and Romans on one side, and Anglicans on the other, is: In what sense is this regular ministry in the church 'priestly'?

According to the Roman and Orthodox Churches priesthood is of two kinds: spiritual and sacramental. For the spiritual priesthood all Christians are equally endowed and they exercise it in common (I Pet. 2:9). The priesthood to which special members are sacramentally ordained in the Church, is that which Christ committed to his Apostles and which is continued down into our day by the Apostolic succession. All who are baptized hold the spiritual priesthood, enabling them to be in union with the ordained priest and to participate in the liturgical worship in which they offer the holy oblation. Thus, to use the words of Pope Pius XII,

The priest acts for the people only because he represents Jesus Christ, who is Head of all members and offers Himself in their stead. Hence he goes to the altar as the minister of Christ, inferior to Christ but superior to the people. The people on the other hand, since they in no sense represent the Divine Redeemer and are not a mediator between themselves and God, can in no way possess the sacerdotal power.[1]

[17] Bicknell, op. cit., p. 341; cf. also Gore, *Orders and Unity*, p. 65. See also below, p. 241.

[1] *Mediator Dei* (Nov. 1947), 84. See above, p. 171.

From an Orthodox point of view[2] the words of this Pope correspond absolutely to Orthodox teaching. According to the Church of England,

The fundamental Christian Ministry is the Ministry of Christ. There is no Christian Priesthood or Ministry apart from this. . . . The Church as the Body of Christ, sharing His life, has a ministerial function derived from that of Christ. In this function every member has his place and share according to his different capabilities and calling. The work of the Church is to bring all the various activities and relationships of men under the control of the Holy Spirit, and in this work each has his part. The particular function of the official Ministry can only be rightly understood as seen against the background of this universal ministry.[3]

This doctrine is elaborated by Gore at many points in his work *The Ministry of the Christian Church*. For example:

. . . all are offerers, but they offer through one who is empowered to this high charge, to 'offer the gifts' for God's acceptance and the consecration of his Spirit. . . . The individual life can receive the fellowship with God only through membership in the one Body and by dependence upon social sacraments of regeneration, of confirmation, of communion, of absolution, of which ordained ministers are the appointed instruments.[4]

And the doctrinal Report says

A layman may, and on occasion should, proclaim the word of God's forgiveness. But it is only the priest who is authorised to pronounce the Word of Absolution in the Church.[5]

As with the question of the transformation, if any, effected in the bread and wine in the Eucharist, the question of sacramental priesthood and its relation to the priesthood of all believers has been the subject of a vast amount of controversy in the history of the Church, at least in the West. But the above quotations suggest that, despite past controversies, there is substantial ground for agreement between

---

[2] Karmiris, *The Symbolic and Dogmatic Mnemeia*, ibid. vol. ii, p. 640, cf. also Trembelas, *Dogmatic*, vol. iii (Athens, 1961), pp. 288–9. See moreover S. Bolshakoff, op. cit., pp. 162–3.

[3] *Doctrine in the Church of England*, p. 114.

[4] Gore, *The Ministry of the Christian Church*, ibid. pp. 93–4. cf. also *Doctrine in the Church of England*, pp. 114 ff, 157–8, 199.

[5] *Doctrine in the Church of England*, p. 158.

Orthodox, Roman, and Anglican thought on the fundamentals of the subject.

One particular point has in the past proved controversial: the question of the 'matter' and 'form' of ordination for the priesthood. Some have maintained that this is the imposition of hands, with the appropriate words of prayer, but some Roman authorities have taught that it was the presentation of the holy vessels, the chalice and paten, symbolizing the authority to celebrate the Eucharist (*porrectio instrumentorum*). On this ground, amongst others, Romans in the past rejected the validity of Anglican Orders. This question was settled, in the Roman Church, by the Apostolic Constitution[6] on Holy Orders issued in 1947. Although this decision had no reference to the past, thenceforth it could no longer be maintained that the presentation of the holy vessels was essential for the ordination of a priest. A point of disagreement between the Churches was thus removed.

9. *Marriage*

Both Romans and Orthodox agree that matrimony is a sacrament which endows the couple with divine grace. According to the Council of Trent[1] marriage was ordained as a Sacrament by Christ, and is a chosen vessel of God's favour.

Anglicans in general would readily agree that marriage has a sacramental character and that in Christian marriage divine grace is given to the couple for their married life. Differences arise, in particular, in regard to the question of the indissolubility of marriage. All the Churches regard this as the ideal and the norm, in accordance with our Lord's words 'What therefore God hath joined together, let not man put asunder' (Matt. 19:6). The Orthodox Church allows divorce on the basis of the words that follow (Matt. 19:9) 'except it be for fornication'; it regards this as a last resource, after all attempts at reconciliation have failed, and in such cases permits remarriage. With this many Anglicans would agree. Other Anglicans, and the consistent teaching of the Roman Church, would allow no form of divorce that permits remarriage, but only, in essential cases, a separation 'from bed and board', the sacramental bond of the marriage remaining unbroken as long as both parties live. Thus Pope Eugenius IV (1421–47) taught, in the *Decretum pro Armenis*, that although such separations

---

[6] B. Leeming, *Principles of Sacramental Theology*, p. 370.
[1] Sess. XXIV, *de Sacram.*, Can. 1.

are allowable 'The bond of lawful wedlock is perpetual'. It has been said that this kind of semi-divorce was unknown in Jewish law or to the Apostolic Church.[2] Critics of the Roman position also point out that the Roman use of the procedure for a decree of nullity (a decision that no indissoluble bond of wedlock existed and the parties are therefore free) has amounted in some cases to something very like the permission of divorce. The Orthodox would prefer that the principle of 'Economy' already mentioned, by which the Church has a certain power to regulate the administration of the Sacraments, is better than the Roman legislation. Anglican thought on the whole prefers to concentrate on fundamental principles while admitting differences of application. Thus the Doctrinal Report emphasizes that marriage has the character which enables St. Paul to draw an analogy between it and the Union of Christ and the Church.[3]

Minor matters, such as the relationships within which marriage is not allowed (the 'prohibited degrees') and the questions concerning the marriage of unbaptized persons, are differently dealt with in the different churches, but are not fundamental to the understanding of marriage.

10. *Confession and Absolution*

The Orthodox and Roman Churches teach that confession followed by absolution is one of the sacraments, but in practice in the West this sacrament had a different development which caused many afflictions to the Church. In the Anglican Church, as has been pointed out in connection with the number of the Sacraments (p. 181 above), Sacramental absolution after Confession to a priest is available but not obligatory. The Commission on Christian Doctrine in the Church of England stated that

the authoritative teaching of the Church of England neither enjoins nor advises the regular and universal practice of auricular confession. Nevertheless, the Church of England does not minimise the need of confession and absolution. Sin is always an act which injures the whole

[2] Hase, op. cit., vol. ii, p. 305.

[3] Op. cit., pp. 200, 201. While adhering to such a fundamental principle as this, the Church of England is at present engaged in a reconsideration of its practice in regard to remarriage after divorce and attention is paid to the Orthodox attitude to the subject. See the Report, *Marriage, Divorce and the Church* (S.P.C.K., 1971).

Body of Christ . . . while the regular practice of auricular confession has now become more frequent, and is by no means confined to one school of thought within the Church of England, it is important to recognise that it is a ministry of the Word which is open to all but obligatory upon none.[1]

The attitude of the Anglican Church towards Confession reflects, as Bishop Ellison says, the whole attitude of Anglicanism towards the conscience of the individual, 'on which Anglicanism places the onus of responsibility, and not upon the dictates of the Church', and 'this requires the greatest effort. This gives opportunity for a higher form of discipline and self-sacrifice than can be called forth by compulsion.'[2]

11. *Holy Unction*

The Roman and the Orthodox Churches regard Holy Unction as one of the sacraments. The only difference is that the Roman Church has in the past performed it as a preparation for death (*extrema unctio*). It was not, however, necessary or advisable to wait until the danger of death was imminent.[1] In this sense Extreme Unction in the Roman Church could, as with the Orthodox, be a sacrament of the living, not a sacrament of the dying (in spite of the decision of the Council of Trent).[2] The Second Vatican Council shows a return to the more correct doctrine that the anointing is for the sick rather than for the dying.[3] It can now, therefore, be repeated. According to the Epistle of James (5:14 ff.) Holy Unction is not a means to a holy death, but is intended for the recovery of the sick by means of faith in connection with the miraculous power of healing possessed by the Apostolic Church. As this power, however great it was, did not work infallibly, for Holy Unction had been administered to those who were seriously ill and followed more frequently by death than by cure, this Sacrament was changed in the Roman Church to a Sacrament of the dying, but still in the Council of Trent[4] it 'maintained a slight trace of cure as its object'. In the Church of England, when the Thirty-Nine Articles

[1] *Doctrine in the Church of England*, pp. 191, 192.
[2] G. Ellison, *The Anglican Communion*, p. 84 ff.
[1] B. J. Kelly, p. 123.
[2] Sess. XIV, *de Sacr. Extr. Unct.* Can. 1.
[3] *Instruction on putting into effect the Constitution on the Sacred Liturgy* (Catholic Truth Society, 1964), pp. 23–24.
[4] Sess. XIV, Can. 2.

were composed and reference was made to Unction it was thought of as introduced by a 'corrupt following of the Apostles', but the Commission on Doctrine said 'we think that what has been said should be present to the minds of those who have to decide whether or not official provision should be made in the Church of England for a rite of Unction; on this point the Commission is divided.'[5] Nevertheless some diocesan bishops in the Church of England do in fact make the Holy Oils available to parish priests for the purpose of anointing the sick. The consecration of the Oils takes place at a celebration of Holy Communion by the Bishop on Maundy Thursday.

[5] *Doctrine in the Church of England*, p. 200.

PART III

Chapter VIII

TOWARDS UNITY

1. *Between Romans and Orthodox: a General Survey*

The greatest obstacle to Roman-Orthodox unity is that from a Roman Catholic point of view the unity of the Church is understood in terms of a 'return' of the Eastern Churches to the 'Catholic Church' considered as the Papal, that is, the Roman Communion. Although during the last one hundred years the attitude of the Roman Church towards the East has undergone a considerable development there is still no common point for Roman–Orthodox unity. Even today the Roman attitude to union with the Orthodox is the same as it has been for a long time. There is only one Church, from which all others have separated themselves. (This applies, writes Canon Bernard Pawley, ironically, even to the Orthodox Patriarchates of the East!) Nevertheless some Protestants think that the decree *De Ecumenismo* 'sets forth for all time *a completely new concept of Ecumenism*'—new at any rate from the Roman point of view. The Orthodox think that the expression 'separated brethren' which appears in the document and the special place which is given to the Roman Church as the centre, 'surrounded by the Churches and Communities as if they were satellites', show that the doctrine of the Roman Church concerning the restoration of Christian Unity is unaltered. Especially 'the chapter concerning the Eastern Churches is unfortunately distorted by its preoccupation with the Uniate Churches'[1]. The dialectical nature of the Orthodox Church differs from the legalistic Roman conception. On the one hand Orthodoxy conceives itself as the Church of Christ, which alone conserves true Orthodoxy, the pure undefiled truth handed down from the days of the Apostles and the early Church of

[1] Bernard Pawley, 'An Anglican views the Council', in *Steps to Christian Unity*, p. 112.

the Fathers and the Councils. On the other hand, it has promoted encounter and co-operation with the Christian Churches which are separated from it.

The Romans emphasize the efforts of the Popes to persuade the Eastern Churches to return to the 'Catholic Church'. They praise all the affection and love of the Popes for Eastern Christians and they instance all the good will on the Papal side concerning respect for the Eastern Churches' privileges.

In the Encyclical *Praeclara Gratulationis* (1894) Pope Leo XIII describes the traditions of the Eastern Churches with appreciation and love. Leo, however, repeated the usual Latin mistake; he did not ask the Eastern and Roman Churches to be united, but he asked the Eastern Church to 'return' to unity. In some other matters he changed the papal vocabulary: he said

the line that separates us is not very wide. Moreover, apart from a few points, there is such a complete agreement on everything else that we often times rely on the authorities and reasons for doctrines, customs, and rites of the Eastern Churches for the defence of the Catholic faith.[2]

The same attitude was displayed by Leo XIII in his encyclicals *Christi Nomen* and *Orientalium Dignitas*. To these the Orthodox Church answered in a letter of the Ecumenical Patriarchate:[3]

The Orthodox Church of Christ is always ready to accept any proposal of union, if only the Bishop of Rome would shake off once for all the whole series of the many and divers anti-evangelical novelties that have been 'privily brought in' to his Church, and have provoked the sad division of the Churches of the East and West, and would return to the basis of the seven Holy Ecumenical Councils, which having been assembled in the Holy Spirit, of representatives of all the Holy Churches of God, . . . *have a universal and perpetual supremacy in the Church of Christ*. And this, both by her writings and encyclical letters the Orthodox Church has never ceased to intimate to the Roman Church, having clearly and explicitly set forth that so long as the latter perseveres in her innovations and the Orthodox Church adheres to the

[2] See Tavard, *Two Centuries of Ecumenism*, p. 87; cf. G. Baum, *The Quest for Christian Unity*, p. 31.

[3] *Encyclical Patriarchal and Synodical of the Ecumenical Patriarchate*. English transl. by E. Metallinos (Oxford, printed by Horace Hart, 1896). This document of the Ecumenical Patriarchate has been published by A. Lowndes, *Vindication of Anglican Orders* (New York, 1899–1900), Vol. ii, pp. cxlviii–clxv.

divine and apostolic traditions and institutions of the first nine centuries of Christianity, during which the Western Churches were of the same mind and were united with the Churches of the East, so long is it a vain and empty thing to talk of union. . . . The union of the separated Churches with herself in *one rule of faith* is a sacred and inward desire of the Holy, Catholic and Orthodox Apostolic Church of Christ, but without such unity in the faith the desired union of the Churches becomes impossible. This being the case, we wonder in truth how the Most Blessed Pope, Leo XIII, though he himself also acknowledges this truth, falls into a plain self-contradiction, declaring, on the one hand, that every Church, even after the union can hold her own dogmatic and canonical definitions, even when they differ from *those of the Roman Church*, as His Holiness declares in a letter encyclical dated November 30, 1894.

The Patriarchal Letter goes on to enumerate the innovations of the Roman Church and says:

These innovations, which have reference to essential points of the faith and of the administrative system of the Church, and which are manifestly opposed to the ecclesiastical conditions of the first nine centuries, make the longed-for union of the Churches impossible; and every pious and Orthodox heart is filled with inexpressible sorrow on seeing the Roman Church disdainfully persisting in them, and not in the least contributing to the sacred purpose of union by rejecting those heretical innovations and coming back to the ancient condition of the one holy, catholic and apostolic Church of Christ, of which she also at that time formed a part.

The Roman Church considers the primacy of the Pope to be the only obstacle in the way of unity between the Eastern and Western Churches, whereas the Orthodox Church believes that there are many doctrinal differences, which the Patriarchal Letter describes. The basic difference is seen in the divergent understanding of the term 'unity' itself; unity to the Eastern Church means unity in faith, as it was in the primitive Church, and not the 'return' of the Orthodox to the Roman jurisdiction. Before the separation between East and West, the Orthodox were united with the Pope and the Pope with the Orthodox, but the Orthodox were never under the authority or jurisdiction of the Pope.

The same attitude towards the East is shown in more recent Papal pronouncements: Pius XI in his *Rerum Orientalium* (1929) and *Nostis Qua* and Pius XII in his *Orientales Omnes* (1945).[4] All these appeals to the East suffer from the same disadvantage that they treat the East as a 'dissident' Church, which ought to 'return' to Rome. All the approaches which Rome made to the East are regarded by the Orthodox Church as a means not to unite the Church but to subject the East to the West. There are, however, some interesting points in the recent encyclicals which we must not overlook. For the first time the Popes have declared that the reconciliation between East and West would be beneficial to the entire Catholic Church, Roman and Orthodox: for example, Pius XII, in his Encyclical *Orientales Omnes* wrote that: 'From the full and perfect unity of all Christians the Mystical Body of Christ and all its members, one by one, are bound to reap great spiritual profits.' Pope John XXIII was the first to acknowledge a degree of Roman Catholic responsibility for Christian disunity.

Having in mind the above antithesis between Rome and the Orthodox we must frankly acknowledge that we cannot at present see any possibility of reconciliation. We know that there are honest people amongst Roman Catholics who look upon their Orthodox brethren with sincere friendship, and I suppose that there are a few amongst the Orthodox who hope for unity with Rome. In the Orthodox East there are still deep anti-Roman Catholic feelings because of the attitude which the Romans adopted until recently,[5] and also because the Roman Church is thought to have changed the Christian Faith.

Roman Catholic theologians appear to think that Rome and

[4] There were many occasions on which Pope Pius XII insisted on the return of the Orthodox to the Roman Church; see, besides the above Encyclical the appeals *Orientalis Ecclesiae decus*, issued on the occasion of the commemorations of the fifteenth centenary of the death of St. Cyril of Alexandria; *Sempiternus Rex* (1951), issued on the fifteenth centenary of the Council of Chalcedon, *Sacro vergente anno* (1952), addressed to the people of Russia, and *Orientales Ecclesias* (1952); cf. 'Pius XII and the East', *E.C.Q.* xi (1956), pp. 232–8. See also, *E.C.Q.* xii (1958–9), pp. 321–2.

[5] It is not correct, as Visser 't Hooft writes (op. cit., pp. 137–8), that up to the period of Pope John XXIII the Roman Church showed no desire to recognize Orthodoxy itself as a genuine and full expression of Christian life. On the contrary, in the authoritative publications emanating from Roman quarters we see that Rome always recognized the Orthodox Church as such, but 'separated from Rome'. See Pope Leo's *Christi Nomen, Orientalium Dignitas, Praeclara Gratulationis*, Pope Pius XI's *Rerum Orientalium, Nostis Qua* and Pius XII's *Orientales Omnes*. See above, p. 69.

8

Orthodoxy 'have the same Faith'[6] and that they need a certain method in theology, and since they have a different way of thinking they must treat the whole question, not dividing up the faith into different treatises, and giving up the practice of selecting particular points in doctrine and discussing them in isolation, and especially of quoting snippets from the Fathers irrespective of the whole context. Only in this way will both sides understand the development of the various subjects which has taken place in one Church or the other. The Orthodox however think differently, believing that in the West the Faith has been changed, and that there are obstacles, which at present appear insuperable, to a sincere *rapprochement*.

(i) *Differences in the way of thinking between East and West*

First of all the two Churches feel deeply their membership in the One Catholic and Apostolic Church. The Romans believe that the faith of the 'dissident' Orthodox is, in its very essence, none other than the Catholic Faith as apprehended previous to the schism. Hence the difference at the present day is not great or essential. The faith of the first seven Councils is seen as essentially that which has developed into the Catholic faith of today. The Orthodox Church remained outside the Western Mediaeval and Reformation disputes and has never known the rationalistic subtleties of Roman scholasticism. The Roman spirit in doctrinal matters is legalistic; the Orthodox have retained the characteristics of the primitive church. Identical theological terms have in the West a juridical colour, whereas in the East they are ontologically understood. Orthodox theology is more speculative, more mystical and more theocentric, whereas Western theology is more practical, more moral and more anthropocentric. The Western theologian is the successor of the legal counsellors of Imperial Rome, the Orthodox of the Greek philosophers. The Eastern Church produced a complete theology, whereas with the exception of Augustine, no really distinguished exponent of Catholic–Orthodox theology appeared in the West.[7] It is sometimes said that the teaching of Eastern and of Western theologians, in regard to the Holy Trinity, for example,

[6] Cf. B. Leeming, 'Orthodox-Catholic Relations', *R.E.C.*, p. 15. Fr. Leeming thinks that both East and West have the same faith deriving from the very same sources and the same authority in interpreting the doctrine prevailing in their respective Churches.

[7] The Romans say that from a theoretical point of view the theological expressions which differ are often complementary rather than contradictory. The

in the Fathers of the fourth century, was fundamentally one, but differed in emphasis and approach, as when the doctrine of the Holy Trinity starts from the three divine Persons and proceeds to consider the Unity, in contrast to starting with the divine Unity and proceeding to the three Persons.[8] This however is not a complete explanation of East/West differences. The Orthodox preserved healthy ancient traditions, where the Romans failed either to maintain or restore them. Orthodox ecclesiology is that of the Fathers of the Church and especially of the Cappadocian Fathers, but post-Tridentine Roman Catholic views are different from this. The Romans consider the extension of the Church and the number of the faithful, whereas the Orthodox see rather the depth of the Church and the quality of its members. . . . Romans view the horizontal plane that covers the face of the earth, while the Orthodox contemplate the perpendicular which joins earth to heaven. For one thousand years, during which union between East and West was maintained, the Orthodox Church practised a system of collegial synods for Church government, without Rome finding anything abnormal in this system, or the East seeing anything unorthodox in the Roman centralism (i.e. papal domination).[9]

(ii) *The main obstacles to Roman–Orthodox unity*

From an Orthodox point of view the two Churches ought, with a sincere desire to know the truth, to examine what the Holy Catholic and Orthodox Apostolic Church of Christ, before the division of the same body throughout the East and West, believed, and to hold this fast, entire, and unaltered. This does not refer to the differences regarding the ritual and hymns, or vestments and the like, which do not in the least injure the substance and unity of the faith; but to those essential differences concerning the divinely transmitted doctrines of the faith, and the divinely instituted canonical constitution of the

Decree on Ecumenism states that 'the authentic theological traditions of the Orientals are remarkably well rooted in the sacred Scriptures, they find their support and their expression in the life of the Liturgy, they draw sustenance from the living traditions of the Apostles and from writings of the Eastern Fathers and spiritual writers, their tendency is towards the right ordering of life and indeed towards a full contemplation of Christian Truth.' (Catholic Truth Society ed. p. 16).

[8] See an article 'Eastern and Western Mentality' in *E.C.Q.* ix (1952), p. 393.

[9] See the article mentioned in the last note, pp. 392–401; this was written by an Easterner who was united with Rome and knew both sides; cf. also Clement Engbert, 'Eastern Orthodox Theology,' *E.C.Q.* xii (1958) p. 173 ff.

Churches and their administration. On the purpose of unity the Patriarchal Letter of 1895 says that

> the Eastern Orthodox and Catholic Church of Christ is ready heartily to accept all that which both the Eastern and Western Churches unanimously professed before the ninth century, if she has perchance perverted or does not hold it. And if the Westerns prove from the teaching of the Holy Fathers and the divinely assembled Ecumenical Councils that the then Orthodox Roman Church, which was throughout the West, ever before the ninth century read the Creed with the addition, or used unleavened bread, or accepted the doctrine of purgatorial fire, or sprinkling instead of baptism, or the immaculate conception of the ever-Virgin, or the temporal power, or the infallibility and absolutism of the Bishop of Rome, we have no more to say. If, on the contrary, it is plainly demonstrated, as those of the Latins themselves who love the truth also acknowledge, that the Eastern and Orthodox Catholic Church of Christ holds fast the anciently transmitted doctrines which were at that time professed in common both in the East and the West, and that the Western Church perverted them by divers innovations, then it is clear, even to children, that the more natural way to union is the return of the Western Church to the ancient doctrinal and administrative condition of things, for the faith does not change in any way with time or circumstances, but remains the same always and everywhere, for 'there is one Body and one Spirit'.

(iii)   *The three main doctrinal obstacles*

(a)   *The Procession of the Holy Spirit.* The Orthodox Church cannot accept the addition of the *Filioque* clause to the original Creed made by the Roman Church and maintained by the Anglican Church. This formulation was first made formally by the Roman Council of Lyons (1274, *De processione Spiritus Sancti*) 'That the Holy Spirit proceeds eternally from the Father and the Son, not as from two principles, but from one, not by two breathings (spirations) but from a single breathing and that this has always been the profession of the Holy Roman Church' and again by the Council of Florence (1439, Decree for the Greeks) 'that when the Holy Fathers and Doctors say that the Holy Spirit proceeds from the Father through the Son they mean thereby to signify that the Son also is the cause, according to the Greek Fathers, or the principle according to the Latins, of the subsistence of the Holy Spirit, just as is the Father'. These assertions are regarded by the Orthodox Church as innovations and alterations to the ecumenical creed of the one Church. This Western innovation has been repeated in the Decree *de Ecumenismo*.[10]

(b) *The Roman Primacy*. It is impossible to achieve unity between East and West without a change in the doctrine concerning the primacy of the Pope in the universal Church and his infallibility. The Roman Church however has recently declared that it cannot abandon the prerogatives of the Pope. Since the Papal claims were declared a dogma of the Catholic faith by the First Vatican Council and have not been changed at all by the Second Vatican Council, this barrier still remains insurmountable to the Orthodox, for Orthodoxy cannot accept the Roman 'dogma' which sanctifies all other doctrinal innovations of the Roman Catholic Church. Whatever explanation might be given for a recognition of papacy, or for a re-examination of the Pope's position within the college of bishops, or of the relationship between the Pope and the bishops,[11] the Orthodox attitude is unanimous and firm. No Bishop or Pope or Patriarch is above the college of bishops. (Much earlier in his letter of 18 January 1924, Cardinal Mercier had written that 'the Papal Primacy was the first thing and the last thing to be discussed'.) In this matter Cardinal Bea is right in saying that there are two obstacles to unity between Rome and Orthodoxy: Roman Primacy and Papal infallibility.[12] The reason is simple; in any approach to unity with Rome, papal prerogatives raise the whole question of the nature of the Church. Papal supremacy in the Universal Church, and papal infallibility, will never be accepted by the Orthodox Church. The Orthodox do more than refuse to accept; they reject such a papacy altogether. It is a great pity that the Second Vatican Council, instead of bridging the gap between the Pope and the bishops, has increased the division by the distinction it made between the bishops as successors of the Apostles, and the Pope as the Successor of Peter. According to the Orthodox Church the primacy of the Pope affects the whole structure of the Church, its ecclesiology, and its administration.[13] The Orthodox Church, said Archbishop

[10] *The Decree on Ecumenism of the Second Vatican Council*. A New Translation by the Secretariat for Promoting Christian Unity with a Commentary by Thomas F. Stransky, C.S.P. (Paulist Press, Glen Rock, N.Y. 1965), p. 75.

[11] cf. Decree *de Ecclesia* (Catholic Truth Society, London, 1965), pp. 27–46, and appendix pp. 91–94.

[12] Bea, *The Unity of Christians*, pp. 161, 175; cf. *C. E.* v (1924), p. 127.

[13] At the present time various suggestions have been made for a fresh examination of the Roman primacy in relation to the Eastern Churches: cf. the following: Fr. Paul Mailleux, S.J., in *Problems before Unity* (Dublin), pp. 46–57. A

Jacovos of America, recognizes the Pope as the first and foremost of the bishops of the world, but having a primacy of honour alone, and equal in jurisdiction to the other bishops, or rather to the other Patriarchs. (*Primus inter pares non primus super omnes.*) Infallibility, the Orthodox claim, is a gift of the Holy Spirit residing in the whole Church, not in the first of the Bishops alone. The doctrine of collegiality contained in the Council's Constitution *On the Church* represents some forward movement from an Orthodox point of view. Collegiality however, as defined by the Council, does not recognize the 'principles of self-government and autonomy guaranteed by the early Councils of the Church'.[14]

(c) *The Mother of God*. The Orthodox Church would agree with the Roman Church on the doctrine of the importance of Mary's role in the Incarnation, but it would not agree with some former Roman teachings about Mary's role in the Redemption. Many Orthodox do however use the equivalent of the term *Mediatrix* (John Damascene, St. Andrew of Crete, Gregory Palamas, etc.).[15] With regard to the Immaculate Conception, and the Corporeal Assumption of the Mother

---

Kartashoff, *Christian Reunion. The Ecumenical Problem in the Orthodox Conscience* [in Russian] (Paris, Y.M.C.A. Press, no date), p. 82. N. Afanasieff, *The Lord's Table* [in Russian] (Paris, 1955) and *La Primauté de Pierre dans l'église Orthodoxe* (Neuchatel, 1960). A. Schmemann, 'The Idea of Primacy in Orthodox Ecclesiology', in *St. Vladimir's Seminary Quarterly*, Vol. 4 (New York, 1960). See also an article by Georges Dejaifve under the title, 'East and West. Two Theologies, One Faith', *R.E.C.* p. 51 ff, which deserved great attention, as revealing the new attitudes of Romans towards the East. As an answer to the above see the articles of Professor Trembelas entitled 'Unacceptable theories concerning Unam Sanctam', *Ecclesia*, 41 (1964), pp. 167 ff.

[14] *Catholic Herald*, 20 Oct. 1965. The Orthodox view was stated by Professor Glubokovsky in 1924: 'I differentiate the historical Papacy from the dogmatised Papacy. The second, of course did not appear *ex abrupto*, and is connected with the first by some genetic succession, but for the Orthodox mind it is a hyperbolic deviation. With such a Papacy—I am saying this with the greatest regret—I do not foresee any peace, and I must sum up the Orthodox frame of mind in regard to it by the celebrated formula *sint ut sunt*. But I accept the historic Papacy, and we Orthodox are ready to return to it. I firmly believe that, if the Papacy will forego its claims, all misunderstanding will disappear, and that even the so-called dogmatic differences will be levelled to a peaceful cohabitation. Thus, the final word lies with the Papacy, and to it I turn with the hearty appeal: *Fiat ex Occidente Pax*!' 'Papal Rome and Orthodox East,' *C.E.* v (1924), p. 167.

[15] *A Patristic Greek Lexicon*, ed. G. W. H. Lampe (Oxford, 1961–8) gives one quotation for *mesités* (mediator) as applied to the Virgin Mary, and this excludes authors later than about A.D. 800.

of God, although there is nothing in the piety of the Orthodox Church which forbids its people to believe them, yet the fact that the Roman Church has defined these dogmas, ignoring the rest of Christendom, and that it commands the Churches to accept its definitions, makes agreement very difficult.

Orthodox Christians, said Archbishop Jacovos of America, feel that the Latin Church 'goes too far' in its Marian theology. But the inclusion of the Virgin Mother in the Second Vatican Council's Decree *On the Church*[16] rather than the issuing of a separate document on Mariology, as some of the bishops wished, is a 'definite advance' which is 'much appreciated by the Orthodox'.

On the dogma of the Immaculate Conception as defined by Pope Pius IX in 1854, the Orthodox teaching is that Christ alone was conceived without being subject to sin, corruption and death, and that only through Mary's acceptance of the Archangel's invitation was she sinless, or completely at one with God. As to the dogma, proclaimed by Pius XII in 1950, of our Lady's Assumption into Heaven, the Orthodox see in it a possible implication that Mary, because of her Immaculate Conception, did not die. 'But if', writes Professor Alivizatos, 'there is no question of any such mischievous intention [viz: that the new dogma had been created out of nothing to raise a new barrier or division], then let this so-called new dogma be considered by us who are outside as at least one of those doubtful points (*dubia*) for which *Libertas* is fitting, in order that we can proceed without interruption in the effort we are making. For this above all things is required *in omnibus caritas*.'[17]

2. *The Dialogue between Rome and the Orthodox*

In spite of many differences and of centuries of mutual hostility, the two Churches have declared that they will come together in dialogue. 'The Orthodox and Roman Catholic Churches share the privilege of defending Catholic principles in the Ecumenical dialogue. No other Church is basically committed to fidelity to Tradition. No other Church is exempt from what the Catholics and Orthodox, in the light of the great councils, judge to be heresies.'[1] Three factors have helped

[16] *Catholic Herald*, 20 Oct. 1965.
[17] H. Alivizatos, 'The New Dogma from an Eastern Orthodox Standpoint', *E.R.* iii (1951), p. 158.
[1] Tavard, op. cit., p. 211.

to bring Romans and Orthodox nearer to one another. For many centuries interpreters who spoke both Latin and Greek were exceedingly rare. This fact made understanding between the two Churches difficult. Today the Churches communicate with one another more easily because of the great improvement in the means of communication. Secondly the election to the Papal throne of Pope John XXIII was an event of significance.[2] Finally, the constant and sincere efforts for Christian unity of Patriarch Athenagoras of Constantinople have been of considerable importance.[3] In order to appreciate fully the Orthodox attitude towards Christian unity we must take into account the attitude of Patriarch Athenagoras's predecessors. Patriarch Joachim III, in his Patriarchal encyclical of 1902, set forth Orthodoxy's principal aim in participating in the Ecumenical Movement.[4]

This attitude of the Ecumenical Patriarchate proved that the Orthodox Church has for a long time had in mind the restoration of disrupted

[2] Cf. *John XXIII, Pope of the Council*, by Zsolt Aradi, M. Derrick and D. Woodruff (London, 1961); cf. also Stephen Neill, *Men of Unity* (London, S.C.M. Press, 1960), pp. 169–80. The writings of Pope John show 'a tension between monologue and dialogue, between the Pope's intention and what might be called Vatican Curialism. It grieved and disappointed many Orthodox Christians to read the Encyclical *Aeterna Dei Sapientia*, published in commemoration of Leo I (A.D. 461) because without careful consideration for the "Brother" it takes up the most delicate question of the old discord. The spirit of superficial monologue, which is not usually a characteristic of the present Pope, seems to have prevailed in this particular encyclical.' K. E. Skydsgaard, 'From Monologue to Dialogue', *E.R.* xiv (1962), p. 435.

[3] Cf. Cary MacEoin, 'Athenagoras, The Orthodox Prophet', in *Sign*, April 1964; also cf. A. Michalenko, 'Athenagoras I, Patriarch-Ecumenist', in *Chrysostom*, Winter 1965–66. See also Francis House, 'The Ecumenical significance of the Patriarchate of Constantinople', in *E.R.* ix (1957), pp. 310–20.

[4] These are the main principles of the Encyclical: 'although our primary task is to watch over our own doctrines, we must nevertheless be also concerned for our Christian brothers and never cease from our prayers for the union of all into one. Difficulties should not discourage us, nor should the thought of the apparent impossibility of it stop us from engaging ourselves in the work of Church unity which is dear to God or from examining existing possibilities for it; we should always remember that it is our duty to walk in wisdom, and to conduct ourselves in meekness towards our separated brothers, for they also believe in the All-Holy Trinity and take pride in being called with the name of our Lord Jesus Christ, hoping also to be saved by the Grace of God.' Cf. Archbishop Jacovos, 'The Contribution of Eastern Orthodoxy to the Ecumenical Movement', *E.R.* xi (1959), pp. 396–397. From a Roman Catholic point of view, the 1920 Encyclical of the Ecumenical Patriarchate was described as having been 'written in an entirely new spirit of moderation and love'. *E.R.* xvii (1965), p. 307.

Christian Unity. This initial movement was followed by another appeal, in 1920, to 'All the Churches of Christ wheresoever they be'. This document is regarded as one of the most significant early records of the Ecumenical Movement and shows that the Patriarchate of Constantinople had never stopped working for the accomplishment of Christ's will. This Encyclical of the Ecumenical Patriarch was called by Leo Zander, the Russian theologian and ecumenist, 'the Golden Charter of Orthodox Ecumenism'.[5] The Encyclical of the Ecumenical Patriarchate issued in 1920 was included in the *Documents on Christian Unity (1920-24)* edited by Bishop Bell.[6] The Patriarchal Letter begins:

Our Church is of the opinion that a closer intercourse with each other and a mutual understanding between the several Christian Churches is not prevented by the doctrinal differences existing between them, and that such an understanding is highly desirable and necessary and in many ways useful in the well-conceived interest of each one of the Churches taken apart and as a whole Christian body, as also for preparing and facilitating the complete and blessed union which may some day be attained with God's help. Our Church, therefore, deems the present time most opportune for bringing forth and considering this important question in common. For although owing to old prejudices, traditions, and even pretensions, it is probable that there may even now arise or be brought forward the same difficulties which have so often frustrated the work of union, nevertheless, seeing that it is now a question of a mere contact and understanding, the difficulties, in our mind, will in any case be less serious, and if there be a good will and disposition, neither can they nor should they constitute an invincible and insuperable obstacle.[7]

[5] *E.R.* i (1949), p. 270.

[6] G. K. A. Bell (ed.), *Documents on Christian Unity* (London, 1924), No. 13, p. 44.

[7] Metropolitan Meliton, 'The Re-encounter between the Eastern Church and the Western Church', *E.R.* xvii (1965), p. 307. According to the former General Secretary of the World Council of Churches, Dr. Visser 't Hooft, this Encyclical has a threefold significance: (a) It shows that the Church of Constantinople, the Church of the Ecumenical Patriarchate, was the first Church which decided officially to propose to the other Churches of Christ a permanent fellowship or a Council of Churches; (b) Above all, the significance of this Encyclical is that it is addressed to all Churches in the World, to fellow-heirs, members of the same body, and partakers of the promise in Christ; (c) Moreover, the Church of Constantinople formulated an important principle by saying in the letter that the contacts which had thus been proposed should not be postponed until complete dogmatic agreement was reached, but that co-operation between the Churches would prepare the way for such union.

Two years later Patriarch Meletios IV (1921–3) published an Encyclical in which he wrote that the Church of Constantinople, 'kindled from the beginning with zeal for Universal Union, . . . has always followed with interest every movement in the separated Churches, and has examined with care and study their any and every expression of faith which might point towards rapprochement with Orthodoxy.'[8]

Likewise Patriarch Athenagoras issued an Encyclical Letter on 31 January 1952, in which he emphasized the witness of Orthodoxy in the World Council of Churches.[9]

Though in these initiatives the Ecumenical Patriarchate had included even the Roman Catholic Church, in the last few years it has addressed itself separately to the various Churches.

For many years the Romans and some Anglicans had asserted that the Orthodox Church could not have a Pan-Orthodox meeting simply because it lacks a primacy. However in the year 1961 (24–29 September) Patriarch Athenagoras convened the first Pan-Orthodox conference on the island of Rhodes, in which it was decided that the Orthodox Church should develop relations with the Roman Catholic Church. This sprang from the spirit of Christian love shown in the Patriarchal Letter of 1920, bearing in mind that the two Churches must study positive and negative points of the faith, administration, and Church activity (against proselytism). Two years later Patriarch Athenagoras called the second Pan-Orthodox Conference on the same island (1963, September 26–30) where it was decided to accept the proposal of the Patriarch expressed in the words 'The Orthodox Church proposes to the Venerable Roman Church to begin a dialogue on equal terms'. 'We are coming out of our isolation,' said Patriarch Athenagoras, 'and in coming out, we are opening the doors which imprison us. Catholics and Greek Orthodox have much in common; traditions, dogmas, the sacraments, the catacombs and the common blood of martyrs. We have decided to engage in a dialogue. Isolation is a disgrace and aloneness is isolation.' Furthermore, we may remember that the Patriarch in his efforts for Christian *rapprochement* had already addressed the Christian Leaders in his Easter Message (1963) when he expressed the following sentiments:

[8] Bell, *Documents on Christian Unity, Second Series, 1924–1930*, (London, 1930) pp. 94–5; cf. also *E.R.* v (1952), pp. 167–169.

[9] Bell, *Documents on Christian Unity, Fourth Series, 1948–1957* (London, 1958), pp. 38–41.

From this Ecumenical See of Saint Andrew, the first[10] of the Twelve Apostles, we joyously extend our most heartfelt Easter greetings to our dearly beloved, respected and most reverend brethren, to leaders, Patriarchs and Primates of all Christian Churches and to all the hierarchy of the Christian Orthodox Church. We pray also that Almighty God will guide us to emerge with decisive steadfastness from all barriers of our life-imposed isolation, and lead our Churches to the unity of the Risen Christ Jesus . . . .

Patriarch Athenagoras was wont to say 'we have to work to make our dreams come true, work untiringly and with faith'. He made his proposal for the Roman-Orthodox Dialogue a reality when he manifested his enthusiasm by meeting Pope Paul during the latter's pilgrimage to the Holy Land (5–6 January 1964). Professor Alivisatos[11] says that the Dialogue between Rome and Orthodoxy properly began with this historic meeting which took place in Jerusalem. As a result, further and more definite commitments were made to set up commissions to enter on the Roman-Orthodox Dialogue. Later the same year Patriarch Athenagoras called the third Pan-Orthodox conference at Rhodes (1–15 November 1964), where delegates were appointed to carry decisions and terms to the Roman Church. While the meetings of the Conference were in progress a very important event took place. A personal message from Pope Paul was sent, through Cardinal Bea, President of the Secretariat for Christian Unity, to this third Pan-Orthodox Conference. The Pope compared the Pan-Orthodox Conference with the Vatican Council and he sent his good wishes for the success of the Conference. In accordance with the decision of the Conference, a delegation of the Ecumenical Patriarchate was sent to the Vatican (14 February 1965), the first for many centuries, in order to bring to the Head of the Roman Catholic Church the decision of the Orthodox Church for the opening of the Dialogue between Orthodox and Romans. As the Pope officially learned the decisions of the third Pan-Orthodox Conference, he said: 'we are happy about the wisdom and realism of the main outlines of the programme that you have produced. Through numerous brotherly contacts, we must try to improve and correct what the centuries of isolation have destroyed, and create a new atmosphere on all levels of the life of our

[10] That is, 'first-called', *prōtoklētos* (see John 1: 40 ff).

[11] 'What motives led you to take an active part in the Ecumenical movement and what do you expect from it in our time?' *E.E.*, p. 3.

Churches, an atmosphere which will enable us at the right time to begin a fruitful theological dialogue.'[12]

On 2 April 1965, a Roman Catholic delegation visited the Ecumenical Patriarch and brought a letter from Pope Paul to Patriarch Athenagoras. The Pope wrote amongst other things: 'Is not the happy similarity which we can so easily perceive between the decisions of the Conference at Rhodes and the decisions of the Vatican Council a new sign of the work of the Holy Spirit?'[13] It is of great importance that the Roman Church should have acknowledged the identity of the decisions of the two Churches concerning the mutual desire for unity and the methods proposed for its accomplishment. In this case the aim of unity between Orthodox and Roman Catholics is connected with the problem of the inner renewal of both Churches. Not only in the Vatican Council but also in the third Pan-Orthodox Conference the problem of Christian Unity is bound together with that of the renewal of the Church. We can see that already the language of communication between the two Churches has changed. The Pope and the Ecumenical Patriarch now exchange letters in a spirit of Christian love and mutual affection.

Those who are following the dialogue between the two Churches are divided over the results they hope for from it. Some theologians maintain that 'the amelioration of social problems should take precedence in the dialogue', whereas others maintain that dogmatic problems must first be settled.[14] Immediate results of the dialogue may take the form of co-operation and collaboration in practical matters. Fr. Florovsky, however, points to the danger that an efficient co-operation of divided Christians on social issues, or in the field of international affairs, without any deeper urge for ultimate union in one Church, can obscure or even destroy the vision of true Christian Unity, which is the unity in Faith and Order, the unity of the Church and in the Church.[15]

(i) No longer excommunicated

A new move to make the relations between Orthodox and Romans closer took place in 1965, when a Roman Catholic mission, headed by

[12] Metropolitan Meliton, *E.R.* xvii (1965), p. 311.

[13] Metropolitan Meliton, ibid., p. 312.

[14] *Chrysostom*, Winter 1965–66, p. 5; cf. also B. Leeming, *The Vatican Council and Christian Unity*, pp. 180–181.

[15] G. Florovsky, 'The Ecumenical Dialogue', *E.E.* p. 43.

Mgr. Willebrands, spent four days (21–25 November) in Constantinople (Istanbul) in discussions with Orthodox representatives—an event
without parallel for many previous centuries. The exchange of views
took place in a very cordial atmosphere, though the greatest discretion
was needed with regard to the content of the discussion. Neither the
Roman nor the Orthodox commission had the power to make
decisions; the results of their studies and negotiations were submitted
to the Pope and to the Ecumenical Patriarch.[16] They discussed how to
revoke the formal cause of their schism—the mutual excommunication
made in 1054. Experts had been divided over the significance of this
proposed move. Some had said the revoking of the excommunication
was not a necessary step in an East–West Dialogue. Others said it was
essential in order to secure the approval of the Greek Orthodox Church
for any real theological dialogue with Rome. Greek theologians,
contrary to the view of the Greek Ecclesiastical authorities, held that
as the 1054 excommunication was issued by the Patriarchal Synod in
Constantinople, that body alone had the right to repeal it. In spite of
various criticisms the Synod of the Ecumenical Patriarchate had
decided on 6 November to lift the excommunication of 1054, whereas
in Rome, a spokesman for the Secretariat said that the commission's
findings so far indicated that the mutual excommunication of 1054 had
not been understood as a definitive break by either side, although the
rift widened until it could be bridged neither by the Council of Lyons
nor by the Council of Florence.[17]

The formal removal of the excommunication took place as follows:[18]
on Tuesday, 7 December 1965, the Bishop of Rome, Pope Paul VI,
and the Bishop of New Rome, Ecumenical Patriarch Athenagoras,
lifted the mutual excommunication exchanged in 1054 by means of a
'joint act' which, in Rome, was read in French at the penultimate
session of the Council. The 'joint act' of Pope and Patriarch reaffirmed
their ultimate goal of Christian unity and said the lifting of the Ex-
communications showed a common desire for justice and charity.
The document was greeted with tremendous applause from the
Council Fathers. A similar ceremony took place at the Ecumenical

---

[16] A statement issued by the Secretariat for Christian Unity in Rome gave the
names of negotiators. *The Tablet*, 4 Dec. 1965, pp. 1368–9.

[17] For a detailed account of the mutual schisms which occurred in 1054 see
S. Runciman, *The Eastern Schism* [sic] (Oxford, 1956). Subtitled 'A Study of
the Papacy and the Eastern Churches during the XIth and XIIth centuries', this
is an important work by an expert on Byzantine history.

[18] *The Tablet*, 11 Dec. 1965, p. 1460.

Patriarchate in Istanbul. It was attended by a papal delegation led by Cardinal Shehan, Archbishop of Baltimore. Here follows the text of the Common Declaration of the Pope and the Patriarch, read in Rome and Constantinople on 7 December 1965:

1. Imbued with gratitude to God for the favour which, in His mercy, He granted to them in their brotherly meeting in the Holy Places where, by the death and resurrection of the Lord Jesus, the mystery of our salvation was consummated, and, by the outpouring of the Holy Ghost, where the Church was born, Pope Paul VI and Patriarch Athenagoras I, have not lost sight of the intention which they formulated from that time onwards, each for his part, of never failing in the future to make whatever gestures possible to nurture charity and to help the development of the brotherly relations thus initiated between the Roman Catholic Church and the Orthodox Church of Constantinople. They were persuaded to respond in this way to the call of divine grace which today concerns the Roman Catholic Church and the Orthodox Church as well as all Christians: to be yet again 'one' as the Lord Jesus asked of His Father for them.

2. Amongst the obstacles found on the road to developing this brotherly relationship of trust and esteem, is numbered the memory of decisions, acts and distressing incidents, which resulted in 1054 in the sentence of excommunication delivered against the Patriarch Michael Cerularius and two other personalities by the legates of the Roman See led by Cardinal Humbert, legates who were themselves in turn the object of a similar sentence on the part of the Patriarch and the Synod of Constantinople.

3. One cannot pretend that these events did not take place in that particularly troubled period of history. But today, now that a more serene and equitable judgement has been brought to bear on them, it is important to recognise the excesses with which they were tainted and which ultimately led to consequences which exceeded, as far as we are able to judge, the intentions and expectations of their authors, whose censures concerned the persons they were aimed at and not the Church, and were not intended to break the ecclesiastical communion between the sees of Constantinople and Rome.

4. This why Pope Paul VI and Patriarch Athenagoras I and his synod, certain of expressing the common desire of justice and the unanimous feeling of charity of their faithful and remembering the precept of the Lord: 'if you are offering your gift at the altar, and there remember that your brother has something against you, leave your gift there before the altar and go; first be reconciled to your brother, and then come and offer your gift' (Matthew v. 23–24), declare with one accord:

(a) They regret the offending words, the reproaches based on no foundations, the culpable acts which, on both sides, have marked or accompanied the sad events of this epoch;

(b) They equally regret and wish to eradicate from memory and the Church's milieu the sentences of excommunication which followed them and the memory of which still works in our days as an obstacle to meeting in charity, and to consign them to oblivion;

(c) Lastly they deplore the troublesome precedents and the ultimate events which, under the influence of various factors, among which were mutual incomprehension and mistrust, finally led to the effective rupture of ecclesiastical communion.

5. This reciprocal gesture of justice and forgiveness, Pope Paul VI and Patriarch Athenagoras I and his synod are aware, will not suffice to put an end to the differences, old or more recent, which continue to exist between the Roman Catholic Church and the Orthodox Church and which, by the action of the Holy Spirit, will be overcome thanks to the purification of hearts, regret for historical errors, as well as an effective will to reach a common expression of the apostolic faith and of its demands.

In accomplishing this deed, nevertheless, they hope that it will be recognised by God, Who is prompt to pardon us when we have forgiven one another, and appreciated by the whole Christian world, but above all by the Roman Catholic Church and the Orthodox Church together, as the expression of a sincere reciprocal desire for reconciliation, and as an invitation to continue, in a spirit of mutual trust, esteem and charity, the dialogue which will bring them, with God's aid, to live anew, for the greater good of souls and the coming of God's kingdom, in the full communion of faith, brotherly concord and sacramental life which existed between them in the course of the first thousand years of the Church.[19]

The mutual revocation of the nine-hundred-year-old excommunication brought unfavourable reactions from the Churches of Russia and Greece. It is however likely that finally both these Churches will accept the decision of the Ecumenical Patriarchate.

For a long time Patriarch Athenagoras had expressed his desire to meet the Pope of Rome. When he first arrived in Constantinople as Ecumenical Patriarch he sent a brotherly message to Pope Pius XII, but it remained unanswered. However, relations with Pope John

[19] *The Tablet*, 25 Dec. 1965, pp. 1452–3 (reprinted by kind permission); cf. also Mario Rinvolucri, 'Revoking the Anathemas. Orthodox Reactions to Vatican II'. *The Tablet*, 5 Feb. 1966, pp. 155–6. cf. 'The Common Declaration of Pope Paul VI and Patriarch Athenagoras I, *O.I.C.*, ii (1966) pp. 167–9.

became more cordial and the Patriarch expressed the desire to meet the Pope. That meeting took place with Pope John's successor, in Jerusalem.

Pope Paul, showing real Christian humility, took the *rapprochement* further by visiting the Patriarch in Constantinople. The Pope's decision to go to Constantinople is of immense importance. 'Power became service, prerogative became humility', wrote Max Thurian (*La Croix*, 1 August 1967). The Pope presented a Latin parchment to Patriarch Athenagoras, which says in part: 'Now, after a long period of division and reciprocal misunderstanding, the Lord gives it to us to rediscover ourselves as sister Churches in spite of the obstacles set between us. In the light of Christ we see how urgent it is to overcome these obstacles to reach fulness and perfection of the already rich communion between us.' In the evening of the same day (Tuesday, 25 July 1967) Pope Paul said: 'We see more clearly that it belongs to the heads of the Churches, to their hierarchies, to lead the Churches along the path to full communion. As they do this they must recognise and respect one another's pastors and the sections of the flock entrusted to them. If unity of faith is a prerequisite for full communion, diversity in practices is no obstacle to it, quite the contrary.'[20] Patriarch Athenagoras replied in equally warm terms. He pledged to make all possible sacrifices and to forget those things which had kept the two Churches apart in the past. The Catholic and Orthodox Churches, he said, must begin to re-unite so that other Churches would follow.

But the climax of the dialogue between the two Churches was the visit of Patriarch Athenagoras to Rome (November, 1967). The result of the efforts of the two leaders is reflected in the final communiqué issued at the end of the meeting which took place in Rome. It contains these words:

Pope Paul VI and the Ecumenical Patriarch Athenagoras I . . . while they recognise that in the journey of all Christians towards unity, a long road has still to be traversed, and that, between the Roman Catholic Church and the Orthodox Church, there are still points to be cleared up and obstacles to be overcome before reaching that unity in the profession of faith that is necessary for the re-establishment of full communion, they rejoice in the fact that their meeting has been able to contribute to making their Churches discover each other again as sister Churches.

[20] See the texts of the speeches in *O.I.C.* iii (1967), pp. 467–71.

In the prayers they offered, in their public declarations, and in their private discussions, the Pope and the Patriarch have underlined their conviction that an essential contribution towards the restoration of full communion between the Roman Catholic Church and the Orthodox Church, is to be found in the renewal of the Church itself and of all Christians, in faithfulness to the traditions of the Fathers and the inspiration of the Holy Spirit.

They recognise that the genuine dialogue of charity, at the foundation of all relations between themselves and between their Churches, must be rooted in a total loyalty to the one Lord Jesus Christ, with mutual respect for the traditions of the other. Every element that can strengthen the bonds of charity, of communion, and of joint activity is a cause of spiritual joy and should be encouraged. Whatever could harm this charity, communion, and joint activity should be eliminated with the grace of God and the creative strength of the Holy Spirit.

Pope Paul VI and the Ecumenical Patriarch Athenagoras I are convinced that the dialogue of charity between their Churches should bear the fruit of disinterested collaboration on the level of joint action in the pastoral, social, and intellectual spheres. They would like it to be possible for regular deep contacts to be made between Catholic and Orthodox pastors for the good of their faithful. The Roman Catholic Church and the Ecumenical Patriarchate are ready to study concrete ways in which pastoral problems can be solved, especially where marriages between Catholics and Orthodox are concerned. They desire a better collaboration in works of charity, to help refugees and those who suffer, and to promote justice and peace in the world.

In order that faithful contacts may be prepared between the Roman Catholic Church and the Orthodox Church, the Pope and the Patriarch give their blessing and their pastoral support to every attempt at collaboration between Catholic and Orthodox scholars in the fields of history, the traditions of the Churches, patristics, the liturgy, and a presentation of the gospels which corresponds both to the authentic message of the Lord and to the needs of the world today. . . .'[21]

(ii) *Fears and hopes for the Dialogue*

The commencement of the dialogue on equal terms presupposes that the Roman Church should give up the claim to primacy and be content that its head on earth, the Pope, should rank as *Primus inter pares honoris causa*. When the Orthodox decided to start the Dialogue, the decision was made under certain terms. These were not accepted by the Vatican Council; on the contrary, from what was stated in the

[21] *The Tablet*, 11 Nov. 1967.

Council, and in the Papal Encyclical *Ecclesiam Suam*, it seems that the
Roman Church continues to regard herself as the one Church, insisting on the 'return' of the 'separated brethren'. The Orthodox
Church has a real desire for a *rapprochement* with the Roman Church
but it is determined to stand on two principles, *truth and love*. If the
Roman Church is unable to respond to these principles the dialogue
will be fruitless.

As regards the two dogmas on Mary, there are positive indications
that they will not hinder the dialogue. But there are fundamental
differences on the meaning of the Church, on the authority of the
bishops in the Church and in the Councils; on the relationship of
bishops to the Pope; on the infallibility of the Councils in relation to
the Pope; on the laity, and on the nature of unity (the Orthodox are
not satisfied by the appeals of the Popes for the Orthodox 'to go back
to Rome'). Although the Decree on Ecumenism makes it seem that
compromise is possible by its frank and friendly attitude to the
Oriental Churches, the Orthodox are anxious because no distinction
was drawn between the Orthodox Church and the Non-Chalcedonian
Eastern Churches.

Another very important obstacle to the Dialogue is the question
of the Uniate Churches. The Orthodox at Rhodes asked that before
the Orthodox started any Dialogue, the Romans should abolish their
propaganda and efforts at conversion through the '*Unia*', and cease to
regard the Orthodox Churches as *terrae missionis*. Unfortunately the
emphasis given by the Decree on Ecumenism that these Churches
express the Eastern heritage 'more faithfully and completely' just
because 'they live in full Communion with their brethren who
follow the tradition of the West' shows that the *Eastern Tradition in
itself* is not considered to express 'the full Catholic and Apostolic
character of the Church'.[22] The Second Vatican Council attributes this
character only to those who are in communion with Rome. An
Orthodox theologian writes that the Chapter of the Decree on
Ecumenism on the Eastern Churches is unfortunately distorted by its
preoccupation with the Uniate Churches. This is a serious error which
casts a shadow of uncertainty. It must be made clear once and for all
that 'Uniatism' is a method which has proved abortive, and it is
better not to mention it in an ecumenical dialogue. The relationship

---

[22] Decree *de Ecumenismo*, 16. These 'Uniate' Churches cannot be considered as
'Eastern' in communion with Rome. They are Roman Catholics; at least they
became so.

between Rome and the Roman Churches in Eastern countries is a matter for its own inner structure. The Uniates are not in the same category as the non-Roman Churches of Eastern Christendom.[23]

A Rome correspondent of the American agency, Religious News Service, stated that, in the opinion of certain circles in the Roman Council, the Orthodox were adopting an attitude of reserve because, they felt that 'although there has been a change of heart in Romanism its mentality frequently continues to be imperialistic, western, juridical and self-sufficient'. The same point was made in even clearer and more definitive terms by Cardinal Lercaro, Archbishop of Bologna, in an address at the Greek (Uniate) College in Rome.[24] The Cardinal called on Roman Catholics to make an act of self-abasement, and to recognize the fact that the Catholic Church is not yet entirely ready 'to be looked at closely by the Orthodox'. He continued:

we must once more reveal in its fulness the conciliar nature of the Church and realize its conciliarity in our ecclesiastical life. Only then can we proclaim officially to the Orthodox that we are prepared to respect in its full integrity one of the more impressive forms in which this conciliar spirit is expressed in the genuine traditions of the East— namely, the institution of the Patriarchate and the institution of Autocephalous Churches ... Only then will it be possible to invite Eastern representatives to look closely at us.

[23] P. Evdokimov, 'Comments on the Decree on Ecumenism', *E.R.* xvii (1965), p. 98. See also H. S. Alivizatos, 'La codification des saints canons des Eglises orientales unies à l'Eglise romaine', *Proche-Orient Chrétien*, April-June 1960, pp. 136–45. Professor Alivizatos reflects the serious complaints raised by the Orthodox hierarchy about a series of blunders by the Roman authorities. Pope Leo XIII, in the Apostolic Letter *Orientalium Dignitas*, thought that 'the Catholics of Eastern rites should live in such a way that they be regarded as true messengers and reconcilers of the Unity between the Eastern Churches and the Roman Church'. Fr. Baum sees in all the Roman documents on the Eastern Churches, since Pope Leo's time, a friendly and brotherly tone and a gentle call to reconciliation; but he overlooks the very fact that the Pope, though eager for reconciliation, asks the Easterns 'to return to Unity with Rome'. Baum, *The Quest for Christian Unity*, p. 35.

[24] 'The Decree *de Ecumenismo* and the Dialogue with the Non-Catholic Eastern Churches'. *C.* v (1965), pp. 83. From an Orthodox point of view the address of Cardinal Lercaro deserves special consideration. Does the Roman Church as a whole approve it? Cardinal Lercaro himself asks the whole Roman Catholic Church, both leaders and faithful, to adopt the right attitude towards the East, otherwise, the symbolic gestures between Romans and Orthodox would be meaningless. See also *La Croix* 13 and 16 Nov. 1964.

Another Roman Catholic theologian[25] enumerates the points in the conciliar documents which make the Orthodox hesitant to start the Dialogue: (i) The constant stress on Papal primacy. (ii) The choking of the conciliar spirit of the Church by codified legal rules which remain unduly inflexible. According to these rules, the Council of Bishops is in the last resort no more than an auxiliary organ, intended simply to give advice to the central religious authority, i.e. the Pope. (iii) The basic refusal on the part of Rome to undertake a summit conference with the Eastern Patriarchs on equal terms. (iv) The Roman Curia which remains, as ever, all-powerful. (v) The greatest difficulty however, is of a purely theological nature: it is the absence of a real pneumatology, of teaching on the Holy Spirit. As a result the statements of the Council are given no more than a superficial veneer of spirituality: remarks about the Holy Spirit are added, as a sort of decoration, to statements which remain basically and fundamentally juridical.

It is very interesting that in the very centre of the Orthodox Church in Istanbul a similar voice was raised by the French-language newspaper *Journal D'Orient*,[26] where the author attributes the present unwillingness and distrust on the Orthodox side to the fact that the fundamental Orthodox objection still remains unanswered:

No one succeeded in explaining to them how it is that the role of the Orthodox Church as a judge of the truth—a role still ascribed to her for many centuries even after the schism—has today been reduced to that of a mere observer, one amongst many, at the second Vatican Council . . . how it is possible for Orthodox to accept the fact that the Council discusses and legislates for the Eastern (i.e. Uniate) Churches, in the absence of the Orthodox? It seems to be an indication that these Churches have been assimilated by the Roman Church, or else have been completely subjected to her.[27]

The facts however do not allow us to be very optimistic, although there are certain events which give courage, and hope. The Roman Church has given back the relics of St. Andrew to the Orthodox Church of Patras (Peloponnesus), of St. Saba to the Patriarchate of Jerusalem and of St. Titus to the Church of Crete. Although the

[25] Fr. Maurice Villain writing in *Le Figaro*, 18 Dec. 1964.

[26] 15, 16, 17 Nov. 1964.

[27] Quoted in the periodical *Zoe* (Athens), 1 Jul. 1965. Cf. *The Orthodox Herald* (London), 1965, pp. 7–8. Cf. Decree *De Ecclesiis Orientalibus Catholicis* (Catholic Truth Society, London, 1965).

Decree on Ecumenism[28] disappoints the Orthodox, it does give instruction to the Romans to co-operate with the Orthodox and also with the approval of local authorities to take part in Orthodox sacraments. A further decree of the Congregation for the Oriental Churches, approved by the Pope and published in *L'Osservatore Romano*, 22 February 1967, says that the Holy See will recognize the validity of marriages contracted in an Orthodox ceremony between Latin-Rite Catholics and members of the Orthodox Church. Although they will still be considered contrary to the Church Law, they will be considered true sacramental marriages. The same recognition was given to marriages between Oriental-Rite Catholics and Orthodox Church members contracted in the presence of an Orthodox Priest.

The new legislation goes further than the Council did, in giving local Bishops power to dispense Catholics from the 'canonical form' required for marriage. With the new decree a Bishop can allow a Catholic under his authority to marry an Orthodox in the presence of an Orthodox Priest in cases where circumstances make it very difficult for the marriage to be held in a Catholic Church. It will do away with the previous arrangements whereby in such cases dual ceremonies were often held, one in a Catholic Church and another in an Orthodox.[29] The *Directorium*, issued by the Vatican Secretariat for Promoting Christian Unity, in two parts (first part May 1967), for the guidance of Roman Catholics in implementing the Decree on Ecumenism, should also be consulted for its bearing on Roman Catholic/Orthodox relations.

Sharing in sacraments is a very important question for the Orthodox, because it has been thought that *Communicatio in Sacris* would hinder the dialogue.[30] But Cardinal Lercaro explains clearly what the Decree

[28] 'Turn the Schema upside down, shuffle the pages, read the things backwards, the conclusion is still the same, and ecumenism means only one thing: there is only one Church, and all the rest of us are separated from it (the Roman Church) and the sooner we all get back into it (Patriarchs of Jerusalem, Antioch, Alexandria, and all) the better. In fact, there is not such a thing as ecumenism commonly understood at all.' These are the words of Bernard Pawley, *An Anglican Views the Council*, p. 123, concerning the Schema or draft for this Decree.

[29] *O.I.C.* ii (1966), pp. 416–19 and iii (1967) pp. 363–5 with the translation of the decree issued on 22 Feb. 1967.

[30] Professor Evdokimov, of the Orthodox Institute of St. Sergius in Paris, thinks that *Communicatio in Sacris* makes the dialogue more difficult. He thinks also that 'Rome's conception of itself as the centre—something often described by observers as Romanocentrism—remained the greatest problem in a fruitful dialogue between the Eastern and Western Church'. *The Tablet*, 8 January, 1966.

no (ch. ii, para. 8) means by *Communicatio in Sacris*. Firstly,
'unicatio in Sacris is a sign of unity, it cannot be applied
nity does not exist; however, there are cases where to
...ain from intercommunion could be a scandal for the faithful and
harden divisions which are but superficial'. Secondly, 'in no case
must it be a matter of isolated individuals. It necessarily involves the
leaders of the two Churches in question. To be a step towards full
communion between us and our Eastern brothers, it must be explicitly
agreed to by the Catholic and Orthodox bishops'.[31] In a speech at the
Vatican Council by Cardinal Bea[32] Catholics were asked to pray with
non-Catholics for that unity which Christ desired for his Church, and
leave it to God to decide when and how this will be achieved.[33] This
may mean that there will be unity within a framework different from
the present Roman one.

3. *The Dialogue between Romans and Anglicans*

(i) *Four centuries of separation*

Between Romans and Anglicans there exists a misunderstanding
about the nature of the Reformation in England. Romans have often
found it difficult to accept the fact that there were important reasons
which account for the Anglican position.[1] Anglicans on the other
hand, have unhappy memories, particularly in more recent times,
connected with the condemnation of Anglican Orders in 1896 by
Pope Leo XIII.[2] This action of the Roman Church was a great blow
to the advocates of Anglo-Roman unity in both Churches, who hoped
that a positive decision might mean the first important step towards
ultimate reunion between Canterbury and Rome.

If the Anglicans have sometimes admired the Roman Church for
her achievements, discipline, and obedience, they cannot in conscience

---

[31] Cardinal Lercaro, ibid., p. 90.

[32] *Council Speeches of Vaticcn II*, pp. 109–111.

[33] For the realization of co-operation between Romans, Orthodox, Non-
Chalcedonians, Anglicans and Protestants a new Institute for higher theological
studies is to be set up in Jerusalem. 'The studies should be carried out in an
atmosphere of piety and religious service.' *The Tablet*, 8 Jan. 1966.

[1] Jaeger, *The Ecumenical Council*, pp. 152–62.

[2] See above, Ch. V. Sect. 1, pp. 93–8. The Papal Bull has been criticized not
only as cruelly contemptuous but also as unscholarly. Cf. Visser 't Hooft, op. cit.,
p. 135.

pay the price which the Romans have paid for these—the price of
freedom.[3] Again there are historical events connected with the English
domination in Ireland which gave rise to bitterness. Since the Roman
Catholic community in England is largely of Irish origin, the conflict
remains.[4] The situation is perhaps best illustrated from a letter of
Newman, which, although it was written over a century ago, still
maintains its importance. In his *Apologia*, Newman quotes a letter
which he wrote on 12 September 1841 to a zealous Catholic layman:
'Suspicion and distrust', he wrote, 'are the main causes at present of
the separation between us, and the nearest approaches in doctrine will
but increase the hostility, which, alas, our people feel towards yours,
while these causes continue. . . . I am sure, that, while you suffer, we
suffer too from the separation; *but we cannot remove the obstacles;* it is
with you to do so. You do not fear us; we fear you. Till we cease to
fear you, we cannot love you.'[5]

This passage reveals the tenacious suspicion with which the Roman
Catholics were regarded by Anglicans. The reasons are obvious; the
Roman Church was seen as a strictly authoritative body, as a well-
organized and often effective power.

It may have been the spirit rather than the doctrine of the Church of
Rome which has prevented the return of the Anglican Church to the
Roman obedience. A learned Anglican bishop wrote: 'The repudiation
of liberty in human knowledge and human conduct is a far more
serious matter. If historical questions like the relation of St. Peter to
the primitive Roman Church, or literary questions like the com-
position of the books of the Bible, are to be determined not by
criticism but by dogmatic authority, there is an end of historical or
literary scholarship.'[6]

Nevertheless, if in some of her sons the Anglican Church has shown
respect for the great Roman Church, she has also lost no opportunity
of declaring that she is a bridge Church between East and West. As
early as 1920 the Lambeth Conference felt that it was impossible to
make any report on reunion with Episcopal Churches without some
reference to the Church of Rome. The report recalls the statement of
1908, which had reminded the Anglican bishops of the fact 'that there

[3] 'An Anglican's Thoughts on Rome' in *Intercommunion and Christian Unity* by
N. Hook and D. L. Edwards (London, 1962), p. 14.
[4] B. Pawley, *Looking at the Vatican Council*, p. 28.
[5] Newman, *Apologia* (Fontana ed., 1959), p. 241.
[6] J. E. C. Welldon, *The English Church* (London, 1926), p. 54.

can be no fulfilment of the Divine purpose in any scheme of reunion which does not ultimately include the great Latin Church of the West, with which our history has been so closely associated in the past, and to which we are still bound by many ties of common faith and tradition.' But, the bishops continued: 'any advance in this direction is at present barred by difficulties which we have not ourselves created, and which we cannot of ourselves remove'. It was further declared: 'should, however, the Church of Rome at any time desire to discuss conditions of reunion, we shall be ready to welcome such discussions'.[7] At the Lambeth Conference in 1930 the hope was expressed that some day Rome would show a positive attitude towards the Church of England: 'in any attempt at reunion, the whole Church must be in our minds, and we are not without hope that the attitude of the Church of Rome may, in some parts of the world at any rate, change in the not very distant future'.[8]

According to the Anglican view the Roman Catholic theories of Church unity are unacceptable; the Roman view of the unity of the Church is based upon absolutism, every kind of power deriving from a single head, the Pope. But Anglicans consider that every element in the Church has its part; the Pope is only one amongst many bishops (although Bishop of a great and historic see) of the Church. 'On the Roman theory', wrote Bicknell, 'unity is, as it were, imposed from without by external authority; on the Catholic theory it grows from within, as the spontaneous product of the one life that works in all members of the body of Christ'. 'We believe', he continues, 'that neither historically nor theologically can the papal theory of unity be justified by an appeal to Scripture, and therefore we are free to reject it without forfeiting our Catholic inheritance'.[9]

Long before the Malines Conversations, which failed partly because of the reaction of the English Roman Catholics, Anglicans in England had begun to turn to Roman Catholics abroad in search of what is now called ecumenical dialogue. A complaint about this was made by

[7] *Conference of Bishops of the Anglican Communion* (London, S.P.C.K., 1920), p. 144.

[8] *Lambeth Conference, 1930*, p. 131.

[9] Bicknell, op. cit., p. 350. Cf. Gore, *Roman Catholic claims*, 'The Papacy represents the triumph of imperial absolutism over representative, constitutional authority, and of centralisation over consentient witness and co-operation'. 'The Eastern Churches on the whole stand for the older view of confederation'; quoted by Bicknell, ibid., note 2.

Cardinal Heenan, Archbishop of Westminster.[10] In a speech in the Vatican Council, he said 'as far as they [the English Roman Catholics] are concerned they are ready to come into dialogue with the Anglicans in England and Wales, but the separated brethren in England have turned to Catholics outside their country in search of Ecumenism.' This implies that at the very centre of Anglicanism there exists a hostility between Romans and Anglicans. Very recently, however, there are signs that the two Churches have at last begun to co-operate. 'We are in the beginning of Christian Unity', declared Cardinal Heenan:

The Council decree was a little more than one year old, and we are only now beginning to instruct our people on the deeper meaning of this work for Christian Unity. . . . Progress must be slow because it must be honest. Deep religious convictions cannot change overnight. . . . Ecumenism means not that we deny the differences but that we stress the beliefs we hold in common. . . . There is nothing incompatible in wishing all men to be united in the fold of St. Peter while having sincere and genuinely ecumenical relations with them. The essentials of the faith are much fewer than most people realize. What is so often forbidding to those outside the Church is the presentation of our faith.

Before a Roman-Anglican *rapprochement* can start, the nature of the Dialogue should first be clarified. In the Decree on Ecumenism (Ch. iii, para. 13) there is only one phrase concerning the Anglican Communion, noting that it 'has a special place amongst those which continue to retain, in part, Catholic tradition and structure'. There would appear to be therefore no specific objections to the commencement of Dialogue. Although Rome today is deeply different from the Rome of the sixteenth century in respect of both discipline and doctrine, these differences do not on the whole tend to make reunion easier. 'I cannot pretend', wrote Gore, 'to see any way at present opening through the dogmatic obstacles between us'.[11] Gore was writing more than thirty years ago, but even now, apart from courtesy and kind words, there has been no substantial progress in Roman-Anglican relations. This remains true, although a series of meetings of a Joint Preparatory Commission has been held, since it is not yet known what progress, if any, these confidential discussions have made. The starting point from which the Churches approach one another has

[10] *Council Speeches of Vatican II*, pp. 106–8.
[11] *The Anglo-Catholic Movement*, p. 47.

not yet been defined by either. One possible starting point at present could be the Malines Conversations, though Bishop Stephen Neill thinks that the significance of these Conversations has been enormously exaggerated.[12] The main obstacle is still the reluctance of Roman Catholicism to acknowledge that Anglicanism is the legitimate heir of the historic *Ecclesia Anglicana*. Anglicanism, presented merely as a rite similar to the Uniate rites, might possibly solve the difficulties raised by present Roman Catholics, but for many reasons this does not go to the heart of the problem.[13]

As we have said previously, very little concerning Anglicanism has come from the second Vatican Council. It must be noticed also however that Pope Paul speaking on Holy Thursday, 1964, emphasized that with sincere charity and hope he looks forward to seeing Anglicanism one day honourably take up its place in the one and only fold of Christ.[14] Nevertheless there are Anglicans who express their satisfaction at phrases contained in Chapter iii of the Decree on Ecumenism. They acknowledge that these documents are 'Roman Catholic'. They come from Rome, but from a progress of struggle. They thankfully acknowledge the justice of describing the Council as 'a miracle'.[15]

Like the Orthodox, the Anglicans would recognize the primacy of honour, if the Pope would be content with it.[16] Today Anglicans no

[12] *Twentieth Century Christianity* (1961), p. 353.

[13] 'It is quite possible', wrote Gore, 'that, if the Church of England were prepared to submit to the Roman central doctrinal and disciplinary requirements the Roman authority would be prepared to accept Anglicanism as a Uniate Church with its own Liturgy and its own discipline, for example, as regards the marriage of the clergy'. *The Anglo-Catholic Movement*, p. 39. Recently, such a possibility has been put forward again by Bishop B. C. Butler (Auxiliary R.C. Bishop of Westminster, and former Abbot of Downside) in a broadcast talk: *The Listener*, 2 April 1970, pp. 441–2. Nevertheless, many Anglicans would not be 'prepared to submit' to the 'requirements'.

[14] Leeming, *The Vatican Council*, p. 279.

[15] Oliver Tomkins, Bishop of Bristol, 'Comments on the Decree on Ecumenism', *E.R.* xvii (1965), pp. 108–9.

[16] The present Archbishop of Canterbury, Dr. Michael Ramsey, said that 'a primacy should depend upon and express the organic authority of the body; and the discovery of its precise functions will come not by discussions of the Petrine claims in isolation but by the recovery everywhere of the body's organic life, with its bishops, presbyters and people. In this body Peter will find his due place, and ultimate reunion is hastened not by the pursuit of the papal controversy but by the quiet growth of the organic life of every part of Christendom'. Cf. *The Gospel and the Catholic Church* (2nd ed., London, 1965), p. 228; cf. also *R.E.C.*, p. 45.

longer have their old fear of papacy; they do not regard it as being as formidable as in the past.

From the Anglican point of view the two Churches could develop their mutual relations by removing things which cause bitterness. One of these is the Roman attitude to mixed marriages,[17] and there is no real sign that the Roman Church is prepared to change the existing law. On 19 March 1966 the *Osservatore Romano* published the new Instructions of the Roman Church on mixed marriages. The main points are as follows:[18]

1. The Roman Catholic partner has a grave obligation to provide for the [Roman] Catholic baptism and education of any children of the marriage, and will be required to make the 'promises' as before. The non-[Roman] Catholic is to be 'invited' to promise not to interfere in the Roman partner's duties. But if the non-Roman conscientiously objects to this the Bishop is to consult the Holy See about it. In ordinary circumstances the promises are to be given in writing, but in some cases the marriage partners may give them orally.

2. In countries where the law forbids religious education, the marriage can still be allowed so long as the Roman Catholic partner guarantees 'to take every possible step' towards Roman Catholic baptism and education of the children, and the non-Roman makes a guarantee of good will in the matter.

3. In order that a mixed marriage should be valid, it must be celebrated before a Roman Catholic priest; but exceptional cases can be referred to Rome.

4. Bishops can now allow the solemnization of a mixed marriage.

5. Joint celebrations by Roman Catholic and non-Roman

[17] The matter of mixed marriages was transferred to the Pope by the Bishops in order to speed legislation. Cf. *Catholic Herald*, 24 Sept. 1965. Cardinal Heenan of Westminster played a big part in the consultations. He said that although the Pope promised to make an early pronouncement on the subject 'we must never forget that mixed marriages by their very nature are bound to pose a problem. We cannot therefore expect that the Pope will be able to solve all difficulties. But Ecumenism teaches us to respect each other's convictions even though we cannot share them.' *The Tablet*, 29 Jan. 1966, p. 146.

[18] See the full text in *The Tablet*, 26 Mar., 1966. The suggestion that the instruction is not the last word on this subject is contained in the introduction. It states that if the changes work well in practice they will be introduced into the Code of Canon Law, which is now under revision. Further modifications in the Roman regulations were announced in a *Motu Proprio* at the end of April 1970, to come into force on 1 October.

ministers must be 'absolutely avoided'. The Bishop may allow a non-Roman minister to give an address in the Church after the Roman ceremony, and prayers may be recited with non-Romans.

6. Bishops and Parish priests are to be 'attentively vigilant' that mixed marriages actually conform to the promises made.

7. There is no longer a penalty of excommunication attached to 'attempting marriage' in a non-Roman Church. This relaxation is retrospective.

This instruction, which is a compromise between the major changes sought by the Anglicans and the 'no major change' line followed by Hierarchies like that in Britain, was regarded as a prologue to Archbishop Ramsey's visit to Rome. From the non-Roman point of view the instruction on mixed marriages was not at all encouraging. The periodical *New Christian*[19] wrote that 'the Roman Catholic Church has refused to abandon a view of marriage which is theologically unsound and pastorally absurd'. It said that the Vatican decision represented a great victory for the reactionary English Roman Catholic hierarchy and was 'an acute disappointment to those, both within and without the Roman Communion, who had hoped that the recently concluded Council would lead to enlightened deeds as well as pious words. The refusal of Rome to abandon its untenable position over mixed marriages indicates a real blindness to the fact that the increasing number of sophisticated men and women of the twentieth century are not prepared to accept this kind of nonsense.' The Archbishop of Canterbury told reporters that he had 'made it clear to everyone with whom he had spoken in Rome that the Vatican instruction would not satisfy Anglican consciences'. After a careful study of the document, however, he believed that it was not meant to be a final settlement. It allowed difficult cases to be referred to Rome.[20]

Cardinal Bea explained clearly the intentions of the Roman Church on this point. He said, 'It is necessary to say frankly that in a certain sense no solution will ever be able to give complete satisfaction; the case of mixed marriages reveals the whole paradox of the separation of Christians. They inevitably suffer the repercussions of this separation. The only true solution is the unity of Christians. While this is lacking the difficulty, the cross, will remain, and will call for much patience and charity.'[21] The question of mixed marriages is a great

[19] 24 Mar. 1966.
[20] *Church Times*, 1 Apr. 1966.
[21] ibid.

problem between Romans and Anglicans. It is not a theological question but a matter of discipline, and since more than half of the marriages contracted in Roman Churches in Britain are mixed it is really a delicate matter.[22] The Archbishop of Canterbury said that 'the goal of actual unity of these Churches is still a long way off and it is no use planning for final goals unless they meanwhile get on with matters which affect practical attitudes. This is something they could begin now, by working for a solution of doctrinal and theological problems. Many of us', the Archbishop continued, 'have great hopes of better relations between the Church of England and the Roman Catholic Church. The first step in these relations must be in terms of practical Christian brotherhood. Moreover, the members of the two Churches must get away from any habit of regarding one another with hostility, as a sort of enemy. They must find themselves to be fully brother Christians. That must be expressed in the way they treat one another . . . . Then, it is important that they should take steps to remove things which cause bitterness. I am sure', continued Dr. Ramsey, 'that in our Church of England we have to get rid of a good deal of sheer partisan bitterness and irrational hostility to Roman Catholics inherited from the past. We, on our part, would like to see the Roman Catholic Church taking steps which would immensely help our practical relations.'[23] A joint Roman Catholic/Anglican Sub-Commission on the Theology of Marriage and its application to mixed marriages met twice during 1968.[24]

Bearing in mind that in the Encyclical *Mortalium Animos* (1928), the Roman Church once declared itself against any participation in the Ecumenical Movement, we cannot but now be happier with the new developments concerning the Roman Church's attitude to those outside its own visible boundaries. The work for Christian Unity in Britain, the very centre of Anglicanism, is only beginning. 'We had to wait until the Council was over before giving full attention to this new form of apostolate', said Cardinal Heenan, the Archbishop of Westminster. 'The time has come to seek friendly intercourse with the whole of the Church of England.'[25] The Westminster Diocese now has an Ecumenical Centre for the training of clergy and laity in

---

[22] According to statistics between 1958 and 1962 the proportion of mixed marriages rose from 47.8 per cent to 50.6 per cent. In 1962, out of 46,010 marriages in Roman Churches 23,305 were mixed. Cf. *Catholic Herald*, 18 Mar. 1966.

[23] *Catholic Herald*, 17 Sept. 1965.

[24] The first meeting was reported in *The Tablet*, 27 Apr. 1968, p. 433.

[25] *The Times*, 17 Jan. 1966.

Ecumenical work and for establishing dialogue with the Orthodox, Anglican and Free Churches.[26] The Church of England has the Archbishop of Canterbury's Commission on Roman Catholic Relations specially established for this specific purpose. The Roman Catholics have their Ecumenical Commission for England and Wales which deals, but not exclusively as the Archbishop's Commission does, with Anglican-Roman relations. A first joint meeting of these two commissions was held at the end of 1968.

(ii) *The bridging of the 400-years-old rift*

After the visit of Dr. Geoffrey Fisher in 1960,[27] Dr. Ramsey was the second Archbishop of Canterbury to visit the Vatican since the Reformation, but he was the first to hold official conversations. This visit was regarded as similar to the meeting in Jerusalem between the Pope and the Ecumenical Patriarch Athenagoras.

On 23 March 1966 the Pope and the Archbishop, with warm dignity and emotion, exchanged the kiss of peace before the altar of the Sistine Chapel. Both Pope Paul and Dr. Ramsey spoke of the obstacles which still stand in the way of unity. In strong tones the Archbishop greeted the Pope as his dear brother in Christ, pointing out that he had come as President of the Lambeth Conference of Bishops from all parts of the Anglican Communion throughout the world. This is the full text of Dr. Ramsey's address:

Your Holiness, dear Brother in Christ, it is with heartfelt gratitude and brotherly affection in Christ that I greet you as your guest in this Vatican City. I greet you in my office as Archbishop of Canterbury and as President of the Lambeth Conference of Bishops from every part of the Anglican Communion throughout the world. Peace be unto you, and unto all Christians who live and pray within the obedience of the Roman Catholic Church.

I have come with the longing in my heart which I know to be in your heart also, that we may by our meeting together help in the fulfilment of the prayer of our Divine Lord that all his disciples may come to unity in the truth. All Christendom gives thanks to Almighty God for what was done in the service of unity by the greatly loving and greatly loved Pope John XXIII.

It is with the same divine inspiration that Your Holiness works and prays for unity, and to that end you met with the Ecumenical Patriarch Athenagoras in Jerusalem and you now receive me here in Rome. May

---

[26] *Catholic Herald*, 28 Jan. 1966.
[27] See Ch. III, Sect. 3, pp. 62–3, above.

the grace of God enable us to serve his divine purpose by our meeting, and enable Christians everywhere to feel the pain of their divisions and to seek unity in truth and holiness.

On the road to unity there are formidable difficulties of doctrine. All the more therefore it is my hope, and the hope of Your Holiness too, that there may be increasing dialogue between theologians, Roman Catholic and Anglican, and of other traditions, so as to explore together the divine revelation. On the road to unity there are also difficult practical matters about which the consciences and feelings of Christian people can be hurt. All the more therefore must such matters be discussed together in patience and charity.

If the final goal of unity is yet some way ahead, Christians can rejoice already in the fact of their common baptism into the name of the Triune God, Father, Son and Holy Spirit, and they can already pray together, bear witness to God together, and together serve humanity in Christ's name.

It is only as the world sees us Christians growing visibly in unity that it will accept through us the divine message of peace. I would join my voice to the voice of Your Holiness in pleading that the nations agree to abandon weapons of destruction, to settle their quarrels without war, and to find a sovereignty greater than the sovereignty of each separate state. So may the song of the angels be echoed in the wills and actions of men: Gloria in Excelsis Deo et in terra pax.[28]

The Archbishop did not hesitate to state the formidable difficulties in doctrine which still separate Anglicans and Roman Catholics. And in his reply, the Pope went further, emphasizing not only the doctrinal difficulties, but also the grave and complex problems raised by the meeting. The Pope, replying in Latin, said:

We greet with emotion, with joy and with hope your most welcome visit. With a sincere heart we thank you, and we reciprocate the Christian salutation: The peace of the Lord be with you, with the worthy personages who accompany you, and with all those whom you gather about you and represent.

In the light of Christ we advert to the singular importance of this encounter between the Roman Catholic Church and the Church of England, together with the other Churches of the Anglican Communion; believers in Christ are spiritually present, the world observes, history will remember.

You are repeating the act of great courtesy performed by your illustrious and revered predecessor, His Grace Dr. Fisher, in regard to

[28] *Church Times*, 25 Mar. 1966; *Catholic Herald*, 25 Mar. 1966.

our predecessor, the lamented Pope John XXIII of happy memory; and you rebuild a bridge which for centuries has lain fallen between the Church of Rome and the Church of Canterbury: a bridge of respect, of esteem and of charity. You cross over this yet unstable viaduct, still under construction, with spontaneous initiative and sage confidence— May God bless this courage and this piety of yours!

We would wish that your first impression, upon crossing over the threshold of our residence, should be this: your steps do not resound in a strange house; they come to a home which you, for ever valid reasons, can call your own. We are happy to open its doors to you and, together with its doors, our heart; for, applying to this event the words of St. Paul, we are both happy and honoured to welcome you not as 'strangers and sojourners, but . . . fellow-citizens with the saints and members of the household of God' [cf. Ephesians ii, 19–20]. Surely from heaven, St. Gregory the Great and St. Augustine look down and bless. Hence we are well aware of the various aspects of this event, and, in the first place, we do not hesitate to note the historical value of this hour. It appears to us great, almost dramatic and fortunate if we think of the long and sorrowful story which it intends to bring to an end and of the new developments which this hour can inaugurate in the relations between Rome and Canterbury—from now on, friendship must inspire and guide them.

We see also the civil importance which this example of well initiated concord, and this proposal of practical collaboration, can have, for peace among the nations of the world and for the promotion of Christian brotherhood among men.

Moreover, we see the ecumenical value of this our meeting. We do not forget the grave and complex problems which it raises, and which it is not intended now to resolve; but these problems are here presented in their essential terms, which are always very difficult, formulated, however, in such a way as to be studied and meditated together— henceforth, without any resentment of human pride, without any shadow of earthly interests in accordance with the word of Christ and the assistance of the Holy Spirit.

Finally, we see the truly spiritual and religious value of our common quest for a common profession of fidelity to Christ, and of a prayer old and new which may harmonise minds and voices in celebrating the greatness of God and his plan of salvation in Christ for all mankind.

In the field of doctrine and ecclesiastical law we are still respectively distinct and distant; and for now it must be so, for the reverence due to truth and to freedom; until such time as we may merit the supreme grace of true and perfect unity in faith and communion. But charity can, and must, from now on be exercised between us, and show forth its mysterious and prodigious strength: 'Where there is charity and love, there is God.'

This, then, is a great day, this day which, through the divine good-
ness, you enable us to live: *'Exsultemus et laetemur in ea'*. 'Let us on
this day rejoice and be glad together!'[29]

There was a very optimistic atmosphere on both sides and a feeling
that something very important might be declared by the Pope and the
Archbishop.[30] Amongst the matters which could have been discussed
was the question of the re-examination of the validity of Anglican
Orders,[31] on which the Pope had already expressed his willingness to
go further, and mixed marriages. The Archbishop of Canterbury
stressed that the dialogue between Romans and Anglicans must
consider practical matters over which the conscience and feelings of
Christian people could be hurt. Dr. Ramsey may have discussed
questions such as these with the Pope in their private meeting in the
afternoon of 23 March. On the following day the Pope and the
Archbishop presided together at a Service of Prayer in the Basilica of
St. Paul-without-the-Walls, after which in the adjacent Abbey they
signed a common declaration which was read in English and in Latin
on behalf of both leaders. The full text of the Declaration is as follows:

In this city of Rome, from which St. Augustine was sent by St.
Gregory to England and there founded the cathedral see of Canterbury,
towards which the eyes of all Anglicans now turn as the centre of their
Christian Communion, His Holiness Pope Paul VI and His Grace
Michael Ramsey, Archbishop of Canterbury, representing the Angli-
can Communion, have met to exchange fraternal greetings.

[29] *Church Times*, 25 Mar. 1966 and *Catholic Herald*, 25 Mar. 1966. See also
The Archbishop of Canterbury's Visit to Rome, March 1966 (Church Information
Office, London).

[30] Accompanying the Archbishop were the Bishop of Cariboo, Canada (the
Rt. Rev. Ralph Dean), Executive Officer of the Anglican Communion; the
Bishop of Ripon (the Right Rev. John Moorman), the Rev. Dr. J. N. D. Kelly,
Principal of St. Edmund Hall, Oxford, and Chairman of the Archbishop of
Canterbury's Commission on Roman Catholic Relations, Canon J. R. Satter-
thwaite, General Secretary of the Church of England Council on Foreign
Relations, and Canon John Findlow, the Archbishop's personal representative in
Rome.

[31] Bishop Luxton of Ontario, Canada, sent a formal communication to Pope
Paul VI asking him to appoint a commission to examine the validity of Anglican
Orders. Bishop Luxton had a private meeting with the Pope on 20 Nov. 1965,
and explained why he suggested a Roman review of the question. The Pope
then asked that the matter be set out in a formal request. Cf. *Church Times*,
7 Apr. 1966.

At the conclusion of their meeting they give thanks to Almighty God, who, by the action of His Spirit, has in these latter years created a new atmosphere of Christian fellowship between the Roman Catholic Church and the Churches of the Anglican Communion.

This encounter of March 23, 1966, marks a new stage in the development of fraternal relations, based upon Christian charity, and of sincere efforts to remove the causes of conflict and to re-establish unity.

In willing obedience to the command of Christ who bade his disciples love one another, they declare that, with his help, they wish to leave in the hands of the God of mercy all that in the past has been opposed to this precept of charity, and that they make their own the mind of the Apostle which he expressed in these words: Forgetting those things which are behind and reaching forth unto those things which are before, I press towards the mark for the prize of the high calling of God in Christ Jesus (Philippians iii. 13–14).

They affirm their desire that all those Christians who belong to these two communions may be animated by these same sentiments of respect, esteem and fraternal love; and, in order to help these develop to the full, they intend to inaugurate between the Roman Catholic Church and the whole Anglican Communion a serious dialogue which, founded on the gospels and on the ancient common traditions, may lead to the unity in truth for which Christ prayed.

The dialogue should include not only theological matters such as scripture, tradition and liturgy, but also matters of practical difficulty felt on either side.

His Holiness the Pope and His Grace the Archbishop of Canterbury are, indeed, aware that serious obstacles stand in the way of a restoration of complete communion of faith and sacramental life; nevertheless, they are of one mind in their determination to promote responsible contacts between their communions in all those spheres of Church life where collaboration is likely to lead to a greater understanding and a deeper charity, and to strive in common to find solutions for all the great problems that face the Church in the world of today.

Through such collaboration, by the grace of God the Father and in the light of the Holy Spirit, may the prayer of our Lord Jesus Christ for unity among his disciples be brought nearer to fulfilment; and, with progress towards unity, may there be a strengthening of peace in the world, the peace that only he can grant who gives 'the peace that passeth all understanding', together with the blessing of Almighty God, Father, Son and Holy Spirit, that it may abide with all men for ever'.[32]

---

[32] *Church Times*, 1 Apr. 1966. *The Tablet*, 2 Apr. 1966 and *Catholic Herald*, 1 Apr. 1966.

This common declaration by the Pope and the Archbishop of Canterbury is to be regarded as more than just a gesture. It is really the foundation of a bridge which will span the rift of four hundred years of separation. The work of the joint preparatory theological commission set up as a result of this meeting is described in outline below (p. 238).

There were some who thought that the Archbishop 'came home empty-handed so far as any definite agreement between the two Churches is concerned, and apparently without a single hint of any concession, on the Roman side, on the issues which divide these two Churches'.[33] This is true, but the essential success of Dr. Ramsey's visit to Rome lies in the opening of a Roman–Anglican dialogue in a climate of friendliness. It is a mistake to expect that the Roman Church will make any concession on its doctrine or prerogatives. It may relax its discipline only when it thinks that there is no danger for the stability of the Roman Church, but not otherwise. This is obvious. The Roman Church has opened dialogue with non-Christians and non-believers. Would anybody expect that such a dialogue means concession as far as the Roman Church is concerned? Any thought of Dr. Ramsey's 'failure' in his mission comes from the suspicion that his visit to Rome was to raise the question of mixed marriages. On this point it was said by a commentator that 'he has been unable to get any sense out of the English hierarchy on this and other matters'.[34]

From an Orthodox point of view, the inauguration of the Anglican–Roman dialogue will increase the possibilities for a thorough Orthodox–Roman and Anglican theological dialogue with the object of exploring together the divine revelation.[35] Already the Archbishop in his speech made mention of the Ecumenical Patriarch's meeting with the Pope, and newspapers compared the 'reconciliation' between Rome and Canterbury with that between Constantinople and Rome. On the other hand, if the Roman Church has its own doctrines on which it is not willing to compromise, there are equally those Anglican doctrines on which the Anglicans are uncompromising. There is only

[33] *Church Times*, 1 Apr. 1966.

[34] *New Christian*, 10 Mar. 1966.

[35] Bishop Luxton has already suggested such a co-operation between Romans, Orthodox and Anglicans. This was revealed in the *Canadian Churchman*, the national newspaper of the Anglican Church of Canada. His suggestions to the Pope included proposals towards an 'ultimate federation of the three Churches, the Roman Catholic, the Eastern and Orthodox Churches and the Anglican Communion'. *Church Times*, 8 Apr. 1966.

one solution at present to these problems, as the former Archbishop of Canterbury, now Lord Fisher of Lambeth, writes:

The only kind of Union at present of general interest for all Churches is that of Full Communion, in which two or more Churches, finding themselves in general agreement about the essentials of the Christian Faith, are able, while retaining their own separate freedoms as Churches within the one Universal Church, to be in full sacramental fellowship with one another.[36]

The question of unity between Anglicans and Romans and of inter-communion looks almost as far away today as ever. There are difficulties in the way of further Roman–Anglican relations on both sides. There were even criticisms from Roman Catholics who were upset by the warmth of welcome given to the Archbishop of Canterbury.

The Pope and the Archbishop had announced their intention 'to inaugurate between the Roman Catholic Church and the whole Anglican Communion a serious dialogue, which, founded on the gospels and on the ancient common traditions, may lead to the unity in truth for which Christ prayed'. The first step to this was the announcement early in November 1966 of the names of the delegates appointed to serve on the Anglican–Roman Catholic 'joint preparatory Commission'. Once the problems at issue were defined, full scale Commissions would get down to the real dialogue. The first meeting of this Commission was held in January 1967.

The members of the Commission were as follows:

Anglicans. Dr. J. Moorman, Bishop of Ripon, Chairman; Dr. W. G. H. Simon, Bishop of Llandaff; E. G. Knapp-Fisher, Bishop of Pretoria; C. H. W. de Sousa, Bishop of Colombo; Canon James Atkinson; Canon Eric Kemp; Professor Howard Root; Professor Dr. Massey H. Shepherd, Professor E. R. Fairweather. *Secretaries*, Canon John Findlow and Canon John Satterthwaite.

Roman Catholics. The Bishop of Kansas City, C. H. Helmsing, Chairman. The Titular Bishop of Porlais, Auxiliary to the Archbishop of Bombay, W. Gomes; Mgr. J. G. M. Willebrands; the Titular Bishop of Maura and Auxiliary to the Bishop of Menevia, Wales, L. D. Fox; Professor L. Bouyer; Professor G. Tavart; Professor C. Davis; Rev.

---

[36] From a letter of Lord Fisher to *The Times*, 2 Apr. 1966.

John Keating; Rev. Prof. A. Hastings. *Secretary*, Canon W. A. Purdy.[37]

The resulting conversations were begun on 9 January 1967, at Gazzada, in North Italy. The nine Roman and nine Anglican delegates, with the three secretaries, met together to determine exactly which doctrines keep them apart. They met not knowing what to expect of one another but apparently soon discovered that a common devotion to a common cause brought them nearer to each other than they might have expected.

The delegates discussed tradition and revelation, papal infallibility, the validity of the sacraments of each Church, and the two Marian dogmas. It was apparent that the main obstacles to greater fellowship between the two Churches are the Roman position on mixed marriages and the cult of the Blessed Virgin.

The recommendations made by the joint Catholic–Anglican preparatory Commission in Gazzada were submitted to the Pope and to the Archbishop of Canterbury, and once again it was clear that real difficulties exist between the two Churches.[38] This was made explicit later[39] when the Bishop of Ripon urged Anglican caution on Church unity moves. He warned the Roman Catholic Hierarchy that if it did not listen to the Anglican case, 'we shall have to bring the hopeful experiment of permitting Roman Catholics to preach in Anglican Churches to an end'. Dr. Moorman added that, whereas most member Churches of the World Council of Churches would describe the move towards unity as 'coming together', Rome would say the only possible solution would be 'coming in', insofar as those outside the 'true Church' found their way back into the fold.

A second meeting of the Preparatory Commission met at Huntercombe Manor, Berkshire, England, from 31 August to 4 September 1967. The points discussed were: the sources of Church authority, the place of the Mother of God in Christian belief, the problem of mixed marriages, episcopacy, papal primacy and infallibility, Anglican

---

[37] *Catholic Herald*, 4 Nov. 1966; *Church Times*, 4 Nov. 1966. Professor C. Davis, who was at that time on the staff of Heythrop College in England, shortly afterwards left the Church and of course ceased to serve on the Commission; he is now known as Mr. Charles Davis.

[38] *Catholic Herald*, 20 Jan. 1967.

[39] *Catholic Herald*, 16 Jun. 1967.

Orders and problems connected with intercommunion.[40] This second communiqué is more promising than that of Gazzada.

The third and final meeting of the Joint Preparatory Commission was held in Malta from 30 December 1967 to 3 January 1968. Malta saw St. Paul's shipwreck. It also saw, nearly two thousand years later, the temporary end of a new beginning in potentially fruitful Anglican-Roman relations.

The Commission produced a report which was submitted to the respective heads of churches and accepted (albeit with somewhat qualified approval on the Roman side) in principle. The recommendations include:

1. A possible declaration of the faith which is common to both communions.
2. Greater collaboration, where this is considered feasible, in practical matters.
3. Deeper consideration of controversial matters still outstanding.
4. The appointment of a permanent joint commission, to consider these and other questions of mutual concern.[41]

The Lambeth Conference of 1968 endorsed these recommendations and, in spite of potential grounds for possible pause provided by two papal pronouncements made in the summer of that year (the 'Credo of the People of God' and the Encyclical Humanae Vitae), decided still to proceed at a positive pace in the way of better Anglican-Roman relations. The Conference also approved in a practical manner the Anglican Centre established during the Archbishop of Canterbury's visit in 1966, for information and study in Rome.[42]

The death of Cardinal Bea in November 1968 meant that there was considerable delay in the practical arrangements for the setting up of the Permanent Joint Commission, but in October 1969 the names of those appointed to the Commission were announced, and it met for the first time at Windsor in January 1970 (when its name was changed to the Anglican–Roman Catholic International Commission). There it began work on the three subjects of Church and Authority, Ministry, and the Eucharist, which was continued in Sub-Commissions in England, U.S.A. and South Africa, and which led to the production

[40] See the full text of the joint communiqué in The Tablet, 9 Nov. 1967.
[41] For details see Herder Correspondence (London, Dublin, New York), Dec. 1968 pp. 372–6.
[42] Lambeth Conference 1968: Resolutions and Reports (London, S.P.C.K. and New York, Seabury Press) pp. 36–7, 43–4, 132, 134–5.

of three 'working papers' at the Commission's second meeting at Venice in September 1970. These were published in February 1971 in *Theology*, *The Clergy Review* and *One in Christ* and their titles are: 'Church and Authority', 'Church and Eucharist', 'Church and Ministry'. The third meeting of the Commission took place at Windsor in September 1971, when it produced an Agreed Statement on Eucharistic Doctrine, described as a 'substantial agreement' on the subject.[43] The Commission said that it would next seek to produce a similar statement on the doctrine of the ministry.

4. *The Dialogue between Orthodox and Anglicans*

The desire for unity between Orthodox and Anglicans is deep and strong and has a long history. That is why the third Pan-Orthodox Conference in 1966 decided not to start, but to *continue* the dialogue with the Anglican Church. Certainly the last fifty years have seen a great increase in contacts between the two Churches, as Archbishop Ramsey pointed out: 'The relations between the Church of England and the Holy Orthodox Church were before the first world war informal and spasmodic; now they are far more frequent and on a number of occasions official'.[1] And many factors have contributed to the progress of their relations, not least the fact that

the Church of England has never quarrelled with the Orthodox Church. There is no rivalry, there are no catalogues of wrongs inflicted, no smouldering memories of wars of religion, no feeling that the other's real purpose is to undermine one's position. In conversation between Anglicans and Presbyterians or Anglicans and Roman Catholics, there are so many feelings, such as a deep suspicion on all sides. When Orthodox and Anglicans meet, there is very little suspicion, very little temptation to get angry about them.[2]

Nevertheless we must acknowledge that for a long time in the East the idea prevailed that the ecclesiastical body called the Anglican Church was no other than a Protestant branch which, as a remnant of the ancient Church, preserved episcopacy. In England on the other hand,

---

[43] Press release of 31 December 1971, published by S.P.C.K., London, and also in *Theology*, *Clergy Review* and *O.I.C.*, Jan. 1972.

[1] *D.E.W.* p. 12; cf. J. Karmiris, 'The Third Pan-Orthodox Conference in Rhodes. The dialogue between the Orthodox, Catholic and Anglican Churches'. *Eccl.* 42 (1965), pp. 12 ff.

[2] J. Lawrence, 'Anglicans and Orthodoxy', *R.E.C.* p. 120.

as elsewhere in the West, the Orthodox Church was considered as a dead branch of the ancient and undivided Church, which retained some elements of its doctrine but so buried under a mass of superstitions that it was impossible to distinguish the hidden kernel of truth.

In intellectual and ethical outlook Anglicans are usually closer to the Romans than to the Orthodox. They distinguish between ideas and imagery and the reality behind them, while the Orthodox hold together symbols and the things they signify. Anglicans are 'western-minded' in their emphasis on systems and organization, whereas the East is less interested in organization than in the guardianship of the truth. Anglicans, like Romans, still think of the Church as 'Catholic' in character and extent, while the Orthodox—as their name implies— are more concerned for 'right doctrine' and 'true glory'. Between Orthodox and Anglicans there remain doctrinal differences, but unity can be achieved through doctrinal unity,[3] not by the indiscriminate receiving of each other's Sacraments.[4] Yet though Sacramental union is not yet possible, the Orthodox Church is ready to co-operate with other Christian Churches, especially the Anglican and Roman, in common practical and other ways. It is to be hoped, however, that the Anglican Church *will* achieve doctrinal agreement with Orthodoxy through the re-statement of its teaching on certain points and the enrichment of its worship. For then the way will be open to Sacramental communion with the Orthodox.[5]

The Orthodox also need to realize that the Anglican Church is not what many of them imagine it to be. The old idea that Anglicanism is nothing other than a branch of Protestantism should be dispelled.[6] Although within the Anglican Church there are Protestant elements some of whom are violently opposed to Roman Catholicism, they do not constitute an obstacle to unity with the Orthodox Church.

[3] For instance Anglicans for the most part still follow Pusey in insisting on retaining the *Filioque* in the Creed: Shaw, *Early Tractarians*, p. 89, Note 72.

[4] There have been many instances of this in the past, but the Orthodox have never officially approved of their members receiving Communion in Anglican churches—except at the Anglican-Orthodox discussions of 1930, for which the delegates were strongly criticized afterwards. See Istavridis op. cit., pp. 52–3.

[5] cf. Archbishop Germanos, 'Hopes and Fears' in *The Anglican Communion, past, present and future*, H. A. Wilson (London, 1929), pp. 361–6.

[6] 'The Catholic revival was not begun to propagate Ritualism: its primary purpose was to revive in men's minds a knowledge of the Church's Doctrine and Discipline, without which her ceremonial could have no meaning or value.' C. Kelway, *The Story of Catholic Revival* (London, 1915), p. 110.

The old state of affairs when Anglicanism was divided into three apparently irreconcilable parties has changed somewhat, particularly through the influence of the Liturgical Movement and the emergence of a 'radical line' in theology and practice, both of which cut across all previous 'party' boundaries. Nor should we underestimate the great importance given by Anglicanism to Christian unity, or the fact that discussions about unity are carried on by representatives of all shades of opinion rather than by one group in the Anglican Church, as has happened in the past. Anglicans are certainly as variegated as ever in their interpretations of doctrine and in their pastoral and liturgical practice, yet we should not overlook the things they hold in common or the 'common mind' which they are capable of achieving over major issues.

Professor S. L. Greenslade has well expressed the Anglican position in this respect. Anglicans, he says, are ready to learn from the East about authority. This is a matter on which the Anglican Church is highly critical of the Roman Church, which exercises authority in a legalistic way. The Anglicans are willing to learn from the Orthodox tradition about the spirit of worship; about the *consensus fidelium;* and the holding together of all faithful people. However, Anglicans will ask the Orthodox not only to state the content of their faith, but at the same time to discuss it. Anglicans are not prepared to be assimilated by the Orthodox. The Anglicans expect that the Orthodox will discuss even the total dogmatic Faith of the early undivided Church and they expect the Orthodox 'to be prepared to listen to criticism of the notion and to enter into discussion of that formulation'. The Orthodox must trust the Anglicans 'to be conversing with them as fellow-Christians with fellow-Christians, not as in any way secret enemies'. The Anglicans will ask the Orthodox to join in a 'very serious scrutinising of the human element in the Church'. Besides these there are so many other points which the Anglicans think must be discussed. There are for example particular doctrines where the Orthodox have not needed to go through the process that Anglicans have been compelled to, for instance, the doctrine of justification and Grace, which has been much discussed in the West, whereas the East has had no necessity to discuss it.[7] The Anglicans, admiring as they do the

---

[7] Lecture by Prof. S. L. Greenslade, *D.E.W.*, pp. 33–40. When the Orthodox say that 'our teaching is formulated in the decisions of the Universal Councils and we are not prepared to deviate' they show that they are unable to rediscuss and develop the very same catholic truth in terms of our day. 'We shall discuss',

defence of the Christian Faith and Christian doctrine by the Orthodox, expect the Orthodox not to stay on the defensive but to come out towards them as brothers and children of the same God and members of the same body of Christ.

Though it was not the first visit to the Ecumenical Patriarch made by an Archbishop of Canterbury,[8] the visit of Dr. Fisher in 1960 was of great importance because it was made in an ecumenical era and the Archbishop asked the Patriarch to set up a commission which should continue the doctrinal discussions of the Joint Anglo-Orthodox Committee of 1930 and 1931 which were halted because of the war.[9] Following the official request of the Anglican Church the Ecumenical Patriarchate put this question on the agenda for the third Pan-Orthodox Conference (November 1964) which, after appropriate consideration, decided:

1. To authorize the immediate formation of an inter-Orthodox theological committee and to ask the Orthodox Churches to appoint their own representatives.
2. To introduce the list of questions to be discussed.

---

said Patriarch Meletios, 'not our teaching, but the question whether the Anglican Church is or can be in agreement with the Orthodox Church'. The Anglicans complain that by these statements the Orthodox use the same method as the Roman Church, asking them to become gradually assimilated by the Orthodox. 'That Orthodoxy is bound by the decisions of the Ecumenical Councils does not mean that new dogmatic formulas cannot be fixed by future Ecumenical Councils, because some doctrinal aspects in dogmas have acquired the force of law, although the Orthodox have not expressly formulated them'. These aspects are expressed in the Liturgy, and in the writings of the great theologians known as *Theologumena*. There is a similar process in the doctrinal teaching of the Anglican Church.

[8] Cosmo Lang had, in 1939, visited Benjamin the Ecumenical Patriarch: cf. J. G. Lockhart, *Cosmo Gordon Lang*, pp. 324–6.

[9] Besides the 1930 and 1931 Anglo-Orthodox discussions there were similar discussions in Bucharest in 1935 and in Moscow in 1956. (Cf. *Sobornost*, Series 3, No. 23, 1958, and H. M. Waddams (ed.), *The Anglo-Russian Theological Conference Moscow, July 1956* (1958).) Dr. Visser 't Hooft, says that before the last war the Church of England had a 'maximum programme' of reunion for the Orthodox and a 'minimum programme' for the Protestants. In the 1930 Lambeth Conference the Anglican Bishops were willing to favour relations with Orthodoxy at the expense of relations with their fellow-countrymen. This is apparent in the broader perspective of Christian unity. Orthodoxy and Anglicanism did not make progress in their relations with Roman Catholicism on the one hand, nor with Protestantism on the other. This is because both Churches hold fast to their common Catholic heritage in the historical and ecumenical sense of the word.

3. That the inter-Orthodox Committee should arrange the general outline of the Orthodox attitude towards the Anglican position.

4. To start theological discussions between Anglicans and Orthodox after a thorough preparation by the Orthodox Church after consultation with the Anglican Church.

5. That all the above decisions should be communicated to the Anglican Church by the Ecumenical Patriarch, according to Orthodox tradition.

As a consequence of the Rhodes Conference in 1964, meetings were held in Belgrade during 2–15 September 1966, of the two inter-Orthodox Theological Commissions to draw up the agenda for the dialogue between Orthodox and Anglicans on the one hand and Orthodox and Old Catholics on the other.

These Orthodox discussions in Belgrade proved once again that the Orthodox still have more or less confused ideas about the Anglican Church. This derives, perhaps, from the fact that many amongst the delegates there were not sufficiently prepared to face the important theological subjects which were to be discussed, because some Churches had appointed as delegates persons who had not specialized in these problems.[10] On the other hand, we realize that the Orthodox insisted on discussing certain points regarding the Anglican Church which are not acceptable to them, such as the relations between the Anglican Church and the State,[11] the existence of various schools of thought within the Anglican Church, and the principle of comprehensiveness. We notice again that the two Churches begin from different starting points, which makes their differences difficult to reconcile. The Anglicans start from the Bible and sometimes ignore its traditional interpretation, whereas the Orthodox follow strongly the life of the Church through the centuries. The Orthodox still have difficulties in understanding the spirit which prevails in Anglican thought. Even the term 'comprehensiveness' cannot be properly understood nor even properly

[10] See I. Karmiris, 'The Fourth Pan-Orthodox Conference in Belgrade', *Eccl.* 43 (1966), p. 559, note 2.

[11] Though Professor Trembelas overlooks, apparently, the fact that the Church of England, though the biggest, is only one of the Churches which make up the Anglican Communion. And he may not know that even in Great Britain, the Churches of Wales, of Ireland and the Episcopal Church of Scotland are disestablished from the State. P. Trembelas, 'The Pan-Orthodox Conference in Belgrade', *Eccl.* 43 (1966), pp. 543–7, 572–5, 615–16 ff.

translated by the Orthodox.[12] Professor Trembelas, when he spoke at the Pan-Orthodox Conference at Belgrade, repeated the same arguments which he elaborates in his book *The Reformation in the Anglican Church* and the points which are stated by Professor Bratsiotis in his book *The Anglican Ordinations from an Orthodox point of view*. It is needless to say again that these points are antiquated, as I have pointed out in my previous Chapters.[13]

It is now the task of the Theological Commissions to study the points of disagreement between the two Churches and explain them plainly to their respective bodies.

After long and unfruitful discussions the two Theological Commissions issued the following communiqué:

Having formed this Pan-Orthodox Theological Conference in Belgrade entrusted to us by our Churches, we all heartily thank God, the Holy Trinity, Who enabled us to carry out our task to a favourable conclusion. Having confessed in faith the truth of the Christian Revelation, united in love, not in hastiness, but with patience, we have investigated the subjects which had been entrusted to us and we humbly submit the results of our study to His All-Holiness the Ecumenical Patriarch who according to the decision of the third Pan-Orthodox Conference at Rhodes has invited us here. We are doing the same to the venerable Primates of the most Holy Oriental Orthodox Churches.

Reviewing the work done in organising the forthcoming dialogue of the Orthodox Church with the Venerable Anglican and Old Catholic Churches, we declare, that in a spirit of love and reverence we all have investigated all the points in which we agree,[14] and we acknowledge all the elements which show the rapprochement which exists between the Venerable Anglican and the Old Catholic Churches and our Orthodox Churches.

The problems which we discussed prove the relationship in faith, and the co-operation in love which characterise the relations of the Orthodox, Anglican and Old Catholic Churches which have existed for over a century.

We believe that the Holy Spirit, who in the past guided the thoughts of the delegates of both sides to confess agreement in some chapters of the Christian faith, will prepare in future all those who may take part in the dialogue, in order that with patience they may enlarge the

---

[12] See Professor Greenslade's lecture, *D.E.W.*, ibid., pp. 33-40.

[13] See above, Ch. IV, Sect. 4 (pp. 87-8), etc.

[14] There were no new subjects to be discussed at Belgrade. The delegates were guided by the results of the Anglo-Orthodox discussions in the years 1930, 1931, 1936 and 1948, for which see the previous Chapters.

frontiers of love and agreement which exist between Anglicans, Old Catholics and Orthodox. Moreover they will make clear with sincerity those points which need further interpretation, in order that one Faith, one Baptism, one Lord and Saviour, may be confessed by all with one heart and mind.

We do not hesitate to declare our admiration for the leaders of the Anglican and Old Catholic Churches, because it has been proved in the past, as it is now, that they have never ceased to declare their sincere love for our Church, their respect and attachment towards the One, Holy, Catholic and Apostolic Church of the Eastern Orthodox Christians, acknowledging, in spite of their historical circumstances, the favour which they feel towards Orthodoxy.

We consider this spirit of mutual respect as an indication of the guidance of the Holy Spirit, Who will lead us, in due time, though this is known only to God, towards the end which we seek. Our most Holy Church has declared its duty to contribute towards the union of the Churches and the peace of all people.

... We expect that our Churches will confirm the list of the subjects, which, we thought, in the future should be involved in the dialogue. . . .[15]

From an Orthodox point of view, there are two views as to the meaning of unity. According to the first, the broad view, all Christian communities, which have the same origin, Jesus Christ, can establish an external communion of fellowship and co-operation. This view was inaugurated by the Patriarchal Encyclical of 1920. And the formation of the World Council of Churches may well have taken that Patriarchal and Synodal Encyclical as its pattern. According to the second, the narrower view, there is one Holy Catholic and Apostolic Church, and this is the original Church. All who accept the teaching of this Church are internally united with it and form a dogmatic union. If they are also externally united, i.e. in canonical communion, they form an organic union. Such an organic and dogmatic unity is formed by the various parts of the Orthodox Communion. It is not necessary however to have absolute uniformity. For the principles of Patriarch Photius in his Letter to Pope Nicolas are maintained in the Orthodox Church: 'If the question is not one of Faith, nor one concerned with a universal decision, that is, taken from an Ecumenical Council, but one of customs and habits, then he would be blameworthy who would pretend that those who follow them are doing wrong or who would condemn those who do not follow them'.[16]

[15] I. Karmiris, *Eccl.* 43 (1966), pp. 562–3.
[16] *The Letters of the most wise and most Holy Patriarch Photius of Constantinople* by J. N. Valetta (London, 1864), pp. 154–5.

The Orthodox Theological Commission held two meetings. The first in Chambésy, Switzerland from 1 to 8 October 1970 and the second in Helsinki, Finland from 7 to 11 July 1971. In Helsinki it was decided that an unofficial meeting between Anglicans and Orthodox might take place in 1972 in Cyprus, provided that the Orthodox Churches approved this suggestion. (The writer of this book represents the Church of Alexandria in this Commission.)[17]

The Anglican Theological Commission held four meetings: first in Oxford from 5 to 7 February 1968, second in Jerusalem, at St. George's College, from 15 to 19 September 1969, third at Chichester Diocesan Conference and Retreat House, Haywards Heath, from 20 to 24 July 1970, and fourth at Haywards Heath from 26 to 30 July 1971. The Orthodox Commission plans to hold a third meeting at the Orthodox Centre in Chambéry, Switzerland in July 1972, before the first Anglican-Orthodox meeting in Cyprus later that year.

5. Communicatio in Sacris

Communicatio in sacris is the technical term in current Roman Catholic usage, referring to the participation of Christians in the worship of churches other than their own. 'Participation' in this context must be understood in the fullest sense, of attending as a worshipper who shares, for the time being, the privileges of Church membership. In the early centuries, at the end of the Mass of the Catechumens, all unbaptized persons were dismissed, and even to be present at the most sacred part of the Eucharist was a privilege limited to the faithful. In modern conditions of divided Christendom, especially in large cities and cosmopolitan places, and when Christians find themselves in countries where their own church is not represented, non-Roman Catholics may in fact be present at the Roman Catholic Mass, and non-Orthodox people at the Orthodox liturgy; without, of course, receiving Holy Communion. This, naturally, does not amount to *communicatio in sacris*, since the other Christians may attend from various motives ranging from curiosity, through respectful attention, to real devotion and Christian fellowship, but they are not admitted to the privileges of Church membership. Since the greatest of these privileges is to receive Holy Communion, in English the term *intercommunion* is normally used where the Latin would be *communicatio in sacris;* but the Latin term is more exact since it includes all the

[17] See the minutes of both meetings in *Ekklesiastikos Pharos*, 53 (1971), pp. 612–46.

privileges of sacramental worship such as admission to confession and absolution, the right to be married in the Church (subject to regulations about marriage), to have one's children baptized, and so on, without actually leaving one's own Church, in which one was brought up, and 'going over' to the other. A notable example of such intercommunion is that which exists between the Anglican and the Old Catholic Churches according to the 'Bonn Agreement' of 1931.[1]

According to the Orthodox Church, where the totality of the faith is absent there can be no *communicatio in sacris*. Intercommunion cannot be separated from Dogmatic Union. Nevertheless the Committee appointed (1930) by the Ecumenical Patriarch and the Archbishop of Canterbury decided to recommend that each Church (Anglican and Orthodox) should agree to accept members of the other Church as participants in their Sacraments. On the Anglican side, this was not difficult; for the Orthodox, there was some difficulty, but in fact there are cases where Orthodox have accepted Anglicans as participants in Orthodox Sacraments.[2]

Within Anglicanism, the attitude to intercommunion varies between different traditions and schools of thought. Those of the Evangelical and Liberal traditions would accept intercommunion with all Christians who believe in the authority of Scripture and the fundamentals of the Christian faith, or even with all sincere followers of Jesus Christ. Others, of the High Church and Catholic tradition, would require much greater agreement, not only in faith, but in Church order, particularly the possession of the historic ministry of Bishops, Priests, and Deacons, and the practice of episcopal Ordination and Confirmation. As regards the Orthodox—and also Roman Catholics if they desired to receive Communion from Anglicans—their possession of the Catholic order and ministry could make this acceptable; but with Protestants, since they lack the historic episcopal ministry, the Church of England, and most Anglican churches, have not in general been

---

[1] '1. Each Communion recognizes the catholicity and independence of the other and maintains its own. 2. Each Communion agrees to admit members of the other Communion to participate in the Sacraments.' Bell, *Documents on Christian Unity, Third Series, 1930–1948*, p. 60, No. 167. See also Archbishop Jacovos, 'The Contribution of Eastern Orthodoxy to the Ecumenical Movement', *E.R.*, xi (1959), p. 397.

[2] J. A. Douglas, *Relations of the Anglican Churches with the Eastern Orthodox.* (London, 1921), esp. pp. 40–62: 181–3. Also 'Economy and the Communion at Belgrade', by J. A. Douglas, *C.E.* ix (1928), pp. 16–23; cf. also *Pantainos* (Alexandria), 19 Jan. 1928, p. 48; see also J. Cotsonis, *Intercommunio* (Athens, 1957), pp. 96, 100, 109 ff.

willing to establish intercommunion. The Anglican-Methodist Scheme of Union, rejected in 1969, was an attempt to overcome this difficulty, by introducing an episcopal ministry in Methodism, but it has so far failed to obtain sufficient support on the Anglican side.

The Roman Catholic Church, like the Orthodox and High Church Anglicans, naturally insists on the existence of the historic episcopal ministry—that is, of the Apostolic Succession—as a pre-requisite of intercommunion. But where this is not in doubt, it has not been very strict in this matter. For various reasons it has permitted *communicatio in sacris* not only with the Orthodox, but with almost all the non-Chalcedonian Churches of the East. The Decrees on Ecumenism and on the Eastern Catholic Churches (i.e. of Eastern Rite) encourage the faithful, in certain cases, to frequent Orthodox Churches and ask for the Sacraments, and *vice versa* for Orthodox in Roman Catholic Churches. From a Roman Catholic point of view participation in the Eucharistic Liturgy with Orthodox Christians is 'not merely possible but is encouraged', because the faith common to Orthodoxy and Catholicism explicitly includes the exercise of the Sacramental priesthood—'by apostolic succession—in a full common Liturgy'.[3] At the present stage of relations, *communicatio in sacris* is imperative for the establishment of full communion between East and West.[4] For this reason the Decree on the Catholic Eastern Churches advises the responsible hierarchs that this 'flexible approach to sharing in sacred rites with brothers of the separated Eastern Churches is entrusted to the watchful control of local hierarchs. They are to co-ordinate their plans and, should there be occasion, give hearing to hierarchs of separated Churches and direct the association of Christians by means of precepts and rules which meet the case and are effective'.[5] This attitude of the Second Vatican Council indicates that the Roman Church 'recognizes the ecclesial character of Eastern Orthodox Churches' and 'it is precisely their recognition which makes it possible for Rome to propose intercommunion to them as a means of grace by which they can come closer together in view of full and final union. In the past', says Cardinal Lercaro, 'Churchmen were wrong in this matter of reunion with the East in that they laid down conditions which were the object of diplomatic negotiations which, it was hoped, would lead to an agreement to restore intercommunion. But

---

[3] *Decree on Ecumenism* (Catholic Truth Society ed.), p. 23–4.
[4] John F. Long, S. J. 'East and West in the Decree on Ecumenism', *Unitas*, xvii (1965), i, p. 16.
[5] Op. cit., p. 18.

when one has realized that theologically the marks of the true Church
are sufficiently, though from our point of view incompletely, present
among our Brothers of the East, one is entitled to suggest intercommunion if the circumstances are opportune. With the help of
God's grace in us we can then try to find the formula which will make
full and unconditional intercommunion possible.'[6]

But Professor Evdokimov is of the opinion that 'the Roman Catholic
decisions concerning *communicatio in sacris* merely make the dialogue
more difficult, confusing the issues and obscuring the ecclesiological
bases by taking premature steps; these steps are fragmentary, local and
exceptional, and offer no solution for the basic problem.'[7] Professor
Evdokimov's opinion is the opposite to that of Patriarch Athenagoras.
According to *La Croix*, in a Roman Catholic 'Uniat' ceremony in
Istanbul to mark the feast of St. John Chrysostom, it is reported that
'the Liturgy ended with the traditional invocation intoned by the
choir which mentioned both the Pope and the Patriarch Athenagoras'.
It was revealed in a paper there that 'the next gesture from the Patriarchate will be the mention of Pope Paul's name in the Liturgy of the
Orthodox Mass in his position as Patriarch of the West and the First
amongst the Patriarchs.'[8]

The Decree on Ecumenism does not make any special reference to
intercommunion between Romans and Anglicans. If Anglicanism be
included amongst the separated Churches and Ecclesial Communities
in the West, full participation in such eucharistic celebrations cannot
be recommended, because the Romans do not believe that the Protestants have preserved 'the whole, authentic substance of the mystery
of the Eucharist, especially in view of their lack of the Sacrament of
Order'.[9] There are also, from an Anglican point of view, certain
reservations about intercommunion between Anglicans and Romans
since some Anglicans 'would feel insuperable difficulty in receiving
Communion at a Roman Mass, or in reciting with Roman Catholics
prayers to the Virgin Mary or to Saints. . . .'[10] Things are changing

---

[6] Cardinal Lercaro, ibid., pp. 90–91, cf. also *O.I.C.* i (1965), p. 188.

[7] P. Evdokimov, ibid. p. 98. In fact 'the Orthodox and Romans firmly believe
that unity in the faith is an essential pre-requisite for unity in Sacramental life,
and that to compromise this is to make shipwreck of the Faith'. B. Leeming,
'An Anglo-Catholic on the Recovery of Unity', *E.C.Q.* xii (1958–9), p. 334.

[8] *The Tablet*, 5 Mar. 1966, p. 288.

[9] Catholic Truth Society, p. 29.

[10] 'Intercommunio: A personal opinion', in *Intercommunion* (London, 1952),
p. 229; cf. M. Bévenot, S.J. 'Communicatio in Sacris' in 'Christian Unity, A
Catholic View,' ibid. p. 133.

10

rapidly and the relationship between Romans and Anglicans will surely come to a stage in which the Roman Church will show greater charity towards Anglicanism, above all by recognizing Anglican ordinations. The best gesture possible for the Roman Church would be to do as some of the Orthodox Churches have done, and accept the validity of Anglican orders. Since, on the Anglican side, no doubts exist about the fact that both the Roman and Orthodox episcopates stand in the historic succession, there is nothing that would be more fruitful for the coming-together of these three churches than the complete mutual recognition of their ministries. It must be admitted that this cannot be given merely as a matter of expediency, but requires very careful consideration on grounds of history, theology, and the whole doctrine of the Church. But should this result in the removal of all remaining objections that would indeed be a joyful day for the whole of Christendom.

APPENDIX

Terms of Intercommunion suggested between the Church of England and the Churches in Communion with her and the Eastern Orthodox Church

These suggested terms of intercommunion were communicated in 1921 to the Ecumenical Patriarch with the approval of Archbishop Davidson by his Eastern Churches Commission as a *ballon d'essai* in order to provoke discussion. Consequently, they are not the formal and authenticated proposals of the Anglican Episcopate. It is to be deplored that although such a long period has elapsed since the publication of the above terms, no reaction has yet been expressed by the Orthodox Church. The text was published in G. K. A. Bell, *Documents on Christian Unity* [First Series] 1920-4 (London, 1924), No. 17, pp. 77-87. See also *C.E.* xii (1931), pp. 49-56.

1. *Of the Christian Faith*

We accept the Faith of Christ as it is taught us by the Holy Scriptures and as it has been handed down to us in the Creed of the Catholic Church, and as it is expounded in the dogmatic decisions of the Oecumenical Councils as accepted by the Undivided Church.

2. *Of the Canon of Scripture*

We accept the Canon of Scripture as it is defined by St. Athanasius,[1] and as it has been received by the whole Catholic Church; namely, the twenty-two books of the Old Testament which are contained in the Hebrew Canon, and the twenty-seven books of the New Testament. As regards the other books, which are called sometimes Deuterocanonical, sometimes *Anaginōskomena*, sometimes *Apocrypha*, we also accept the teaching of St. Athanasius: 'for greater exactness I add this also . . . that there are other books besides these [books], not indeed included in the Canon, but appointed by the Fathers to be read by

[1] *Festal Epistle* 39.

those who newly join us, and wish to be instructed in the word of godliness . . . the former [books] . . . being included in the Canon, the latter being [only] read',[2] and the teaching of St. Jerome 'that the Church may read them for the edification of the people, not for the confirmation of the authority of ecclesiastical dogmas'.[3]

3. *Of the Sufficiency of Holy Scripture*

We believe that Holy Scripture contains all things necessary to salvation, as St. Athanasius says, 'The sacred and inspired Scriptures are sufficient to declare the truth.'[4] And elsewhere, 'These are the fountains of salvation, that he who thirsts may be satisfied with the or-acles contained in them. In these [books] alone is proclaimed the doctrine of godliness. Let no man add to them, nor take aught from them';[5] and, as St. Augustine says: 'In those things which are plainly laid down in Scripture all things are found which comprise faith and morals'.[6] As touching Tradition, we accept it, in the words of the *Longer Catechism* of the Russian Church, 'as a guide to the right understanding of Holy Scripture, for the right ministration of the Sacraments, and the preservation of sacred rites and ceremonies in the purity of their original institution'; and 'we must follow that tradition which agrees with the divine revelation and with Holy Scripture'.[7]

4. *Of the Creed of the Church*

We accept as the creed of the Catholic Church that which is some-times called the Creed of Constantinople, and in the formularies of the Church of England is called the Nicene Creed; which was put forth by the Council of Chalcedon and has been accepted by the whole Catholic Church.

5. *Of the Exposition of Faith of the Council of Chalcedon*

We accept also as explaining the Creed the Exposition of Faith which was put forth by the Council of Chalcedon.

[2] ibid.
[3] *Prol. in Libros Salom.*
[4] *Contra Gentes* I § 3; cf. *de Synod.* 6, *ad Episc. Aegypt.* 6.
[5] *Festal Epistle* 39.
[6] *De Doctrina Christiana*, ii, 9.
[7] *Longer Catechism*. English Translation in *The Doctrine of the Russian Church*. By the Rev. R. W. Blackmore (Aberdeen, 1845), p. 36.

6. *That no one may put forth any other Creed*

Whereas it is stated in the Exposition of faith of the Council of Chalcedon that 'these things having been defined by us with all possible accuracy and care, the Holy and Oecumenical Synod hath decreed that it is unlawful for any one to present, or compile, or compose, or believe, or teach to others, any other creed; and that those who dare either to compose another creed, or to bring forward, or to teach, or to deliver another symbol to those wishing to turn from paganism or from Juadaism or from heresy of what sort soever, to the full knowledge of the truth, these, if bishops or clerics, be deposed, the bishops from the episcopate and clerics from the clerical office; and, if monks or laics, they be anathematized'.[8] We recognize that it is unlawful for a Church to demand any further statement of faith as a necessary condition of intercommunion; but that it is not unlawful for the several Churches to use as their baptismal creed some other creed agreeable to the tradition of the Church, as in the Western Church that which is called the Apostles' Creed is and always has been so used. Nor is it unlawful for a Church to use any other similar document in the services of the Church, or for the instruction of the Faithful, provided that it is agreeable to orthodox doctrine.

7. *Of the Doctrine of the Holy Spirit*

Whereas there has been a difference, as between the East and the West, in the language used concerning the eternal procession of the Holy Spirit, so that it has been the custom in the East to say that the Holy Spirit proceeds from the Father, and in the West that He proceeds from the Father and the Son, we recognize that both forms of expression may rightly be used, and that they are intended to express the same faith. While we reject every conception or form of expression which implies the existence of two principles or *archai* or *aitiai* in the Holy Trinity, we accept the teaching of St. John of Damascus and of the earlier Greek Fathers that the Holy Ghost proceeds from the Father through the Son.

8. *Of the* Filioque *Clause*

And whereas in the Western Church at some time in the sixth or seventh century the words *Filioque* were added to the Creed, we agree

[8] *Expos. fidei Conc. Chalc.* (Mansi, *Concilia*, vii. 116).

in acknowledging that this addition was not made 'in an ecclesiastically regular manner'; and that in assemblies of Easterns and Westerns the one Creed of the Universal Church ought to be recited without those words; but we are also agreed that, since the added words are used in an orthodox sense, it is lawful for any Church which has received the Creed as containing these words to continue to recite it in the Services of the Church.

9. Of Variety of Customs in the Church

St. Augustine divides the usages of the Church into three classes: viz. (1) those customs which have the authority of our Lord and of the Scriptures, of which he says 'Our Lord Jesus Christ has put us under a light yoke and an easy burden as He says Himself in the Gospel; and therefore He has bound together the society of the New People by sacraments in number very few, in observance most easy, and in meaning most excellent: as Baptism consecrated in the Name of the Trinity, the Communion of His Body and Blood, and anything else that is commended in the Canonical Scriptures'; (2) 'those things which we hold on the authority, not of Scripture, but of tradition, which are observed throughout the whole world', and of these he says it is to be understood that they are retained 'as commended and enacted either by the Apostles themselves or by plenary Councils whose authority in the Church is most salutary'; and (3) 'those things which are different in different places and countries. ... All such things are free to be observed or not; and there is no better rule for a serious and prudent Christian than to act in such wise as he sees that church to act in which he chances to find himself'.[9] The Patriarch Photius also writes: 'In cases where the thing disregarded is not matter of faith and does not involve a falling away from any general or catholic decree, where different customs and usages are observed in different places, a man who knows how to judge would be right in deciding that neither do those who observe them act wrongly, nor those who have not received them break the law'.[10] We agree, therefore, to recognize those customs which have the authority of our Lord, of Scripture, and of the Universal Church; while, as to those which are different in different parts of the Christian world and for

[9] S. Aug. Ep. liv ad Ianuarium 1–3.
[10] J. N. Valetta, op. cit., p. 156.

which there is not the authority of Scripture or of any general Council, we agree that each Church do retain its own customs.

10. *Of the Number of the Sacraments*

Inasmuch as the number of the Sacraments has never been authoritatively fixed either by tradition from the Apostles or any decision of an Oecumenical Council, their number has been differently reckoned in the Church at different periods. It was not until the sixteenth century that the number was defined in the Roman Church, or until the seventeenth century in the Eastern. We recognize that the two Sacraments of Baptism and the Holy Eucharist are pre-eminent above the rest. In the Book of Common Prayer of the Church of England the title Sacrament is only used of these two as (1) having an outward visible sign ordained by Christ Himself, and (2) as generally necessary for salvation. But we agree further that the title Sacrament may be used of other rites and ceremonies in which there is an outward and visible sign and an inward and spiritual grace, and in that sense it is rightly used of other institutions, such as ordination, penance, confirmation, marriage, and the anointing of the sick; and in relation to some of these Sacraments, since the customs of the different Churches have varied and still vary, we agree that each Church have liberty to retain its own usages.

11. *Of the Holy Eucharist*

The Church has at all times desired to fulfil the Lord's command by the celebration of the Holy Eucharist, and we desire in all things to obey the teaching of Scripture and the regulations of the Universal Church. But whereas there has been much controversy, and many divisions have arisen, as to the more exact definition of the nature of the presence of the Body and Blood of our Lord in the Holy Eucharist; and whereas there is no decree of any Oecumenical Council touching the manner of the presence of Christ; and whereas some of the terms that have been used have been used with different significations in different parts of the Church: we agree that this is a Divine Mystery which transcends human understanding, and that the Church has expressed sufficiently its belief in its Liturgies; and we agree further that the doctrine of the Holy Eucharist, as it is taught in the Liturgies of the Orthodox Church, and in the Liturgies of the Church of England

and those of the Churches in communion with the Church of England, is adequate and sufficient.

12. Of the Holy Orders of the Church

In order that the Word of God might be preached and the Sacraments duly administered our Lord instituted a Ministry for His Church and the Apostles ordained ministers by the laying on of hands with prayer, and the Catholic Church has laid down rules for the continuation and ordering of the Ministry. We desire always to fulfil the commands of Christ, the intention of the Apostles, and the rule of the Church. We agree that 'from the Apostles' time there have been these Orders of Ministers in Christ's Church—Bishops, Priests, and Deacons'—and it has always been our intention that these Orders 'be continued and reverently used and esteemed';[11] and we agree that in accordance with our common usage and the canon of the Council of Nicaea every bishop be consecrated by three other bishops at least, and that all priests and deacons be ordained by bishops with the laying on of hands and prayer; and that in Ordination the Holy Spirit is given for the work of the Ministry; and we consider that the forms of Ordination used in the Orthodox Church and in the Church of England are adequate and sufficient.

13. Of the Sacred Ikons

Since there has been much difference of opinion touching the use of ikons, and since there are differences of usage between the East and the West, we express our agreement with the Second Council of Nicaea that the tradition of 'making pictorial representations is agreeable to the history contained in the Evangelic Message, for a confirmation of the real incarnation of God the Word, and serves to our profit in this regard';[12] and we agree further that worship (*latreia*) pertains to the Divine Nature alone, and we accept the words used by the bishop at his consecration in the Russian Church: 'I will take care

[11] *The Form and Manner of making, ordaining, and consecrating of Bishops, Priests, and Deacons, according to the order of the Church of England*, Preface. Compare also the words used by the Bishops in the Lambeth Conference of 1908 and 1920: 'We who speak are bearers of the sacred commission of the ministry given by our Lord through His Apostles to the Church.'

[12] *Definitio Conc. Nicaen. II* (Mansi, *Concilia*, xiii, 377).

that the homage due to God be not transferred to holy images nor false miracles be ascribed to them whereby the true worship is perverted and a handle given to adversaries to reproach the Orthodox; on the contrary I will study that images be respected only in the sense of the Holy Orthodox Church as set forth in the Second Council of Nicaea.' And for other matters we agree that each Church may have liberty to preserve its own distinctive customs, and that in the Western Church figures of Christ and the Saints be allowed which are carved and sculptured contrary to the custom of the Eastern Church; and that the Eastern Church should show reverence to the Sacred Ikons in accordance with its own customs and the teaching of the Second Council of Nicaea; and that neither Church should accuse the other of idolatry or false teaching.

BIBLIOGRAPHY

Works of the Fathers of the Church are not mentioned in this Bibliography. The Bibliography concerning Anglican Orders can be found in Chapter V. This list does not exhaust all the material relevant to the subjects of this book; it is a list of those works which I have consulted in the writing of it.

I. Books

Androutsos, Ch. *An Essay of Symbolic. From an Orthodox Point of View*. Athens, 1901. [In Greek].
— *The Validity of English Ordinations. From an Orthodox Point of View*. Tr. by F. W. Groves Campbell, London, 1909.
— *Dogmatic of the Orthodox Eastern Church*. Athens, 2nd ed. 1956. [In Greek].
Anglican Congress Report (1954). Minneapolis.
Anglican Communion, The. London, Church Information Office, 1962.
Allchin, A. M. (ed.) *We Belong to One Another*. Methodist, Anglican and Orthodox Essays. London, 1965.
Arseniev, N., and French, R. *The Anglican and the Orthodox Churches*. Two Essays published in connection with the Anglican and Eastern Churches Association Centenary Year. London, 1964.
Baum, G. *The Quest for Christian Unity*. London, 1963.
Bea, Augustine, Cardinal. *The Unity of Christians*. Ed. by B. Leeming, London, 1963.
Bell, G. K. A. (ed.) *Documents on Christian Unity, [First Series], 1920–1924*, London, 1924. *Second Series*, London, 1930. *Third Series, 1930–1948*, London, 1948. *Fourth Series, 1948–57*, London, 1958.
— *Randall Davidson, Archbishop of Canterbury*. London, 2 vols., 1935, (3rd ed. bound in 1 vol., 1952).
— *Christian Unity: The Anglican Position*. London, 1948.
Bettenson, H. (ed.) *Documents of the Christian Church*. London, 1943; 2nd ed., 1963, paperback ed., 1967.
Bicknell, E. J. *A Theological Introduction to the Thirty-Nine Articles of the Church of England*. 3rd ed., revised by H. J. Carpenter, London, 1961.

Bolshakoff, S. *The Doctrine of the Unity of the Church in the Works of Khomyakov and Möhler.* London, 1946.
Boyer, C. *Christian Unity and the Ecumenical Movement.* London, 1962.
Broomfield, G. W. *Revelation and Reunion.* London, 1942.
Bulgakov, S. *The Orthodox Church,* London, 1935.
Bull, George. *Works,* ed. E. Burton, vol. ii, Oxford, 1827.
Canisius van Lierde, P. *The Holy See at Work.* Tr. by James Tucer, London, 1964.
Cavert, S. McCrea. *On the Road to Christian Unity.* New York, 1961.
Chadwick, O. *The Mind of the Oxford Movement.* London, 1960.
Churton, E. see Pearson.
Conference of Bishops of the Anglican Communion. [*The Lambeth Conference Report*]. London, 1920.
Conferinţa Română Orthodoxă-Anglicană ţinută la Bucureşti 1–8 Iunie 1935 şi Călătoria i.p.s. Patriarch D. D. Dr. Miron în Anglia 28 Iunie–7 Iulie 1936. Bucharest, 1938.
Congar, Y. *Divided Christendom.* London, 1939.
Congar, Y., H. Küng, and D. O'Halton, (eds.) *Council Speeches of Vatican II.* London, 1964.
Daniel-Rops, H. *The Second Vatican Council.* Tr. by A. Guinan, New York, 1962.
Davidson, R. (ed. under the direction of), *The Five Lambeth Conferences.* London, 1920.
Dixon, R. W. *History of the Church of England from the abolition of the Roman Jurisdiction.* Vol. ii, London, 1884; Vol. iv, London, 1891.
Doctrine in the Church of England. The Report of the Commission on Christian Doctrine Appointed by the Archbishops of Canterbury and York in 1922. London, 1938.
Douglas, J. *The Relations of the Anglicans with the Eastern-Orthodox.* London, 1921.
Dvornik, F. *The Photian Schism. History and Legend.* Cambridge, 1948.
— *Byzance et la Primauté Romaine.* Paris, 1964. (Unam Sanctam, 49).
Ecumenical Patriarchate. *Encyclical Patriarchal and Synodical of the.* Tr. by E. Metallinos, Oxford, 1896.
Ellison, G. *The Anglican Communion.* New York, 1960.
Evangelische Kirche Deutschland (Hrsg.) *Dokumente der Orthodoxen Kirchen zum Oekumenischen Frage.* Heft 1. Die Moskauer Orthodoxe Konferenz vom Juli 1948.Witten, n.d.
Every, G. *The Byzantine Patriarchate.* London, 1962.
— *Misunderstandings between East and West.* Ecumenical Studies in History No. 4, ed. by A. M. Allchin, Martin E. Marty and T. H. L. Parker, London, 1965.
Fisher of Lambeth, Lord. *The Archbishop Speaks.* Ed. E. Carpenter, London, 1958.

Flew, R. Newton. (ed.) *The Nature of the Church*. Papers presented to the Theological Commission appointed by the Continuation Committee of the World Conference on Faith and Order. London, 1952.

Fortescue, A. *The Orthodox Eastern Church*. 2nd. ed., London, 1908.

Fremantle, A. *The Papal Encyclicals in their Historical Context*. New York, 1956.

Garbett, C. *The Claims of the Church of England*. London, 1960.

Gasparri, Cardinal. *The Catholic Catechism*. 5th ed., London, 1934.

Gore, Charles. *The Ministry of the Christian Church*. London, 1888.

— *Orders and Unity*. London, 1909.

— *Roman Catholic Claims*, 10th ed., London, 1909.

— *The Holy Spirit and the Church*. London, 1924.

— *Belief in Christ*. London, 1922.

— *The Anglo-Catholic Movement Today*. London, 1925.

Guillon, M. J. Le. *The Tradition of the Eastern Church*. London, 1962.

Hanson, R. P. C. *Tradition in the Early Church*. London, 1962.

Halifax, Viscount. *Leo XIII and Anglican Orders*. London, 1912.

Hase, K. von. *Handbook to the Controversy with Rome*. Tr. from the 7th German edition by A. W. Streane, Vols. i–ii, London, 1906.

Headlam, A. C. *The Doctrine of the Church and Christian Reunion*. London, 1920.

Healing, The Ministry of. Report of the Committee Appointed in accordance with resolution 63 of the Lambeth Conference, 1920. London, 1924.

Heenan, J. C. (ed.) *Christian Unity*. *A Catholic View*. London, 1962.

Heiler, F. *Altkirchliche Autonomie und Papstlicher Zentralismus*, 1941.

Hodges, H. A. *Anglicanism and Orthodoxy*. *A Study in dialectical Churchmanship*. London, 1955.

Hooft, W. A. Visser 't. *Anglo-Catholicism and Orthodoxy*. London, 1933,

Hook, W. Farquhar. *Lives of the Archbishops of Canterbury*. Vol. i. London, 1860.

Horton, W. M. *Christian Theology*. *An Ecumenical Approach*. London, 1956.

Ionescu, D. G. *Relaţiile Ţărilor Române cu Patriarchia de Alexandria*. Bucherest, 1935.

Iremonger, F. A. *William Temple, Archbishop of Canterbury, His Life and Letters*. London, 1948.

Istavridis, V. *Orthodoxy and Anglicanism*. Published by the Anglican and Eastern Churches Association. The Faith Press. London, n.d.; cf. *The Greek Orthodox Theological Review* 5 (1959), pp. 9–26.

Jaeger, L. *The Ecumenical Council. The Church and Christendom*. London 1961.

— *A Stand on Ecumenism. The Council's Decree*. London, 1965.

Jasper, R. *Arthur Cayley Headlam*. London, 1960.

Karmiris, J. *The Dogmatic and Symbolic Mnemeia of the Orthodox Catholic Church*. Athens, Vol. i, 1960; Vol. ii, 1953. [In Greek].

— *The New Dogma*. Athens, 1951. [In Greek].

Karrer, O. *Peter and the Church. An examination of Cullman's Thesis*. London, 1963.

Kelly, B. J. *Apologetics and Catholic Doctrine*. Part iii, Dublin, 1951.

Kelly, J. N. D. *Early Christian Doctrines*. 2nd ed. London, 1960.

Kelway, C. *The Story of the Catholic Revival*. London, 1915.

Küng, H. *Changing Church*. London, 1965.

Lambeth Conference: see under *Conference*.

Lathbury, Th. *A History of the Non-Jurors, their Controversies and Writings, with remarks on some of the Rubrics in the Book of Common Prayer*. London, 1845.

Leeming, B. *Principles of Sacramental Theology*. 2nd ed., London, 1960.

— *Vatican Council and Christian Unity*. London, 1965.

Lockhart, J. G. *Cosmo Gordon Lang*. London, 1949.

Lubac, H. de. *Catholicism*. A Study of Dogma in relation to the Corporate Destiny of Mankind. London, 1962.

Mackey, J. P. *The Modern Theology of Tradition*. London, 1962.

Mendieta, E. A. de. *Rome and Canterbury*. Tr. by C. Quin, London, 1962.

Metallinos, E. (Tr.). See under Ecumenical Patriarchate.

Meyendorff, J. A., A. Schmeman, N. Afanasieff, and N. Kolomzine, *The Primacy of Peter*. London, 1963.

Meyendorff, J. *The Orthodox Church*. Tr. from the French by J. Chapin, London, 1962.

Möhler, J. A. *Die Einheit der Kirche, oder das Princip des Katholizismus dargestellt in Geiste der Kirchenväter der drei ersten Jahrhunderte*. Mainz, new ed., 1925.

— *Symbolism: or exposition of the doctrinal differences between Catholics and Protestants as Evidenced by their Symbolic Writings*. Tr. by J. B. Robertson, Vols. i–ii, London, 1843.

Molland, E. *Christendom*. The Christian Churches, their doctrines, constitutional forms and ways of worship. London, 1961.

Moorman, J. R. H. *A History of the Church in England*. 3rd ed., London, 1958.

More, P. E., and F. L. Cross. *Anglicanism*. The thought and practice of the Church of England, illustrated from the Religious literature of the seventeenth Century. London, 1935; repr. 1957.

Neander, A. *History of the Church*. Edinburgh, vols. i–ix, 1847–55.

Neill, S. (ed.) *Twentieth Century Christianity*. London, 1961.

Newman, J. H. *Apologia Pro Vita Sua*. London, 1864; repr. Fontana Books, 1964.

Newman, J. H. *An Essay on the Development of Christian Doctrine.* London, 1845; repr. New York (Image Books) 1960.

Niesel, W. *Reformed Symbolics.* Tr. by D. Lewis, London, 1962.

Overton, J. H. *The Non-Jurors.* Their Lives, Principles and Writings. London, 1902.

Papadopoulos, Ch. *The Question of the Validity of the Anglican Orders.* Tr. by J. Douglas, London, 1931.

— *The Primacy of the Bishop of Rome.* Athens, 1930 [In Greek].

Pawley, B. C. *Looking at the Vatican Council.* London, 1962.

Pearson, John. *Works,* ed. E. Churton, vol. ii, Oxford, 1844.

Pope, H. *St. Augustine of Hippo.* New York (Image Books), 1961.

Potessaro, G. *The Orthodox Doctrine of the Apostolic Eastern Church.* London, 1857.

Prestige, G. L. *The Life of Charles Gore.* London, 1935.

— *Fathers and Heretics,* London, 1940.

Puller, F. W. *The Continuity of the Church of England.* 3rd ed., London, 1913.

Ramsey, A. M. *The Church of England and the Eastern Orthodox Church.* London, 1946.

— *From Gore to Temple.* The Development of Anglican Theology between *Lux Mundi* and the Second World War, 1889–1939. London, 2nd impr., 1961.

Report of the Conference at Bucharest from June 1st to June 8th, 1935 between the Rumanian Commission on relations with the Anglican Communion and the Church of England Delegation appointed by the Archbishop of Canterbury. Bucharest, 1966.

Ricaut, P. *The Present State of the Greek and Armenian Church.* London, 1679.

Richardson, C. C. *The Sacrament of Reunion.* London, 1940.

Runciman, S. *The Eastern Schism.* London, 1956.

Sartory, T. *The Ecumenical Movement and the Unity of the Church.* Tr. by Hilda C. Graef, Oxford, 1963.

Sayegh, M. *The Eastern Churches and Catholic Unity.* London, 1963.

Scharp, H. *How the Catholic Church is governed.* London, 1960.

Shaw, P. E. *The Early Tractarians and the Eastern Church.* London, 1930.

Slenczka, R. *Ostkirche und Oekumene.* Die Einheit der Kirche als dogmatische Problem in der neueren Ostkirchlichen Theologie. Göttingen, 1962.

Schmaus, M. *Katholische Dogmatic.* München, vol. iii, 1958.

Southgate, W. M. *John Jewel and the Problem of Doctrinal Authority.* Cambridge, Mass., 1962.

Stoker, R. B. *The Legacy of Arthur's Chester.* London, 1965.

Stransky, Th. F. *The decree on Ecumenism, with a Commentary.* Paulist Press. New York, 1965. [The same under the title, 'The Decree on Ecumenism: An Analysis, *O.I.C.* ii (1966), pp. 5–26.]

Tavard, G. H. *Two Centuries of Ecumenism*. London, 1960.
— *La Poursuite de la Catholicité. Etude sur la pensée anglicane*. Paris, 1965. (Unam Sanctam, 35.)
Trembelas, P. *Dogmatic of the Orthodox Catholic Church*. Vols i–iii, Athens, 1959–61 [in Greek].
— *The History of the Reformation in the Anglican Church*. Thessaloniki, 1956 [in Greek].
Tomos Agapis, Vatican-Phanar (1958–1970), Rome-Istanbul 1971.
Valetta, J. N. *The Letters of Patriarch Photius*. London, 1864 [in Greek].
Vatican Council II: *Decree 'de Ecumenismo'*. London, 1965. [See also L. Jaeger, *supra*, Fr. Stransky, *supra*, Fr. Leeming, *supra*, and *O.I.C.* i (1965), pp. 169–186.]
— *Decree 'de Ecclesia'*. London, 1965.
— *Decree 'de Ecclesiis Orientalibus Catholicis'*. London, 1965. [See also *O.I.C.* i (1965), pp. 334–338; cf. moreover ibid. pp. 394–401.]
Vidler, A. R. *The Church in an Age of Revolution*. London, 1961.
Villain, M. *Unity. A History and some Reflections*. Tr. by J. R. Foster, from the third revised and augmented edition, London, 1963.
Welldon, J. E. C. *The English Church*. London, 1926.
Williams, G. *A Collection of Documents relating chiefly to the Visit of Alexander, Archbishop of Syros and Tenos, to England in 1870*. London, 1876.
Woodward, D. *Our Separated Brethren*. London, 1961.
Zernov, N. *The Christian East*. London, 1956.

II. Articles

Afanassieff, N. 'The Ministry of the Laity in the Church'. *E.R.* x (1958), pp. 255–263.
Alberico, G. 'The Council of Trent: New Views on the occasion of its Fourth Centenary'. *C.* vii (1965), pp. 38–48.
Alivisatos, H. 'The New Dogma from an Eastern Orthodox standpoint'. *E.R.* iii (1951), pp. 151–158.
— 'Roma Locuta est'. *C.E.* ix (1928), pp. 127–130.
— 'The Proposed Ecumenical Council and Reunion'. *E.R.* xii (1959), pp. 1–10. The same in *Orthodoxos Skepsis* ii (Athens, 1959), pp. 187–192.
— 'The Canon Law of the Orthodox Church'. *TH.* xviii (1940), pp. 29–58.
— 'Can a Council be summoned in the way proposed by the Pope?' *To Vima* (Athens) 1 Febr. 1959. The same *Orthodoxos Skepsis* ii (Athens, 1959), pp. 119–121.
Antony, Metropolitan, 'Why Anglican Clergy could be received in their Orders'. *C.E.* viii (1927), pp. 60–69.

Arseniev, N. von. 'The Slavophil Doctrine of the Church'. *C.E.* ix (1928), pp. 130–136.

Armstrong, A. H. 'Membership of the Church'. *E.C.Q.* viii (1949), pp. 231–40.

Athenagoras, Metropolitan of Elaia. 'Tradition and Traditions', *TH.* xxxiv (1963), pp. 42–57.

Berdyaev, N. 'The Unity of Christendom in the Strife between East and West'. *E.R.* i (1948), pp. 11–24.

Bévenot, M. 'The recent Instruction on the Oecumenical Movement'. *E.C.Q.* viii (1950), pp. 357–364.

Borovoy, V. 'The Meaning of Catholicity'. *E.R.* xvi (1963), pp. 26–32.

Brandreth, H. R. T., O.G.S. 'Approaches of the Churches towards each other in the nineteenth Century'. *H.E.M.* pp. 263–306.

Bratsiotis, P. 'The Fundamental Principles and main Characteristics of the Orthodox Church'. A Faith and Order Dialogue. *Faith and Order Paper No. 30* (W.C.C. Geneva, 1960), pp. 7–16. The same in *E.R.* xii (1960), pp. 154–163.

— 'The Authority of the Bible from an Orthodox Point of View'. *TH.* xxiii (1952), pp. 505–516.

Bulgakov, S. 'Does Orthodoxy possess an outward Authority on Dogmatic Infallibility?' *C.E.* vii (1926), pp. 12–24.

— 'The Papal Encyclical and the Lausanne Conference'. *C.E.* ix (1928), pp. 116–127.

— 'One Holy, Catholic and Apostolic Church'. *C.E.* xii (1931), pp. 90–104

Christophilopoulos, A. 'The Reception of the non-Christian and non-Orthodox by the Orthodox Church'. *TH.* xxvii (1956), pp. 53–60. 196–205.

Chrysanthos, Metropolitan of Trebizond. 'The Relations of the Constantinopolitan and Anglican Churches'. *C.E.* i (1920), pp. 64–71.

Chrysostom, Archbishop of Athens. 'The Nature of the Church'. *C.E.* viii (1927), pp. 139–146.

Church of Constantinople. 'Unto all the Churches of Christ Wheresoever they be'. *C.E.* i (1920), pp. 58–61.

Clément, O. 'A Misunderstanding at Rhodes? An Orthodox Viewpoint'. *E.R.* xii (1960), pp. 223–230.

Congar, Y. 'The historical development of Authority in the Church. Points for Christian Reflection'. *P.A.* pp. 119–156.

— 'My first step in Ecumenism'. *E.E.* pp. 25–32.

Constantinidis, CH. 'The significance of the Eastern and Western Traditions within Christendom'. *Faith and Order Paper*, No. 30, pp. 62–72. The same in *E.R.* xii (1960), pp. 143–153.

Cotsonis, I. 'The Validity of the Priesthood of the Anglicans from the

Point of view of Orthodox Canon Law'. *TH.* xxviii (1957), pp. 354–375, 532–549.

Davis, H. Francis 'A Commentary on *De Ecumenismo*'. *O.I.C.* i (1965), pp. 118–125.

Dejaifve, G. 'East and West: Two Theologies, One Faith'. *R.E.C.* pp. 51–62.

— 'The Third Pan-Orthodox Conference in Rhodes'. *O.I.C.* i (1965), pp. 140–156.

Dvornik, F. 'The authority of the State in the Ecumenical Councils'. *C.E.* xiv (1933), pp. 95–108.

— 'The Patriarch Photius; Father of the Schism or Patron of Reunion?' in *Report of the proceedings at the Church Unity Octave.* Oxford, 1942.

Douglas, J. A., 'Reservation in the Eastern Orthodox Church'. *C.E.* vii (1926), pp. 86–96.

— 'Economy and the Communion at Belgrade'. *C.E.* ix (1928), pp. 16–23.

— 'Archbishop Germanos on Anglicanism'. *C.E.* x (1929), pp. 11–20.

— 'The Orthodox Delegation to the Lambeth Conference of 1930.' *C.E.* xi (1930), pp. 49–64.

— 'The Purport of the Recent Orthodox Delegation'. *C.E.* xi (1930), pp. 97–126.

— 'The Limits of agreements reached by the Orthodox delegates to the Lambeth Conference'. *C.E.* xi (1930–31), pp. 145–181.

— 'The Orthodox Principle of Economy, and its exercise'. *C.E.* xiii (1932), pp. 99–109.

Dumont, C. J. 'The decree on the Eastern Catholic Churches'. *O.I.C.* i (1965), pp. 334–338.

Duquoc, CH., O. P. 'The Believer and Christian Existence in History'. *C.* ix (1965), pp. 66–72.

Englert, C. 'Eastern Orthodox Theology'. *E.C.Q.* xii (1958), pp. 173–181.

Espine, H. D. 'The Apostolic Succession as an Ecumenical issue'. *E.R.* iv (1951), pp. 151–160.

Every, E. 'Khomyakoff and the Encyclical of the Eastern Patriarchs in 1948'. *S.* Series 3: No. 3 (1948), pp. 102–104.

Every, G. 'The Schism—Solutions and Problems'. *E.C.Q.* xi (1956). pp. 305–313.

Fedotov, Prof. 'The Orthodox Church and her History'. *C.E.* x (1929), pp. 104–113.

Florovsky, G. 'The Ethos of the Orthodox Church'. *Faith and Order Paper* No. 30, pp. 36–51. The same in *E.R.* xii (1960), pp. 183–198.

— 'The Work of the Holy Spirit in Revelation'. *C.E.* xiii (1932), pp. 49–64.

— 'The Orthodox Churches and the Ecumenical Movement prior to 1910'. *H.E.M.* pp. 171–215.

— 'The Problem of Ecumenical Encounter'. *R.E.C.* pp. 63–76.

— 'The Ecumenical Dialogue'. *E.E.* pp. 39–45.

Florovsky, G. 'The Way of Russian Theology'. *Theologia, Aletheia and Zoë. A Spiritual Symposium* (Athens, 1962), pp. 15–59.

Fransen, P. 'The Authority of the Councils'. *P.A.* pp. 43–78.

Franzen, A. 'The Council of Constance: Present State of the Problem'. *C.* vii (1965), pp. 17–37.

Geiselmann, J. R. 'Scripture, Tradition, and the Church: An Ecumenical Problem' in *Christianity Divided*, ed. by Küng, Cullman, and others (Sheed and Ward, London, 1961), pp. 39–72.

Germanos, Metropolitan of Thyateira. 'Anglican and Orthodox Reunion'. *C.E.* iv (1923) pp. 123–128.

— 'Towards Reunion'. *C.E.* xiv (1933), pp. 8–29.

— 'Progress towards the Reunion of the Orthodox and the Anglican Churches'. *C.E.* x (1929), pp. 20–31.

Glubokovsky, N. 'Papal Rome and the Orthodox East'. *C.E.* iv (1923), pp. 180–186.

— 'The Modern Papacy and the Reunion of the Orthodox East with the Roman Catholic West'. *C.E.* v (1924), pp. 124–131, 155–167.

— 'Eastern Orthodoxy and Anglicanism'. *C.E.* iii (1922), pp. 20–28.

Gore, C. 'Committee on our Relations with the Eastern Churches, Orthodox and Separated, Appointed by the Archbishop of Canterbury'. *C.E.* i (1920), pp. 62–64.

Gregory of Thessalonica. Homily Preached on the Occasion of the Feast of the Entry of our Most Pure Queen, the Mother of God, into the Holy of Holies. *E.C.Q.* x (1954–55), pp. 378–384.

Hajjar, J. 'The Synod in the Eastern Church'. *C.* viii (1965), pp. 30–34.

Harrison, C. G. 'Re-union and the Holy See'. *C.E.* ix (1928), pp. 27–33.

House, F. 'The Ecumenical Significance of the Patriarchate of Constantinople'. *E.R.* ix (1957), pp. 310–320.

Jacovos, Greek Archbishop of America, 'The Contribution of Eastern Orthodoxy to the Ecumenical Movement'. *E.R.* xi (1959), pp. 394–404.

James, V. 'Essays towards the Ecumenical Method.' *E.C.Q.* v (1942), pp. 7–19.

Joannou P.-P. Die Einheit der Christen in Vergangenheit und Gegenwart. *Ostkirchliche Studien*, 19 Band, 2–3 Heft 1970, Würzburg pp. 113–134.

Karmiris, J. 'The Second Vatican General Council of the Roman Catholic Church'. *Eccl.* 40 (1963), pp. 479–482, 496–499, 576–578; 41 (1964), pp. 15–18, 34–38, 57–63, 137–143; 42 (1965), pp. 221–225, 251–255, 309–313.

— 'The Pan-Orthodox Conference at Rhodes (Sept. 24–Oct. 1) 1961'. *TH.* xxxii (1961), pp. 497–536.

— 'The Third Pan-Orthodox Conference at Rhodes'. *Eccl.* 41 (1964), pp. 588–591, 607–611, 633–638. 42 (1965), pp. 12–21, 49–56, 80–87.

Kartachoff, A. 'Orthodox Theology and Ecumenical Movement'. *E.R.* viii (1955), pp. 30–35.

— 'The Reunion of Orthodoxy'. *Tserkovnyi Vestnik* 5–6 (1956), pp. 4–12.

King, A. A. 'The Assumption of Our Lady in the Oriental Liturgies'. *E.C.Q.* viii (1949), pp. 198–205, 255–231.

Lambeth Conference, 1930. *C.E.* xi (1930), pp. 64–73.

— Conferences, *C.E.* xi (1930), pp. 73–85.

Lawrence, J. 'Anglicans and Orthodox'. *R.E.C.* pp. 119–134.

Leeming, B. 'Orthodox–Catholic Relations'. *R.E.C.* pp. 15–50.

— 'The Doctrine of the Mystical Body and its Connection with Oecumenical Work'. *E.C.Q.* vii (1948), pp. 519–537.

— 'An Anglo-Catholic on the Recovery of Unity'. *E.C.Q.* xii (1958), pp. 263–278, 323–334.

Lercaro, Giacomo Cardinal. 'The Decree *De Ecumenismo* and the dialogue with non-Catholic Eastern Churches'. *C.* v (1965), pp. 83–91.

— '*Communicatio in Sacris* with the Orthodox'. *O.I.C.* (1965) pp., 187–189.

Lescrauwaet, J. F. 'The Reformed Churches'. *C.* vi (1965), pp. 57–67.

Lialine, C. (Dom.) 'Concerning the Eirenic Method'. *E.C.Q.* iii (1939), pp. 443–460.

Mackenzie, K. 'The Orthodox Mind and Re-union'. *C.E.* ix (1928), pp. 152–157.

Marot, H., O.S.B. 'The Primacy and the decentralization of the Early Church'. *C.* vii (1965), pp. 9–16.

Meletios, Patriarch of Alexandria. A Statement to the Holy Synod of the Patriarchate in regard to the contact in London of the Orthodox and Anglican Churches. *Pantaenos* (Alexandria) 11 Dec. and 18 Dec., 1930. See the translation made by Canon J. A. Douglas, *C.E.* xi (1930–31), pp. 181–192.

— Letters, concerning the Anglican Ordinations. *C.E.* xii (1931), pp. 1–4.

Melia, E. 'An Orthodox Point of View on the Problem of Authority in the Church'. *P.A.* pp. 104–116.

Meliton, Metropolitan. 'The Re-Encounter between the Eastern Church and the Western Church'. *E.R.* vii (1965), pp. 303–320.

Meyendorff, J. 'Tradition of the Church and Traditions of the people'. *Theologia, Aletheia and Zoë.* (Athens, 1962), pp. 131–151.

Meyer, Albert Cardinal. 'The Scandal of a Divided Christendom'. *S.C.U.* pp. 29–38.

Michalenko, A. 'Athenagoras I, Patriarch-Ecumenist'. *Chrysostom* 1965–1966.

Michaud, E. 'Ecclesiologie de St. Gregoire de Nazianze'. *Revue Internationale de Theologie*, xii (1904), pp. 570 ff.

Minutes of the Conference between the Orthodox Delegation and the Anglican Bishops, *C.E.* xii (1931), pp. 27–45.

Mikat, P. 'Collaboration between Clergy and Laity'. *C.* ix (1965), pp. 34–38.

Naronha, S. 'The Nature of the Church according to the teaching of the Greek Orthodox'. *E.C.Q.* xii (1957), pp. 51–61.

Nectarie, Metropolitan (Rumanian Church). Report. *C.E.* xii (1931), pp. 6–26.

Neill, S. C. 'Division and the Search for Unity prior to the Reformation'. *H.E.M.* pp. 1–24.

— 'Plans of Union and Reunion 1910–1948'. *H.E.M.* pp. 445–505. Especially, 'The Orthodox Churches and other episcopal Churches'. pp. 486–489.

— 'Intercommunion'. *H.E.M.*, Appendix ii, pp. 741–4.

Nicolas of Hermupolis (Alexandria). Report upon the First Session of the Orthodox and Anglican conjoint Doctrinal Commission. *C.E.* xiii (1932), pp. 87–91.

Nikolai, Bishop of Ochrida, 'The Sacraments from the point of view of the Eastern Church'. *C.E.* ix (1928), pp. 80–83.

Pailler, A. 'Consideration on the Authority of the Church'. *P.A.* pp. 13–26.

Pawley, B. 'An Anglican Views the Council'. *S.C.U.* pp. 109–126.

— 'The First two sessions of the Vatican Council through Anglican Eyes'. *E.E.* pp. 100–112.

Rawlinson, A. E. J. 'An Anglican Comment on intercommunion'. *E.R.* v (1953), pp. 382–384.

Reardon, M. 'Church Authority in Ecumenical perspective'. *O.I.C.* i (1965), pp. 339–356.

Rees, Gr. R. (Dom.) '1054–1954'. *E.C.Q.* xi (1955), pp. 5–12.

Report of the Delegation of the Patriarchate sent to the Conference at Lambeth, 1920. *C.E.* iii (1922), pp. 2–19.

Rich, E. C. 'The Idea of Doctrinal Development'. *E.C.Q.* xii (1958), pp. 221–227.

Richards, M. 'Understanding Anglicans'. *E.C.Q.* x (1954), pp. 342–345.

Rigby, Th. (Dom.) 'Reunion and the Episcopate'. *E.C.Q.* vii (1948), pp. 471–476.

Rinvolucri, M. 'Revoking the Anathemas. Orthodox Relations to Vatican II'. *The Tablet* Feb. 1966, pp. 155–156.

Rios, Romanus (Dom.) 'The Liturgy and Dennion'. *E.C.Q.* iv (1940), pp. 97–104.

Schlink, E. 'The Significance of the Eastern and Western Traditions for the Christian Church'. *Faith and Order Paper*, No. 30, pp. 52–61. The same in *E.R.* xii (1960), pp. 133–142.

— 'Changes in Protestant thinking about the Eastern Church'. *E.R.* x (1958), pp. 386–400.

Simpson, J. Sparrow, 'A Russian Layman on Reunion'. *C.E.* i (1920), pp. 86–94.

Skydsgaard, K. E. 'From Monologue to Dialogue'. *E.R.* xiv (1962), pp. 429–436.

Schmeman, A. ' "Unity", "Division", "Reunion", in the light of Orthodox Ecclesiology'. *TH.* xxii (1951), pp. 242–254.

— 'Theology and Eucharist'. *Theologia, Aletheia and Zoë.* (Athens, 1962), pp. 89–127.

Stavridis, V. 'Orthodoxy and Anglicanism'. *TH.* xxii (1961), pp. 475–495, 410–436, 582–607; xxxiii (1962), pp. 273–290, 355–375, 520–547; xxxiv (1963), pp. 58–83.

Stephan, Archbishop of Sofia. 'Fundamental Conditions for the unification of the Christian Churches'. *C.E.* viii (1927), pp. 121–139.

Sykes, N. 'The Ecumenical Movement in Great Britain in the 17th and 18th Centuries'. *H.E.M.* pp. 123–167.

Szepticky, A. 'Eastern and Western Mentality'. *E.C.Q.* ix (1952), pp. 392–401.

Tavard, G. H. 'The Authority of Scripture and Tradition'. *P.A.* pp. 27–42.

Thurian, M. 'Walking Together to Christ'. *S.C.U.* pp. 129–144.

Todd, J. M. 'The Authority of the Layman'. *P.A.* pp. 217–235.

Terbovich, J. B. 'Mary's Last End in Byzantine Tradition'. *E.C.Q.* xii (1958), pp. 228–242.

'Terms of Intercommunion suggested between the Church of England and the Churches in Communion with her and the Eastern Orthodox Church'. London, 1921. See Appendix to this book, pp. 253–9.

Tomkins, O. S. 'The Roman Catholic Church and the Ecumenical Movement'. *H.E.M.* pp. 677–693.

Trembelas, P. 'The Apostolic Tradition and the Life of the Church'. *Eccl.* xl (1963), pp. 442–443.

— 'Theories concerning Unam Sanctam which are unacceptable'. *Eccl.* 41 (1964), pp. 167–168, 198–200, 235–237, 268–270, 296–298, 318–320, 351–353.

Urresti, T. J. 'The Ontology of Communion and Collegial Structures in the Church'. *C.* viii (1965), pp. 5–10.

Vellas, V. 'The Authority of the Bible according to the teaching of the Orthodox Church'. *TH.* xxii (1951), pp. 602–616.

Villain, M. 'The Third Session of Vatican II. Collegiality and the Ecumenical Dialogue'. *O.I.C.* i (1965), pp. 133–139.

Vries, W. de. 'Communicatio in Sacris'. *C.* iv (1965), pp. 11–22.

— 'The College of Patriarchs'. *C.* viii (1965), pp. 35–43.

— 'The origin of the Eastern Patriarchates and their relationship to the power of the Pope'. *O.I.C.* ii (1966), pp. 50–69, 130–142.

Waal, V. de. '*De Ecclesia*. An Anglican Comment'. *O.I.C.* ii (1966), pp. 31–43.

Weiler, A. 'Church Authority and Government in the Middle Ages. A Bibliographical Survey'. *C.* vii (1965), pp. 65–71.

Willems, L. E. (Dom). 'A Study on the Church'. *E.C.Q.* xi (1955–56), pp. 153–170.

Williams, G. H. 'The Role of Layman in the Ancient Church'. *Greek and Byzantine Studies* (Cambridge, Mass.) i (1958), p. 21 ff.

Zander, L. 'The Ecumenical Movement and the Orthodox Church'. *E.R.* i (1949), pp. 267–276.

Zernov, N. 'The Eastern Churches and the Ecumenical Movement in the Twentieth Century'. *H.E.M.* pp. 645–674.

III. Additional Periodicals

The Tablet. London.
Catholic Herald. London.
Chrysostom. London.
Church Times. London.

INDEX